# THE BREXIT CHALLENGE FOR IRELAND AND THE UNITED KINGDOM

Since the 1950s, European integration has included ever more countries with ever-softening borders between them. In its apparent reversal of integration and its recreation of borders, Brexit intensifies deep-seated tensions, both institutional and territorial, within and between the constitutional orders of the United Kingdom and Ireland. In this book, leading scholars from the UK and Ireland assess the pressures exerted by Brexit, from legal, historical, and political perspectives. This book explores the territorial pressures within the UK constitution, connecting them to the status of Northern Ireland before exploring how analogous territorial pressures might be addressed in a united Ireland. The book also critically analyses the Brexit process within the UK, drawing on Irish comparative examples, to assess unresolved tensions between popular mandate, legislative democracy, and executive responsibility. Through practical application, this book explores how constitutions function under the most intense political pressures.

Oran Doyle is a Professor in Law at Trinity College Dublin, Ireland. He is the author of The Constitution of Ireland: A Contextual Analysis (2018) and a member of the Working Group on Unification Referendums on the Island of Ireland.

Aileen McHarg has published widely on UK and Scottish public law. Previous edited books include *The Scottish Independence Referendum: Constitutional and Political Implications* (2016). She is joint general editor of the journal *Public Law*.

Jo Murkens is Associate Professor in the Department of Law at the London School of Economics and Political Science. He has published in the areas of public law, EU law, and comparative constitutional law, and is a member of the editorial board of *Public Law*.

# The Brexit Challenge for Ireland and the United Kingdom

CONSTITUTIONS UNDER PRESSURE

*Edited by*

**ORAN DOYLE**

Trinity College Dublin

**AILEEN MCHARG**

University of Durham

**JO MURKENS**

London School of Economics and Political Science

# CAMBRIDGE
UNIVERSITY PRESS

University Printing House, Cambridge CB2 8BS, United Kingdom

One Liberty Plaza, 20th Floor, New York, NY 10006, USA

477 Williamstown Road, Port Melbourne, VIC 3207, Australia

314–321, 3rd Floor, Plot 3, Splendor Forum, Jasola District Centre, New Delhi – 110025, India

79 Anson Road, #06–04/06, Singapore 079906

Cambridge University Press is part of the University of Cambridge.

It furthers the University's mission by disseminating knowledge in the pursuit of education, learning, and research at the highest international levels of excellence.

www.cambridge.org
Information on this title: www.cambridge.org/9781108832922
DOI: 10.1017/9781108966399

© Cambridge University Press 2021

This publication is in copyright. Subject to statutory exception and to the provisions of relevant collective licensing agreements, no reproduction of any part may take place without the written permission of Cambridge University Press.

First published 2021

*A catalogue record for this publication is available from the British Library.*

ISBN 978-1-108-83292-2 Hardback

Cambridge University Press has no responsibility for the persistence or accuracy of URLs for external or third-party internet websites referred to in this publication and does not guarantee that any content on such websites is, or will remain, accurate or appropriate.

# Contents

| | |
|---|---|
| List of Figures | page vii |
| List of Tables | viii |
| List of Contributors | ix |
| Preface | xi |

The Constitutional Tensions of Brexit
*Oran Doyle, Aileen McHarg and Jo Murkens* — 1

### PART I  TERRITORIAL PRESSURES IN IRELAND AND THE UNITED KINGDOM

1 Subsidiarity, Competence and the UK Territorial Constitution
*Jo Hunt* — 21

2 Brexit and the Mechanisms for the Resolution of Conflicts in the Context of Devolution: Do We Need a New Model?
*Elisenda Casanas Adam* — 43

3 Beyond Matryoshka Governance in the Twenty-First Century: The Curious Case of Northern Ireland
*Sylvia de Mars and Aoife O'Donoghue* — 64

4 Political Parties in Northern Ireland and the Post-Brexit Constitutional Debate
*David Mitchell* — 86

5   The Constitutional Significance of the People
    of Northern Ireland
    *C. R. G. Murray*                                                108

6   The Constitutional Politics of a United Ireland
    *Oran Doyle, David Kenny and Christopher McCrudden*              129

7   The Minority Rights Implications of Irish Unification
    *James Rooney*                                                   153

   PART II   INSTITUTIONAL PRESSURES AND CONTESTED LEGITIMACY

8   Populism and Popular Sovereignty in the UK and Irish
    Constitutional Orders
    *Eoin Daly*                                                      175

9   Party, Democracy, and Representation: The Political
    Consequences of Brexit
    *Malcolm Petrie*                                                 195

10  Westminster versus Whitehall: What the Brexit Debate
    Revealed About an Unresolved Conflict at the Heart
    of the British Constitution
    *David Howarth*                                                  217

11  Brexit and the Problem with Delegated Legislation
    *Adam Tucker*                                                    239

12  Litigating Brexit
    *Christopher McCorkindale and Aileen McHarg*                     260

13  The Law Officers: The Relationship between Executive
    Lawyers and Executive Power in Ireland and the
    United Kingdom
    *Conor Casey*                                                    292

14  In Search of the Constitution
    *Martin Loughlin*                                                313

Index                                                                336

# Figures

1: *Governance 'nests' impacting on Brexit* (where the white tiers represent the 'sub'-level, and the light grey tiers represent the 'super'-level of actors) — *page 73*
2: *Governance 'nests' impacting on Northern Ireland under the Withdrawal Agreement* (where the white tiers represent the 'sub'-level, and the light grey tiers represent the 'super'-level of actors) — 80

# Tables

| | | |
|---|---|---|
| 1: | Brexit-Related Strategic Litigation (by year of commencement) | *page* 263 |
| 2: | What Was Being Litigated? | 267 |
| 3: | Who Was Litigating? Claimants/Petitioners, Interested Parties and Interveners | 270 |
| 4: | Political Motivation | 272 |
| 5: | Legal Outcomes | 275 |
| 6: | Expert Involvement | 286 |
| 7: | Litigation Funding | 289 |

# Contributors

ELISENDA CASANAS ADAM, Lecturer in Public Law and Human Rights, University of Edinburgh

CONOR CASEY, Max Weber Postdoctoral Fellow, European University Institute

EOIN DALY, Lecturer Above the Bar, School of Law, NUI Galway

SYLVIA DE MARS, Senior Lecturer in Law, Newcastle University

ORAN DOYLE, Professor in Law, Trinity College Dublin

DAVID HOWARTH, Professor of Law and Public Policy, University of Cambridge

JO HUNT, Professor of Law, Wales Governance Centre, Cardiff University

DAVID KENNY, Assistant Professor in Law, Trinity College Dublin

MARTIN LOUGHLIN, Professor of Public Law, London School of Economics and Political Science

CHRISTOPHER MCCORKINDALE, Senior Lecturer in Public Law, University of Strathclyde

CHRISTOPHER MCCRUDDEN, Professor of Human Rights and Equality Law, Queen's University Belfast and William W. Cook Global Law Professor, University of Michigan

AILEEN MCHARG, Professor of Public Law and Human Rights, Durham University

DAVID MITCHELL, Assistant Professor, Conflict Resolution and Reconciliation, Trinity College Dublin at Belfast

JO MURKENS, Associate Professor of Law, London School of Economics and Political Science

C. R. G. MURRAY, Reader in Law, Newcastle University

AOIFE O'DONOGHUE, Professor of International Law and Global Governance, Durham University

MALCOLM PETRIE, Lecturer in History, University of St Andrews

JAMES ROONEY, Adjunct Assistant Professor, Trinity College Dublin

ADAM TUCKER, Senior Lecturer in Law, University of Liverpool

# Preface

This book originated in a conference of the British Irish Chapter of the International Society of Public Law (ICON-S) held at the University of Strathclyde in April 2019. The decision of the United Kingdom to leave the European Union had, perhaps ironically, illustrated the extent to which the constitutional futures of Ireland and the United Kingdom are intertwined. There has never been greater need for comparative constitutional scholarship that explores the relationships between and within Ireland and the United Kingdom. The ICON-S Chapter will continue that work, and this book is an attempt to bring some of that work to a wider audience.

We are grateful to all who presented papers at the Strathclyde conference, including those whose papers did not fit the theme upon which we settled for this book. We are also grateful to those authors who joined the project after the conference, helping us to provide a fuller account of the relevant issues. Strathclyde University and ICON-S provided financial support for the conference, without which it could not have proceeded. Cambridge University Press have provided impeccable and unstinting support for the project. In particular, we are grateful to Finola O'Sullivan, Marianne Nield, Becky Jackman, Malini Soupramanian, and Emma Sullivan.

The book proposal was approved in April 2020 as the world went into lockdown. Notwithstanding these most difficult circumstances, all authors worked with us to deliver a complete manuscript on schedule to Cambridge University Press on 1 September 2020. This date marks the cut-off point for the legal analysis in the book but it does raise significant issues. Eight days later, the UK government published the United Kingdom Internal Market Bill (now act), raising issues relevant to the analysis in many of the chapters. Rather than ask the authors to adapt their chapters to take account of the bill as it worked its way through the legislative process, we instead highlight here the ways in which the chapters in the book both anticipate the issues raised by the Internal Market Act and are affected by it.

For those outside the United Kingdom, the most striking feature of the bill as initially drafted were the provisions in Part V which authorised, in disregard of international law, UK government ministers to override aspects of the Withdrawal Agreement ratified by the United Kingdom and endorsed by the UK Parliament only eight months previously. In his chapter, Casey provides an account of how legal advice is deployed by the executive to enhance the legal credibility and political legitimacy of contested and controversial political positions. In some ways, the Internal Market Bill challenges this analysis, with the UK government making a virtue of its law-breaking, in defence of what it deemed the United Kingdom's national interests and its territorial integrity. In other ways, however, the damage caused by the resignation of legal advisors and Law Officers alongside the attempts – however unpersuasive – of other Law Officers to provide legal justifications for the bill, supports Casey's observations about the role played by government lawyers in legitimising executive decisions.

If implemented, the threat to breach the Northern Ireland Protocol – the product of months of careful negotiation between actors in the EU, the United Kingdom, Ireland, and Northern Ireland, as documented by de Mars and O'Donoghue in their chapter – would likely have led to the re-introduction of a border between Ireland and Northern Ireland. This in turn would probably have further increased support for a united Ireland – as analysed in the chapter by Doyle, Kenny, and McCrudden and the subsequent chapter by Rooney. In early December 2020, agreement was reached between the chairs of the EU-UK Joint Implementation Committee which allowed the provisions in Part V to be withdrawn, and these potential adverse consequences to be averted. Nevertheless, the very threat to break international law calls into question the United Kingdom's commitment to all international treaties, including the Belfast/Good Friday Agreement. It raises real doubts as to whether the United Kingdom – or at least the current UK government – would respect a decision of the Irish people, ratified in referendums north and south, in favour of unification.

The Internal Market Act also exerts significant pressure on the devolution settlement within the United Kingdom. It creates new legal supports for frictionless trade within the United Kingdom, to replace the homogenising effects of EU law, but in ways which are likely to restrict the ability of the devolved institutions to regulate their own territories in accordance with local needs and local political priorities, to a significantly greater extent than EU law. The Act also empowers UK ministers to spend in devolved policy areas, again prioritising UK-wide objectives above devolved autonomy. As with other Brexit legislation, the Internal Market Act amounts to a unilateral rewriting of the devolution settlement by the UK government, over-turning the consensual process of development of devolved governance that had hitherto prevailed. Hunt's chapter most directly anticipates the Internal Market Act, noting that the approach in the preceding Internal Market White Paper was 'markedly less collaborative, more top-down, and potentially damaging to the scope and exercise of devolved competence'. The bill's enactment process more than bears out this assessment. Although both the Scottish and Welsh Parliaments, once again, voted to withhold their consent, the Bill was enacted anyway, with only minimal compromises offered by the UK government, providing further evidence of Casanas Adam's analysis of the way in which the Brexit process has strained the Sewel Convention almost to breaking point.

The legislation's liberal use of Henry VIII clauses, threatening to allow ministers to put the United Kingdom in breach of international law, as well as to alter the scope of the internal market principles, bears out Tucker's claim that 'a likely legacy of the Brexit process will be (and perhaps already is) the exacerbation of the already troubling constitutional position of delegated legislation'. By the same token, as Howarth's analysis also suggests, the Act marks a further assertion of Whitehall's power at the expense of Westminster. Here, however, the legislation raised new issues (as regards the Brexit process) – in the context of a UK government which once again has a strong majority in the House of Commons – about the ability and willingness of the House of Lords to defend constitutional values and act as a brake upon the executive. Although peers significantly amended the Bill in order to defend devolved autonomy, and - usually - insisted on those amendments through several rounds of parliamentary 'ping pong', they ultimately dropped their opposition in return for relatively limited concessions by the government.

Part V of the bill also contained a sweeping ouster clause, no doubt intended to deter the kind of constitutional litigation that McCorkindale and McHarg identify in their chapter as having been such a notable feature of the Brexit process. Nevertheless, given the Welsh Government's unprecedented threat to seek judicial review of the Act, it seems like litigation (even where, as in this instance, it appears highly speculative) remains an attractive prospect where political channels of influence seem to be closed off.

In his chapter, Loughlin identifies six phases of constitutional development, with the final phase (2015–19) described as 'Paralysis'. It may be that we are witnessing an attempt to move beyond paralysis, by centralising power in the hands of a UK executive intolerant of constraints upon its power, whether these come from Parliament, the courts, the devolved institutions, or international agreements. However, the fate of the bill so far suggests that such centralising attempts are likely to continue to be resisted, highlighting an ongoing mismatch between the constitutional ambitions which motivated Brexit and the reality of constrained and dispersed constitutional power.

In sum, the UK Internal Market Act provides a vivid illustration of the constitutional pressures that continue to be exerted by Brexit on the constitutions of both the United Kingdom and Ireland, and on relationships between them. The constitutional implications of Brexit did not come to an end on 31 January 2020, when the United Kingdom finally left the EU; nor did they end when the implementation period elapsed. Rather, Brexit is likely to shape and condition the constitutional futures of these islands for many years to come.

# The Constitutional Tensions of Brexit

Oran Doyle, Aileen McHarg and Jo Murkens

INTRODUCTION

The United Kingdom's departure from the European Union on 31 January 2020 ran counter to recent trends of European history. Since the 1950s, European integration has included ever more countries with ever-softening borders between them. Progress was intermittent; the final destination both unclear and contested. But the direction of travel was set. In its apparent reversal of integration and its recreation of borders, Brexit is first and foremost a territorial event. The EU has lost one of its most powerful member states. The future relationship between the United Kingdom and the EU, while still unclear at the time of writing, will be markedly different from what has pertained hereto; the movement of people, goods, services, and capital (the four freedoms of the European Single Market) across borders will be considerably more difficult. Unsurprisingly, these effects are experienced most directly in the United Kingdom itself and in those EU member states closest to it, particularly Ireland, with whom it shares a land border and whose land-bridge to the rest of the EU now traverses a non-member state.

The consequences of Brexit will unfold across a myriad of domains over the next several decades, but constitutional consequences for the United Kingdom and Ireland have already come into focus. Within the United Kingdom, Brexit has involved the removal of a source of law – which the UK Supreme Court described as a 'fundamental legal change'[1] – and its replacement with a new legal category: 'retained EU law'.[2] It has also involved the removal of a layer of governance, and the consequent reallocation of internal decision-making competences. This has meant the disturbance of

---

[1] *R (Miller)* v. *The Secretary of State for Exiting the European Union* [2017] UKSC 5 at para. 83.
[2] European Union (Withdrawal) Act 2018. EU law continued to apply in the United Kingdom until the end of the so-called implementation period – i.e., 31 December 2020.

settled policy communities and familiar modes of regulation, creating considerable uncertainty about the future direction of legal and policy development, particularly given the removal of a major legal constraint on the powers of the UK Parliament. It has altered the status of EU nationals resident in the United Kingdom and of UK nationals living in other member states, and means that all UK nationals lose the citizenship rights flowing from EU membership – most notably, but by no means limited to, rights to free movement within the EU. And it has also entailed a reorientation of the United Kingdom's external relationships, away from the relatively stable and predictable obligations and incidences of EU membership towards a new relationship with the EU and its member states, as well as new and unpredictable trade relations with the rest of the world.

Though less immediately and dramatically affected by Brexit, in Ireland too there have been significant political, and potentially also profound constitutional, implications. Ireland's land border with the United Kingdom and the geographical interposition of the United Kingdom between Ireland and the rest of the EU would on their own suffice to render Ireland uniquely affected by Brexit. But the significance of these factors is overshadowed by the delicate relationship between Ireland, Northern Ireland and the rest of the United Kingdom brokered by the Belfast/Good Friday Agreement 1998 (the 1998 Agreement). The reintroduction of a hard border on the island of Ireland threatened to undermine the 1998 settlement and, in the view of the Irish government, posed an existential threat to the Irish state.[3] Given the terms on which the United Kingdom ultimately departed the EU, Brexit has not had immediate constitutional implications for Ireland. It has, however, placed the issue of a united Ireland on the political agenda.

All of this was foreseeable in advance of the EU referendum of 23 June 2016, and the implications of Brexit – and it is advantages and disadvantages – have been widely debated before and since, even if considerable uncertainties remain. What, though, was less foreseeable – or at least not foreseen – was the considerable strain that the *process* of leaving the EU would place on the United Kingdom's constitutional order. One dimension of this was the EU's adoption of Ireland's concerns in relation to Northern Ireland as a critical negotiating objective. This was among the factors that made it difficult for the UK government to secure a parliamentary majority for a form of withdrawal that would be widely seen as respecting the referendum result. That three-way constitutional tussle between parliament, executive, and popular mandate,

---

[3] Tom McTague, 'How the UK Lost the Brexit Battle', Politico.eu, 27 March 2019, www.politico.eu/article/how-uk-lost-brexit-eu-negotiation/.

exacerbated by the developing territorial tensions within the United Kingdom, meant that the Brexit process itself amounted to a full-spectrum test of the resilience of the UK constitution.

The three and a half years between the referendum and the United Kingdom's eventual – thrice postponed[4] – formal withdrawal from the EU were punctuated by a series of disagreements over the location and proper exercise of constitutional authority, both to trigger withdrawal and to determine the consequences of withdrawal (see chapters by Petrie and Howarth). These included disputes about the constitutional authority and legitimacy of the referendum result (see chapter by Daly); about relations between the UK Parliament and executive (see chapters by Petrie, Howarth, and Tucker); about the principles of territorial authority and territorial consent (see chapters by Mitchell; Murray; Hunt; and Casanas Adam); and about the role of the courts as constitutional decision-makers, and the UK government's commitment to the rule of law (see chapters by Casey, and McCorkindale and McHarg). While the potential for a serious crisis of constitutional legitimacy[5] has been averted by the eventual implementation of the referendum result, and the restoration of executive dominance in the UK Parliament following the December 2019 general election, the repercussions of these various constitutional conflicts rumble on. In particular, Brexit's reinvigoration of secessionist and irredentist pressures in Scotland,[6] Wales,[7] and Northern Ireland[8] still has the potential to threaten the continuation of the UK state in its current form.

---

[4] The negotiation period triggered the United Kingdom's formal notification of its intention to withdraw from the EU under Art. 50 TEU was initially supposed to expire on 29 March 2019. This was postponed initially to 12 April 2019, then until 31 October 2019, and finally until 31 January 2020.

[5] See Aileen McHarg, 'Navigating Without Maps: Constitutional Silence and the Management of the Brexit Crisis' (2018) 16 *International Journal of Constitutional Law*, 952–68. For a sceptical view of the risk of constitutional crisis posed by Brexit see Eoin Daly, 'Constitutionalism and Crisis Narratives in Post-Brexit Politics' (2020) *Political Studies* (forthcoming); and see also Daly, in this volume.

[6] Since the beginning of 2020, a series of opinion polls have put support for independence in Scotland at or above 50 per cent – see https://whatscotlandthinks.org/questions/how-would-you-vote-in-the-in-a-scottish-independence-referendum-if-held-now-ask/?removed.

[7] According to the YouGov/ITV Welsh Barometer Poll in June and October 2020, 25 and 27 per cent of those surveyed backed a fully independent Wales – the highest level of support for Welsh independence ever recorded. Gareth Wyn Williams, 'Surge in support for Welsh independence gives hope to campaigners', *Daily Post*, 5 June 2020, https://docs.cdn.yougov.com/lvbjz3q4w9/Results_WelshBarometer_October2020_W.pdf.

[8] Opinion polls in Northern Ireland over 2019 and 2020 show support for unification ranging between 25 and 46%. '51% of people in Northern Ireland support Irish unification, new poll finds', thejournal.ie, 11 Sept. 2019, www.thejournal.ie/lord-ashcroft-irish-unification-poll-4804

At one level, the constitutional upheavals occasioned by Brexit can be attributed to the way in which the EU referendum was conceived and conducted:[9] the party political rather than constitutional motivation for the referendum; the relatively short and poor quality referendum campaign; the failure to take seriously the implications of a territorially divided result;[10] the lack of planning for how withdrawal would be implemented; and the narrowness of the majority in favour of Leave.[11] These weaknesses may have contributed to a significant absence of 'losers' consent' amongst Remain voters,[12] as well as a lack of realism about the choices and compromises that would need to be made in order to secure a withdrawal agreement. But these essentially procedural factors, important as they were, reflected and exacerbated much deeper tensions within the UK constitutional order. Indeed, Loughlin's chapter in this volume traces the origins of what he calls the current period of 'constitutional anxiety' in the United Kingdom in certain persistent and deeper-seated ambiguities about the nature of the English and then UK state dating back as far as the Revolution of 1689. The 2016 referendum result also represents the culmination of at least two decades' worth of increasing anti-European sentiment. In this introductory chapter, we explore these deeper tensions, addressing the United Kingdom's position in the EU; the territorial tension within the United Kingdom; Ireland's relationship with the UK; and the developing tensions at the core of the UK constitution.

## THE UNITED KINGDOM IN THE EU: AN UNEASY MEMBERSHIP

In order to join the European Economic Community in 1973, alongside Ireland and Denmark, the United Kingdom had to overcome political and psychological obstacles that are encapsulated in the observation by US Secretary of State Dean Acheson in 1962 that Britain had lost an empire and had not yet found a role. When the United Kingdom looked to the East, it expressed reservations about supranationalism and about full-hearted support for European cooperation and integration. These misgivings were shared by President de Gaulle, who twice – in 1963 and in 1967 – vetoed the UK

---

372-Sep2019/; ARK Northern Ireland Life and Times Survey: www.ark.ac.uk/nilt/2019/Political_Attitudes/REFUNIFY.html.
[9] See Saskia Hollander, 'The Politics of Referendum Use in European Democracies' (London: Palgrave Macmillan, 2019) chap. 7; McHarg, 'Navigating Without Maps', p. 956.
[10] 62% of voters in Scotland and 56% of voters in Northern Ireland voted to remain in the EU.
[11] 52% of voters overall opted to leave the EU.
[12] See Richard Nadeau, Éric Bélanger and Ece Özlem Atikcan, 'Emotions, Cognitions and Moderation: Understanding Losers' Consent in the 2016 Brexit Referendum' (2020) 30 *Journal of Elections, Public Opinion and Parties* (forthcoming).

government's applications to join the EEC. When the United Kingdom looked to the West, it envisioned transatlanticism and a special relationship with the USA. That vision was shared in Washington, on condition, however, that the United Kingdom join the EEC and embrace European integration. For the USA, until the Trump presidency began in 2017, non-EU membership of the United Kingdom has always been 'politically awkward'.[13]

In the second half of the twentieth century, Britain's role in the world lay in managing the tension between European integration and American domination. British political leaders have carefully nurtured the United Kingdom's self-perceived outsider status with respect to European policy formation resulting in fault lines that continue to run through the main political parties. In the 1970s, the Labour party was divided on the question of accession to the EEC and on holding a referendum on the issue. From around the time of the Maastricht Treaty (1993) onwards, the Conservative Party has been in a 'near permanent civil war on the issue of membership of the European Union'.[14] The 'Maastricht Rebels' subsequently operated alongside single-issue political parties that were advocating withdrawal from the EU: the Referendum Party in the 1990s; the UK Independence Party (especially from 2004–2016); and the Brexit Party (since 2019).[15] Euroscepticism is also readily apparent in the editorial stances of the British press, with their phony wars against Euromyths (from bent bananas and curved cucumbers to banning prawn cocktail crisps), and their hostility towards European institutions and politicians (from Jacques Delors to Jean-Claude Juncker). Whereas the press was virtually unanimous in its support for UK membership of the common market during the 1975 referendum, after the Maastricht Treaty (1993), British politicians effectively handed over leadership on European matters to 'a uniquely powerful and Eurosceptic popular press'.[16] The splits in the electorate in 2016 were mirrored in the divisions in the party-political landscape and in British newspapers (with the Eurosceptic tabloids reaching a larger audience),[17] which in

---

[13] Desmond Dinan, *Europe Recast: A History of European Union* (Houndsmills: Palgrave Macmillan, 2014), p. 100.
[14] Martin Holmes, 'The Conservative Party and Europe', *The Bruges Group*, Paper No. 17.
[15] Julie Smith, 'The European Dividing Line in Party Politics' (2012) 88:6 *International Affairs* 1277–95.
[16] Charles Grant, 'Why is Britain Eurosceptic?' *Centre for European Reform*, Dec. 2008; Oliver Daddow, 'Performing Euroscepticism: The UK Press and Cameron's Bloomberg Speech', in Karine Tournier-Sol and Chris Gifford (eds.), *The UK Challenge to Europeanization: The Persistence of British Euroscepticism* (London: Palgrave Macmillan, 2015).
[17] Georgi Gotev, 'Britain's newspapers take sides on Brexit', euractiv.com, 22 June 2016, www.euractiv.com/section/uk-europe/news/britains-newspapers-take-sides-on-brexit/.

turn reflected the indecisive attitudes towards Europe that British political leaders have always adopted.

Although the United Kingdom was technically an insider for the duration of its membership, it saw itself, and was viewed by other member states, as an 'awkward partner'.[18] The United Kingdom signed up to the *acquis communautaire* and to the supervisory jurisdiction of the Court of Justice of the EU like every other member state. However, more than any other member state, the United Kingdom negotiated and obtained opt-outs and special clauses. It demanded its 'money back' and fought symbolic battles, for instance against the inclusion of the word 'federal' in the draft European Constitution, but then acquiesced to text which referred to the functionally identical concepts of 'subsidiarity' and 'communautaire'.[19] No other member state was as detached from the core project of integration.

The United Kingdom's fraught relationship with the project of European integration is partly explained as an attempt to manage the geopolitical pressures exerted by Europe and the USA. But it also has a domestic dimension characterised by tension between economic necessity, national identity, and constitutional politics. The economic case for membership has not changed. After World War II, the United Kingdom's per capita GDP was almost a third larger than the average of the original six member states. It declined steadily until 1973, when it had fallen to 10% below the average. Membership in 1973 put an end to the decline, and per capita GDP was relatively stable between 1973 and 2010.[20] In 2016, the EU was the United Kingdom's largest trading partner and its largest export market for services. The London School of Economics' Centre for Economic Performance estimated that the long-term cost to the United Kingdom from reduced trade and lower productivity after withdrawal could be as high as 9.5% of GDP – a figure similar to the United Kingdom before accession.[21] In Autumn 2019, UK in

---

[18] Stephen George, *An Awkward Partner: Britain in the European Community* (Oxford: Oxford University Press, 1990).

[19] Valéry Giscard-d'Estaing: 'I knew the word "federal" was ill-perceived by the British and a few others. I thought that it wasn't worth creating a negative commotion, which could prevent them supporting something that otherwise they would have supported. ... So I rewrote my text, replacing intentionally the word "federal" with the word "communautaire", which means exactly the same thing', cited in *Wall Street Journal*, 7 July 2003, www.wsj.com/articles/S B105752135945040000. See generally, Steven G. Calabresi and Lucy D. Bickford, 'Federalism and Subsidiarity: Perspectives from U.S. Constitutional Law (2014) 55 *Nomos* 123–89.

[20] Nauro F. Campos and Fabrizio Coricelli, 'EU Membership, Mrs Thatcher's Reforms and Britain's Economic Decline' (2017) 59:2 *Comparative Economic Studies* 169–93.

[21] Swati. Dhingra et al., *'The Consequences of Brexit for UK Trade and Living Standards* (London: LSE, 2016).

a Changing Europe (an independent research organisation on United Kingdom-EU relations) calculated that the negative impact over ten years would be 8.1% of GDP for no deal or 6.4% for the deal then advocated by Boris Johnson.[22]

The economic argument was determinative for the United Kingdom joining the common market. Prime Minister Harold Macmillan identified economics as the focus of the Treaty of Rome. The common market was exactly that: a common market, not a political entity: 'I ask hon. Members to note the word "economic". The Treaty of Rome does not deal with defence. It does not deal with foreign policy. It deals with trade and some of the social aspects of human life which are most connected with trade and production.'[23]

But the economic case, although still clear, was not determinative in 2016. One die-hard Leaver captured the mood at the time: 'I don't think we'll be poorer out, but if you told me my family would have to eat grass I'd still have voted to leave'.[24] The motivation to vote leave was governed by something stronger than money. It was primarily a matter of national identity, specifically – as we shall see below – English national identity within a weakening Union.

The question of (British) national identity had featured in every major speech on Europe given by a prime minister since 1945. Even the most pro-European prime minister, Edward Heath, balanced the recognition of 'our common European heritage, our mutual interests and our European destiny' by stressing 'our national identity and ... the achievements of our national history and tradition'.[25] A whole raft of binary divisions were subsequently subsumed underneath the two EU and UK mastheads. Margaret Thatcher's Bruges speech in 1988, for instance, developed the oppositions that were nascent in Heath's speech, with Europe characterised as liberal, intergovernmental, bureaucratic and formal, protectionist and parochial, and politically unstable, whereas the United Kingdom is seen as free, independent, pragmatic and democratic, free trading and global, and politically stable.[26]

Brexit has not made the task of 'finding a role' any easier. For a start, the USA's dominance is no longer unrivalled. China has emerged as another player of great-power politics, and the United Kingdom once again finds itself

---

[22] 'The Economic Impact of Boris Johnson's Brexit Proposals', The UK in a Changing Europe, October 2019.
[23] Hansard, Harold Macmillan, HC Deb, vol. 645, col. 1481, 2 August 1961.
[24] Reported in 'Brexit: the Conservatives and their thirty years' war over Europe', Financial Times, 14 December 2018, www.ft.com/content/0dee56c0-fdfa-11e8-ac00-57a2a826423e.
[25] Speech by Edward Heath, Brussels, 22 January 1972, www.cvce.eu/content/publication/2001/9/14/45bb74bd-554c-49d4-8212-9144cc2c8c1d/publishable_en.pdf.
[26] Chris Gifford, The Making of Eurosceptic Britain: Identity and Economy in a Post-Imperial State (Farnham: Ashgate, 2nd edn., 2014), p. 97.

caught in the middle. In January 2020, the UK government decided to allow the Chinese telecoms giant Huawei to help build the domestic 5G network. The decision angered the US administration and it was reversed in July 2020, meaning that UK mobile providers are now banned from buying Huawei equipment in the future. The United Kingdom may have taken control back from Brussels but exercising sovereignty in a globalised world still requires difficult decisions and strategic alliances.

### THE UNITED KINGDOM: AN UNEASY UNION

Certain members of the British political class always claimed that national identity was threatened by Europe and only secured through rebates, opt-outs, vetoes, and ultimately through the threat and actualisation of withdrawal. However, the United Kingdom that left the EU was a much more complex territorial entity than the one that joined in 1973. The programme of devolution to Scotland, Wales, and Northern Ireland in the late 1990s had heightened consciousness of regional identities – in England as well as in the devolved territories[27] – and brought in its wake significant political divergence[28] and markedly differentiated attitudes towards the EU.[29] Far from revealing a coherent national unit capable of 'taking back control of our borders, money and laws',[30] the 2016 referendum result revealed instead a set of divisions that represented different attitudes towards EU membership, and also reflected deep splits with respect to education, age, geography, and political citizenship.[31] 70% of voters whose only academic qualification was GCSE or lower voted to leave, and 68% of voters with a university degree voted to remain. As many voters under the age of fifty voted to remain (62.5%) as those above fifty voted to leave (62%). It also represented geographical divisions: in England, every region apart from London voted to leave, whereas Northern Ireland and Scotland voted to remain.

---

[27] See Richard Wyn Jones, Guy Lodge, Charlie Jeffery, Glenn Gottfired, Roger Scully, Ailsa Henderson and Daniel Wincott, *England and its Two Unions: The Anatomy of a Nation and its Discontents* (London: Institute for Public Policy Research, 2013).

[28] By 2016, there were different political parties in power in each of the United Kingdom's four governments.

[29] Ailsa Henderson et al., 'How Brexit was Made in England' (2017) 19:4 *British Journal of Politics and International Relations* 631–46.

[30] HM Government, 'EU Exit: Taking back control of our borders, money and laws while protecting our economy, security and Union', November 2018, Cm 9741.

[31] 'How Britain voted at the EU referendum', YouGov, 27 June 2016.

As a post-imperial identity, Britishness does not have the force of an 'overarching, civic national identity'.[32] Instead, it has become a byword for English dominance. Ultimately, 'Brexit was made in England'.[33] It is true that Wales also voted to leave; however, the final result was not dependent on the Welsh vote. Regional divergences notwithstanding, Prime Minister Theresa May interpreted the referendum result as a decision by 'the people of the United Kingdom' to 'restore, as we see it, our national self-determination'.[34] Yet ignoring regional disparities was not a long-term strategy. That kind of crude nation building from the centre may have succeeded in late nineteenth century Europe. But as an imperial identity, 'Britishness' sits alongside sometimes stronger regional identities in Scotland and Wales, and especially Northern Ireland, where European and Irish identities are thrown into the mix.[35] Come 2016, the project of restoring self-determination and identity from the centre was not going to work.

Furthermore, the United Kingdom still operates as a highly centralised state on the world stage. The doctrine of the legislative supremacy of the UK Parliament and the absence of a written constitution still buttress the Westminster model of government. EU withdrawal was a matter of high (foreign) policy, tightly controlled and determined by central government. Whilst Theresa May initially promised that the devolved governments would be fully involved in determining the timing and shape of Brexit,[36] the Art. 50 withdrawal process was triggered without consulting – let alone securing the agreement of – the devolved governments. Key pieces of legislation – the European Union (Withdrawal) Act 2018 and the European Union (Withdrawal Agreement) Act 2020 – were enacted in the face of the express refusal of devolved consent (see Chapter 2 by Casanas Adam); and proposals for post-Brexit legislation to bolster the United Kingdom's internal market present a significant threat to devolved autonomy (see Chapter 1 by Hunt). Since the process of EU withdrawal affects state and society at every level, the involvement of the Celtic regions, and especially the Northern Ireland question, has added layers of constitutional complication that cannot be resolved

[32] Eva-Maria Asari, Daphne Halikiopoulou and Steven Mock, 'British National Identity and the Dilemmas of Multiculturalism' (2008) 14:1 *Journal Nationalism and Ethnic Politics* 1–28.
[33] Henderson et al., 'How Brexit was Made in England'.
[34] Prime Minister's letter to Donald Tusk triggering Art. 50, gov.uk, 29 March 2017, www.gov.uk/government/publications/prime-ministers-letter-to-donald-tusk-triggering-article-50.
[35] See, e.g., Patricia Burke Wood and Mary Gilmartin, 'Irish Enough: Changing Narratives of Citizenship and National Identity in the Context of Brexit' (2018) 22 *Space and Polity*, 224–37.
[36] See Akash Paun and George Miller, *Four-Nation Brexit: How the UK and Devolved Governments Should Work Together on Leaving the EU* (London: Institute for Government, 2016), p. 7.

by the resurgence of a particularly muscular and centralising form of unionism[37] that brooks no opposition to the authority of UK-level institutions in their attempt to assert 'national identity' and 'take back control'. Tensions between the assumptions of centralised governance and the devolution of primary law-making power to Scotland, Wales, and Northern Ireland, as well as the acceptance of the principle of popular consent in the context of future constitutional changes, have been exacerbated by Brexit and will continue to characterise the United Kingdom's territorial constitution. These territorial tensions are particularly intense in Scotland, where the Brexit vote followed a narrow loss for Scottish nationalists in the 2014 independence referendum (and where the question of continued EU membership had been an important part of that referendum debate), and in Northern Ireland, where a new land border between the EU and the United Kingdom would resuscitate disagreements on the island of Ireland that had largely been silenced by the 1998 Agreement.

## IRELAND AND THE UNITED KINGDOM: AN UNEASY RELATIONSHIP

Brexit was the most significant territorial event in the United Kingdom's constitution since the departure of twenty-six counties of southern Ireland in 1921. It is perhaps unsurprising therefore that the terms of Ireland's departure from the United Kingdom should have exerted so much influence, nearly 100 years later, on the terms of the United Kingdom's departure from the EU. Legislatively united with Great Britain in 1800, Ireland was a separate and restive part of the United Kingdom. Irish MPs at Westminster advanced the cause of 'home rule' from the 1870s onwards, against intense opposition from unionists in the northeast of Ireland. The religious-demographic make-up of this part of Ireland was markedly different, reflecting the success of plantations in Ulster of British Protestants some 250 years previously.[38] The province of Ulster consisted of nine counties, four with a large Protestant majority, two with a narrow Catholic majority and three with a large Catholic majority. The Liberal government eventually used the Parliament Act 1911 to force through the Government of Ireland Act 1914, establishing home rule for the entirety of Ireland. However, by this point, World War I had commenced. Prime

---

[37] See Michael Kenny and Jack Sheldon 'When Planets Collide: the British Conservative Party and the Discordant Goals of Delivering Brexit and Preserving the Domestic Union, 2016–2019' (2020) 68 *Political Studies* 1–20.
[38] Jonathan Bardon, *A History of Ulster* (Belfast: The Blackstaff Press, 2nd edn., 2001), chap. 5.

Minister Asquith presented a Suspensory Act for Royal Assent at the same time as the Government of Ireland Act. This deferred implementation of home rule until after the end of the war, alongside a political promise that some solution would be found for Ulster.

In 1919, Irish nationalist MPs refused to take their seats in Westminster, instead establishing a new assembly (the first Dáil) in Dublin. A war of independence was fought from 1919 to 1921. In 1920, Westminster established separate Parliaments for Northern Ireland – consisting of the four counties of Ulster with a large Protestant majority and the two counties with a narrow Catholic majority – and for the remaining twenty-six counties in the South. The Anglo-Irish Treaty of 1921 granted self-governing dominion status to Ireland, similar to that of Canada, but allowed Northern Ireland, through its Parliament, to opt out of the new Irish Free State and remain in or return to the United Kingdom, which it duly did. The Treaty, reflected in the Constitution of the Irish Free State 1922, maintained several constitutional connections between the Irish Free State and the United Kingdom, subordinating the autonomy of Irish institutions to UK-based institutions such as the Crown and the Privy Council. These were successively dismantled by Éamon de Valera's government between 1932 and 1936, prior to the enactment of the current constitution in 1937.

With its opening words, 'We, the people of Éire ... hereby adopt, enact, and give to ourselves this Constitution', the 1937 Constitution marked a definitive rupture with Westminster. In Arts. 2 and 3, it made a territorial claim to the entire island of Ireland, while providing that 'pending the re-integration of the national territory', laws made by the Oireachtas (the Irish Parliament) would not have effect in Northern Ireland. In 1949, Ireland formally declared itself a Republic, precipitating its withdrawal from the British Commonwealth of Nations. Notwithstanding the constitutional and territorial tension with the United Kingdom, close relationships between the two states continued – before, during and now after their common membership of the EU. A common travel area allows citizens of each state to move and live freely in the other; and British citizens resident in Ireland may vote in Irish general elections, and vice versa.

The most significant change to the constitutional structure of the Irish State occurred in 1973 with accession to the then European Communities. This required a constitutional amendment, approved at referendum by over 83 per cent, to provide authorisation for the European Communities Act 1972. Successive Taoisigh (prime ministers) had advocated for Ireland's membership since the early 1960s, but it was not realistically achievable until the French veto on UK membership was lifted; the Irish economy was too intertwined with that of the United Kingdom to allow Ireland enter on its own. But membership has never been as controversial in Ireland as in the United Kingdom. Successive treaties, granting further competences to the European Communities and then to the EU, have been approved at referendum. True, the Nice Treaty (2001) and Lisbon Treaty (2008) were both rejected at the first time of asking, but each was subsequently approved by a higher margin on a higher turnout.

While Ireland could not have joined the European Communities without the United Kingdom, there was never any prospect that it would follow the United Kingdom's decision to leave the EU. Membership of the EU allowed Ireland much greater political and economic independence from the United Kingdom. It operated as an equal and independent state, differentiating itself from the United Kingdom in its support of European integration, most clearly through its membership of the Eurozone. In economic terms, Ireland's dependence on the United Kingdom considerably reduced, the proportion of its exports to the United Kingdom falling from 55% in 1973 to 18% in 2003,[39] and to just 9% in 2019.[40] Irish support for EU membership increased to 92% during the Brexit process.[41]

The Brexit referendum, however, brought the border between Ireland and Northern Ireland into sharp focus. The 1998 Agreement saw the establishment of devolved, power-sharing government in Northern Ireland; north-south bodies addressing a number of issues of common concern; and a British-Irish Inter-Governmental Conference alongside a British Irish Council. While the EU did not play a direct role in the peace settlement, Ireland and the United Kingdom's common membership of the EU's single market was a critical factor, removing the need for any border checks. For those living on either side of it, the border became a practical irrelevance, reducing nationalist unease at Northern Ireland's continued constitutional status within the United Kingdom.

The EU made the avoidance of a hard border on the island of Ireland a core objective for the Withdrawal Agreement. The British government also committed itself to this objective (see Chapter 3 by de Mars and O'Donoghue), but

---

[39] Central Statistics Office, 'Ireland and the EU 1973–2003: Economic and Social Change', www.cso.ie/en/media/csoie/releasespublications/documents/statisticalyearbook/2004/ireland&theeu.pdf.

[40] Cliff Taylor, 'Irish Exports Reach a Record €152.5bn as Trade with Britain Declines', *Irish Times*, 14 February 2020, www.irishtimes.com/business/economy/irish-exports-reach-a-record-152-5bn-as-trade-with-britain-declines-1.4173714.

[41] Patrick Smith, 'More than 90% of Irish people want to stay in EU, poll reveals', *Irish Times*, 8 May 2018, www.irishtimes.com/news/politics/more-than-90-of-irish-people-want-to-stay-in-eu-poll-reveals-1.3488112.

found it difficult to reconcile with the other objectives set by Prime Minister May: withdrawing the United Kingdom from the single market and customs union, and avoiding any border between Northern Ireland and the rest of the United Kingdom. The Brexit process involved many issues, but what R. Daniel Keleman identified as the 'Brexit Trilemma' – the promise to leave the EU single market and customs union while simultaneously avoiding a hard border either between Ireland and Northern Ireland or between Northern Ireland and Great Britain – was critical.[42] May sought in the first attempt to secure a Withdrawal Agreement to resolve the trilemma by leaving the entire United Kingdom in de facto alignment with much of EU law. However, the indefinite duration of this arrangement, confirmed in legal advice by the Attorney General (see Chapter 13 by Casey), fuelled intense parliamentary opposition and ultimately cost her premiership. It was only with Boris Johnson's capitulation, accepting a border between Northern Ireland and Great Britain in order to allow much greater divergence from EU law by the remainder of the United Kingdom, that a Withdrawal Agreement could be concluded that would achieve parliamentary approval after the 2019 general election. This crystallised English nationalism – in opposition to British unionism – as the dominant force of Brexit.[43]

At the same time that Ireland posed a territorial challenge to the implementation of Brexit, Brexit posed a territorial challenge to Ireland. The 1998 Agreement built a new model of power-sharing politics on the foundation of a territorial compromise. On the one hand, Ireland and Irish Nationalists accepted the legitimacy of Northern Ireland's status as a component part of the United Kingdom. They thereby relinquished a territorial claim to the whole island of Ireland that had been advanced in different ways since independence and partition in 1921–2. On the other hand, the UK and Ulster Unionists accepted that Northern Ireland would only remain part of the United Kingdom for as long as a majority of people in Northern Ireland so wished it. They thereby relinquished the right of the United Kingdom to preserve its own territorial boundaries.

In 1998, Irish unification – like Scottish independence – seemed a distant prospect. The priority for most Irish nationalists – and certainly for all Irish governments – was to make the new political arrangements work, not to advocate for a united Ireland. But demographic change was slowly producing an electorate more open to unification, and Brexit has now dramatically

---

[42] See R. Daniel Keleman, @rdanielkelemen (24 May 2019). Twitter Page. https://twitter.com/rdanielkelemen/status/1131860434234085376?lang=en.

[43] Kenny and Sheldon, 'When Planets Collide'.

increased the attractiveness of a united Ireland that comes with EU membership. As a result, although opinions on the likelihood of a united Ireland diverge widely, the territorial compromise of 1998 is under pressure. This has raised questions over how well equipped the Irish Constitution is to manage both the processes of unification and the recalibration of a state sympathetic to the interests of those from Ulster Scots and Ulster British traditions.[44] While Ireland amended Arts. 2 and 3 of the Constitution in 1998, withdrawing its territorial claim to Northern Ireland, many other constitutional provisions were predicated on an Irish nation or people largely defined by its struggle against what it perceived as British oppression. The possibility of unification has raised significant questions (see Chapter 6 by Doyle, Kenny, and McCrudden and Chapter 7 by Rooney) over how the Constitution could manage the incorporation of a significant minority community, geographically concentrated in the northeast of the island.

## THE UNITED KINGDOM: AN UNEASY CONSTITUTION

These issues of conflicting and intertwined territorial identities and governance provide part of the explanation why Brexit has placed such pressure on the United Kingdom's constitution. But in other ways too it was unduly simplistic to think that, by leaving the EU, the United Kingdom's constitutional clock could be reset to 31 December 1972. Over the course of the United Kingdom's membership of the EU, its constitution has changed significantly, and these changes help to explain the multiple constitutional challenges that have arisen during the Brexit process.

Put simply, since the 1970s, the United Kingdom's constitution – famously unwritten, highly flexible, and power-hoarding; perhaps not even worthy of the term 'constitution'[45] – has been significantly modernised and in the process has become much more *constitutionalised*. Thus, we have seen the increased use of referendums as a constitutional change device. There is more explicit attention to, and greater legal protection of, constitutional principles – the rule of law, separation of powers, and fundamental rights – which mediate and constrain the hitherto unlimited sovereignty of Parliament. And there is greater emphasis not only upon the dispersal of power through devolution but also the control of power through an increasingly assertive Parliament,[46] the

---

[44] On this terminology, see Chapter 6 by Doyle, Kenny, and McCrudden.
[45] See, e.g., F. F. Ridley 'There is No British Constitution: A Dangerous Case of the Emperor's Clothes' (1988) 41 *Parliamentary Affairs* 340–61.
[46] See, e.g., Meg Russell and Philip Cowley, 'The Policy Power of the Westminster Parliament: The "Parliamentary State" and the Empirical Evidence' (2016) 29 *Governance* 121–37.

expansion of judicial review reconceived as a 'constitutional fundamental',[47] strengthened judicial independence,[48] and an accountability revolution manifested in freedom of information legislation and the proliferation of 'regulation inside government'.[49]

EU membership itself has been an important driver of these changes – both directly and indirectly. For example, the first UK-wide constitutional referendum was held in 1975 on the question whether the United Kingdom should remain a member of the then EEC. Taking inspiration from the use of referendums in other EU member states, Euro-sceptic politicians advocated the use of further referendums as a means initially of constraining deeper European integration, through the referendum lock contained in the European Union Act 2011, and ultimately of side-stepping a pro-European political elite in order to withdraw from the EU altogether.[50] EU membership was also the first constitutional development to place significant pressure on the constitutional centrality of the principle of parliamentary sovereignty. While constitutional lawyers may argue about the precise impact of the European Communities Act 1972 on parliamentary sovereignty, it is undeniable in practice that EU membership limited Parliament's legislative freedom and gave domestic courts new powers to reinterpret,[51] or even set aside Acts of the UK Parliament in order to give effect to the supremacy of EU law.[52] EU membership also had a more pervasive effect on UK public law. For instance, judicial protection of fundamental rights first arrived in the United Kingdom via EU law, and the CJEU's principled approach to adjudication, using standards of proportionality, legal certainty, reason-giving, and effective protection, provided an important source of inspiration for domestic lawyers and judges seeking to break free of the limited and subordinate role for public law

---

[47] William Wade, *Constitutional Fundamentals* (London: Stevens and Sons, revised edn., 1989), chap. 5. See also *R (Jackson)* v. *Attorney General* [2006] 1 AC 262 per Lord Steyn at para. 102.
[48] See e.g. Constitutional Reform Act 2005, s. 3(1) and the inauguration of the UK Supreme Court in 2009.
[49] See Christopher Hood, Oliver James, George Jones, Colin Scott and Tony Travers, *Regulation Inside Government: Waste Watchers, Quality Police and Sleaze Busters* (Oxford: Oxford University Press, 1999).
[50] See Mark D'Arcy, 'Brexit: How Rebel MPs Outfoxed Cameron to Get an EU Referendum', BBC News website, 29 December 2016, www.bbc.co.uk/news/uk-politics-parliaments-38402140.
[51] E.g., *Macarthys Ltd.* v. *Smith* [1980] 3 WLR 929; *Litster* v. *Forth Dry Dock & Engineering Co. Ltd.* [1990] 1 AC 546.
[52] *R* v. *Secretary of State for Transport ex p. Factortame Ltd. (No 2)* [1991] 1 AC 603; *R* v. *Secretary of State for Employment ex p. Equal Opportunities Commission* [1995] 1 AC 1; *Thoburn* v. *Sunderland CC* [2003] QB 151; *Benkharbouche* v. *Sudan* [2015] 3 WLR 301; *Secretary of State for the Home Dept.* v. *Watson* [2018] EWCA Civ 70.

prescribed by the Diceyan orthodoxy.[53] And the EU has also been an important driver of the development of a regulatory state – more rule-bound, and with an increased role for independent experts – in place of the system of 'club government' which characterised the British state in the 1970s.[54] More indirectly, we can also see membership of the EU – a limited legal order, bound by its own constitutional framework – as engendering broader shifts in constitutional thinking, about the dividing and sharing of governmental power and about the role of law in constraining the state, which paved the way for later constitutional developments, such as devolution, the Human Rights Act, and the creation of the Supreme Court.

Nevertheless, though the constitutional impact of EU membership has been profound, it has not been wholly unambiguous. While the United Kingdom may have shifted away from a largely 'political' towards a more 'legal' constitution, with an increased role for legal regulation and judicial control, there has been no wholesale change in constitutional methodology. The constitution remains unwritten, unentrenched, and marked by significant areas of political rather than legal regulation and by extensive constitutional silence.[55] Similarly, constitutional development remains ad hoc, uncoordinated and driven by considerations of political advantage rather than constitutional principle. While this may be true to a degree of all constitutional orders (see, for example, Daly's Chapter 9), the UK constitution is nevertheless one that is unusually free of formal constraints on constitutional change beyond the need to secure a parliamentary majority (and sometimes not even that). Thus, neither joining the EEC in 1973, nor voting to leave the EU in 2016 was expressly presented as a 'constitutional' decision. As noted above, joining the EEC was understood to be about trade, whereas, for the UK government, leaving the EU was conceived as a matter of foreign affairs – and therefore a matter for the royal prerogative rather than Parliament,[56] and one on which the devolved governments had no legitimate say. Similarly, the use of referendums on matters of European integration was not born of a principled belief in the role of the people as the authors of constitutional change, but purely as a means of resolving political problems. More generally, the new constitutional dispensation has not fully embedded itself in the United Kingdom's

---

[53] See e.g. Jeffrey Jowell and Anthony Lester, 'Beyond *Wednesbury*: Substantive Principles of Administrative Law' (1988) 14 *Commonwealth Law Bulletin* 858–70.
[54] See, e.g., Giandomenico Majone, 'The Rise of the Regulatory State in Europe' (1994) 17 *West European Politics* 77–101; Michael Moran, *The British Regulatory State: High Modernism and Hyper-Innovation* (Oxford: Oxford University Press, 2003).
[55] See McHarg, 'Navigating Without Maps'.
[56] Though this characterisation was rejected by the Supreme Court in *Miller 1*.

political culture. Parliamentary sovereignty remains at the heart of the constitution – as demonstrated by the lengths to which judges have gone to limit and domesticate the impact of EU law. Moreover, many of the constitutional reforms undertaken in recent years remain politically controversial and for some at least, as Theresa May put it in her Lancaster House speech, the implications of EU membership sat 'very uneasily in relation to our political history and way of life'.[57]

The result has been the creation of a substantially more complex constitutional order, but one which has struggled to establish a coherent alternative constitutional narrative sufficient to dislodge the Diceyan orthodoxy. In these circumstances, there was plenty of scope for political conflict over Brexit to spill over into clashes between competing constitutional visions. On one side, a UK government determined to use the constitutional power afforded to it to implement the result of referendum, and thereby restore the authority of the central state. On the other, opponents asserting in various, and not always consistent, ways the existence of constitutional constraints conditioning the effect of the referendum mandate and limiting the government's power to act upon it. That so many of these disputes ended up in the courts, as documented in McCorkindale and McHarg's chapter (Chapter 12), illustrates the extent to which the UK constitution has changed. At the same time, the likely backlash that Brexit litigation has produced against 'political interference' by the courts suggests those changes may have shallow roots.

## CONSTITUTIONS UNDER PRESSURE

The underlying constitutional tensions that contributed to Brexit have themselves been exacerbated by Brexit. While it is probably too early – and beyond the scope of this book – to analyse the United Kingdom's new role in Europe, possible constitutional futures have already come into focus. The chapters in this book seek not merely to document some of the myriad constitutional issues that have arisen in the course of the Brexit process, but also to consider its longer-term constitutional implications in both the United Kingdom and Ireland. Part I explores the intersecting territorial pressures created by Brexit for both the United Kingdom and Ireland, including the implications of possible Irish unification, as well as the future development of the United Kingdom's devolution arrangements. Part II then considers the various

---

[57] 'The government's negotiating objectives for exiting the EU: PM speech', gov.uk, 17 Jan. 2017, www.gov.uk/government/speeches/the-governments-negotiating-objectives-for-exiting-the-eu-pm-speech.

institutional pressures and issues of constitutional legitimacy exposed by Brexit, from friction between government and parliament, to the implications of popular sovereignty, and the constitutional role of the courts. The focus in Part II is primarily on the United Kingdom, but comparative reference is made to Ireland where relevant. These territorial and institutional dynamics continue to unfold during a global pandemic that has, if anything, exacerbated the pre-existing constitutional tensions and instabilities. Whether the UK and Irish constitutions can respond effectively will be a significant question for constitutional actors and scholars over the next decade.

# PART I

# TERRITORIAL PRESSURES IN IRELAND AND THE UNITED KINGDOM

# 1

# Subsidiarity, Competence, and the UK Territorial Constitution

## Jo Hunt

### INTRODUCTION

New Labour's 1997 manifesto commitment to devolution drew parallels with the European Union's own moves towards a reinforced commitment to decentralisation. 'Subsidiarity' it declared, 'is as sound a principle in Britain as it is in Europe'.[1] The principle of subsidiarity was first anchored into the EU system by the member states over thirty years ago, in large measure as a defensive bulwark against competence creep from the supranational EU legislature,[2] and it has since become a defining element of the multileveled EU governance architecture.[3] The principle comprises a substantive dimension, that decisions should be taken at the lowest effective level, as well as a procedural dimension, which includes structured opportunities for both *ex ante* political and *ex post* judicial assessment of subsidiarity compliance by the EU legislature. Importantly, the principle operates beyond the two levels of the EU and the nation state. The devolved, or regional level is also implicated. The EU system's openness to regional concerns has opened up the decision-making structures to regional interests, and carved out a space for the exercise of devolved competence and local autonomy within a system of cooperative multilevel governance.

Now as the United Kingdom embarks on the process of leaving the EU, its own existing internal distribution of power is being subjected to reassessment, and to a potential recentralisation of competence. The allocation of

---

[1] *New Labour: Because Britain Deserves Better* (London: Labour Party, 1997).
[2] On the history of the principle in the EU order, see, amongst many others, Antonio Estella, *The EU Principle of Subsidiarity and Its Critique* (Oxford: Oxford University Press, 2002); Robert Schütze, *From Dual to Cooperative Federalism: The Changing Structure of European Law* (Oxford: Oxford University Press, 2009).
[3] S. Pazos-Vidal, *Subsidiarity and EU Multilevel Governance: Actors, Networks and Agendas* (Abingdon: Routledge, 2019).

competence between the UK central authorities and the devolved level has been a continual work-in-progress throughout the history of devolution.[4] In the main, this has involved a progressive expansion of those areas falling within the sphere of devolved competence. The UK system has conventionally been described as one in which shared or concurrent competence is eschewed in favour of a binary approach to competence, so much so that it has been defined as 'hyper-dualist'.[5] However, this model of near *autonomous coexistence* of the different governments within the UK nation state has operated within a broader EU governance framework which takes a more cooperative approach to governance and has an active commitment to subsidiarity.

This chapter provides a reassessment of competence allocation and exercise under the UK constitution. It is submitted, that this needs to be understood through the prism of EU membership, and the supports that were provided by the EU's broader governance framework – including the active commitment to subsidiarity. Drawing in particular on a literature from comparative federalism studies, the first section presents an outline of the issues raised by competence allocation in multilevel states, and shows how subsidiarity exists in a variety of guises across many federal and otherwise decentralised states.[6] Subsidiarity is particularly called into service in areas where competences are shared by different levels of government, and assists in determining the appropriate level to act where powers are concurrent. The second section re-evaluates prevailing understandings of competence under the UK constitution. It identifies the spaces and practices of concurrency, but sees subsidiarity as having little formal presence as a tool to manage the exercise of competence. The third section then brings into sharper focus the way EU membership and its system of governance has provided a framework for the cooperative exercise of shared or concurrent competence. It will demonstrate how this EU commitment to subsidiarity has been incorporated into the UK system. Finally, the chapter will consider how issues of competence are being

---

[4] See e.g., David Torrance, "A Process, Not an Event": Devolution in Wales 1998–2020', HC Briefing Paper CBP-8318 (6 April 2020); David Torrance, '"The Settled Will"? Devolution in Scotland 1998–2020', HC Briefing Paper CBP-8441 (6 April 2020).

[5] Mark Sandford and Cathy Gormley-Heenan, '"Taking Back Control': The UK's Constitutional Narrative and Schrodinger's Devolution' (2020) 73 *Parliamentary Affairs* 108–26.

[6] See, for examples drawn especially from North America, James E. Fleming and Jacob T. Levy (eds.), *Federalism and Subsidiarity* (New York: Nomos, 2014); from Australia, Brazil and Germany, Michelle Evans and Augusto Zimmerman (eds.), *Global Perspectives on Subsidiarity* (Dordrecht: Springer, 2014); and for a consideration of national (including Nigeria and Italy) and international institutional responses (including the EU and ECHR), see Rosa Mulé and Günther Walzenbech (eds.), 'Spaces of Subsidiarity: Diverging Politics and Policies' Special Issue (2019) 57 *Commonwealth and Comparative Politics* 141–259.

approached in the post-Brexit context, and the prospect for subsidiarity as a feature of the UK system. The chapter argues that, following the United Kingdom's withdrawal, there is a need for an effective domestic replacement for the shared competence space that was previously provided by the EU system of governance. Though there are some steps being taken towards this, there are powerful challenges to it because of an attachment to the model of autonomous co-existence of central and devolved levels of government in the UK state.

## COMPETENCE ALLOCATION AND EXERCISE IN MULTILEVEL SYSTEMS OF GOVERNANCE

The capacity for sovereignty to be shared is the defining hallmark of a federal system, as distinct from a unitary state where sovereignty remains at the centre. Whilst the United Kingdom does not fall within any conventional definition of a federal state, approaching its constitutional arrangements through a comparative federalist frame is nonetheless instructive.[7] As Leyland observes, both federalism and devolution are 'essentially addressing the same question, namely, how to define the political organization prevailing within separate polities while maintaining the union of the overarching political system'.[8] Though differences exist, there is sufficient commonality to merit the exploration of the concepts, principles, and practices found in federal orders which keep the tension between centralisation and decentralisation in balance. Whether the United Kingdom is set on a federalising course through the process of devolving power to Northern Ireland, Scotland, and Wales is clearly an open question. Certainly, though, there are some aspects of the current competence settlement which resemble those found in federal systems. Identifying these resemblances, as well as the differences will assist in diagnosing the limits of the UK system, and the causes of the tensions within it.

A common set of questions[9] may be asked about the allocation of competence in federal, and federal-type systems, with each system providing its own unique set of answers. A first question concerns the locus of sovereignty in the

---

[7] See, for example Robert Schütze and Stephen Tierney (eds.) *The United Kingdom and the Federal Idea* (Oxford: Hart, 2018).
[8] Peter Leyland, 'The Multifaceted Constitutional Dynamics of UK Devolution' (2011) 9 *International Journal of Constitutional Law* 251–73, p. 256.
[9] These questions are derived from the approach taken by George Bermann and Kalypso Nicolaidis, 'Basic Principles of Federal Allocation of Competence' in Kalypso Nicolaidis and Robert Howse (eds.), *The Federal Vision: Legitimacy and Levels of Governance in the United States and the European Union* (Oxford: Oxford University Press, 2001).

system, and whether it exists and is exercised at more than one level. Whilst federal states acknowledge a shared sovereignty across levels of governance, in other forms of multilevel governance, sovereignty may be located in the people as whole, or in specific institutions at one particular level. From this, consequences will flow for understandings of the origins of law-making authority in the system, and the relations between the orders. The next set of questions look to the terms on which competences are allocated. This may be substantive allocation by subject matter, with the different levels responsible for different policy areas. This scheme of dual or coordinate legislative federalism is used to describe the original approach under the US Constitution.[10] In comparison, the approach originally adopted in Germany was instead one of assigning different roles to different levels within the same policy sphere. This has been described as being closer to a form of executive or administrative federalism.[11] The Länder were in effect compensated by being afforded a place in the creation of the legislation through their representation in the Bundesrat. As to which powers are assigned to which level, certain commonalities in approach emerge across multilevel orders. As Hueglin and Fenna explain, a key concern in the creation of many federal orders was to 'remove from local particularisms those policy fields concerned with the functioning of the market economy: customs tariffs, money, patents, weights and measures, and trade. These were also the policy areas with extensive spill-over effects'.[12] Policy areas which, at least at the point in time when the federation was formed, were able to be more locally contained, were more apt to lie at the subnational level. These have tended to include the realm of social affairs, including health care, education, and social policy.

The form that the enumeration of powers takes raises another set of questions. These include whether powers are enumerated for one or both levels, whether enumerated powers extend to include implied powers, and where any residual powers lie. The answer to this last question has had a tendency to track the locus of original sovereignty. In federations which have been created by constituent states, any power not expressly identified and allocated has generally remained with the original source. This was the approach adopted under the US Constitution, which deployed a single list of only a limited number of areas of responsibility for Congress, everything else remaining at state level. The Canadian Constitution however, which has lists of both state and federal

---

[10] Thomas O. Hueglin and Alan Fenna, *Comparative Federalism: A Systematic Inquiry* (Toronto: University of Toronto Press, 2nd edn., 2015), p. 136.
[11] Ibid., p. 138.
[12] Ibid., p. 138.

level powers, provides that any residual powers lie with the centre. In both cases, subsequent judicial interpretation has led to a rebalancing of the original settlement: in the USA towards greater centralisation,[13] and in Canada towards greater decentralisation.

Whilst some settlements assign powers to a particular level to be exercised exclusively, others set out powers to be concurrent. As Steytler observes, 'In federations across the world it is widely accepted that few policy fields remain the exclusive domain of either the centre or the constituent units.'[14] Where concurrence exists, questions will arise about how those concurrent powers are managed, about whether one level rather than the other is the preferred decision-maker or legislator in any given situation,[15] and about the consequences of action in that concurrent space. The solutions commonly adopted include a principle of priority, with supremacy afforded to the laws adopted by one level over another in cases of inconsistency. A principle of pre-emption, meanwhile, sees action by one level in an otherwise concurrent space thereby occupying the field, precluding further action by the other level, effectively rendering the powers of that level exclusive.

In a range of systems, the principle of subsidiarity is seen as going some way towards providing an answer to which level should act in situations of concurrence. In the more familiar version derived from Catholic social doctrine,[16] subsidiarity is directed at establishing a hierarchical, vertical order between different social units, with priority afforded to the level closest to the individual. Applied to the context of political governance, a commitment to subsidiarity provides a means of achieving the 'unity in diversity' which is the hallmark of federal and non-unitary states. It is also presumed to enhance the democratic life of the state, by 'encouraging decision-making closer to the region or problem at hand'.[17] Whilst at times 'complex and double-edged',[18] it is, in essence, a decentralising principle, which conceives of the centre as subsidiary to that of its regional units. The default position is one of a presumption of local action,

---

[13] Through the 'elastic' power of Congress to take such action as 'necessary and proper', particularly when tied to the clause for Congress to regulate commerce.

[14] Nico Steytler, 'The Currency of Concurrent Powers in Federal Systems', in Nico Steytler (ed.), *Concurrent Powers in Federal Systems: Meaning, Making and Managing* (Nijhoff: Brill, 2017), p. 1.

[15] See further, Steytler, ibid., and Anna Dziedzic and Cheryl Saunders 'The Meanings of Concurrency' in Steytler (ed.), *Concurrent Powers*.

[16] As opposed to the horizontal sphere sovereignty approach of Protestant Calvinist teaching, see Rosa Mulé and Günter Walzenbech, 'Introduction: Two Spaces of Subsidiarity' (2019) 57 *Commonwealth and Comparative Politics* 141–52, p. 141.

[17] Evans and Zimmerman, *Global Perspectives*, p. 2.

[18] Mulé and Walzenbech 'Introduction: Two Spaces of Subsidiarity', p. 144.

unless this is dislodged by the case made for centralised action. In Germany, for example, though most federal law once enacted has a pre-emptive effect in areas of concurrent competence,[19] the Federation's right to legislate is subject to a national interest necessity test. This is enforceable by the Federal Constitutional Court, and operates to restrict the federal legislator to acting in certain concurrent fields when this is necessary in the interests of legal or economic unity, or the maintenance of equivalent living conditions.[20] Subsidiarity is also a feature of the (non-federal) Italian Constitution, introduced into the constitutional order by its Constitutional Court in 2003, though its use has been more centralising than decentralising. It has been used to endorse executive and legislative action by the centre, across otherwise regional powers. The principle is described as a 'factor for flexibility'[21] in meeting the Italian state's unitary needs. As a counterbalance to this, though, there is an emphasis on the procedural and consensual dimension of subsidiarity in the decision-making process.[22]

The move to more concurrent powers in non-unitary systems may be explained as a response to the increasing complexities and interconnectedness of modern governance. It is a shift that has been charted in federal literature: from the dominant model of dual federalism, to one of cooperative federalism, with its metaphors of layer cakes and marble cakes.[23] An approach based on the mutually exclusive spheres of dual federalism has been replaced by one in which 'governments must cooperate, that is, work and function together'.[24] Here, considerations of legal competence connect with the related, but separate political concepts of self and shared rule. Coined first by Elazar,[25] and subsequently developed most notably by Hooghe, Marks, and Schakel in their construction of a 'Regional Authority Index',[26] self-rule refers to the

---

[19] Art. 72(1) Grundgesetz (Basic Law) establishes pre-emptive effect, subject to the exclusion of certain areas under Art. 72(3) GG which permit the Länder to take different measures.

[20] Art. 72(2) GG; Carlo Panara 'The Enforceability of Subsidiarity in the EU and the Ethos of Cooperative Federalism: A Comparative Law Perspective' (2016) 22 *European Public Law* 305–32.

[21] Corte Constituzionale, 1 October 2003, Sentenza 303/203, Considerato in Diritto, para 2.2.

[22] See for discussion Laura Ronchetti, 'The Judicial Construction of Italian Regionalism' in Stelio Mangiameli (ed.), *Italian Regionalism: Between Unitary Traditions and Federal Process* (Switzerland: Springer, 2014).

[23] Morton Grodzins, 'The Federal System' in Daniel J. Elazar (ed.), *The American System: A New View of the Government of the United States* (New York: Rand McNally, 1966), p. 74.

[24] Daniel J. Elazar, 'Cooperative Federalism' in Daphne A. Kenyon and John Kincaid (eds.), *Competition Among States and Local Governments: Efficiency and Equity in American Federalism* (Washington DC: Urban Institute Press, 1991), p. 69.

[25] Daniel J. Elazar, *Exploring Federalism* (Tuscaloosa: University of Alabama Press, 1987).

[26] Liesbet Hooghe, Gary N. Marks and Arjan H. Schakal, *The Rise of Regional Authority: A Comparative Study of 42 Democracies* (London and New York: Routledge, 2010).

decision-making autonomy that regional sub-units possess. Shared rule, meanwhile, refers to the involvement of regional institutions in decision making for the whole state – the degree to which they are represented and their interests and prerogatives protected. The balance between self and shared rule differs from system to system. Taken as a whole, this combination of legal and political institutions, structures, processes and principles will provide each state with its own dynamic model of how power is shared across the territorial constitution.

## COMPETENCE ALLOCATION AND EXERCISE UNDER THE UK CONSTITUTION

Turning to the United Kingdom, some of the questions on competence posed above have been answered differently for different parts of the Union state. They are also contested – starting most obviously with the locus of sovereignty. The claims to an absolute Westminster parliamentary sovereignty have been challenged by Scotland in particular, both politically and judicially,[27] and arguments have been advanced concerning the continued sovereignty of the Scottish people.[28] So far, however, the concept of divided sovereignty has not been endorsed within the legal and judicial institutions of the wider state such that it has dislodged the conventional constitutional orthodoxy.[29]

Competence is allocated broadly by subject matter, with specific policy areas assigned to the centre. The main areas assigned to the centre follow those seen elsewhere – foreign affairs, defence, and the constitution.[30] Beyond this common core, the specific reservations differ across the devolved regimes, which reflect their different legal histories.[31] Traces of an earlier functional administrative model of devolution are still evident, especially in the model of devolution seen for Wales, where responsibility for different elements within

---

[27] The famous *obiter dictum* of Lord President Cooper in *MacCormick v. Lord Advocate*, 1953 SC 396: 'the principle of the unlimited sovereignty of Parliament is a distinctively English principle which has no counterpart in Scottish constitutional law'.
[28] See Aiden O'Neill, 'The Sovereignty of the (Scottish) People: 1689 and All That' (2013) 18 *Judicial Review* 446–63.
[29] See Gordon Anthony, 'Devolution Issues, Legislative Power, and Legal Sovereignty' in A. Antoine (ed.), *Le Droit Public Britannique: État des Lieux et Perspectives* (Société de Législation Comparée/Lextenso, 2015).
[30] Northern Ireland Act 1998, Schedule 2 (Excepted Matters); Scotland Act 1998, Schedule 5 (Reserved Matters); Government of Wales Act 2006, Schedule 7A (Reserved Matters).
[31] Though there are now significant commonalities in approach across the three settlements, differences remain. In NI, the first layer of reservations is referred to as 'excepted' matters. There is a further set of 'reserved' matters which may be removed from central control at some later point.

the same policy area is more regularly divided across the levels of government. This reservations-with-exceptions approach creates a degree of policy interdependency between the levels that might imply systems of effective cooperation and coordination, rather than autonomous activity.[32] However, it is a well-observed feature of the devolution arrangements that the necessary machinery of shared governance has never been created for the United Kingdom.[33]

The enumeration of a list of reserved powers is now the common approach taken for all three devolved orders. This has only recently been adopted for Wales, which operated under a conferred model basis until the Wales Act 2017.[34] The devolution statutes now each contain a set of exclusive powers reserved to the centre, and the devolved Parliaments are precluded from legislating in these reserved areas. A further set of restrictions limit the scope of devolved legislative action, by specifying a series of UK Acts of Parliament which cannot be modified. As the Supreme Court made clear in the *Scottish Continuity Bill* reference,[35] areas covered by the 'protected enactment' do not wholly exclude action by the devolved level, only such action as amends, modifies, or repeals the protected enactment. In contrast, where a matter is reserved, the UK level 'occupies the field', and devolved legislation is not permitted except where it has a loose or consequential connection.

These provisions aside, UK legislation in a non-reserved policy area does not benefit from any automatic rule of hierarchical priority –and it will not pre-empt devolved legislative action in that space. Though *sovereign*, the Westminster Parliament is not necessarily automatically *supreme*, in that its laws may be overridden by later devolved legislation. A series of *ex ante* and *ex post* controls over the devolved legislatures provide checks on the boundary line between reserved and non-reserved competence. Anything adopted in violation of the reservation is 'not law' as a consequence of being outside

---

[32] See, for a discussion of the unmet requirement for greater shared governance to match the interconnected policy allocation, Nicola McEwen and Bettina Petersohn, 'The Challenges of Shared Rule After the Scottish Referendum' (2015) 86 *Political Quarterly* 192–200.

[33] Adam Tomkins, 'Shared Rule: What the UK Could Learn from Federalism' in Schütze and Tierney (eds.), *The UK and the Federal Idea*; Nicola McEwen, Michael Kenny, Jack Sheldon, and Coree Brown Swan, 'Intergovernmental Relations in the UK' (2020) 91 *Political Quarterly*, 632–40.

[34] See Richard W. Rawlings, 'The Strange Reconstitution of Wales' (2018) *Public Law*, 62–83; David Moon and Tomos Evans, 'Welsh devolution and the problem of legislative competence' (2017) 12 *British Politics*, 335–60.

[35] *The UK Withdrawal from the European Union (Legal Continuity) (Scotland) Bill – A Reference by the Attorney General and the Advocate General for Scotland* [2018] UKSC 64.

legislative competence.[36] In addition to these 'federal' restrictions delineating competence, [37] a set of 'constitutional' restrictions operate over devolved competence. These ensure that law makers comply with obligations arising under ECHR, and, until the end of the transition period, EU law.

How then should those powers that have not been centrally reserved be categorised? Should they be seen as exclusive to the devolved level, or are they held concurrently? If concurrent, are there principles determining how that concurrence should operate? The devolved governments certainly present such powers as 'theirs', though there is, as a matter of strict law, no area from which the Westminster Parliament is excluded. There are no devolved legislative competences reserved exclusively to that level. The devolution statutes make this explicit, with a common provision recognising the continued sovereignty of Westminster: devolution 'does not affect the power of the Parliament of the UK to make laws' for any part of the UK. [38] That said, there is much to suggest that an assumption of exclusivity is not misplaced. The Memorandum of Understanding that contains an agreed (though not legally binding) set of principles for intergovernmental relations (IGR) identifies a bifurcated approach, with matters either 'devolved' or 'non-devolved'. It acknowledges that devolved areas are 'the primary responsibility of devolved legislatures and administrations in these fields' and says the UK government will encourage the Westminster Parliament to recognise that it is a consequence of its own decision to 'devolve certain matters that Parliament itself will in future be more restricted in its field of operation'.[39] The sense of devolved ownership over these levels has been reinforced through the endorsement in legislation of the Sewel Convention. [40] This provides that Westminster will not normally legislate on devolved matters without devolved consent. Certainly, whilst Westminster has continued to legislate in devolved space, until the very particular pressures of Brexit, it has always done so respecting the Sewel Convention.[41] This has seen it amending legislative proposals to accommodate devolved concerns, or redefining the territorial scope of the problematic elements of proposed legislation.[42] As Elliott

---

[36] Northern Ireland Act, s. 6(1); Scotland Act, s. 29(1); Government of Wales Act, s. 108(1).
[37] Christopher McCorkindale, Aileen McHarg and Paul Scott, 'The Courts, Devolution and Constitutional Review' (2017) 36 *University of Queensland Law Journal*, 289–310.
[38] Northern Ireland Act, s. 5(6); Scotland Act, s. 28(7); Government of Wales Act, s. 107(5).
[39] MoU para. 15.
[40] Through the Scotland Act 2016 and Wales Act 2017.
[41] For discussion of how the Sewel Convention has been strained by Brexit, see Casanas Adam, in this volume.
[42] Graeme Cowie and David Torrance, 'Devolution: The Sewel Convention', HC Briefing Paper CBP-8883 (13 May 2020).

identifies, 'the modern territorial Constitution is premised upon constitutional actors' mutual respect for each other's constitutional spheres of authority'.[43] For Tierney, the recent formal legislative statement of the Sewel Convention and the permanence of the devolved institutions appeared 'to have created the near complete protection for self-rule'.[44]

The UK model of competence allocation thus appears to be effectively one of an exclusive and autonomous coexistence of powers within the nation state. This exclusivity, as far as the powers of the devolved level are concerned, remains conditional, partial and shorn of the constitutional protections usually found in systems of divided sovereignty. A more constitutionally coherent conceptualisation of competence allocation might be to consider the sphere of devolved powers as concurrent, though with a strong presumption of devolved responsibility. Does this presumption of devolved responsibility translate to support for, and the operationalisation of a principle of subsidiarity at work within the UK constitution? Certainly, the terminology and spirit of the principle has been appealed to throughout the recent history of devolution, starting with the introduction of the devolution proposals in the Labour Party manifesto by Prime Minister Blair, ahead of the 1997 general election. However, despite the many references to it as a guiding principle for the UK's constitutional order,[45] there is an absence of any explicit articulation of subsidiarity as an operational principle within the United Kingdom's governance system. There may indeed be entirely convincing reasons consistent with subsidiarity concerns why Westminster would wish to legislate across devolved areas.[46] However, though the legislative consent process may provide the framework for raising subsidiarity concerns, there is no shared language around this, or common understandings of when a UK-wide measure is more appropriate than one at devolved level.[47] Furthermore, the principle of

---

[43] Mark Elliott, 'The Supreme Court's Judgment in *Miller*: In Search of Constitutional Principle' (2017) 76 *Cambridge Law Journal* 257–88, p. 277.

[44] Stephen Tierney 'Drifting Towards Federalism?' Appraising the Constitution in the Light of the Scotland Act 2016 and the Wales Act 2017' in Schütze and Tierney (eds.), *The UK and the Federal Idea*, p. 112.

[45] The specific language of subsidiarity is not a feature of the Conservative government's lexicon. It does appear in many Parliamentary Select Committee reports, e.g., HL Select Committee on the Constitution, 'The Union and Devolution 2015–16' (10th Report), HL Paper 149; and thinktank recommendations, e.g., 'Draft Charter of the Union' Bingham Centre for the Rule of Law (London: British Institute of International and Comparative Law, May 2015).

[46] For an account of the reasons for Westminster legislation in the early days of devolution, see Alan Page and Andrea Batey, 'Scotland's Other Parliament: Westminster Legislation About Devolved Matters in Scotland Since Devolution' (2002) *Public Law*, 501–23.

[47] Any case that may be made for Westminster action would be found in the relevant bill's Explanatory Memorandum and related bilateral ministerial letters. These will follow the communications of officials backstage.

subsidiarity has not received much in the way of support from the courts. In successive cases about the extent of devolved competence before the Supreme Court, the observation has been made that 'it is not for the courts to say whether legislation on any particular issue is better made by the Scottish Parliament or by the Parliament of the United Kingdom at Westminster'.[48] This agnosticism is repeated in relation to concurrent *executive* powers. These powers are particularly a feature of the devolution scheme for Wales, and they are appearing more frequently in the Brexit-related primary legislation. In determining the meaning of concurrence as being that either the UK or Welsh minister could exercise the relevant powers, the Supreme Court in the *Byelaws (Wales)* case did not search for any ordering principles, saying merely that it was 'left to their good sense to decide which should exercise a particular function in a particular case'.[49]

Whilst there may be little in the way of constitutional recognition of an operational principle of subsidiarity, or a de facto recognition of concurrent competence, the superimposition of the EU system of governance brings a different picture into focus.

## THE EUROPEAN UNION: A MULTILEVEL SHARED GOVERNANCE REGIME

The European Union is a multilevel system of governance which, as Schütze argues, increasingly reflects a model of cooperative, rather than dualist federalism.[50] The process of transition from a binary division between national and supranational spheres of exclusive responsibility, to a system which promotes shared governance, has been effected in a number of steps. Crucial to this process has been the constitutionalisation of the principle of subsidiarity, 'as a safeguard for decentralised federalism'.[51] Introduced by the Maastricht Treaty, this cross-cutting governance principle originally operated on a two-level basis. Its first formulation provided that, outside the realm of its exclusive competence, 'the Community shall take action, in accordance with the principle of subsidiarity, only if and in so far as the objectives of the proposed action cannot be sufficiently achieved by the Member States, and can therefore, by reason of their scale or effects of the proposed action, be

---

[48] *Martin v. HM Advocate* [2010] UKSC 40 at para. 5; *Imperial Tobacco Ltd. v. Lord Advocate* [2012] UKSC 61 at para. 12.
[49] *Attorney General v. National Assembly for Wales Commission, Local Government Byelaws (Wales) Bill* [2012] UKSC 53 at para. 41.
[50] Schütze, *From Dual to Cooperative Federalism*.
[51] Ibid., p. 242. Schütze additionally cites the importance of the demarcation of the sphere of complementary competences, where the role of the EU is to support member state action.

better achieved by the Community'.[52] From the start though, the subnational dimension has been apparent. The pressure for a commitment to subsidiarity had in particular come from the German Länder, as a response to the hollowing out of their competences through EU governance as a two-level endeavour.[53] Since then, the regional and local dimensions have continued to command attention,[54] and a series of initiatives have contributed to the creation of an infrastructure which is receptive to (and can be protective of) the subnational level of governance. Not least, the subsidiarity principle was reformulated by the Lisbon Treaty to incorporate a consideration of sufficiency of the regional and local level to meet policy objectives, alongside the member states.[55] In addition to the question of which level should act, the subsidiarity principle is also understood as containing a proportionality dimension, which checks whether, if action lies with the EU legislator, there is no measure available that could impact less on decentralised powers, whilst achieving the objectives of the policy in question.[56]

The limits of a *justiciable* subsidiarity principle have been well documented, especially given the centralising way it has been interpreted by the European Court of Justice.[57] However, it has, by some assessments, been successfully 'internalised'[58] by the European Commission, which must explicitly articulate the case for EU level action when introducing legislative proposals. Of particular significance has been the introduction of the 'Early Warning System', which provides a formal role for national parliaments to perform a subsidiarity check on draft legislation. Running through the Protocol[59] that sets out this procedure is an

---

[52] The 1986 Single European Act had introduced the principle into the field of environmental governance, but it was the Maastricht Treaty that introduced it as a horizontal principle.

[53] Charlie Jeffery, 'The Länder Strike Back. Structures and Processes of European Integration Policy-Making in the German Federal System', *Leicester University Discussion Papers in Federal Studies*, No. FS94/4 (1994).

[54] A '2017 Task Force on Subsidiarity' established by President Juncker had as one of its three tasks 'to find ways to better involve regional and local authorities in EU policy making and delivery', insisting that Europe must deliver at the level closest to its citizens. Michael Schneider, 'Subsidiarity: Past, Present and Future' (2019) 18 *European View* 16–25.

[55] Art. 5(3) TEU.

[56] This exists alongside the broader conception of proportionality in Art. 5(4) TEU, which is a more frequently and more successfully pleaded ground than subsidiarity. See Vasiliki Kosta, 'The Principle of Proportionality in EU Law: An Interest Based Taxonomy' in Joana Mendes (ed.), *EU Executive Discretion and the Limits of Law* (Oxford: Oxford University Press, 2019).

[57] Jacob Öberg, 'Subsidiarity as a Limit to the Exercise of EU Competences' (2017) 36 *Yearbook of European Law* 391–420.

[58] Oxana Pimenova, 'Subsidiarity as a 'Regulation Principle' in the EU' (2016) 4 *The Theory and Practice of Legislation* 381–98.

[59] Protocol (No. 2) on the Application of the Principles of Subsidiarity and Proportionality, Official Journal of the EU 115, 09/05/2008 P. 0206–0209.

appreciation of the regional and local level, and national parliaments are directed to consult regional parliaments with legislative powers.[60] This engagement with national parliaments reinforces the democratic element of the principle. The recognition of regional parliaments as participants, albeit indirectly, in EU policy processes[61] joins a variety of other mechanisms which provide for subnational involvement in EU governance. These include various direct and indirect routes into the process,[62] such as through the Committee of the Regions, through regional ministers representing the relevant member state in the Council of Ministers, through Commission consultation ahead of legislative proposals, and more informally, through lobbying and participation in networks, facilitated by having representations based in Brussels.[63] These formal and informal channels into the 'upstream' aspects of the policy process are accompanied by a 'downstream' role for subnational regions in policy implementation. Many legal measures, especially those in areas such as the Common Agricultural Policy (CAP) and environmental law, explicitly create space for a local determination of how policy is to be implemented, which can result in managed variation.[64] As de Conincke and van Hecke explain, directives in particular 'grant the governments some leeway in how to fulfil their obligations ... This allows the member states, and thus also the regions to take into account their specific situation, traditions and existing laws when deciding on how to reach the aims of the directives'.[65] The role played by regional governments and legislatures is consistent with the German model of cooperative federalism, with the different levels participating in shared roles and responsibilities.

---

[60] Protocol (No. 2) Art. 6(2).
[61] Gabriele Abels and Annegret Eppler (eds.), *Subnational Parliaments in the EU Multi-Level Parliamentary System: Taking Stock of the Post-Lisbon Era* (Innsbruck: Studienverlag, 2016).
[62] Carlo Panara, *The Subnational Dimension of the EU: A Legal Study of Multilevel Governance* (Switzerland; Springer International, 2015); Serafin Pazos-Vidal, *Subsidiarity and EU Multilevel Governance: Actors, Networks and Agendas* (Routledge, 2019). For accounts that are less convinced by the space provided for subnational regions in EU governance, see e.g., Michèle Finck, 'Challenging the Subnational Dimension of Subsidiarity in EU Law (2015) 8 *European Journal of Legal Studies* 5–17; Piet Van Nuffell, 'Does EU decision-making take into account regional interests?', in Elke Cloots, Geert De Baere and Stefan Sottiaux (eds.), *Federalism in the European Union* (Oxford: Hart Publishing 2012).
[63] Carolyn Rowe, *Regional Representations in the EU: Between Diplomacy and Interest Mediation* (London; Palgrave Macmillan, 2011).
[64] Jens Newig and Tomas M. Koontz, 'Multi-level governance, policy implementation and participation: the EU's mandated participatory planning approach to implementing environmental policy' (2014) 21 *Journal of European Public Policy* 248–67.
[65] Isabelle De Coninck and Steven Van Hecke, 'The regional transposition of EU directives: a comparison of Flemish, Walloon and Scottish performances' (2018) 19 *European Politics and Society* 79–102, p. 80.

When this EU context is layered over the UK governance system, the picture emerges of greater concurrent competence, greater cooperation, and a greater role for the principle of subsidiarity than is otherwise the case. Though relations with the EU are defined as falling within the exclusive, reserved competence of the UK Parliament,[66] the devolved administrations were certainly not excluded from either upstream or downstream dimensions of the policy process. Significant areas of EU policy activity correspond with areas recognised as falling within devolved competence, including agriculture, environment, and regional economic development. As the Memorandum of Understanding between the governments of the United Kingdom acknowledges, the devolved governments 'have a particular interest in those many aspects of European Union business which affect devolved areas, and a significant role to play in them'.[67] A specific Concordat on the Coordination of European Union Policy Issues made the commitment that devolved administrations would be involved 'as directly and fully as possible in decision making on EU matters',[68] with the 'full and continuing involvement of ministers and officials' extending across 'policy formulation, negotiation, and implementation'.[69] This commitment goes beyond that found in the Concordat on International Relations, which is limited to ensuring 'close cooperation' between the UK government and ministers from the devolved governments in the conduct of international relations.[70] This cooperation is expected to take place through the Joint Ministerial Committees.[71] Though these have rightly received heavy criticism, the specific formation for European affairs, JMC (E) was the most functional. It continued to meet regularly through the lengthy hiatuses encountered by the other JMCs, had a clear remit linked to upcoming European Council meetings and provided an opportunity for influence to be exerted.[72] The Concordat also explicitly recognises that ministers from the devolved governments could represent the United Kingdom in Council of the European Union.[73] In addition, the

---

[66] Northern Ireland Act, Schedule 2 s. 3; Scotland Act, Schedule 5 s. 7(1), Government of Wales Act, Schedule 7A ss. 10(1) and (2).
[67] Memorandum of Understanding, October 2013, para. 18. This MoU is a revised version of the original agreed in December 2001 (Cm 5240).
[68] B Concordat on the Coordination of European Union Policy Issues, October 2013, B1.5 (Scotland); B2.5 (Wales); B3.5 (Northern Ireland).
[69] B Concordat, B1.6 (Scotland); B2.6 (Wales); B3.6 (Northern Ireland).
[70] D Concordat on International Affairs, D1.5 (Scotland); D2.5 (Wales); D3.5 (Northern Ireland).
[71] For JMC (Europe) see B Concordat, B4 Common Annex, B4.5–12.
[72] Nicola McEwen, 'Still better together? Purpose and power in intergovernmental councils in the UK' (2017) 27 *Regional & Federal Studies* 667–90.
[73] B Concordat, B4 Common Annex, B4.13.

devolved Parliaments had a role to play in developing a UK line on EU policy development, specifically, since its introduction under the Lisbon Treaty, through the system of subsidiarity monitoring. Formalised monitoring procedures were established within the regional parliaments, and though the UK Parliament did not create any legally mandated procedures for managing the subsidiarity checking process, it demonstrated a receptiveness to the submissions that were passed to them.[74]

In relation to the downstream aspects of policy implementation, the devolution statutes all explicitly recognised that, whilst relations with the EU may be reserved, implementing and observing EU legal obligations was devolved.[75] The approach of the United Kingdom has been to accommodate the local variation that EU law permits. The Concordat presents implementation by the devolved administrations in their sphere of competence as the default position. Alternatively, they could opt for participation in a GB- or UK-wide approach.[76] Where the default applies, the Concordat identifies the need for 'consistency of effect',[77] though this certainly does not mean uniformity and leaves wide space for divergence. This was confirmed following the *Horvath* case, which contains one of the few mentions of subsidiarity in the UK courts.[78] The High Court[79] made a reference to the European Court of Justice, on the question whether the different legislatures in the United Kingdom could lawfully implement EU rules (here, under the CAP) differently, which resulted in different obligations being placed on farmers in different parts of the United Kingdom. Horvath, a farmer in England, was subject to the most onerous regime, and challenged the implementation. The relevant regulation provided for possible alternative choices in implementation, and the question was whether this internal variation was

---

[74] The House of Lords has demonstrated particular receptiveness. On regional parliaments and EWS see Karolina Borońska-Hryniewiecka (2017) 'Regional parliamentary empowerment in EU affairs. Building an analytical framework' (2017) 23 *The Journal of Legislative Studies* 144–61; Anna-Lena Högenauer, 'The Scottish Parliament – Active Player in Multilevel European Union' in Abels and Appler (eds.), *Subnational Parliaments*.

[75] Northern Ireland Act, Schedule 2 s. 3(c); Scotland Act, Schedule 5, s. 7(2)(a); Government of Wales Act, Schedule 7A s. 10(3). This division was confirmed by the Supreme Court in the *Scottish Continuity Bill Reference*.

[76] B Concordat, B4 Common Annex, B4.17.

[77] B Concordat, B4 Common Annex, B4.18.

[78] Outside the use of the principle as an instrument in human rights cases, as recognised under the ECHR system, and separate from this territorial constitutional context. An attempt to defend non-implementation of a directive by Northern Irish authorities on the ground that the subsidiarity principle gave them room to manoeuvre was rejected by the High Court in *Seaport Investments* [2007] NIQB 62, though no discussion of the principle was entered into.

[79] *R (Horvath)* v. *Secretary of State for Environment, Food and Rural Affairs* [2006] EWHC Admin 1833.

discriminatory and would require objective justification, or whether it was automatically lawful. The decision to refer was appealed against, and the Court of Appeal confirmed that the reference should be sent.[80] A key ground highlighted by the court in support of the decision to refer the question was 'the developing nature of the concept of subsidiarity', which the European Court should be given the opportunity to consider. Though the Court of Justice ultimately decided the case without express reference to the principle,[81] it confirmed the lawfulness of differential implementation by legislatures within a state as a matter of EU law, recognising that 'each Member State is free to allocate powers internally and to implement [EU law] by means of measures adopted by regional or local authorities'.[82] It equated the regional legislature with a national legislature, recognising its competence to adopt measures which result in divergent implementation, if such divergences would be permitted as between member states under the terms of the legislation. Case law from the Court of Justice has also upheld specific pieces of legislation adopted independently by the devolved executives and legislatures against challenges that the legislation offends against the free movement principle under EU law. Legislative choices have been justified under the EU laws concerning public goods which can trump considerations of economic efficiency, such as public health, animal health, and environmental protection.[83]

Whilst the practice under the UK constitution has been to treat de jure concurrent competences as de facto exclusive, and to ignore the need for effective shared governance, the EU governance context reveals a different picture. Here, competences are more evidently exercised concurrently, in a system which demonstrates a strong commitment to subsidiarity.

## SUBSIDIARITY AND COMPETENCE POST-BREXIT

On the United Kingdom's departure from the EU, it leaves the cooperative shared governance framework that has formed the context for the exercise of swathes of devolved competences since the coming into force of the 1999 settlements. The Supreme Court in *Miller* characterised this as a removal of

---

[80] [2007] ECWA Civ 620, per Lady Justice Arden, paras. 73–5.
[81] C-428/07, [2009] ECR I-6355. Advocate General Trstenjak's opinion, which went the same way as the court's judgment, did draw on subsidiarity to approve the United Kingdom's arrangements, at para. 94.
[82] At para. 50.
[83] E.g., *R (Petsafe)* v. *The Welsh Ministers* [2010] EHWC 2908; *Sinclair Collis Ltd.* v. *Lord Advocate* [2012] CSIH; *Scotch Whisky Association* v. *Lord Advocate and Advocate General* [2017] SC 465.

constraints, which, in the absence of new restraints, would result in enhancements to the scope of devolved competence.[84] The period since the 2016 vote has seen successive UK governments attempt to determine how much of the framework previously provided by the EU would need to be replicated within the United Kingdom. The overwhelmingly dualist, bifurcated system of governance which has operated between the centre and the devolved institutions would appear to provide unpromising ground upon which to build this replacement for EU frameworks. The autonomous coexistence resulting from the latitude afforded to the devolved institutions in what were treated as effectively 'their' exclusive competences, and the absence of effective shared competence machinery in the United Kingdom, mean that any attempts to redefine the relationship are likely to be controversial. There have been trenchant reassertions of sovereignty by the Westminster Parliament which have revealed starkly the limits of shared rule. The two key pieces of withdrawal legislation were marked by these limits as they came into force: with the Scottish Parliament refusing consent to the EU (Withdrawal) Act 2018, and all three devolved legislatures refusing consent to the EU (Withdrawal Agreement) Act 2020. The confirmation of the lack of legal enforceability of the Sewel Convention meant that the consequences of legislation in the face of a negative Legislative Consent Motion are political, rather than legal.[85] It has also seen the UK government double down on its sphere of exclusive powers and its zone of self-rule, especially as regards competence over international relations.

Further, there has been no commitment by the UK government to maintain any role for the EU principle of subsidiarity. The EU Withdrawal Act 2018 makes provision for the retention of general principles of EU law, but only those general principles that have been recognised as such by the European Court of Justice are carried over.[86] While academic commentators and practitioners conventionally refer to subsidiarity as a general principle, the court has rarely used this language in relation to subsidiarity. In contrast to its description of proportionality, legal certainty, and non-discrimination as general principles, subsidiarity is repeatedly defined as simply a 'principle'.[87]

---

[84] *R (Miller and another) v. Secretary of State for Exiting the European Union* [2017] UKSC 5 at para. 130.
[85] *R (Miller)* [2017], see Casenas Adam, in this volume; Aileen McHarg, 'Constitutional change and territorial consent: The *Miller* Case and the Sewel Convention' in Mark Elliott, Jack Williams and Alison Young (eds.), *The UK Constitution After Miller* (Oxford: Hart Publishing, 2018).
[86] EU (Withdrawal) Act 2018, Schedule 1 at para. 2.
[87] But cf. Case C-110/03, *Belgium v. Commission* ECLI:EU:C:2005:223 at para. 58.

Whether this is sufficient for national courts to consider themselves able to draw on the principle is unclear, and in any case the Act limits the use of general principles in various ways, such as restricting them to being used only when interpreting retained EU law.

Despite the unpromising terrain, there has been some notable, positive progress towards a shared governance system. This has included significant appeals to the principle of subsidiarity, albeit couched in other terms, in particular through the programme of work on common frameworks. These are the UK-wide replacements for the governance frameworks previously provided under EU law that set the parameters for domestic legislative variation. The starting point for this transformation in governance was unpromising. The UK government had originally proposed maintaining existing EU provisions,[88] precluding future unilateral action in those policy areas by the devolved governments and parliaments, unless and until such a time that the UK government decided it was possible. Through a series of coordinated steps, the devolved institutions in Scotland and Wales sought to prevent these constraints being imposed.[89] The resultant changes to the draft legislation were such that the Welsh Parliament – but not the Scottish – gave its legislative consent. Rather than automatic control over repatriated competences flowing to Whitehall and Westminster, the Withdrawal Act provides the power for UK ministers to freeze such EU law measures that may need to be maintained ahead of the agreement of new UK-wide frameworks.[90] The decision to freeze EU retained legislation would 'not normally' be taken without devolved consent, and an associated Intergovernmental Agreement (IGA)[91] between the Welsh and UK governments provides that the resultant freeze would apply to both parties, as it includes a political commitment not to change the law for England. In practice, no freezing regulations have so far been adopted. With retained EU law continuing to apply until the end of the transition period, the room for manoeuvre, or for disruption, was much less than was envisaged at the start of the process. Instead, work has proceeded on the common frameworks, with the IGA setting out principles as to how and when these would be created. Despite its refusal to sign up to the IGA, the Scottish government has nonetheless participated in this work, which had,

---

[88] EU (Withdrawal) Bill, clause 11.
[89] See Nicola McEwen, 'Negotiating Brexit: power dynamics in British intergovernmental relations' (2020) *Regional Studies*, forthcoming.
[90] EU (Withdrawal) Act, s. 12.
[91] Intergovernmental Agreement on the European Union (Withdrawal) Bill and the Establishment of Common Frameworks, 24 April 2018.

until the Covid outbreak, been progressing in a positive way, demonstrating clear elements of a shared rule approach to governance.

The IGA identifies a set of reasons when and why cooperation across the four nations is required, which effectively introduces a principles-based approach to the exercise of concurrent competence. These principles were first agreed in 2017, and they foresee joint working for the creation of common frameworks for the following purposes:

- 'the functioning of the UK internal market, while acknowledging policy divergence';
- 'compliance with international obligations';
- 'the UK's ability to negotiate, enter into and implement new trade agreements and international treaties';
- 'the management of common resources';
- 'the administration of and provision of access to justice in cases with a cross-border element';
- 'the security of the UK'.

There is also agreement that 'frameworks will respect the devolution settlements and the democratic accountability of the devolved legislatures', and will therefore: 'maintain, as a minimum, equivalent flexibility for tailoring policies to the specific needs of each territory as is afforded by current EU rules; [and] lead to a significant increase in decision-making powers for the devolved administrations'.[92] The process of creating these joint frameworks has progressed through close working relations between officials, and includes the clarification of which areas require a legislative response, and those which need no, or only loose coordination,[93] again reflecting an appreciation of subsidiarity concerns. Legislation has started to be introduced,[94] and design principles for non-legislative frameworks agreed – including a role for inter-ministerial agreement through JMC (EN) and new dispute resolution processes.[95] Though the common frameworks activity is seen as a discrete piece of work in the EU governance space, there is the potential for emerging

---

[92] These were agreed under the auspices of the Joint Ministerial Committee (EU Negotiations), Communique 16 October 2017. JMC (EN) was established to provide a forum for consideration of Brexit related issues, though it has not always met regularly, nor provided an effective means for communication and cooperation.
[93] Cabinet Office, 'Breakdown of Areas of EU law that Intersect with Devolved Competence in Scotland, Wales and Northern Ireland', March 2018; and 'Revised Breakdown', April 2019.
[94] E.g., the Fisheries Bill, 2019–21 [HL-7] revised and reintroduced on 29 January 2020 after a previous version fell on the prorogation of Parliament.
[95] Cabinet Office, 'An Update on Progress on Common Frameworks', July 2019.

elements of best practice in intergovernmental work to be mainstreamed across broader IGR.

The impetus propelling common frameworks activity was, however, displaced during the Covid pandemic, and the work programme ceased to be on track for Implementation Period Completion day. In the meantime, the UK government took steps to reinforce the guarantees of free movement which had been secured through EU law pre-Brexit. In addition to rolling over and adapting some vertical legislative provisions under the frameworks programme, a White Paper introduced over Summer 2020[96] proposed to introduce horizontal cross-cutting measures in the interests of maintaining the UK internal market, and ensuring no new barriers to trade emerge through unmanaged policy divergence. The approach is markedly less collaborative, more top-down and potentially damaging to the scope and exercise of devolved competence. Its relationship with the common frameworks work is also unclear. The White Paper proposes a principle of mutual recognition, along with a principle of non-discrimination, which together form a 'market access commitment'. It suggests that these measures will run alongside and fill the gaps between frameworks. However, many of the examples given for why action is needed come from areas where common frameworks are proposed, such as pesticides, animal health, and labelling. The concerns with subsidiarity seen in relation to common frameworks are not as evident here. The commitment to allow the same scope for diversity as under EU rules is not replicated as it is under the common frameworks. Instead, the principle of mutual recognition which is proposed appears to be automatic and absolute, and does not seem to envisage the same range of justifications for not accepting a product as equivalent as currently exist under EU law, and which have been successfully pleaded by the devolved governments in the past.

There will evidently be a strong push back from the devolved governments against these proposals.[97] The rationale for having horizontal rules is not accepted by devolved ministers, who favour proceeding through cooperation and agreement. The proposals are likely to be a response to concerns by UK government about being able to satisfy potential international trade partners that they will face no internal barriers to trade which may limit the attraction of a trade deal. However, the devolution legislation already provides a power

---

[96] Department for Business, Energy and Industrial Strategy, White Paper UK Internal Market, July 2020, CP278.

[97] Though Northern Ireland is in a special position, covered as it is by the NI Protocol. See generally Katy Hayward, David Phinnemore and Milena Komarova, 'Anticipating and Meeting New Multilevel Governance Challenges in Northern Ireland after Brexit', ESRC, UK in a Changing Europe Initiative, 2020.

for the secretary of state to intervene if proposed legislation is 'incompatible with any international obligation'[98] as well as a power to oblige the devolved governments to take action to implement international obligations.[99] In general, the approach taken to international relations has been to cede little in the way of a shared rule approach, and to emphasise the exclusivity of this reserved area of competence. In successive legislative proposals dealing with devolved areas including agriculture and fisheries, the UK government has sought to define particular provisions as being outside devolved competence due to the international relations reservation – despite the clear policy overlap.[100] This is a more expansive interpretation of the scope of the international relations reservation than recognised by the Supreme Court in the *Scottish Continuity Bill Reference*. In this way, the international relations argument has been used to bypass the requirement for devolved consent, thus undermining further an already weakened legislative consent convention.

## CONCLUSION

The EU order is one that operates along cooperative federalist lines. This approach extends not only to the level of the member state government, but, in a more attenuated though still significant form, to the regional and local level too. In the United Kingdom, the past two decades have witnessed progressive evolution of devolution and devolved competences, at the same time as the EU context has become more receptive to the regional dimension of governance. However, the cooperative, shared governance approach which operates between the devolved administrations and the EU level is not repeated domestically in the relations between the devolved and UK institutions. Attempts to replicate this model at the national level come up against ingrained positions and practices, not least a resurgent principle of Westminster parliamentary sovereignty. The prevailing model of autonomous coexistence, based around the two spheres of de jure (for the UK government) and de facto (for the devolved governments) exclusive self-rule is not suited to the overlapping, interdependent allocation of competences. It leaves little scope for the effective operation of a principle of subsidiarity, as the

[98] Scotland Act, s. 35(1); Government of Wales Act 2006, s. 101 (d).
[99] Scotland Act, s. 58; See also s. 82 of the Government of Wales Act 2006, s. 82; Northern Ireland Act 1998, s. 26.
[100] Tom Mullen and Jo Hunt, Review of Implications of Brexit-Related UK Legislation for Devolved Competence, Report for Scottish Parliament Finance and Constitution Committee, August 2019.

open, dynamic nature of competence allocation it suggests is anathema to a binary model. Moving towards a shared rule model, closer to a cooperative federalist system, will require both sides to make compromises and shift from often politically entrenched positions. As difficult as that may be, it is perhaps the only way to successfully maintain the Union.

# 2

# Brexit and the Mechanisms for the Resolution of Conflicts in the Context of Devolution: Do We Need a New Model?

Elisenda Casanas Adam

INTRODUCTION

The referendum vote in 2016 to leave the European Union (Brexit) and the process for its implementation have had a significant impact on the devolution framework, and in particular on its legal mechanisms for ensuring harmonious relations between Westminster and the devolved legislatures, and for resolving conflicts between them. Prior to Brexit, there had been very few conflicts between the United Kingdom and the devolved institutions over the distribution of competences set out in the devolution settlements, and any disagreements were resolved primarily through political means. Since the vote, however, a significant breakdown in trust has been followed by a shift to the resolution of disputes through litigation in the courts. The *Miller* and *Scottish Continuity Bill* cases are particularly significant in this sense.[1] These cases have, in turn, highlighted the problems arising from the use of the mechanisms established in the devolution settlements, primarily designed to ensure that the devolved legislatures do not act ultra vires, for the legal resolution of competence conflicts between both orders of government. Taking into consideration the significant role that the courts play in federal or quasi-federal systems by providing an independent and balanced interpretation of the constitutional framework, this chapter reflects on the effectiveness of these mechanisms in the UK system and considers if, in the light of recent developments, they need to be reformed.

The chapter begins with some brief comparative considerations on the role of courts in the resolution of competence disputes in federal or quasi-federal systems. It then highlights particularities of the UK model within the

[1] *R (Miller) v. Secretary of State for Exiting the European Union* [2017] UKSC 5; [2017] 2 WLR 583 and *The UK Withdrawal from the European Union (Legal Continuity) (Scotland) Bill – A Reference by the Attorney General and the Advocate General for Scotland* [2018] UKSC 64.

devolution framework, and the problems arising from the use of its existing mechanisms for the legal resolution of conflicts between both orders of government. Next, it considers the significant impact of Brexit on these mechanisms, with a focus on the *Miller* and *Scottish Continuity Bill* cases from the perspective of the territorial constitution. Finally, it makes some proposals for the development of a new model for dealing with competence disputes. Overall, the chapter argues that, depending on the final Brexit outcome and if the increasingly litigious political climate continues, this model will become unsustainable and new mechanisms will need to be considered.

The focus of the chapter will be primarily on Scotland, but some references will also be made to Wales and Northern Ireland where necessary, and some of the wider considerations in the chapter also apply across all three devolution settlements.

## THE RESOLUTION OF CONFLICTS OF COMPETENCE IN FEDERAL, QUASI-FEDERAL, AND DEVOLVED STATES

A defining element of a federal, quasi-federal, or devolved system is the territorial distribution of competences between the federal nationwide unit and federated sub-units.[2] While there is a diversity of models of multilevel states, and of systems of distributions of competences, what is common to all these systems is the distribution of power based on the federal principle. A second key element in a majority of these systems is that courts are given the final decision on the interpretation of these norms that distribute competences among the different orders of government.[3] In many cases, this will enable the courts to review the legislation enacted by both the federal parliament and those of the component units, and their powers may also involve the striking down of the challenged legislation, if this is found to be outwith their competence.[4]

When considering the role of courts in a federal system, much of the focus is on their power to strike down legislation. However, this chapter will focus on

---

[2] Akhtar Majeed, Ronald Watts, Douglas Brown and John Kinkaid (eds.), *Distribution of Powers and Responsibilities in Federal Countries* (Quebec: McGill-Queen's University Press, 2006); Francesco Palermo and Karl Kössler, *Comparative Federalism: Constitutional Arrangements and Case Law* (Oxford: Hart Publishing, 2017).

[3] Nicholas Aroney and John Kinkaid, 'Introduction: courts in federal countries', in Nicholas Aroney and John Kinkaid (eds.), *Courts in Federal Countries: Federalists or Unitarists?* (Toronto: University of Toronto Press, 2017).

[4] See, for example, the different case studies included in Aroney and Kinkaid (eds.), *Courts in Federal Countries*.

their role as the final *interpreter* of the competence norms, which is related to, but significantly distinct from their power to overturn legislation. Indeed, the main justification for conferring these powers on the courts is the need for some dispute settlement mechanism, or for an independent arbiter (or set of arbiters) to police and uphold the distribution of powers against disagreement between political forces who may be tempted to alter this distribution in a more centralist or decentralist direction.[5] By their very nature, competence clauses will always have a degree of generality or indeterminacy which may lead to disagreements on specific definitions or on the scope or content of specific clauses. This is common in most federal or quasi-federal systems. Disagreements may also arise in relation to new developments and the updating of previously defined clauses. When carrying out this role as final interpreters of the distribution of competences, courts can ensure that the balance between the positions of the federation and the federated units is maintained, and that any new developments remain faithful to the federal principle.[6]

As in other contexts, there is a lively debate about the benefits or shortcomings of the intervention of courts in this area.[7] There are, of course, many arguments put forward against the judicial intervention in federal competence questions.[8] Some are specific to the functioning of federal polities, such as the fact that courts tend to favour the federation and show bias against the sub-state units; other arguments are more general, noting a democratic deficit in relying too heavily upon an unelected judiciary, for example, or highlighting the problems arising from the legalisation of political conflicts. However, despite these theoretical debates, from an empirical perspective the conferral of this role on the courts is widespread across federal systems, with few exceptions, and even scholars who would not consider that this role needs to be performed by the courts would defend the need for some form of impartial arbiter for resolving disagreements between both orders of government.[9] On the other hand, there are risks for the position and perception of legitimacy of the courts

---

[5] Aroney and Kinkaid (eds.), *Courts in Federal Countries*, and Jean-François Gaudreault-DesBiens, 'The Role of Apex Courts in Federal Systems' (2017) 17:1 *Jus Politicum* 171–91.

[6] Koen Lenaerts, 'Constitutionalism and the Many Faces of Federalism' (1990) 38 *Am. J. of Comp. Law* 205–63 and Gerald Baier, *Courts and Federalism. Judicial Doctrine in the United States, Australia and Canada* (Vancouver: UBC Press, 2006).

[7] For example, Gaudreault-DesBiens, 'The Role of Apex Courts'.

[8] Ibid.

[9] Cheryl Saunders, 'Legislative, Executive, and Judicial Institutions: A Synthesis', in Katy Le Roy and Cheryl Saunders (dir.), *Legislative, Executive and Judicial Governance in Federal Countries*, vol. 3 (Montreal & Kingston, Forum of Federations/IACFS, McGill-Queen's University Press, 2006); and Kenneth C. Wheare, *Federal Government* (New York: Oxford University Press, 1947), p. 66.

themselves, if their decisions are not sufficiently balanced and responsive to both the arguments of the federation and sub-state units in conflict.[10]

In practice, we can see the impact of the courts' interpretative function on the development of specific federal or quasi-federal models, where litigation over competence divisions is an ordinary part of the working of the system. Thus, in Spain, for example, many of the constitutional provisions concerning the 'State of the Autonomies', especially the competence provisions, have been developed and fleshed out by hundreds of decisions of the Spanish Constitutional Court.[11] In this way, the Constitutional Court has contributed significantly to the establishment and development of the system, and in the initial years of self-government, helped to protect the sphere of autonomy of the Autonomous Communities by resisting the strongest centralising tendencies of central government.[12] More recently, however, the court has adopted a much more restrictive and centralised interpretation of the constitutional framework, largely endorsing the arguments put forward by central government.[13] As a result, it is no longer seen as an independent arbiter by many Autonomous Communities. This example therefore also highlights the importance of courts taking a thoughtful and balanced approach to the interpretation of the constitutional framework in this context.

## THE UK MODEL IN THE CONTEXT OF DEVOLUTION

The UK model is one of devolution and therefore not of federalism in a strict sense. The distinction between a devolved and a federal model is that while in a federal system the division of competences is constitutionally entrenched, in a devolved model the central parliament retains ultimate law-making authority in all matters, including the power of unilateral revocation.[14] In the United Kingdom, this is included specifically in each of the devolution settlements and marks a constitutional asymmetry between the sovereign Westminster

---

[10] Elisenda Casanas Adam and François Rocher, '(Mis)recognition in Catalonia and Quebec: The Politics of Judicial Containment' in Jaime Lluch (ed.), *Constitutionalism and the Politics of Accommodation in Multinational Democracies* (London: Palgrave Macmillan, 2014).

[11] Elisenda Casanas Adam, 'The Constitutional Court of Spain: From system balancer to polarizing centralist.' in Aroney and Kinkaid (eds.), *Courts in Federal Countries*.

[12] Ibid.

[13] Ibid.

[14] Michael Keating and Guy Laforest 'Federalism and Devolution: the UK and Canada', in Michael Keating and Guy Laforest (eds.), *Constitutional Politics and the Territorial Question in Canada and the United Kingdom: Federalism and Devolution Compared* (London: Palgrave Macmillan, 2017).

Parliament and the non-sovereign devolved legislatures.[15] However, despite these provisions, there are contrasting views on the constitutional impact and significance of the devolution settlements, and in particular, on whether they represent a constraint on Westminster's parliamentary sovereignty understood in its traditional sense.[16] As McHarg notes, the status of devolution within the UK constitution is therefore ambiguous and contested.[17] More generally, in their introduction to the comparative discussion of the multi-level systems in the United Kingdom and Canada, Keating and Laforest highlight that in the twenty-first century, the distinction between unitary (devolved) states and federal ones is less clear cut.[18] Similarly, Tierney states that federalism, understood in general terms as a means of accommodating territorial pluralism in a constitutional system, is a 'useful prism' through which to assess the United Kingdom's territorial model.[19]

In common with the models discussed above, the distribution of competences between the UK Parliament and the devolved legislatures is set out in statute. Thus, the legislative competence of the Scottish Parliament is defined in ss. 28 and 29 of the Scotland Act 1998.[20] These follow a 'reserved powers' model whereby the Scottish Parliament is given plenary power to make laws by s. 28(1), but this is subject to the limits set out in s. 29, most notably the list of policy areas 'reserved' to the Westminster Parliament.[21] Also in common with the models above, the Scotland Act 1998 contains a range of mechanisms designed to ensure that the Scottish Parliament remains within competence when carrying out its legislative functions. These include political controls, such as requirements on the minister or other member introducing a bill to state that its provisions are intra vires, as well as an independent requirement

---

[15] Scotland Act 1998, s. 28(7); Government of Wales Act 2006, s. 93(5); Northern Ireland Act 1998, s. 5(6).
[16] Christopher McCrudden and Daniel Halberstam, '*Miller* and Northern Ireland: A Critical Constitutional Response' (2016) 8 *The UK Supreme Court Yearbook* 299–343.
[17] Aileen McHarg, 'Devolution in Scotland', in Jeffrey Jowell and Colm O'Cinneide (eds.), *The Changing Constitution* (Oxford: Hart, 9th edn., 2019).
[18] Keating and Laforest, 'Federalism and Devolution'.
[19] Stephen Tierney, 'The territorial constitution and the Brexit process' (2019) 72 *Current Legal Problems*, 59–83.
[20] Parallel provisions apply in Wales; see ss. 107 and 108A of the Government of Wales Act 2006, as amended by s. 3 of the Wales Act 2017. The Northern Ireland devolution settlement is more complex, distinguishing between 'transferred', 'reserved' and 'devolved' matters, in reflection of the particular nature of the Northern Irish Constitution. For a discussion in the context of the issues considered in this chapter, see Gordon Anthony, 'Sovereignty, Consent, and Constitutions: The Northern Ireland References', in Mark Elliot, Jack Williams and Alison Young (eds.), *The UK Constitution after* Miller: *Brexit and Beyond* (Oxford: Hart, 2019).
[21] Scotland Act 1998, ss. 28 and 29 and Schedule 5.

on the Parliament's Presiding Officer to state her opinion as to the competence of the bill.[22] They also include judicial controls which allow a bill or an Act of the Scottish Parliament to be referred to the courts, and in final instance to the Supreme Court, to consider its compatibility with the Scotland Act 1998. Before a bill receives Royal Assent, this power is conferred on the UK or Scottish government Law Officers.[23] Once an Act has entered into force, post-enactment competence challenges may be initiated by the UK Law Officers or by private parties, under the 'devolution issues' procedures.[24] The Scotland Act states clearly that an Act of the Scottish Parliament is not law in so far as any provision of the Act is outside its legislative competence.[25]

In contrast with the federal or quasi-federal models considered above, however, there are no equivalent procedures to question whether the Westminster Parliament remains within its sphere of reserved competences when legislating for Scotland. The lack of such procedures is a manifestation of the Westminster Parliament's sovereignty, and of the retention of its competence to legislate for devolved matters despite empowering the devolved legislatures to do so.[26] From the perspective of the issues considered in this chapter, there are two significant consequences that flow from this. The first is that in the UK model, while the courts are given the final decision on the interpretation of the devolution settlements (as they are currently set out in statute)[27] in the context of a legislative conflict, a question regarding the interpretation or scope of the competence provisions included in the Scotland Act 1998 can only reach the courts if it is raised in relation to legislation of the Scottish Parliament (or other devolved legislature). The second consequence is that the devolved governments therefore have very limited options to enable them to raise competence questions for consideration and clarification by the courts. Although the Scottish Law Officers could refer a Scottish bill to the Supreme Court before its coming into force for the court to certify that it is within the competence of the Scottish Parliament, in order to avoid it being challenged once it comes into force, in the majority of cases these cases will be the result of a direct challenge to the Scottish Parliament's exercise of legislative power either by the UK Law Officers or by a private party. When considered from this perspective, it

[22] Ibid., s. 31(1) and (2).
[23] Ibid., s. 33.
[24] Ibid., s. 98 and Schedule 6.
[25] Ibid., s. 29(1).
[26] McHarg, 'Devolution in Scotland'.
[27] The UK Parliament is free to amend the devolution statutes, including the reversal of an interpretation given by a court.

becomes evident that in the UK model, rather than establishing a dispute resolution mechanism between both orders of government, these processes are designed to ensure that the devolved institutions stay within their sphere of competences, and to apply punitive consequences if they do not.

However, there does exist a political constraint on the legislation of the Westminster Parliament: the Sewel Convention, which states that the UK Parliament will not normally legislate in respect to devolved matters without the consent of the Scottish Parliament.[28] As is well known, the convention originated from a statement by the Scottish Office minister, Lord Sewel, during a parliamentary debate on the Scotland Bill 1998.[29] His statement has since been included and further developed in the Memorandum of Understanding between the UK and devolved governments and various Devolution Guidance Notes, and was codified in s. 28(8) of the Scotland Act 1998, as amended by s. 2(2) Scotland Act 2016. It is currently understood that the consent of the Scottish Parliament is *normally* required for legislation which 'contains provisions applying to Scotland and which are for devolved purposes' *or* 'which alter the legislative competence of the Parliament or the executive competence of the Scottish Ministers'.[30] The same convention also applies in Wales, where it was codified in s.2 of the Wales Act 2017, and with some differences, in Northern Ireland, where it remains uncodified.[31]

The Sewel Convention is the United Kingdom's own distinct model of incorporation or safeguarding of the federal principle in general terms, and of recognising that, in ordinary circumstances, despite its overarching legislative sovereignty, the Westminster Parliament will respect and comply with the distribution of competences as agreed and established in the devolution settlements. Furthermore, in a situation where it deemed it necessary to legislate within devolved competences, Westminster will not do so without the consent of the corresponding parliament. As McHarg explains, the convention therefore performs a defensive function, providing devolved legislatures with reassurance that Westminster will normally gain the consent of the

---

[28] On the Sewel Convention see Graeme Cowie and David Torrance, 'Devolution: The Sewel Convention', HC Briefing Paper CBP-8883 (13 May 2020).

[29] During the second reading debate, Lord Sewel said: 'we would expect a convention to be established that Westminster would not normally legislate with regard to devolved matters in Scotland without the consent of the Scottish parliament'. *Hansard*, HL Deb, vol. 592, col. 791, 21 July 1998.

[30] See Devolution Guidance Notes 8–10, 14 and 17, www.gov.uk/government/publications/devolution-guidance-notes.

[31] On Wales, see now Government of Wales Act 1998, s. 107(6). On Northern Ireland, see, for example, the decision of the High Court of Northern Ireland in *Re McCord* [2016] NIQB 85 at para. 119, where the court stated that only the narrower dimension of the convention applied.

relevant devolved legislature before legislating on devolved matters.[32] In the light of the initial comparative discussion above, the question then arises concerning what happens when there is a disagreement between the UK and devolved governments (and/or parliaments) over whether, in the ordinary functioning of devolution, a specific matter falls within the reserved competence of Whitehall, and cannot be resolved through political negotiation. While the Westminster Parliament can theoretically legislate on any matter, the model would be unsustainable if all potential conflicts were to end in this way. Yet, the devolved governments or legislatures cannot refer the matter to the courts; nor can the UK government do so, even if it legitimately believes that in this case the specific matter is within the Westminster Parliament's sphere of reserved competences. In these situations, therefore, the only option available is for the devolved legislature to legislate on the matter and for the devolved bill to then be referred to the Supreme Court for consideration.

The incorporation of the Sewel Convention into statute led to some discussion (and significant uncertainty) over whether this would make it legally enforceable.[33] If this were to be the case, it would have resulted in a new and distinctive UK mechanism for bringing questions of competence arising from Westminster legislation before the Supreme Court: the devolved legislatures could not challenge a UK bill because the UK Parliament was legislating within the sphere of devolved competence, but they *could* challenge the fact such a bill had been enacted without their consent. However, the consideration of the consent question would necessarily require the court to consider whether the bill was indeed within devolved powers, and as such would enable the Scottish Parliament to bring issues regarding the interpretation of the competence provision before the court. As will be discussed below, though, this possibility was rejected by the Supreme Court in the *Miller* case.

The lack of legal security (or lack of entrenchment) afforded to the devolved settlements in the current constitutional arrangements has already been highlighted as one of the problems of the UK model of devolution, as have other potential models to overcome this, and the obstacles to achieving such models.[34] A fully federated UK model would, of course, overcome these

---

[32] Aileen McHarg, 'Constitutional change and territorial consent: The *Miller* Case and the Sewel Convention', in Elliott, Williams, and Young (eds.), *The UK Constitution after* Miller, p. 159.

[33] Chris Himsworth, 'Legislating for permanence and statutory footing' (2016) 20 *Edinburgh Law Review*, 361–7.

[34] Aileen McHarg, 'The future of the United Kingdom's territorial constitution: can the Union survive?', in Alberto López-Basaguren and Leire Escajedo San-Epifanio (eds.), *Claims for Secession and Federalism. A Comparative Study with a Special Focus on Spain* (Heidelberg: Springer, 2019).

problems, and may be the only sustainable solution in the long term. Yet this chapter aims to put forward a different argument in relation to the model in its current form. While the principle of parliamentary sovereignty as it applies to the Westminster Parliament is a justification for not giving the courts the power to strike down its legislation in the context of the devolution settlements, the principle is not necessarily a justification for limiting the access of the devolved governments and legislatures to the courts, in the case of a conflict over the interpretation of the corresponding devolution framework itself. In other words, there is an interest in establishing with clarity and certainty *when* the UK Parliament is legislating within devolved competences, even if under the devolution settlements it may legally do so. Furthermore, even if understood in very general terms, the federal principle would seem to require a degree of symmetry of access to the courts for the devolved and UK governments for the resolution of conflicts over the interpretation of the competence provisions. In the context of intransigent disagreement between the devolved and UK governments, it is also only with this certainty that the Sewel Convention as a political mechanism can work effectively.

However, prior to the Brexit vote, the limited access of the devolved institutions to the courts in this context was not a matter of significant concern due to the small number of disagreements over the interpretation of the competence provisions in the devolution settlements.[35] In the case of Scotland, no Scottish Acts had been referred to the Judicial Committee of the Privy Council, or later to the Supreme Court, by the Law Officers and no cases had reached the courts that involved a disagreement on competences between the Scottish and UK institutions.[36] Of the cases raised by private parties, only three involved a challenge regarding devolved/reserved boundaries.[37] Various reasons have been put forward to explain the lack of challenges and disagreements.[38] These include the initial harmony between a Labour-led government in Holyrood and Westminster in the initial years of devolution (1999–2007); yet the situation continued with the first minority (2007–11, 2016–present) and then majority (2011–16) SNP governments that have followed. It is also suggested that the attention paid to these matters

---

[35] Christopher McCorkindale, Aileen McHarg and Paul Scott, 'The courts, devolution and constitutional review' (2018) 36 *University of Queensland Law Journal*, 289–310; and Eugenie Brouillet and Tom Mullen, 'Constitutional jurisprudence on federalism and devolution', in Keating and Laforest (eds.), *Constitutional Politics*.
[36] Ibid.
[37] McCorkindale, McHarg, and Scott, 'The Courts, Devolution and Constitutional Review' and McHarg, 'Devolution'.
[38] Ibid.

during the process of parliamentary review of a bill, and in particular the cooperation between the Scottish and UK governments during this period contributed to the lack of challenges. Indeed, disagreements on competence questions are resolved in on-going dialogues between officials and legal advisors acting on behalf of the UK and Scottish governments, and the Scottish Parliament.[39] However, it is also worth noting that such discussions are conducted taking the existing jurisprudence of the Supreme Court as one of their main points of reference.[40] Therefore, even despite the lack of conflict, this confirms the significance of the role of the Supreme Court in this context, and also of the type of issues it considers and decides on, and brings the question of access back into focus.

A final explanation for the lack of conflict over the competence provisions is the willingness of both governments to make use of the flexibility of the devolution settlement to transfer more competences or provide consent for UK-wide legislation where necessary.[41] There is no doubt that despite the constitutional asymmetries of the model, in its initial years it has functioned largely on a trust basis between the UK institutions and the devolved institutions, with a clear preference for the political resolution of disputes over the use of courts. A clear example of this is, as McHarg notes, that the most important function performed by the Sewel Convention in the initial years of devolution has been a facilitating function, enabling the cooperation between the UK and devolved governments to achieve their policy goals, when the devolved legislatures are constrained by competence provisions or a UK-wide approach is more beneficial.[42] As the next section will argue, this context has changed significantly with the Brexit process.

### THE IMPACT OF BREXIT AND ITS WIDER IMPLICATIONS

The impact of the Brexit vote and the developments that have followed upon all the above cannot be overstated.[43] In the lead-up to the vote, the territorial differences on EU membership were already notably evident, leading the SNP (with the support of Plaid Cymru) to argue for the adoption of a principle of

---

[39] Christopher McCorkindale and Janet Hiebert, 'Vetting bills in the Scottish Parliament for legislative competence' (2017) 21 *Edinburgh Law Review* 319–51.
[40] Ibid.
[41] Ibid., and McHarg, McCorkindale, and Scott, 'The Courts, Devolution'.
[42] McHarg 'Constitutional change', p. 159; and see also Andrea Batey and Alan Page 'Scotland's other parliament: Westminster legislation about devolved matters in Scotland since devolution' (2002) *Public Law* 501–23.
[43] See McHarg 'Devolution', and also Sionaidh Douglas-Scott, 'Brexit, Art. 50, and the Contested British Constitution' (2016) 79 *Modern Law Review* 1019–40.

parallel consent to secure a Leave victory: a majority of votes across the United Kingdom as well as in each of its constituent nations.[44] This was rejected by the UK government and the territorial divisions were then confirmed on the day of the vote, when Scotland and Northern Ireland voted strongly to remain, in contrast to the victory for Leave in England and Wales.[45] In relation to Scotland, the UK government then also refused to consider proposals for a 'differentiated Brexit' and for a second independence referendum which could allow Scotland to remain in the EU.[46] Two subsequent developments, however, had a particular impact on the processes for regulating the division of competences.

The first resulted from the challenge regarding the requirements for the activation of the Art. 50 TEU withdrawal process, which developed a devolution dimension.[47] The discussion over the need for legislation by Westminster then led to the argument that, under the Sewel Convention, the consent of the devolved legislatures was also required, as the process of withdrawing from the EU would affect their devolved competences (by removing the obligation to act in accordance with EU law). This argument was first raised in Northern Ireland, in the *McCord* case, where it was rejected by the High Court of Northern Ireland (NIHC), which also adopted a very restrictive interpretation of the convention.[48] This was also the position of the UK government. In the Supreme Court, the appeals and devolution references requested by the Attorney General for Northern Ireland were joined with the analogous English *Miller* case, appealed from the Divisional Court.[49] Concerned that the Supreme Court might follow the NIHC's restrictive interpretation of the convention, the Scottish and Welsh governments then decided to intervene in defence of the application of the convention and the need for the consent of the devolved legislatures, although the Northern Irish government intervened in support of the UK government's position. Therefore, *Miller* became the first case that reached the Supreme Court involving a direct conflict between the UK and Scottish governments. *Miller* also became the first test of the legal consequences of the statutory recognition

---

[44] Ibid.
[45] Scotland voted to remain by 55.8% and Northern Ireland by 62%; England voted to leave by 53.4% and Wales by 52.5%.
[46] Tobias Lock, 'Taking Stock: Scotland and Brexit', Centre for Constitutional Change Blog, 6 September 2018, www.centreonconstitutionalchange.ac.uk/opinions/taking-stock-scotland-and-brexit.
[47] On this case from the devolution perspective see McHarg, 'Constitutional Change'.
[48] *McCord and Agnew* [2016] NIQB 85.
[49] *R (Miller) v. Secretary of State for Exiting the European Union* [2016] EWHC 2768 (Admin); [2017] 1 All ER 158 at para. 102.

of the Sewel Convention. From the perspective of the territorial constitution it became a highly significant case.

In contrast with the cases where devolved legislation was challenged by a private party, the *Miller* case put the Supreme Court at the centre of the tensions between Westminster and Holyrood. As is common in such cases in other federal or quasi-federal systems, both sides put forward strongly diverging interpretations of the contested provision; in this case, the provisions in the Scotland Act 1998 providing recognition of the Sewel Convention, and also of the convention itself. In brief, the Lord Advocate and the Counsel General for Wales adopted a broad interpretation of the Sewel Convention and argued that it not only applied to devolved competences, but also to situations where Westminster legislated to alter the devolved competences.[50] As the triggering of Art. 50 and leaving the EU would alter the competences of the devolved legislatures and governments, their consent was required for any legislation enacted with this purpose. In the case of the Scottish Parliament, the argument was reinforced by the recognition of the convention in the Scotland Act 1998. On the other hand, the UK government adopted a much narrower interpretation of the convention, arguing that it only applied when Westminster legislated on a devolved matter, and that foreign affairs (and the relationship between the United Kingdom and the EU) were not devolved.[51] Furthermore, it argued that even if the Sewel Convention did apply in this case, statutory recognition had not made the convention legally justiciable, and accordingly, as a convention it could not be legally enforced by the courts.

As is well known, while the Supreme Court decided that legislation by the Westminster Parliament was required to trigger Art. 50, it also unanimously held that, as a matter of convention rather than law, the Sewel Convention did not give rise to legally enforceable obligations, nor could the courts give rulings on its operation or scope[52]. Regarding the statutory recognition of the convention in the Scotland Act 2016, the court held that this had not rendered it any more justiciable and that this mechanism remained primarily a political one.[53] In a small number of not extensively reasoned paragraphs, the court largely deactivated much of the potential significance or impact of the legal recognition of the Sewel Convention that had been carefully negotiated and

---

[50] See the written submissions of the Lord Advocate, Counsel General for Wales, www.supremecourt.uk/news/article-50-brexit-appeal.html.
[51] See the written submissions for the UK government by the Advocate General, www.supremecourt.uk/news/article-50-brexit-appeal.html.
[52] *Miller* at paras. 136–52.
[53] Ibid., at paras. 147–9.

agreed in a multi-party consultation process in Scotland which had then been crystallised in an Act of Parliament at Westminster. It also left the devolved institutions notably weakened at a time of constitutional turmoil. As a result, in contrast to responses to its previous decisions on the devolution settlements, where it was considered overall to have contributed positively to the development of the model, the court found itself under criticism both for its approach to, and the impact of its decision upon, the devolved settlements. For example, Welikala highlighted that 'it may have been possible to articulate a more imaginative interpretation of these provisions that was more responsive and sensitive to both the historical traditions and the contemporary needs of our multination Union'.[54] McCrudden and Halberstam put it more strongly: 'The devolution aspects of the Supreme Court's judgment in *Miller* will come to be seen as a significant misstep, in that it failed to live up to the challenge of becoming a truly constitutional court for the UK as a whole.'[55]

The second development of significance to the discussion in this chapter arose from what can be described as 'the Continuity Bill saga'.[56] The disagreement between the UK government and the devolved governments continued into the enactment of what became the European Union (Withdrawal) Act 2018, designed to regulate the domestic consequences of the United Kingdom's withdrawal from the European Union. The Scottish and Welsh governments described the bill's impact on devolved competences as a 'naked power grab', and recommended that consent to the bill under the Sewel Convention be withheld.[57] The Scottish Parliament then proceeded to pass its own UK Withdrawal from the European Union (Legal Continuity) (Scotland) Bill which regulated the domestic consequences of the withdrawal for Scotland, and the Welsh Assembly passed its own analogous bill for Wales. Both were referred to the Supreme Court by the UK government's Legal Officer. Before the court heard the case, the Welsh government reached an

---

[54] Asanga Welikala, 'The Need for a "Cartesian Cleaning of the Augean Stables"? *Miller* and the Territorial Constitution', UK Constitutional Law Blog, 7 February 2017, https://ukconstitutio nallaw.org/2017/02/07/asanga-welikala-the-need-for-a-cartesian-cleaning-of-the-augean-stables

[55] Christopher McCrudden and Daniel Halberstam, 'Northern Ireland's Supreme Court Brexit Problem (and the UK's too)', UK Constitutional Law Blog, 21 November 2017, https://ukcon stitutionallaw.org/.

[56] Christopher McCorkindale and Aileen McHarg, 'Continuity and Confusion: Legislating for Brexit in Scotland and Wales (Part II)', UK Constitutional Law Blog, 7 March 2018, https:// ukconstitutionallaw.org/. Also Christopher McCorkindale and Aileen McHarg, 'Continuity and Confusion: Legislating for Brexit in Scotland and Wales (Part I)', UK Constitutional Law Blog, 6 March 2018, https://ukconstitutionallaw.org/.

[57] 'Nicola Sturgeon claims Brexit repeal bill is a "power grab"', BBC News website, 18 July 2017, www.bbc.co.uk/news/uk-scotland-scotland-politics-40586269/comments.

intergovernmental agreement with the UK government on the Withdrawal Bill, the Welsh Assembly granted its consent, and the referral was withdrawn.[58] While the Welsh bill then received Royal Assent, it was repealed shortly after. However, the Scottish government stood its ground and, following its recommendation, the Scottish Parliament voted to refuse its consent to the UK bill.[59] The Scottish Parliament's 'Withdrawal Bill' therefore became the first Scottish bill to be referred to the Supreme Court by the UK Law Officers for being outwith its competence and, again, the Supreme Court found itself at the centre of the tensions between Westminster and Holyrood.[60]

As McCorkindale and McHarg explain, the passing of the Scottish bill is significant because it was the culmination of an approach by the Scottish government (initially in coordination with the Welsh government) to negotiate with the UK government over the contested aspects of the Withdrawal Bill. It also served the political purpose of adding pressure on the UK Parliament in relation to the Westminster Withdrawal Bill; and from a practical perspective, it was the logical consequence of their decision to refuse to give their consent to the UK bill.[61] In this sense, it was a defensive move to ensure the Scottish legislation was in place before the enactment of the UK Act, to avoid Westminster proceeding with the bill as originally put forward without the Scottish Parliament's consent. This can be seen in statements by both Nicola Sturgeon and Mike Russell, defending the need to proceed with the Scottish Act as something they were required to do to 'protect the interests of the parliament' and to assert its 'right to legislate for itself'.[62] From the perspective of the issues considered in this chapter, the enactment of the Scottish Parliament's own legislation on the matter also resulted in the escalation of the conflict with the UK government for consideration by the Supreme Court.

Again, as is common in cases of conflicts of competence, the UK Law Officers challenged the Scottish bill on numerous and notably expansive grounds. For example, they argued that the Scottish bill was 'contrary to the constitutional principles underpinning the devolution settlement' and that the Continuity Bill as a whole was outwith competence because it related to

---

[58] Manon George, 'Agreement Reached on Amendments to the EU (Withdrawal) Bill', Senedd Research Blog, 1 May 2018, https://seneddresearch.blog/2018/05/01/agreement-reached-on-amendments-to-the-eu-withdrawal-bill/.
[59] SP OR 18 May 2018, cols. 9–76.
[60] *The UK Withdrawal from the European Union (Legal Continuity) (Scotland) Bill – A Reference by the Attorney General and the Advocate General for Scotland* [2018] UKSC 64.
[61] McCorkindale and McHarg 'Continuity and Confusion I'.
[62] 'MSPs agree emergency timetable for Scottish Brexit bill', BBC News website, 1 March 2018, www.bbc.co.uk/news/uk-scotland-scotland-politics-43248551.

the reserved matter of relations with the EU.[63] This is relevant as during the passage of the UK Withdrawal Bill, the UK government had conceded that some devolved competences were affected and therefore had requested the Scottish Parliament's consent. The Lord Advocate, meanwhile, defended the Scottish Parliament's competence to legislate for the legal consequences in Scotland of the UK leaving the EU.[64] The Counsel General for Wales and the Attorney General for Northern Ireland also intervened in support of the competence of the bill. Notably, the referral of the Scottish bill had the effect of delaying it being granted Royal Assent. The UK Parliament then proceeded to enact the UK Withdrawal Act with effect also for Scotland, becoming the first Act to be enacted where the Scottish Parliament had withheld its consent under the Sewel Convention. The UK Withdrawal Act also amended the Scotland Act so that it became a 'protected statute' which the Scottish Parliament could not modify.[65] Accordingly, the court had to consider if the bill was within competence when it was passed, and – if so – whether it still would be within competence when it received Royal Assent.

The challenges to the competence of the bill were unsuccessful on the majority of grounds, and the court therefore ruled that, when it was passed, the bill was largely within the competence of the Scottish Parliament. The only provision found to be outwith its competence at that point was s. 17, which required the consent of the Scottish Ministers for the exercise of delegated legislative powers conferred on UK ministers under UK Acts enacted after the Continuity Bill, in areas of devolved competence.[66] However, the court also decided that the competence of a bill was to be judged at the point it would have received Royal Assent, rather than when it was passed.[67] As a result, the enactment of the UK Withdrawal Act and its nature as a 'protected statute' meant that, by the time of the decision, many of the Scottish bill's provisions had been rendered outwith competence.[68] Nevertheless, the judgment was much more balanced from the perspective of the territorial constitution than the Supreme Court's previous decision in *Miller*. On the one hand, the court reaffirmed the reserved powers model, stating that 'the Scottish Parliament is a democratically elected legislature with a mandate to make laws for people in

---

[63] See the arguments of the Attorney General and the Advocate General for Scotland, www.supremecourt.uk/cases/uksc-2018-0080.html.
[64] Ibid., see the arguments of the Lord Advocate.
[65] European Union Withdrawal Act 2018, Schedule 3, Part 3, 21(1) (2).
[66] *The UK Withdrawal from the European Union (Legal Continuity) (Scotland) Bill – A Reference by the Attorney General and the Advocate General for Scotland* [2018] UKSC 64 at paras. 37–65.
[67] Ibid., at paras. 91–7.
[68] Ibid., at paras. 98–124.

Scotland. It has plenary powers within the limits of its legislative competence'.[69] On the other, 'in contrast to a federal model, a devolved system preserves the powers of the central legislature of the state in relation to all matters, whether devolved or reserved'.[70]

The court's decision was also much better received from the perspective of its approach to, and its impact upon, the territorial constitution. For example, Elliott highlights that, 'In some respects, the judgment reaffirms the importance of the constitutional position occupied by devolved institutions', and at the same time, 'serves to reaffirm that the UK's territorial constitutional settlement continues to be ... a devolved, not a federal, model, of which the sovereignty of the UK Parliament remains a cardinal feature'.[71] McCorkindale and McHarg describe the case as 'a landmark in the developing devolution jurisprudence, with the Court having taken the opportunity to reaffirm established principles, as well to address a number of novel questions, which are relevant across the UK's devolved jurisdictions'.[72] These assessments confirm the important role that courts can play, the Supreme Court in particular, in providing a balanced interpretation of the constitutional framework in the context of a conflict between different orders of government, even within the United Kingdom's model of devolution.

From the perspective of the Scottish institutions, despite numerous provisions of the Scottish Continuity Bill having ultimately been declared ultra vires, the Supreme Court's decision provided the symbolic recognition that the bill had initially been within the Scottish Parliament's competence. Furthermore, the court's strong affirmation of the reserved powers model will strengthen the Scottish Parliament's position when considering new areas of legislation in the future. But it must also be noted that the only means the Scottish Parliament had to bring these issues before the court in the context of an ongoing dispute regarding a Westminster bill was to draft its own competing legislation in order for it to be challenged. The shortcomings of the UK model discussed in the previous section are therefore clearly highlighted in this case. The case also highlights the extreme vulnerability of the model to unilateral changes to legislative competence, with Sewel offering little protection.

---

[69] Ibid., at para. 12.
[70] Ibid., at para. 41.
[71] Mark Elliott, 'The Supreme Court's Judgement in the Scottish Continuity Bill Case', Public Law for Everyone, 14 December 2018, https://publiclawforeveryone.com/2018/12/14/the-supreme-courts-judgment-in-the-scottish-continuity-bill-case/.
[72] Aileen McHarg and Christopher McCorkindale 'The Supreme Court and Devolution: the Scottish Continuity Bill Reference' (2019) *Juridical Review* 190–97.

## LOOKING TO THE FUTURE: DO WE NEED A NEW MODEL?

The litigation discussed above has highlighted both the unsuitability of the existing UK mechanisms for the resolution of competence disputes between the United Kingdom and devolved levels and also the importance of the role of the courts, in particular, the Supreme Court, in this context. It is also worth highlighting that this litigation forms part of a wider increase of litigation of constitutional issues before the courts. Indeed, as highlighted by McCorkindale and McHarg's contribution to this volume, the Brexit process has been characterised by 'hyper-litigation'. And this trend seems set to continue beyond the Brexit context, as can be seen in the surge in litigation challenging different aspects of the first Covid lockdown in 2020.[73] Similarly, the *Miller* and *Scottish Continuity Bill* cases highlight a clear loss of trust between the UK government and the devolved governments which has continued throughout the Brexit process. In response to the UK Parliament enacting the EU Withdrawal Act 2018 without the Scottish Parliament's consent, the Scottish government declared that it would not seek consent from the Scottish Parliament for any further Brexit bill and has not done so, with the exception of the Healthcare (International Agreements) Bill.[74] More recently, all three devolved legislatures refused consent for Westminster's Withdrawal Agreement Bill (now Act), which was required to implement the UK government's Brexit deal, and which was again passed despite the refusal of consent.[75] Both of these wider developments seem to indicate that the conflicts that led to both of the cases discussed above may become much more common in the future, therefore resulting in a significant change in the dynamics of the devolution model.

In the light of the above, it seems likely that the UK government will start taking a much more restrictive approach to when devolved consent is required. Following the Scottish Parliament's refusal to grant consent to the EU Withdrawal Bill, the UK government wrote to the Scottish government reiterating its commitment to the Sewel Convention, and justifying proceeding with the bill under the exception the convention itself

---

[73] Joe Tomlinson, Jo Hynes, Jack Maxwell and Emma Marshall, 'Judicial Review during the COVID-19 Pandemic (Part II)', 28 May 2020, https://adminlawblog.org/2020/05/28/joe-tomlinson-jo-hynes-jack-maxwell-and-emma-marshall-judicial-review-during-the-covid-19-pandemic-part-ii/.

[74] Jess Sargeant, 'Sewel Convention', Institute for Government Blog, 21 January 2020, www.instituteforgovernment.org.uk/explainers/sewel-convention.

[75] Jess Sargeant, 'The Sewel Convention has been broken by Brexit – reform is now urgent', Institute for Government Blog, 21 January 2020, www.instituteforgovernment.org.uk/blog/sewel-convention-has-been-broken-brexit-reform-now-urgent.

provides.⁷⁶ In this sense, it stated that while the Sewel Convention holds that the Westminster Parliament should not *normally* press ahead with legislation without the consent of the devolved legislatures, the circumstances of the United Kingdom's departure from the European Union are 'specific, singular and exceptional'.⁷⁷ Because of the largely uncontroversial way the convention has functioned until recently, there is a lack of clarity as to when the 'normally' exception applies, and some proposals for reform have been put forward in this regard.⁷⁸ Yet, at the same time, for the functioning of the model to be sustainable, the recourse to this exception cannot become the general rule when there is a disagreement between the UK government and the devolved administrations. It seems, therefore, that in a new context of ongoing tensions, the UK government may take a much narrower approach to the interpretation of the content of devolved matters which may be affected by proposed Westminster legislation, and would accordingly require devolved consent. In this way, it can avoid the complex negotiations to secure consent for the bill at the devolved level, and also the political consequences of proceeding with the enactment of the bill if consent is denied. There is already a recent example of a disagreement between the UK and Scottish governments over whether devolved consent is required for Westminster's Agriculture Bill.⁷⁹ Under the current legal framework, the Scottish government and Parliament have no way of challenging the UK government's interpretation, despite the final decision on the competence question ultimately lying with the Supreme Court. It seems, therefore, that some form of reform of the model is desirable.

A third element to consider when looking to the future are the changes to the devolution settlement that are going to result from the overall Brexit process itself, as are discussed in Hunt's contribution to this volume. Indeed, the repatriation of competences that will result from EU law ceasing to be binding in the United Kingdom will enhance the autonomy of the devolved administrations in important areas of policy, in some of which the boundaries between reserved and devolved competences are not

---

⁷⁶ Letter from the Rt Hon Steve Barclay MP to Michael Russell MSP, 17 January 2020, https://assets.publishing.service.gov.uk/government/uploads/system/uploads/attachment_data/file/859145/2020–10-20_Letter_to_Michael_Russell_MSP.pdf.
⁷⁷ Ibid.
⁷⁸ Scottish Government, 'Strengthening the Sewel Convention: Letter from Michael Russell to David Lidington', 12 September 2018, www.gov.scot/publications/strengthening-the-sewel-convention-letter-from-michael-russell-to-david-lidington/. Also Welsh Government, 'Reforming our Union, Shared Governance in the UK' 2019, https://gov.wales/sites/default/files/publications/2019–10/reforming-our-union-shared-governance-in-the-uk.pdf.
⁷⁹ Sargeant 'Sewel Convention'; Cowie and Torrance 'The Sewel Convention', p. 29.

clearly delimited.[80] Furthermore, the proposed establishment of UK-wide frameworks to provide a level of common standards across the United Kingdom, and most recently of a UK internal market, will further increase the overlap between reserved and devolved competences and the potential for disagreement over the scope and boundaries of each.[81] This has led Hunt and others to argue for the need to enhance the 'shared rule' dimension of the model, and to strengthen and reform the mechanisms of inter-government cooperation and political dispute resolution between the UK and devolved governments.[82] In response to the 'deactivation' of the significance of the legal recognition of the Sewel Convention, there have also been proposals to strengthen its effectiveness, such as creating an outright or a suspensive veto for the devolved parliaments (in the latter case, for example, the Westminster Parliament could overcome the veto after a year), or requiring a super-majority at Westminster to overrule their objections.[83] Similar proposals have been put forward by the Scottish and Welsh governments.[84] While all of these proposals would be extremely beneficial for the development of the current model, their impact would be further enhanced by increasing the access of devolved institutions to the courts, thus also contributing to the development of clarity and legal certainty in the interpretation of the devolution legal frameworks.

As a result, all the above seems to point to the need for a review of the current mechanisms for the resolution of conflicts of competences in the United Kingdom, and for the introduction of some form of procedure that would enable the devolved governments and parliaments to obtain a legal answer from the courts, and more specifically, from the Supreme Court, on

---

[80] Tierney, 'The territorial constitution' and Alan Page , 'Brexit, the Repatriation of Competences and the Future of the Union' (2017) 39 *Juridical Review* 38–47.

[81] Akash Paun, 'Common UK Frameworks after Brexit', SPICe Briefing, Scottish Parliament, 2 February 2018, https://sp-bpr-en-prod-cdnep.azureedge.net/published/2018/2/2/Common-UK-Frameworks-after-Brexit/SB%2018–09.pdf. Also 'Policy Paper. UK Internal Market', gov.uk, 16 July 2020, www.gov.uk/government/publications/uk-internal-market/uk-internal-market.

[82] Hunt, Chapter 1, this volume; Nicola McEwen, Michael Kenny, Jack Sheldon and Coree Brown Swan, 'Intergovernmental Relations in the UK: Time for a Radical Overhaul?' (2020) *The Political Quarterly* 632–40.

[83] Akash Paun, 'Saving the Union from Brexit will require bold thinking about the constitution', Institute for Government Blog, 13 September 2018, www.instituteforgovernment.org.uk/blog/saving-union-brexit-will-require-bold-thinking-about-constitution). Also Paul Reid, 'Time to Give the Sewel Convention Some (Political) Bite?', UK Constitutional Law Blog, 26 January 2017, https://ukconstitutionallaw.org/.

[84] Scottish Government, 'Strengthening the Sewel Convention' and Welsh Government, 'Reforming Our Union'.

the interpretation of the competence and related clauses in the devolution settlements. In the case of Scotland, such a mechanism could enable the Scottish and UK Law Officers to refer to the Supreme Court the question whether a bill or any provision of a bill introduced in the Westminster Parliament would make changes to the law in a devolved area of competence. In addition, the Supreme Court could also consider the issue of whether a bill would alter either the legislative competence of the Scottish Parliament or the executive competence of the Scottish government. The referral could take place as soon as the bill was introduced, and the disagreement on the competence question between the UK and Scottish governments was established. This would enable further negotiation and amendment if, in accordance with the Supreme Court's decision on the competence question, the bill or one of its provisions required devolved consent. It would also enable the activation of the different mechanisms that have been suggested to strengthen the functioning of Sewel Convention, for example within Westminster's own parliamentary procedure, should these be adopted. The analysis which the Supreme Court would be required to make of the disputed competence provisions in these cases would be very similar to the analysis it already carries out when considering challenges to devolved legislation under the current legal framework, and would provide not only an answer to the specific competence conflict, but also clear guidance on the interpretation of these provisions for the future.

A final point to highlight is that such a mechanism would not be completely new in the United Kingdom's constitutional framework. Indeed, a similar mechanism is included in s. 4 of the Human Rights Act 1998, which enables certain courts to make a declaration of incompatibility, when they consider that a provision of an Act of the Westminster Parliament is incompatible with a convention right. This declaration does not, as such, affect the validity of the Act and is therefore respectful of Westminster's parliamentary sovereignty. Similarly, in the case of the mechanism proposed in this chapter, the Supreme Court's declaration on the competence question would not be binding on the Westminster Parliament, as the legislation could still be enacted under its overarching competence to legislate across devolved matters. However, it would provide clarity and certainty regarding whether the legislation did indeed encroach on devolved competences, and in those cases where it did and consent under the Sewel Convention was not obtained, it would provide the symbolic recognition of the devolved government's grievances. More generally, the establishment of such a mechanism would also strengthen the Supreme Court's role as an arbiter between the UK government and the devolved administrations in competence disputes, and as the final interpreter of the devolution settlements.

## CONCLUSIONS

In most federal or quasi-federal systems, courts play a fundamental role in resolving competence conflicts between both orders of government and in providing an independent and balanced interpretation of the constitutional provisions that provide the structure of the federal framework. In the United Kingdom's model of devolution, however, while the different devolution settlements confer the final decision on their competence provisions on the courts, the mechanisms that enable the courts to carry out their functions in this context present significant limitations from the perspective of the devolved governments and legislatures. The changes in the relationship between the UK and devolved governments that have followed the Brexit vote, and the complexity of the future articulation of the devolution competence frameworks that will result from the repatriation of competences from the EU indicate that potential disagreements between the two levels of government over the reserved/devolved boundary will become more common. Together with existing proposals to strengthen intergovernmental relations between the UK and devolved governments and the political mechanisms for ensuring respect for the distribution of competences, mechanisms for enabling access to the courts, and in particular the Supreme Court, must therefore also be considered.

# 3

## Beyond Matryoshka Governance in the Twenty-First Century: The Curious Case of Northern Ireland

Sylvia de Mars and Aoife O'Donoghue

### INTRODUCTION

Retrospective accounts will undoubtedly declare Northern Ireland to have been the linchpin in the United Kingdom's negotiations to leave the European Union: and certainly it was Northern Ireland's distinctiveness that brought down the May government and determined the ultimate shape of the Withdrawal Agreement concluded by the Johnson government. For a long time, the lack of an agreement between the United Kingdom and the EU could be traced directly to the 'red lines' concerning the needs and wants of Northern Ireland.[1] Commentators on Northern Ireland specifically raised concerns about the Belfast/Good Friday Agreement (the 1998 Agreement) and the 'land border' early on[2] – but neither the EU (Ireland aside) nor the United Kingdom considered Northern Ireland as their primary concern.[3] Their 'red lines' concerned issues at the national, if not regional level, not at

---

[1] For a summary of Northern Ireland 'red lines' see Chris Morris, 'Reality Check: Red lines on the Irish border', BBC News website, 4 October 2018, www.bbc.co.uk/news/uk-politics-45737229. In the European Council's Guidelines for the Art. 50 Negotiations, published on 29 April 2017, EU held the 'aim of avoiding a hard border', www.consilium.europa.eu/en/press/press-releases/27/04/29/euco-brexit-guidelines/.

[2] Brendan Donnelly, 'Troubles redux: Brexit would put the Good Friday Agreement in jeopardy', LSE Brexit Blog, 28 April 2016, https://blogs.lse.ac.uk/brexit/2016/04/28/troubles-redux-brexit-would-put-the-good-friday-agreement-in-jeopardy/.

[3] This was the case for the United Kingdom until 2017. See Theresa May, 'The government's negotiating objectives for exiting the EU', gov.uk, 17 January 2017, www.gov.uk/government/speeches/the-governments-negotiating-objectives-for-exiting-the-eu-pm-speech. This references Northern Ireland three times but there is no mention of the land border. See also the European Council's original response to the referendum result, on 29 June 2016, which does not mention Northern Ireland or Ireland explicitly, www.consilium.europa.eu/media/20462/sn00060-en16.pdf.

the relatively 'local' level of one specific part of the United Kingdom, and it was only at Ireland's behest that Northern Ireland became part of the withdrawal negotiations.[4]

The idea that Northern Ireland would play a key role in the Brexit negotiations is anathema to the dominant theories of international governance. Multilevel governance, defined by Marks as 'a system of continuous negotiation among nested governments at several territorial tiers', suggests that while Northern Ireland would have some form of input into the negotiation strategy of the United Kingdom, this input would be limited at best.[5] What we saw in practice, however, was that the 'local' in Northern Ireland shaped the settlement reached between the United Kingdom and 'supranational' EU.[6] Despite the internal wrangling of the Conservative Party, even after the Johnson government took over, settling Northern Ireland remained core. The meeting between Leo Varadkar and Boris Johnson in Thornton Manor in October 2019 set the final parameters.[7] Finding a solution to the Northern Ireland 'red lines' had become core to preventing a no-deal Brexit, with a border in the Irish Sea the final compromise.[8] By this point, Northern Ireland had made itself so central to the United Kingdom's divorce from the EU that even those wishing to shrug it off were required to settle its fate.

Here, the innermost 'nested' governance level (Northern Ireland) had enough influence, and was constitutionally important enough to UK and EU relations, to ensure that the relationship between Ireland and Northern Ireland was an inevitable part of the Brexit process. Deal or no deal, the EU applied pressure downwards to accommodate the demands from Ireland (and, by proxy, parts of Northern Ireland). The United Kingdom, on the other hand,

---

[4] For a detailed account of Irish pressure on the Commission Article 50 Task Force, Tony Connolly, *Brexit and Ireland: the Dangers, the Opportunities, and the Inside Story of the Irish Response* (London: Penguin, 2018), chap. 9; Tom McTague, 'How the UK lost the Brexit battle', politico.eu, 27 March 2019, https://www.politico.eu/article/how-uk-lost-brexit-eu-negotiation/.

[5] Gary Marks, 'Structural Policy and Multi-Level Governance in the EC', in Alan Cafruny and Glenda Rosenthal (eds.) *The State of the European Community: The Maastricht Debate and Beyond* (Boulder: Lynne Rienner, 1993), p. 392.

[6] See the 14 November 2018 *Draft Agreement on the withdrawal of the United Kingdom and Great Britain and Northern Ireland from the European Union and the European Atomic Energy Community* (TF50 (2018) 55), https://ec.europa.eu/commission/sites/beta-political/files/draft_withdrawal_agreement_0.pdf.

[7] 'Brexit: Boris Johnson and Leo Varardkar "can see pathway to a deal"', BBC News website, 10 October 2019, www.bbc.co.uk/news/uk-politics-49995133.

[8] In its final form, see Art. 5 of the Protocol on Ireland/Northern Ireland in the *Agreement on the withdrawal of the United Kingdom of Great Britain and Northern Ireland from the European Union and the European Atomic Energy Community* (2020) OJ L 29/7.

prioritized the concerns of the Democratic Unionist Party (DUP), on whom the Conservative government was reliant for votes. This only changed when the December 2019 election produced the Johnson government, whose outright majority allowed the United Kingdom to secure a deal without the DUP and to compromise on the DUP's red lines by consenting to a border in the Irish Sea.[9] Of course, Northern Ireland is more than the DUP, and other groups in Northern Ireland – both institutional and within civil society – used access across London, Dublin and Brussels to further represent Northern Ireland's interests.[10] Northern Ireland is not a homogenous actor; instead, different actors worked across many levels to produce different outcomes.

The final stretch of the Brexit negotiations saw the re-emergence of traditional, 'nested' players taking decisions that set aside some concerns of the innermost 'nest' and the unionist concerns about a border in the Irish Sea were in effect ignored, albeit with commitments to work to avoid the tangible nature of such a border (and thus separation between Great Britain and Northern Ireland) as much as possible.[11] Meanwhile, the wishes represented by Dublin (as a 'national-level' nest) were foregrounded, even if the final shape of the Protocol on Ireland/Northern Ireland was largely unsatisfactory.

The ultimate shape of the Brexit settlement depended on the specific make-up of the negotiating teams –and the December 2019 UK general election, in sidelining the DUP's voice, has meant that trade from Northern Ireland will be more frictionless with Ireland than it will be with Britain. As such, 'local' concerns in Northern Ireland dominated the direction of travel of the 'federal' and 'supranational' entities in setting out the shape of Brexit, but when that shape proved unacceptable at the 'federal' level in the United Kingdom, the 'local' red lines of the unionist parties were required to accommodate the demands thrown up by the remaining negotiations. The end result is a compromise that neither fits within 'nested' multilevel governance theory nor meets all the concerns of Northern Ireland or any of the main negotiators.

Here we look at the role played by Northern Ireland in the Withdrawal Agreement, before considering what this experience tells us about multilevel

---

[9] This was not unforeseeable: see, e.g., Sylvia de Mars, 'The rise and fall of Northern Ireland's voice in Brexit negotiations'; LSE Brexit Blog, 11 June 2019, https://blogs.lse.ac.uk/brexit/2019/06/11/the-rise-and-fall-of-northern-irelands-voice-in-brexit-negotiations/.

[10] For other voices from Northern Ireland, see 'Brexit: NI parties unite in EU border appeal', BBC News website, 22 May 2018., www.bbc.co.uk/news/uk-northern-ireland-44199212.

[11] Protocol on Ireland/Northern Ireland, Arts. 4–6, which set up Northern Ireland as part of the EU's custom union in language that aims to address unionist concerns: 'Northern Ireland is part of the customs territory of the United Kingdom' (Art. 4) and 'The Union and the United Kingdom shall use their best endeavours to facilitate the trade between Northern Ireland and other parts of the United Kingdom' (Art. 6(1)).

governance: do theories of 'nesting' adequately explain what Northern Ireland achieved in (or wreaked upon) Brexit? We argue that scale theory better describes the manner of the interactions of the different levels of governance – and also captures the fact that the Northern Ireland's voice changed over time.

## SCALE

Scale incorporates a range of ideas useful in considering trade relations: core and periphery, large and small populations, majorities and minorities, both linear and nonlinear temporality, physical size – vast and small as well as local, national, regional, global and universal spaces. Traditionally, scales (concerning large or small populations for instance, or majorities and minorities) were nested into the local, regional, national, regional, global, and universal spheres. This is a recognisable prism for those familiar with trade governance, where multilevel governance debates utilise nested scales that neatly slot into each other like a matryoshka doll to explain the functioning, aptness, and precision of the global trade regime. Even debates that branch into so-called 'noodle/spaghetti bowl' metaphors still slot trade levels in the matryoshka model as part of the logic of the rise of neo- and ordoliberal constructions of trade.[12] As Slobodian argues in *Globalists*, a key attribute of the development of trade since the end of the First World War has been the removal of the domestic and local regulation of trade and its movement upwards to the regional and global level.[13] The intended effect was to push trade regulation away from the sway of domestic democratic shifts and to move it into the technocratic sphere, which was argued to be neutral (though, with its focus on freer and freer trade and its critique of democratic control, any claim to neutrality is spurious).

Yet, scale also includes more complex modular or nodal ideas that incorporate time, space and distance into how we perceive and utilise it as a governance concept. Both modular and nodal frames are used here to fully engage with how Northern Ireland became a core actor of the Brexit negotiations, thus shifting the paradigm of how multilevel governance operates. Networks often displace and circumvent legal and economic orders, producing non-linear nodular scales rather than hierarchical orders.[14]

---

[12] The term was coined by Jagdish Bhagwati in 'U.S. Trade Policy: The Infatuation with Free Trade Agreements', Columbia Discussion Paper, Series No. 726, 1995.

[13] Quinn Slobodian, *Globalists: The End of Empire and the Birth of Neoliberalism* (Cambridge: Harvard University Press, 2018).

[14] Helga Leitner, Claire Pavlik and Eric Sheppard, 'Networks, Governance, and the Politics of Scale: Inter-Urban Networks and the European Union' in Andrew Herod and Melissa W. Wright (eds.) *Geographies of Power: Placing Scale* (Malden, MA: Blackwell, 2002).

Jumping scales, when the local counters the disempowerment of modern governance by jumping to gain attention for localised issues at the global or regional level, is essential to using scalar analysis to its fullest extent, and can be clearly observed in the role Northern Ireland played in the withdrawal stage of Brexit.

Scale is a core geographical concept and the most apparent iteration is cartography, which is itself intimately linked to international law.[15] This 'politics of scale refers to the production, reconfiguration or contestation of particular differentiations, orderings and hierarchies among geographical scales'.[16] Scale is about both governance sites and the relationships amongst them.[17] Mapping, bordering, and delineating territory is fundamentally linked to contemporary trade.[18] Emerging in the 1980s, the earliest scale analysis focused on specific scales. For example, Taylor argued for three – the world, the national and the local – while Smith included the urban, regional, national and global.[19] These static scales have since been problematised and analysis now ranges from the body, to home, to metropolitan areas, to the world scale and beyond, functioning in both nested as well as networked and nodular scales.[20]

Linked to nested analysis is operational scale. Financial services are operationalised on a global scale, but gentrification occurs on a local level within cities.[21] Temporal scales are also relevant, for example legal periodisation (as in Roman, medieval, and modern) as well as personalised views of processes, for instance time-limited political offices such as EU commissioner or unlimited ones such as monarchs. Brenner argues that the traditional Euclidian, Cartesian, and Westphalian notions of geographical scale as a fixed, bounded, self-enclosed, and pre-given container are now superseded by an emphasis on

---

[15] David Pinder, 'Subverting Cartography: The Situationists and Maps of the City' (1996) 28 *Environment and Planning A* 405–27, p. 405.

[16] Neil Brenner, 'The limits to scale? Methodological reflections on scalar structuration' (2001) 25 *Progress in Human Geography* 591–614, pp. 591, 599.

[17] Richard Howitt, 'Scale' in John A. Agnew, Katharyne Mitchell and Gerard Toal (eds.), *A Companion to Political Geography* (Malden, MA: Wiley, 2015) p. 138; David Delaney and Helga Leitner, 'The political construction of scale' (1997) 16 *Political Geography* 93–185, p. 93.

[18] Henry Jones, 'Property, territory, and colonialism: an international legal history of enclosure' (2019) 39 *Legal Studies* 187–203, p. 187.

[19] Peter J. Taylor, 'A materialist framework for political geography' (1982) 7 *Institute of British Geographers* 15–34, p. 15; N. Smith, 'The region is dead! Long Live the region' (1989) 7 *Political Geography* 141–52, p. 141.

[20] Eric Sheppard and Robert B. McMaster (eds.), *Scale and Geographic Inquiry: Nature, Society, and Method* (Malden, MA: Wiley, 2008), p. 5; Julie Cidell, 'The place of individuals in the politics of scale' (2006) 38 *Area* 196–203, p. 196.

[21] Sheppard and McMaster, *Scale and Geographic Inquiry*, p. 6.

process, evolution, dynamism and socio-political contestation.[22] And certainly, trade has rarely limited itself to the boundaries prescribed by national and international law. Borders are porous and since the end of the First World War, both neo- and ordoliberalism have seen it necessary to further remove those borders for the purposes of trade.[23]

Debates on neo-medievalism (the idea that trade was less regulated and thus easier during the European medieval period), may suggest that boundaries no longer have relevance, but as Northern Ireland demonstrates, at any level (local, national, regional, and global) how any nation regulates its border(s) has direct implications for its alignment with key governance orders.[24] The scales at which states have operated evolve and change over time. The United Kingdom at its geographic and population extant, at the height of its empire – including its colonisation and incorporation of Ireland – was one of the largest governance orders and controlled a huge amount of world trade. However, in the contemporary era, other scales such as the extent of extra-territorial control of trade regulation are more critical to controlling world trade than geographic spread.[25] Scales are not static; they alter as a result of territorial, population and governance change.[26] Brexit is one example, and the United Kingdom's aim of projecting itself on the world or the Commonwealth rather than the EU stage is another.[27]

Critically, scales are socially constructed, meaning that the information stored in maps and the scale on which they are represented impact upon our perceptions of both states and the world. The representation of Northern Ireland, the EU and the Commonwealth on maps impacts upon our perceptions of relevance and import. Scale does not capture the totality of governance interaction(s), but rather aspects of its configuration(s) and reconfiguration(s). Even so, the choices made in depicting governance impact on our perceptions of problems, their nature and their solutions.

[22] Brenner, 'The Limits to Scale', p. 592.
[23] Only the EU has included free movement of people in this idea of opening borders, but note that it has done so while also creating Fortress Europe; exploring this polarity, see, e.g., Andrea Schenkler, 'Cosmopolitan Europeans or Partisans of Fortress Europe? Supranational Identity Patterns in the EU' (2013) 27 *Global Society* 25–51, p. 25.
[24] Stephen J Kobrin, 'Back to the future: Neomedievalism and the postmodern digital world economy' (1998) 51 *Journal of International Affairs* 361–86.
[25] Thomas Cottier, Dannie Jost and Michelle Schupp 'The Prospects of TRIPs-Plus Protection in Future Mega-Regionals' in Thilo Rensmann (ed.), *Mega Mega-Regional Trade Agreements* (Basel: Springer, 2017), pp. 191–215.
[26] Sheppard and McMaster, *Scale and Geographic Inquiry*, p. 3.
[27] For an overview of UK government intentions for a 'Global Britain' scale change, see the House of Commons Foreign Affairs Select Committee, 'Global Britain' (6th Report of Session 2017–19), HC 780.

For example, the presence of a sea dividing a country may not be relevant in a local election but becomes significant in a national election. Two locations may appear close but experience diametrically different issues: for instance, Nice and Monaco are close to each other, but life in each is very different. Distance does not explain the differences between them; rather, it is other scales that are necessary to understand their interrelationship on the Mediterranean coast.

Trade presumptions that accompany particular scales, for instance the presumption that there is a size – of territory, population or culture – where trade will be at its freest, alter alongside the rise and fall of empires, and of the WTO and regional and mega-regional trade agreements. Howitt argues that there is no one scale at which justice is most present[28] while Morrill suggests that only the local scale should be privileged within governance.[29] Swyngedouw argues that 'glocalization' – where globalisation and localisation are in a synergic relationship – is essential to creating a full picture of the complex and changing interactions within contemporary economic, political, and cultural contexts that necessitate both nested and nodular scales to fully understand their operation.[30] The construction of a scale can be social, economic, or political.[31] For example, within EU 'movement of people' policy, the amount and relatively risk-free nature of free movement within EU territory can be contrasted with the distances, temporality and risks of refugee migration into the EU. The scale frames employed in this political, legal and social context impact on the governance lenses adopted, and results – alongside other factors – in both extensive free movement rights as well as the creation of Fortress Europe.[32] Further, feminist scale analysis argues that scale construction often obfuscates or ignores issues of welfare, care or the body and that traditional scalar analysis specifically excludes or disregards the gendered character of scale choices and, in particular, patriarchal gender power

---

[28] Howitt, 'Scale', p. 145.
[29] Richard Morrill 'Inequalities of power, costs and benefits across geographic scales: the future uses of the Hanford reservation' (1999) 18 *Political Geography* 1–23, p. 1; Richard Morrill 'The Tyranny of Conventional Wisdom? A response' (1999) 18 *Political Geography* 45–8, p. 45; Peter J. Taylor 'World Systems Analysis and Regional Geography' (1988) 40 *Professional Geographer* 259–65, p. 259.
[30] Erik Swyngedouw 'Neither Global nor Local: "Glocalization" and the politics of scale' in Kevin R. Cox (ed.), *Spaces of Globalization: Reasserting the Power of the Local* (London/New York: Guilford/Longman, 1997), p. 137.
[31] Brenner, 'The Limits to Scale'; Delaney and Leitner, 'The Political Construction of Scale'.
[32] On this disconnect in the EU, see Martin Ruhs, '"Migrants", "mobile citizens" and the borders of exclusion in the European Union' in Rainer Bauböck (ed.), *Debating European Citizenship* (Cham: Springer, 2018).

relations.³³ Looking at both the vertical and horizontal interrelationships within scale as well as nodular non-linear scales gives a fuller account of governance. As such, scale forms the lens through which we will now consider the role Northern Ireland played in the first part of the Brexit negotiations.

### NORTHERN IRELAND AND BREXIT: THE MAY GOVERNMENT

The role played by Northern Ireland was always going to be more expansive than might have been hoped by those in favour of exiting the EU. The anti 'hard border' signs now common on the border between Ireland and Northern Ireland could summarise Brexit in one image. Before the negotiations officially commenced, it had become apparent to the negotiators that while the border physically existed between one member state and one part of a departing member state, the avoidance of a recreation of a border with any kind of physical infrastructure would only be found in the ongoing economic relationship between the United Kingdom and the EU. That Dublin was able to ensure that the border on the island was part of the exit negotiations and not the post-exit trade agreement surprised London, and shaped the settlement that followed.³⁴

Northern Ireland could be described as a 'silent shareholder' in these negotiations because it does not have any devolved powers over its trade policy.³⁵ The negotiations to 'protect' trade in all constituent parts of the United Kingdom were always going to take place in Westminster, regardless of whether Northern Ireland had a functioning executive between 2016 and 2019. This was a similar position to that of Scotland and Wales, and how acknowledged each devolved nation was during the negotiations was disparate and evolving and did not fit neatly into the nature of the United Kingdom's devolved settlement and division of authority. As such, the 'silent shareholder' description seemed apt and, moreover, fits perfectly within theories of nested scales, but the reality turned out to be different.

On the surface, the United Kingdom's position with respect to Northern Ireland is not dissimilar to the EU's approach to the Withdrawal Agreement

---

33 Sallie A. Marston 'The Social Construction of Scale' (2000) 24 *Progress in Human Geography* 219–42, p. 219; Mariana Valverde, *Chronotopes of Law: Jurisdiction, Scale and Governance* (Abingdon: Routledge, 2015), p. 91.
34 Alex Barker and Arthur Beesley, 'How the Irish border backstop became Brexit's defining issue', *Financial Times*, 30 October 2018, https://www.ft.com/content/73ac4a5c-d83f-11e8-a854-33d6 f82e62f8 See also Connolly, *Brexit and Ireland*, chap. 9.
35 Roger Masterman and Colin Murray, *Constitutional and Administrative Law* (Harlow: Pearson, 2nd edn., 2018), chap. 12.

dimension of Brexit. Northern Ireland is primarily of interest to Ireland; it is not inherently a core concern of the other EU member states, even if showing commitment to the remaining state most impacted by Brexit was in the EU's interest for its long-term cohesion. Before the negotiations with the United Kingdom began, successful lobbying by the Irish government within Brussels resulted in its priorities being at the forefront of the negotiations, with a lasting EU commitment to 'do our utmost' to avoid the creation of a hard border between Ireland and Northern Ireland, even in the event of no agreement on withdrawal.[36] The fact that Michel Barnier and his team were not representing Ireland specifically in the negotiations is, in this sense, irrelevant: Irish concerns were adopted by the EU as a whole.[37]

Under traditional multilevel governance theory, then, the Brexit negotiations started with two distinct 'nests', meeting in the middle: the EU, representing Ireland, and the United Kingdom, representing Northern Ireland. However, both of these nests were also absorbed into a more supranational nest, with its own set of policies and rules. This is the WTO, itself also part of a global nest of public international law. The WTO is barely involved in the Brexit negotiations, but as a global or supra-institution, it sets the frameworks within which the 'super'-governments, the EU and the United Kingdom, have to work when trying to come to a settlement that will satisfy the 'sub'-governments of Ireland and Northern Ireland.

The picture gets more complex, and the metaphor of 'nesting dolls' less helpful, when we consider the legally binding bridge between one of the super-governments and one of the sub-governments in these negotiations: the 1998 Agreement.[38] Absent the 1998 Agreement's commitments to peace and equal treatment, the United Kingdom and the EU would find themselves perhaps listening to Northern Ireland and Ireland – but they would not find themselves *bound* to listen.

Rather than resembling distinct nests engaging with each other, the negotiations look more like two unevenly tiered cakes, connected in different ways across different tiers.

At the super-level (here the EU and the United Kingdom, negotiating as equals), there are clear priorities. First, the EU wished to protect the single

---

[36] Lara Marlowe, 'Brexit: EU "obliged" to check goods at Border if no-deal, says Barnier', *Irish Times*, 23 Jan. 2019, www.irishtimes.com/news/world/europe/brexit-eu-obliged-to-check-goods-at-border-if-no-deal-says-barnier-1.3768069. See also Connolly, *Brexit and Ireland*, on Ireland's effective lobbying.
[37] European Council's Guidelines on the Article 50 Negotiations, para. 11.
[38] *Agreement between the Government of the United Kingdom of Great Britain and Northern Ireland and the Government of Ireland* (1998) 2114 UNTS 473.

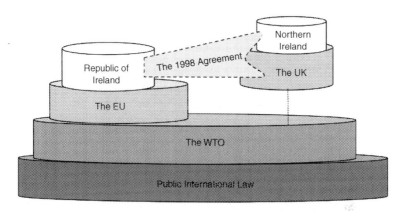

FIGURE 1: *Governance 'nests' impacting on Brexit* (where the white tiers represent the 'sub'-level, and the light grey tiers represent the 'super'-level of actors)

market – meaning the United Kingdom would not get free movement of goods without accepting the other four freedoms.[39] Beyond that, the EU did not have many specific ultimatums – its demands were dependent on what kind of settlement was struck, and more explicit in relation to the post-withdrawal negotiations than the withdrawal negotiations.

The United Kingdom, meanwhile, wanted 'to take back control', which had become loosely defined by the negotiating team as wanting out of the single market, wanting out of the customs union, and withdrawal from Court of Justice jurisdiction.[40] Nonetheless, the exact parameters of what the United Kingdom wanted were nebulous. One example was Prime Minister May's statement of not wanting to 'return to the borders of the past', while maintaining that it was essential the United Kingdom take back control of its laws, including those on borders.[41]

Between the two parties, a broad compromise seemed relatively clear: if the United Kingdom did not want to be in the single market, and the EU did not want to split the single market, the United Kingdom should leave the single market, and the customs union, which by implication would mean no future Court of Justice of the European Union (CJEU) jurisdiction. Instead, trade subsequent to withdrawal would happen under a semi-standard free trade agreement (FTA) that would need to be compliant with WTO rules. Withdrawal would thus end UK single market and customs union

---

[39] See European Council, Guidelines for Brexit Negotiations, para. 1, stressing that the four freedoms are 'indivisible'.
[40] See May, The Government's Negotiating Objectives.
[41] Ibid.

membership and bridge it into this next trade relationship, where the United Kingdom would not be obliged to adopt any EU rules and trade would occur with more friction.

Northern Ireland's priorities were more complicated. Immediately after the referendum, the still functioning Northern Ireland Executive issued a joint letter to the UK prime minister, which set out the unique nature of Northern Ireland's situation, its vulnerable economic position, its reliance on the island-wide energy market, and the impact of EU funding on the region and the border.[42] After power-sharing collapsed in January 2017, the fracturing that followed mapped some of traditional divisions of the two communities. As Mitchell discusses elsewhere in this book, the nationalists foregrounded a frictionless border on the island, whereas the DUP focused on the absence of an economic border in the Irish Sea. The Ulster Unionist Party (UUP) and others had more complicated positions, however, and Northern Ireland farming, agri-food, business, and human rights groups presented a nuanced view of the potential impact of Brexit, and set about making their voices heard.

As Ireland has demonstrated throughout the Brexit negotiations, within some nests, the 'sub' players may have access to and influence on the 'super' players. Connolly details how quickly the Irish government mobilised to get their interests at the forefront of the Commission's strategy; while the EU expected there to be economic consequences, and understood the need for preparation, Ireland stressed that a physical border on the island was both unacceptable and impossible. The Irish Government undertook a series of information campaigns, including bringing influential EU officials to the border region, to ensure that what was happening at the local level was clear at the supranational level.[43]

Communication within nests is not always this smooth, and complications arise when governing parties represent only one part of the public voice. When considering communication within the United Kingdom's nest, it appears at least one party in Northern Ireland wished to ignore the consequences of Brexit on the 'invisible' border on the island of Ireland. The DUP had campaigned for Leave as a unionist policy and while they worked with Sinn Féin immediately after Brexit, once the executive collapsed and then, after the 2017 UK general election (when they entered into a 'confidence and supply agreement' with the Conservative government), they allied their position with

---

[42] See Arlene Foster and Martin McGuinness, Letter to Theresa May, 10 Aug. 2016, https://www.executiveoffice-ni.gov.uk/publications/letter-prime-minister-rt-hon-theresa-may-mp.

[43] Connolly, *Brexit and Ireland*, chap. 9.

the hard Leave parts of the Conservative Party.[44] The voice of other parties in Northern Ireland, more concerned about the preservation of the 1998 Agreement and the invisible border, were largely ignored by the UK government but were listened to both by Dublin and Brussels.[45]

Once Ireland moved the border issue to the top of the EU agenda, the United Kingdom under May's government conceded that a hard border on the island of Ireland had to be avoided.[46] Neither the United Kingdom nor Ireland disputed that resurrecting physical borders would threaten peace – and so the 1998 Agreement surfaced as its own multilevel governance commitment, dictating further specific terms for the negotiations. Here, the nests analogy becomes more tenuous, as Ireland and the United Kingdom were in practice not both 'super' actors in these negotiations, as they had to negotiate on matters involving the Irish trade border directly through the EU.

At the same time, the EU was not a party to any aspects of Brexit that affected the functioning of the Common Travel Area (CTA).[47] While now set out in a non-binding Memorandum of Understanding (MoU) between the UK and Ireland, the CTA supports free movement of UK and Irish nationals between both states, and is accepted within EU law.[48] Though UK government officials frequently offered it up as evidence that Irish and UK citizens in each state did not need to be concerned about Brexit and that it would resolve many issues stemming from Brexit, it became clear that the CTA needed to be put on firmer legal ground. The proposed 2020 UK Immigration Bill and the above MoU resolve some issues,[49] but as the Joint Committee of the Irish Human Rights and Equality Commission and the Northern Ireland Human

[44] Patrick Maguire, 'How the DUP and the ERG shut down one of the few remaining solutions to the Irish border issue', *New Statesman*, 13 September 2018, www.newstatesman.com/politics/staggers/2018/09/irish-border-brexit-dup-european-research-group-theresa-may.

[45] 'NI parties unite in EU border appeal', BBC News website, 22 May 2018, www.bbc.co.uk/news/uk-northern-ireland-44199212; 'Brexit: No withdrawal agreement without a "backstop" for the Northern Ireland/Ireland, European Parliament press release, 27 July 2018, www.europarl.europa.eu/news/en/press-room/20180727IPR08701/brexit-no-withdrawal-agreement-without-a-backstop-for-the-irish-border.

[46] Joint report from the negotiators of the European Union and the United Kingdom Government on progress during phase 1 of negotiations under Art. 50 TEU on the United Kingdom's orderly withdrawal from the European Union, 8 December 2017, https://ec.europa.eu/commission/sites/beta-political/files/joint_report.pdf

[47] The only role EU law has in terms of the CTA is in permitting it in Protocol 20 to the TFEU; see Protocol (No. 20) on the application of certain aspects of Art. 26 of the Treaty on the Functioning of the European Union to the United Kingdom and to Ireland (2012) OJ C326/293.

[48] Ibid.

[49] 'Factsheet 2: Status of Irish citizens', gov.uk, 20 March 2020, www.gov.uk/government/publications/immigration-bill-2020-factsheets/factsheet-2-status-of-irish-citizen; and Memorandum

Rights Commission make clear, more is required.[50] The recent *de Souza* litigation, concerning whether those born in Northern Ireland can reject the British citizenship they are entitled to at birth because of the 1998 Agreement, further underscores the more complicated nature of citizenships and movement that the 1998 Agreement protects.[51]

Local circumstances and conditions set clear brakes on what was possible at both the super-governance and the global WTO governance levels. The United Kingdom's commitments under the 1998 Agreement made its desires for Brexit unachievable: it could not leave all EU infrastructure without creating a hard border. The 1998 Agreement bodies such as the Joint Committee and the Northern Ireland Human Rights Commission represent further statutory and bilateral legal commitments to maintaining rights, and these bodies consistently lobbied Dublin, London, and Brussels on these commitments.[52] Non-diminution of rights and reciprocity on rights across the island became part of the discourse, and the obligations this put on the UK government became a factor.

The EU, in accommodating the Irish position, did not need to change its own red lines. If the United Kingdom were to stay in the single market and the customs union, there would be no new border. But that seemingly simple solution ran into one of the United Kingdom's red lines: and the May government argued that staying in both would not actually amount to a Brexit.[53] Instead, the negotiating parties needed to look further for a compromise that respected the United Kingdom and EU aims, but also accommodated the needs of the sub-governments on the island of Ireland.

Ireland proved to be the key national government that determined the next steps, and it leveraged enough pressure on other EU member states to argue

---

of Understanding between the UK and Ireland on the CTA, gov.uk, 8 May 2019, www.gov.uk/government/publications/memorandum-of-understanding-between-the-uk-and-ireland-on-the-cta. See, for analysis, Sylvia de Mars and Colin Murray, 'With or Without EU? The Common Travel Area after Brexit' (2020) 21:5 *German Law Journal* 815–37.

[50] See, e.g., 'New Research Recommends UK-Irish treaty is best solution to ensure Common Travel Area Rights', NIHRC, 13 November 2018, www.nihrc.org/news/detail/new-research-recommends-uk-irish-treaty-is-best-solution-to-ensure-common-t.

[51] *De Souza* [2019] UKUT 355 (IAC). See, for analysis, Alison Harvey, 'Legal analysis of incorporating into UK law the birthright commitment under the Belfast (Good Friday) Agreement 1998', IHREC, 26 March 2020, www.ihrec.ie/documents/legal-analysis-of-incorporating-into-uk-law-the-birthright-commitment-under-the-belfast-good-friday-agreement-1998/.

[52] See, e.g., 'Joint Committee continues focus on protecting human rights after Brexit', NIHRC, 23 October 2019, https://www.nihrc.org/publication/detail/a-legal-analysis-of-incorporating-into-uk-law-the-birthright-commitment-under-the-befast-good-friday-agreement-1998.

[53] May, The Government's Negotiating Objectives.

for a special deal for Northern Island.⁵⁴ This resulted in the EU budging on one of its core red lines, again suggesting disproportionate influence from one of the sub-governments in a nested governance structure. The EU accepted that the combination of the 1998 Agreement, Irish interests, and the United Kingdom's position meant that either the United Kingdom would leave without a deal and the border that everyone vowed to avoid would emerge, or the EU blurred one of its red lines and a border was avoided.

The December 2017 Joint Report reflects an awkward compromise. It pledged to avoid the border and built in an insurance policy by which Northern Ireland remained in the single market for trade purposes if no alternative means of avoiding a hard border could be found.⁵⁵ There were two problems with this from a UK domestic perspective. First, Northern Ireland would be a de facto EU member state for trade in goods purposes – but it would have no input into EU policy on free movement of goods or trade, via the Common Commercial Policy. Second, if rules relating to trade in Northern Ireland remained (in effect) EU law, and the United Kingdom wished to avoid creating an internal border in the Irish Sea, then all regulation applicable in Great Britain would also have to be compatible with EU law. Several months later, after abandoning some of the rights commitments made in the Joint Report, the United Kingdom and the EU presented an agreed legal text regarding Northern Ireland and Ireland, titled the 'backstop'.

The first draft of the backstop was put forward by the EU; while the UK government prevaricated about technological solutions for avoiding a hard border, the EU proposed a mechanism whereby EU laws on trade would apply in Northern Ireland. The EU appeared to believe that while the 'four freedoms' remained generally indivisible, the case of Northern Ireland was clearly so unique that any special treatment would not constitute a form of 'cherry picking' of the single market rules.⁵⁶ The fact that Northern Ireland was to be covered by EU single market and customs rules, but Britain was not, was anathema to the DUP, however.⁵⁷ It would effectively result in Northern Ireland no longer being part of the economic Union, instead becoming a fully separate

---

54  Connolly, *Brexit and Ireland*.
55  Joint report 8 December 2017.
56  European Commission Draft Withdrawal Agreement on the withdrawal of the United Kingdom of Great Britain and Northern Ireland from the European Union and the European Atomic Energy Community, 28 February 2018, https://ec.europa.eu/commission/publications/draft-agreement-withdrawl-united-kingdom-great-britain-and-nothern-ireland-european-union-and-european-atomic-energy-community-agreed-negotiators-level-14-november-2018_en.
57  'Foster says draft Brexit plans are "unacceptable"' RTE, 28 February 2018, www.rte.ie/news/brexit/2018/0228/944227-brexit-northern-ireland/.

economic operator. There would be custom-related border checks not between Northern Ireland and Ireland, but rather between Northern Ireland and Britain.

The final backstop, which had all of the United Kingdom in a customs arrangement (that is, basically a customs union; Northern Ireland aligned with the EU single market rules that affect trade, and Britain aligned with Northern Ireland so as to absolutely minimise any checks on products moving from Britain to Northern Ireland) was almost entirely shaped by voices originating from the sub-governments, which successfully exerted pressure on the super-governments who were actually negotiating. The innermost nests, in other words, appear to have led the outermost nests. The backstop was a compromise, but it was the only alternative to a hard border or a border in the Irish sea, given WTO rules and the wish to ensure the absence of an economic border in the Irish Sea. Simply not collecting tariffs or running risk-based checks on goods travelling between Northern Ireland and Ireland is not possible. As such, the United Kingdom and the EU, despite effectively holding all the legal cards, ended up caught between two opposing ends: the WTO's basic framework exerting downwards pressure for equal treatment between all their trading partners, and Northern Ireland and Ireland exerting pressure upwards in demanding special consideration for the only land border shared by the United Kingdom and the EU, while the DUP insisted that there be no economic barriers in the Irish sea.

Northern Ireland, and by proxy, Ireland, thus appeared to end up with the best settlements stemming from the withdrawal negotiations conducted by the May government and the EU – and the United Kingdom and the EU ended up not wholly achieving any of their respective goals.

### NORTHERN IRELAND AND BREXIT: THE JOHNSON GOVERNMENT

Despite being largely designed to meet DUP demands, the DUP did not agree with the backstop – believing that Northern Ireland would no longer be a core part of the United Kingdom. They were not the only sceptics: the Westminster Parliament rejected Theresa May's Withdrawal Agreement on three separate occasions, albeit for a range of rationales.[58] Following the final rejection, the May government was brought down – and the Conservative Party's election of Boris Johnson as prime minister meant that different UK negotiators went

---

[58] Rowena Mason and Rajeev Syal, 'May Fails to Convince DUP and ERG "Spartans" to back her Brexit deal', *Guardian*, 27 March 2019, www.theguardian.com/politics/2019/mar/27/may-faces-uphill-battle-as-dup-and-ergs-spartans-will-vote-against-deal.

back to Brussels. The Johnson government returned with a 'new' agreement in October 2019 – different in the sense that the backstop had been removed, and the EU's original proposal for bespoke treatment for Northern Ireland took its place. The other substantial change was to create a mechanism for democratic input from the Northern Ireland Assembly. The Assembly will now vote every four years to maintain or reject the Protocol.[59]

The Johnson deal, however, also looked like it was going to be rejected by Parliament – and so in December 2019, a general election was called, as the only way out of the Northern Ireland stalemate. The outright Conservative Party majority produced by those elections, and the end of the Conservative Party's 'confidence and supply' agreement with the DUP, meant that Northern Ireland's voice in the negotiations changed. It went from having a disproportionate influence as a sub-government to effectively being ignored by a super-government and abandoned by the hard Leavers within the Conservative Party. Once the DUP's votes were no longer needed by the Westminster government, Northern Ireland concerns – i.e., those of the DUP - proved far less important. The election of several Social Democratic and Labour Party (SDLP) and Alliance Party MPs also meant that there were other voices from Northern Ireland represented in Westminster beyond the non-sitting Sinn Féin. Instead, in accommodating the concerns of Ireland (as reflected in the EU negotiating position), it was these other voices in Northern Ireland that proved impactful. When given an unappetising choice between no Brexit, a hard border on the island of Ireland, or a border in the Irish Sea, the UK government ultimately chose to prioritise the land border.

The DUP were not wholly ignored, however, and under the pre-2019 parliamentary arithmetic exerted enough pressure on the UK government for it to commit to several concessions in the October 2019 Withdrawal Agreement. DUP demands that Northern Ireland be part of the Union for trade purposes in the Withdrawal Agreement resulted in a Protocol on Ireland/Northern Ireland that is not a backstop but rather 'the future relationship', and it treats Northern Ireland as a bespoke customs territory, with trade largely governed by EU and WTO rules rather than UK ones, and subjected to checks on the Irish sea. Meanwhile, the United Kingdom, representing only Great Britain in this case, can pursue its own trading relationships with non-EU countries – which Northern Ireland will also benefit from.

---

[59] Protocol on Ireland/Northern Ireland, Art. 18.

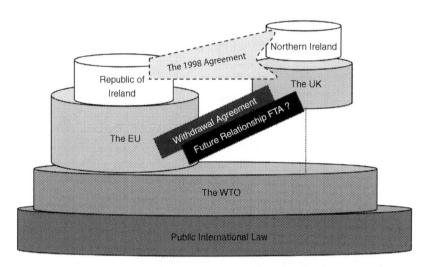

FIGURE 2: *Governance 'nests' impacting on Northern Ireland under the Withdrawal Agreement* (where the white tiers represent the 'sub'-level, and the light grey tiers represent the 'super'-level of actors)

## GOVERNANCE THEORY AND NORTHERN IRELAND

The Withdrawal Agreement negotiations paint a picture that is not captured by classic multilevel governance theory. Marks and Hooghe describe this as 'Type I' multilevel governance, whereby every layer of governance nests within another, but none of the layers have overlapping jurisdictions or memberships; it represents an 'internationalised' version of Westphalian state governance, where formal governments remain the primary actors.[60] Here, instead, we see nested government levels that are in theory distinct, but in practice operate in legal infrastructures that overlap, and compromise political choice. The alternative form of multilevel governance organisation that Marks and Hooghe identify is 'Type II' governance which involves an infinite number of governing actors with overlapping memberships and jurisdictions, taking decisions on sectoral concerns as they arise. While the Brexit process was certainly ad hoc, the governance organisation during the negotiations to date has not been as unstructured as this theory might suggest. What, then, can account for Northern Ireland and its changing voice during these

---

[60] Gary Marks and Liesbet Hooghe, 'Contrasting Visions of Multi-level Governance' in Ian Bache and Matthew Flinders (eds.), *Multi-level Governance* (Oxford: Oxford University Press, 2004).

multilevel negotiations, if neither of these broad strands of multilevel governance theory are able to?

## SCALE, BREXIT, AND NORTHERN IRELAND

Jumping scales encompass more than a binary choice between the local and the global. The concept incorporates a wider context of networks and nodules of governance where the interactions between and amongst scales is essential and the local is often a 'formative part of global processes', and 'cross linkages, awkward juxtapositions, and jumps, and non-hierarchal dialectics' must all be accommodated.[61] Northern Ireland provides a very useful example of this: it jumped its scale, while Ireland juxtaposed its relationships with Northern Ireland, the United Kingdom, and the EU, leading to a nodular negotiations strategy. Cox argues that in political discourse the relationships between scales rather than the jumping of scales is essential, and both Ireland and Northern Ireland benefited from this, while, in relying on nested scales, the United Kingdom missed opportunities and was, at times, outmanoeuvred.[62] Given the role of the 1998 Agreement and Northern Ireland's past, especially the history of the border, temporal jumps, awkward juxtapositions, and a variety of cross linkages of legal and political settlements (from the EU Treaties to the 1998 Agreement to the CTA) each became important.

Jones argues that the construction of particular scales and their entrenchment renders certain questions unaskable.[63] Within trade law, the common-sense rhetoric of freer and freer trade is largely placed 'safely' beyond the regulation of the state and discourses that challenge this are rarely presented as entirely reasonable.[64] Alston famously challenged the co-option of human rights into trade, arguing that human rights would become subsumed by the logic of trade as it moved into that global scale.[65] Indeed, the relationship between the 1998 Agreement (especially its rights requirements), EU rights, and the wish to trade globally are an example of the clash of scales that Alston referred to. It is often assumed that rights will always be the loser in these clashes but this was not necessarily the case in Northern Ireland.

---

[61] Pauline M. McGuirk, 'Multiscaled Interpretations of Urban Change: The Federal, the States, and the Local in the Western Area Strategy of Adelaide' (1997) 15 *Environment and Planning D: Society and Space* 481–98, p. 481; Howitt, 'Scale', p. 145.

[62] Kevin R. Cox, 'Spaces of dependence, spaces of engagement and the politics of scale, or: looking for local politics' (1998) 17 *Political Geography* 1–23, p. 1.

[63] Katherine T. Jones, 'Scale as epistemology' (1998) 17 *Political Geography* 25–8, p. 25.

[64] Slobodian, *Globalists*.

[65] Philip Alston, 'Resisting the Merger and Acquisition of Human Rights by Trade Law: A Reply to Petersmann' (2002) 13 *European Journal of International Law* 815–44, p. 815.

Northern Ireland as a whole managed to push itself forward in a way that few would have expected. In particular, the 1998 Agreement bodies like the Northern Ireland Human Rights Commission and the Joint Committee proved to be essential interlocutors with Dublin, London, and Brussels. Non-diminution and reciprocity on rights became part of super-government trade discourse because of Northern Ireland.

In trade law debates, the Taylor/Smith nested scales of hierarchical models of jurisdiction are foregrounded, and the rich theoretical debates are rarely drawn upon. Northern Ireland demonstrates how these hierarchal scales do not offer neat explanations.[66] Jurisdiction is the most obvious iteration of legal scale, and one where the deliberate choice of scalar formation either broadens or tightens the perspectives taken and the forms of authority assumed. The scale of the CJEU's jurisdiction became a core feature of Brexit and the future relationship negotiations, while the scale of the WTO's Appellate Body has become a key aspect of USA's wish to repatriate control of trade to its own trade representative and to project that out to other states.

Legal debates in environmental law, the law of the sea and in trade law (amongst others) acknowledge that scale is an issue, but do not theorise the scalar construction to operate as part of the analysis; rather, scale is merely a problem to solve or an opportunity to be harness. Davies, de Sousa Santos, Riles, and Valverde provide important exceptions to this limited engagement.[67] De Sousa Santos describes how law demonstrates its exclusivity in order to assert its authority; thus, like maps, law distorts geographical or temporal reality to fit them into its operation.[68] This is most obviously done through jurisdiction, whether this be in an administration area or area of law. The juridification that has accompanied some aspects of globalisation such as trade regulation in the move from GATT to the WTO is an example of this in operation.

Davies describes how scale provides 'dynamic terminology for understanding the ways in which normativity is interconnected through differently imagined frames, from the individual and small groups, to the global order'.[69] She argues that states' domination of law obliterates alternative

---

[66] Howitt, 'Scale', pp. 146–7.
[67] Valverde, *Chronotopes of Law*; Margaret Davies, *Law Unlimited: Materialism, Pluralism and Legal Theory* (Abingdon: Routledge, 2017); Boaventura de Sousa Santos 'Law: A Map of Misreading: Towards a Postmodern Conception of Law' (1987) 14 *Journal of Law and Society* 279–302, p. 279; Annelise Riles 'The View from the International Plane: Perspective and Scale in the Architecture of Colonial International Law' (1995) 6 *Law and Critique* 39–54, p. 39.
[68] De Sousa Santos, 'A Map of Misreading', p. 281; he also describes the use of projection and symbolism to achieve this effect.
[69] Davies, *Law Unlimited*, p. xi.

constructions of law, but this also sidesteps those areas such as trade where increasingly the tendency has been to remove states and, as such, democratic and individual input, from the debate.[70] Valverde argues that temporality is as important as space in understanding the operation of scale and law, suggesting that lived temporalities, ahistorical temporalities, aboriginal, and spiritual temporalities are essential to seeing beyond the bare jurisdictional claims of law.[71] Temporality is an essential element of understanding Northern Ireland: the accumulation of harms, the wish to not return to the borders of the past, and the possibility of a future united Ireland or independent Scotland all play their roles.

For Valverde, scale works across the nested and nodular scales, and it is in seeing law within and amongst these scales that the operation of law is observable. For Northern Ireland, it is essential to see both nested and nodular scales. Law and politics combine to define trading spaces through scale – in spaces that do not exist within a geographical space. An example of this is the existence of Hong Kong and Macau as singular trading spaces outside of the traditional international legal frame of the state. Under the Protocol on Ireland/Northern Ireland, the latter has become a unique trading space with two overlapping regimes that will then impact upon the state it is in, its nearest neighbour, and the regional trading bloc in which it is both outside and within.

Riles argues that in the evolution of international law in the nineteenth century, problems which occurred at local level were 'small' but the resolution of these issues took place at the international 'large' level, where local events became global.

> From the vantage point of the international lawyer's globalising gaze, distant events "on the ground" were "spotted" as international issues and the adjudication of international disputes was understood to take place on an "international plane" different in scale from these events themselves.[72]

Northern Ireland in some ways fits into this pattern but also disrupts it. The Nothern Ireland 'Brexit problem' was discussed and settled away from its source, arguably introducing an element of objectivity. Brussels was the core wherein this local Brexit dispute, at the periphery of both the EU and of the United Kingdom, was resolved, and solutions were adopted at a great distance, not masked by occasional trips by negotiators to the border itself. This was aided by the ever present need to comply with WTO commitments to treat all other

---

[70] Ibid, pp. 94–5.
[71] Valverde, *Chronotopes of Law*, pp. 9–10.
[72] Riles, 'The View', p. 40.

WTO members equally (known as Most-Favoured-Nation and National Treatment). The trade lawyer and the EU lawyer inhabit the global perspective which is itself a 'way of looking that eclipses all others, and a *space* or place'.[73] But conversely, the small, local issue actually became the core: it replaced other, previously projected issues, with Northern Ireland, its people, its peace process, and the all-island economy emerging as the key issue to resolve in the Brexit negotiations.

De Sousa Santos describes local law as large-scale legality, state law as medium-scale and global law as small-scale, arguing that law uses criterion to establish the details and features that are regulated.[74] Law created the unique position of Northern Ireland within both the Irish and UK constitutions;[75] it created a unique space for it within EU law and, with all probability, within WTO law. These different legal forms, both pre- and post-Brexit, create different legal realities which both overlap and interact with each other. Davies argues that law foregrounds the state – but in the Brexit and Northern Ireland example, at times the law sidelined the state in favour of one of its constituent parts.[76] Riles argues that re-scaling and distortion are common international legal practices, and certainly Northern Ireland, utilising both the EU and the 1998 Agreement, used these practices to its advantage.[77]

CONCLUSION

Northern Ireland serves as an excellent case study of ebbs and flows in the extent to which local actors can influence supranational, national and international entities into changing their policies to suit sub-governmental interests. The 1998 Agreement and the post-2017 parliamentary structure tied the United Kingdom's hands, which benefited Northern Ireland, as did the fact that it had what we will call an ally 'of sorts' in Ireland, which has significantly more power in pushing the EU in particular directions. That said, Northern Ireland is, of course, not only one entity with a single view. This became evident once the parliamentary arithmetic was taken away from the DUP in 2019, and Northern Ireland issues suddenly became primarily of interest to Northern Ireland and Ireland, resulting in an altered future agreement rather than the backstop.

---

[73] Riles, 'The View', p. 48, emphasis in original.
[74] De Sousa Santos, 'A Map of Misreading', p. 287.
[75] De Mars and Murray, 'With or Without EU'.
[76] Davies, *Law Unlimited*.
[77] Riles, 'The View', p. 50.

The 1998 Agreement continues to have significant implications for how far the United Kingdom can let Northern Ireland drift from the EU and Ireland, but also ties Northern Ireland to London on account of its unique constitutional function. The Northern Ireland 'problem' has become one of domestic constitutional settlements clashing with international, regional and bilateral commitments. It seems likely that, despite current murmurings about wanting to effectively renegotiate the Protocol,[78] the international and bilateral commitments will win out, simply because they take place at three separate levels and only permit one possible solution that is compatible with all of them: compliance with WTO law requires border checks, the single market requires borders, and the 1998 Agreement requires those borders to not be between Northern Ireland and Ireland. Northern Ireland demonstrates how the matryoshka analogy only ever partially explains those negotiations where a nuanced scaler approach is necessary.

---

[78] See, e.g., David Maddox, 'Brexit SHOWDOWN: Boris vows to fix May's "defective" WA sparking huge outcry in Brussels', *Sunday Express*, 7 June 2020, www.express.co.uk/news/uk/1292372/Brexit-latest-boris-johnson-trade-talks-brussels-news.

# 4

# Political Parties in Northern Ireland and the Post-Brexit Constitutional Debate

## David Mitchell

The implementation of the Belfast/Good Friday Agreement (the 1998 Agreement) entailed the stabilising of Northern Ireland's place within the United Kingdom. Although anti-Agreement unionists and pro-Agreement republicans claimed that the 1998 Agreement was a stepping stone to Irish unity, the addressing of Irish nationalist grievances through the reform of governance in Northern Ireland, alongside growing north-south links and British-Irish cooperation, ensured that northern nationalist interest in Irish unity in the short term remained relatively low. In 2016 this equilibrium was upset by the desire of the United Kingdom – predominantly England – to leave the European Union. This prospect imposed a new binary on Northern Ireland politics which interacted with the constitutional divide in complex ways. This interaction is the focus of this chapter.

The chapter begins by reviewing the positions of the five main parties on Europe prior to 2016. It explains the parties' stances during the referendum campaign and examines how they responded to the referendum result. Following this, the chapter argues that Brexit produced constitutional restlessness in Northern Ireland because the vote lacked legitimacy according to the standards of consent contained in the 1998 Agreement. The chapter then traces how the new constitutional debate became established, highlighting how, although the debate was initiated by Brexit, it was intensified by subsequent developments in British and Irish politics. The chapter also explores key dilemmas that the debate posed for the political parties. The conclusion suggests that constitutional deliberations look set to continue but possibly at a lower intensity. Their direction will be shaped by developments in 2019–20 including the Boris Johnson Brexit agreement, the new Irish government, the restoration of devolution in Northern Ireland and the coronavirus crisis.

## THE NORTHERN PARTIES AND EUROPE BEFORE BREXIT

The thrust of European integration towards the pooling of national sovereignty and the weakening of national borders has had a distinct resonance in a region in which public opinion on sovereignty and borders has been polarised to the point of violence. For at least two decades after the United Kingdom and Ireland joined the European Economic Community (EEC), the militants of the Irish Republican Army (IRA) were engaged in a low-intensity armed conflict against the British state designed to weaken London's commitment to retaining Northern Ireland. Pro-British loyalist paramilitaries sought to defend the status quo through a violent campaign directed at the IRA and what loyalists saw as its Catholic support base. At the same time, the very structure of the Northern Ireland party system was, and still is, based on competing views of the legitimacy of the Irish border. It has been called an 'ethnic dual party system' because most people vote according to their community background and competition for votes mainly occurs within, rather than between, each of the two main blocs.[1] (This description may need updating given the leap of the cross-community Alliance Party from fifth to third largest party in elections in 2019.) Accordingly, Europe and European issues played little role in party politics before Brexit. In a 2010 study of the 'Europeanisation' of politics in Ireland, Murphy and Hayward found that,

> Northern Ireland's political parties have largely proved more resistant to Europeanising influences than their counterparts elsewhere. In this respect, there is little evidence of radically changed attitudes towards Europe among Northern Ireland's political parties, nor is there any strong basis for suggesting that they have treated the EU as an essential arena for broadening political opportunities.[2]

Rather, Europe was refracted through the all-consuming conflict over Northern Ireland's constitutional status.

Despite some policy differences and electoral competition between the Democratic Unionist Party (DUP) and Ulster Unionist Party (UUP) on Europe, the parties' outlooks on Europe have had much in common. To varying degrees, from the debates on initial accession to the EEC in 1974 right up to Brexit, Europe has been perceived by many unionists as a threat to

---

[1] Paul Mitchell, 'Party competition in an ethnic dual party system' (1995) 18:4 *Ethnic and Racial Studies* 773–96.
[2] Mary C. Murphy and Katy Hayward, 'Party politics and the EU in Ireland, North and South', in Katy Hayward and Mary C. Murphy (eds.), *The Europeanisation of Party Politics in Ireland, North and South* (Abingdon: Routledge, 2010), p. 3.

British sovereignty. The threat is twofold. First, unionists are deeply attached to British political institutions, meaning that the possibility of European institutions constraining the primacy of Westminster was viewed as threatening. Second, unionists feared that British sovereignty over Northern Ireland could be weakened through the encroachment of Irish influence across the border, a process potentially facilitated by the EU.

Although religious references have markedly declined in DUP discourse during the party's post 1998 modernisation and expansion,[3] the party's founder, Rev Ian Paisley, was vocally opposed to Europe on the grounds that it was a Roman Catholic plot to extend Vatican influence across the continent, arguing that the EEC was foretold in biblical prophecies of the End Times.[4] At the same time, Paisley voiced secular Euro-sceptic arguments.[5] He topped the polls in the first European Parliament (EP) election in 1979 and every subsequent one until his last election in 1999. Paisley's success indicated how voters treated those elections – the only ones in which Northern Ireland was a single constituency – as proxy constitutional referendums, and demonstrated the wish of the unionists to support a candidate who was self-styled as the stoutest defender of unionism.[6]

Although Paisley understood his role as a member of the European Parliament (MEP) as allowing him to oppose Europe from the inside, the position became a means for the DUP's cooperation with European institutions. This approach was summed up by Paisley in a well-known remark: 'I'm going to get all I can for Ulster, every grant we can possibly get our hands on. Then when we have milked the cow dry, we are going to shoot the cow'.[7] Such pragmatism was evident in how Paisley, John Hume of the Social Democratic and Labour Party (SDLP), and the UUP's Jim Nicholson worked closely to secure funding for Northern Ireland.[8]

After initial opposition to joining the EEC, the UUP accepted the practical benefits of cooperating with other states within a European framework. Murphy sums up the party's orientation to Europe as 'pragmatic but lacking

---

[3] Jonathan Tonge, Maire Braniff, Thomas Hennessey, James W McAuley and Sophie Whiting, *The Democratic Unionist Party: From Protest to Power* (Oxford: Oxford University Press, 2014).

[4] Gladys Ganiel, 'Battling in Brussels: The DUP and the European Union', in Hayward and Murphy (eds.), *The Europeanisation of Party Politics in Ireland*, pp. 161–3.

[5] Dennis Cooke, *Persecuting Zeal: A Portrait of Ian Paisley* (Dingle: Brandon, 1996), p. 189.

[6] Steve Bruce, *Paisley: Religion and Politics in Northern Ireland* (Oxford: Oxford University Press, 2007), p. 109.

[7] John D. Brewer with Gareth L. Higgins, *Anti-Catholicism in Northern Ireland, 1600–1998: The Mote and the Beam* (Basingstoke: Palgrave Macmillan, 1998), p. 108.

[8] Giada Laganà, *The Genesis of the Europeanisation of the Northern Ireland Peace Process*, PhD Thesis, NUI Galway, 2018.

a wholehearted embrace of fundamental EU principles'.[9] Again, that pragmatism focused on harnessing the benefits of Europe to Northern Ireland, given its status as a peripheral, conflict-affected and agriculture-dependent region. The UUP held a seat in the EP from the first European election in 1979 until losing the seat in 2019. In elections to the EP, the DUP presented its Euroscepticism as a selling point, over the UUP's more moderate stance. However, whether this made any impact on voters is unclear since all votes in Northern Ireland tend to be fought on the peace process and/or constitutional question.[10]

Sinn Féin's initial attitude to the EU stemmed from a similar logic to that of the DUP. Surrendering any power to a supra-national body like the EU was highly suspect to a movement dedicated to attaining and maintaining national freedom. However, republicanism's attitude to European integration had a marked, though softening, leftist and anti-imperialist tenor. Republicans opposed Ireland's membership of the EEC, viewing the latter as a threat to Irish sovereignty and neutrality, and as an essentially elitist, capitalist project.[11] These concerns have remained constant in Sinn Féin's European policies; notably, it campaigned against the Nice Treaty in the early 2000s on the grounds that an emboldened European defence and security policy compromised Irish neutrality, and new decision-making rules disempowered individual states.[12] But overall, the party has gradually accepted the Union, moving from being Euro-sceptic to 'Euro-critical'.[13] Elections to the EU have offered an additional – and crucially, all-Ireland – platform for party growth, though this did not bear fruit until 2004 when the party won a seat in Dublin and took John Hume's seat in the north.

The SDLP has been the most unequivocally pro-European party in Northern Ireland. From the beginning of 'the Troubles', John Hume, leader from 1979 to 2001, 'drew upon the integrationist project as an ideological resource, hoping to evoke new ways of thinking about the Northern Ireland problem'.[14] Far from being conditional or pragmatic, the SDLP's support for

[9] Mary C. Murphy, 'Pragmatic politics: The Ulster Unionist Party and European Union' in Hayward and Murphy (eds.), *The Europeanisation of Party Politics in Ireland*, pp. 173–86.
[10] Murphy, 'Pragmatic politics'.
[11] Agnès Maillot, 'Sinn Féin's approach to the EU: Still more critical than "engaged"?', in Hayward and Murphy (eds.), *The Europeanisation of Party Politics in Ireland*.
[12] Agnès Maillot, *New Sinn Féin: Irish Republicanism in the Twenty-First Century* (Abingdon: Routledge, 2005).
[13] Mary Lou McDonald, 'A New Ireland in a new Europe', IACES Annual Lecture, Trinity College Dublin, 30 November 2018.
[14] P. J. McLoughlin, 'The SDLP and the Europeanisation of the Northern Ireland problem', in Hayward and Murphy (eds.), *The Europeanisation of Party Politics in Ireland*, p. 193.

Europe was rooted in a sense of shared values. The European model was instructive for Northern Ireland for several reasons, as summed up in Hume's final speech to the EP in 2004. One was that the achievement of peace between Germany and France in a relatively short time following the Second World War proved that peace was achievable in the most unpromising cases. A second reason was that the EU showed the benefits of building political relationships gradually through practical social and economic cooperation: 'spilling their sweat and not their blood. As they did so, they eroded the divisions of centuries'.[15] A third was that it offered an example of political institutions that could both transcend national borders but accommodate and respect diverse identities.

Hume believed these principles of European cooperation were mirrored in the 1998 Agreement and would have a similar transformational impact.[16] Hume was pivotal in raising the profile of Northern Ireland as a region and as an unresolved political question within the European institutions and, as noted, worked with fellow MEPs from Northern Ireland to secure financial support. In EP elections, the SDLP campaigned on European issues to a much greater extent than other Northern Ireland parties, demonstrating its interest and competence in the European arena as a forum for addressing the concerns of voters and not just the playing out of local battles.[17]

The Alliance Party also regarded itself as ideologically in sync with the European Union through a shared internationalism, liberal outlook, and unifying and reconciliatory ethos. Significantly for Alliance, Europe offered people in the north of Ireland an overarching identity beyond the traditional binaries of unionism and nationalism, Irish and British. These identities, the party believed, needed to be transcended in order for a reconciled and stable society to emerge.[18] At the same time, the regional, as opposed to national, emphasis within the EU was also appealing to Alliance, a party which had always been strongly devolutionist and which saw the unifying potential of a shared regional identification.[19] Traditionally, the fifth largest party, Alliance was never in serious competition for an EP seat until its popular leader, Naomi

---

[15] Hume quoted in Seán Farren (ed.), *John Hume in His Own Words* (Dublin: Four Courts Press, 2017), p. 316.
[16] Farren, *John Hume*.
[17] McLoughlin, 'The SDLP and the Europeanisation of the Northern Ireland problem', p. 191.
[18] David Mitchell, 'Non-nationalist politics in a bi-national consociation: the case of the Alliance Party of Northern Ireland' (2018) 24:3 *Nationalism and Ethnic Politics* 336–47.
[19] Stephen Farry and Seán Neeson, 'Beyond the Band-Aid approach: An Alliance Party perspective upon the Belfast Agreement' (1999) 22:4 *Fordham International Law Journal* 1221–49.

Long, capitalised on Brexit dissatisfaction to win a seat at Northern Ireland's last European poll in 2019.

### THE PARTIES' BREXIT POLICIES

The possibility that the United Kingdom's departure from the EU could undermine peace and stability in Northern Ireland was a very minor point of debate in the Brexit referendum campaign, especially in Britain where the focus was on immigration and the economy. The decision of the then Secretary of State for Northern Ireland, Theresa Villiers, to support the campaign to leave the EU led to – mainly nationalist – calls for her resignation on the grounds that such a position was incompatible with her responsibility to uphold the 1998 Agreement. The former prime ministers, John Major and Tony Blair, campaigned jointly to highlight what they saw as Brexit's threat to the peace process. Pro-Brexit advocates rejected this as scaremongering. Yet all these discussions failed to capture widespread public concern since virtually no-one expected a Leave result.[20]

The DUP was the only main Northern Ireland party to support the Leave campaign. However, the party apparently gave little consideration to the impact of a potential Leave result, especially on the Union. As research by Murphy and Evershed shows,[21] the nature of the EU was not at the forefront of many party figures' thinking. Rather, supporting Leave was viewed as an opportunity to assert Britishness, rediscover the party's Paisley-ite opposition to Europe, and take an opposing stance to that of its traditional rivals, the nationalist parties, Alliance and the British and Irish governments. Supporting Brexit was an 'ideological free-ride'[22] – and no-one in the party foresaw having to deal with the repercussions of their policy.

After the referendum, the party's approach was characterised by two concerns: 1) a hard Brexit for the whole of the United Kingdom involving leaving the single market and customs union; and 2) avoiding any weakening of the link between Northern Ireland and Britain. These were widely viewed as incompatible because the EU, in concert with Ireland, was resolutely opposed to a hard border in Ireland, meaning that either the United Kingdom needed

---

[20] On the campaign see Gerard McCann and Paul Hainsworth, 'Brexit and Northern Ireland: the 2016 referendum on the United Kingdom's membership of the European Union' (2017) 32:2 *Irish Political Studies* 327–42.

[21] Mary C. Murphy and Jonathan Evershed, 'Between the devil and the DUP: The Democratic Unionist Party and the politics of Brexit' (2020) 15 *British Politics* 456–77.

[22] Brendan O'Leary, 'The Twilight of the United Kingdom and Tiochfaidh ár Lá: Twenty Years After the Good Friday Agreement' (2018) 17:3 *Ethnopolitics* 223–42, p. 229.

to pursue a soft Brexit, or Northern Ireland had to be decoupled from the United Kingdom and remain aligned to Ireland and the EU. The June 2017 election, called by Theresa May in order to strengthen her negotiating hand with Europe, left the Conservatives dependent on the DUP for a secure majority and the DUP unexpectedly found itself with extraordinary influence.[23]

Most dramatically, the DUP used its newfound power to stop a UK-EU Withdrawal Agreement at the eleventh hour in December 2017 on the grounds that it could create a border in the Irish Sea. The party consistently opposed the so-called 'backstop', the proposed provision in which Northern Ireland and the entire United Kingdom would remain aligned to whatever EU rules were necessary to avoid a hard border and which would come in to effect if the EU and United Kingdom could not agree a trade deal that could maintain an open border. This opposition placed the party strikingly at odds with the local business and farming communities, with whom the Democratic Unionists usually sought to remain in step. The party opposed May's final Withdrawal Agreement in 2019. The DUP's influence came to an end in December of that year, however, following Boris Johnson's emphatic election victory. Johnson and the DUP had previously courted each other as fellow unionists during the May government, yet Johnson attained his deal with the EU (and the support of Parliament) by overriding the DUP's concerns and conceding a border in the Irish sea in order to prevent a hard land border.

The UUP supported Remain, but, reflecting the party's longstanding ambivalence on Europe, the resolution adopted by the party executive contained two caveats: that the United Kingdom should continue to press for reform of the EU and oppose further political union, and that individual party members could vote as they wished.[24] Party leader Mike Nesbitt's reasons for supporting continued EU membership included the threats to business and to continued peace funding, and the likelihood of a hard border in Ireland, but also two more unionist-informed augments. Brexit could lead to another referendum on Scottish independence, and the prevailing settlement with the EU was advantageous: 'the UK retains a massive degree of sovereignty already. We were not forced into the Eurozone. We did not have to sign up to the Schengen Agreement'.[25]

---

[23] Jonathan Tonge, 'Supplying confidence or trouble? The deal between the Democratic Unionist Party and the Conservative Party (2017) 88 *The Political Quarterly*, 412–16.
[24] Mike Nesbitt, 'EU Poll critical to Northern Ireland's security and prosperity', *Belfast Telegraph*, 7 March 2016, www.belfasttelegraph.co.uk/opinion/mike-nesbitt-eu-poll-critical-to-northern-irelands-security-and-prosperity-34516508.html.
[25] Nesbitt, 'EU poll critical'.

After the referendum, however, this stark policy difference with the DUP faded. The Ulster Unionists accepted the result as a UK-wide decision ('the days of being a "Remainer" or a "Brexiteer" are over') and argued that the Northern Ireland Executive should seek to limit the economic impact of Brexit in Northern Ireland.[26] Yet as the Brexit debate came to focus on the backstop in 2017–18, the UUP saw the same constitutional dangers as those perceived by the DUP. The Ulster Unionists also opposed the Johnson deal, but made sure to point out what they saw as the DUP's responsibility in bringing matters to this point.

From the outset, Sinn Féin, the SDLP, and Alliance Party made clear that they would support remaining in the EU. Their arguments exhibited common themes, both pre- and post- referendum. Sinn Féin reiterated its criticism of the EU, which, the party said, was 'moving away from a social Europe to very much a right-wing agenda'.[27] But the solution was to pursue change from within the structures of Europe rather than support a British Tory exit project. Furthermore, Brexit risked economic damage to the island, undermining labour rights, and causing disruption at the border. Should the United Kingdom vote to leave, the party called for a border poll, and if the north voted to remain while the United Kingdom overall voted to leave, Sinn Féin advocated the north staying in the EU.[28] After the referendum result, Sinn Féin calls for a border poll were immediate. The party's Brexit policy focused on seeking 'special status' for Northern Ireland which could preserve access to the single market and the customs union, and ensure the maintenance of the Common Travel Area, EU standards, and EU funding streams.[29]

The SDLP's pro-Remain campaign was imbued with its strong commitment to the European project and its impact on political relationships in Ireland: 'We are a party with Europe and the Good Friday Agreement at our core'.[30] Following the referendum, the SDLP also called for a special status for the north, but emphasised the potential of the 1998 Agreement structures to

---

[26] 'A Vision for Northern Ireland Outside the EU', Ulster Unionist Party, 2016, p. 1 https://uup.org/assets/images/a%20vision%20for%20ni%20outside%20the%20eu.pdf.

[27] Sarah Bardon, 'Sinn Féin to campaign against Brexit in EU referendum', *Irish Times*, 24 December 2015, www.irishtimes.com/news/politics/sinn-f%C3%A9in-to-campaign-against-brexit-in-eu-referendum-1.2476720.

[28] Bardon, 'Sinn Féin to campaign'.

[29] 'The Case for the North to Active Designated Special Status', Sinn Féin, 2016, www.sinnfein.ie/files/2016/The_Case_For_The_North_To_Achieve_Special_Designated_Status_Within_The_EU.pdf.

[30] *SDLP Westminster Election Manifesto*, 2017, p. 2, https://cain.ulster.ac.uk/issues/politics/docs/sdlp/sdlp_2017-05-30-ge-man.pdf.

facilitate this, especially Strands Two and Three which dealt with the cross-border cooperation and the British-Irish relationship that stood to be undermined by Brexit.[31] The party took a more cautious approach on a border poll to Sinn Féin; it supported such a referendum but highlighted that considerable more debate and clarity on what would be proposed was needed first.

To the Alliance Party, the prospect of Brexit was invidious and polarising, especially given the fact that a majority in Northern Ireland – the polity traditionally prioritised by Alliance over Ireland and the United Kingdom – had voted against it. Like the nationalist parties, Alliance advocated special arrangements that would allow Northern Ireland continued participation in as much of the EU as possible, regardless of what the rest of the United Kingdom opted for, and it contended that access to both the EU and UK single markets could create considerable opportunities: 'Northern Ireland only works based upon sharing and interdependence. Whilst it remains part of the UK in line with the Principle of Consent, it is important that people can live their lives and do business without impediment on both a north-south and east-west axis.'[32]

The nationalist parties, along with Alliance and the Greens, showed a united front at moments during the post-Brexit period, making the case for the backstop as the least bad option for Northern Ireland. A formal Remain electoral alliance did not materialise, but in the general election of December 2019, all of these parties except Alliance (which had long pledged opposition to any form of electoral pact) stood aside in constituencies to boost the Remain candidate who was thought most likely to be successful. These parties were also critical of the DUP's close relationship with the Conservatives, not only due to clashing policies on Europe, but because that relationship was not thought to be conducive to political stability in Northern Ireland and the British government's role as impartial guarantor of the 1998 Agreement. Sinn Féin made much of the instability at Westminster, calling the Commons the 'House of Chaos'.[33] Yet the knife-edge parliamentary drama which began in London after the June 2017 Westminster election placed Sinn Féin under pressure on the matter of abstention, since it appeared that the

---

[31] *SDLP Westminster Election Manifesto*, p. 6.

[32] 'Bridges not borders: Northern Ireland in the Single Market, Alliance Party proposals', Alliance Party, 2017, p. 1, https://d3n8a8pro7vhmx.cloudfront.net/allianceparty/pages/3583/attachments/original/1537972637/bridges-not-borders-northern-ireland-in-the-single-market.pdf?1537972637.

[33] 'Brexit: Sinn Féin hits out at 'House of Chaos' after MPs back Brexit delay amendment', *Belfast Telegraph*, 19 October 2019, www.belfasttelegraph.co.uk/news/northern-ireland/brexit-sinn-fein-hits-out-at-house-of-chaos-after-mps-back-brexit-delay-amendment-38611553.html.

party's eight MPs could have made the difference in some key votes on Europe.

Despite the heatedness of the Brexit debate in Northern Ireland politics, the parties were, in fact, conspicuous by their powerlessness. Except for the DUP which enjoyed influence for two and a half years at Westminster, the Northern Ireland parties' input in the Brexit process was limited to persuasion. This was obviously frustrating for the Remain parties who represented the views of the pro-Remain majority who voted in referendum, although those parties' views were very successfully represented by the Irish government which had considerable sway in the EU-27. The next section examines in greater detail Brexit's constitutional meaning and implications in Northern Ireland in the context of the constitutional provisions of the 1998 Agreement.

## THE CONSTITUTIONAL QUESTION: BREXIT'S CHALLENGE TO THE 1998 AGREEMENT

As has been noted, unionists have traditionally been more Euro-sceptic than nationalists. Yet, as Hayward and Murphy observe, prior to Brexit this difference of opinion was not problematic 'because it did not demand deeper consideration of complex political questions related to UK sovereignty, the unity of the UK and constitutional issues'.[34] The 2016 vote on membership of Europe raised questions about self-determination, legitimacy, and power in Northern Ireland, issues which, for almost a generation since the 1998 Agreement, much of society had been trying move away from. That document offered a political formula which could allow the national question – over which militants had been fighting and which had prevented consensus-based political institutions – to be 'parked', freeing Northern Ireland's leaders to cooperate on socio-economic matters. As the 1998 Agreement itself stated: 'We acknowledge the substantial differences between our continuing and equally legitimate political aspirations. However, we will endeavour to strive in every practical way towards reconciliation.'[35]

The substance of the 1998 Agreement's formula comprised a core trade-off: unionists' primary success was continuing UK sovereignty over Northern Ireland (based on the principle of majority consent) while nationalists' primary success was reform of the governance of Northern Ireland (based on

---

[34] Katy Hayward and Mary C. Murphy, 'The EU's influence on the peace process and Agreement in Northern Ireland in light of Brexit' (2018) 17:3 *Ethnopolitics* 276–91, p. 278.
[35] The Belfast/Good Friday Agreement, 1998, p. 1, www.gov.uk/government/publications/the-belfast-agreement.

cross-community consent). There were, then, two 'standards of legitimacy' in the accord, majoritarian for constitutional matters, cross-community for institutional matters.[36]

The principle of majority consent was clearly a mechanism for managing, not resolving, the constitutional conflict. But in theory this principle allowed both sides to retain their aspirations while preventing both sides from realising those aspirations without taking account of the identity and fears of the other side. Unionists, in order to preserve the Union, would have to ensure that Northern Ireland was a place to which nationalists could feel a sense of belonging, while nationalists, to attain Irish unity, would have to convince unionists of the merits of a united Ireland. As it turned out, this kind of generous convergence was rare during the tumultuous implementation of the 1998 Agreement. Each side held to its own standard of legitimacy as trumping the other's. Thus, for instance, in the relentless post-Agreement dispute over the display of state flags and emblems, unionists argued that the majoritarian standard on sovereignty meant that state symbolism should be unequivocally British. Nationalism countered that state symbolism should have cross-community legitimacy.[37]

Nevertheless, the basic fact that the constitutional status of Northern Ireland depended on majority consent was uncontested after 1998. Indeed, Guelke notes that the 1998 Agreement's constitutional provisions resonated with the post-Cold War international climate on self-determination which was sympathetic to democratically endorsed secession.[38] The removal of the territorial claim on the north from the Irish Constitution – endorsed by the people of the Republic and northern nationalists – ended any doubt over Northern Ireland's legitimacy as an appropriate unit of self-determination. Pro-Agreement unionists welcomed the enshrining of the principle of consent as a bulwark against further nationalist advance since these unionists did not envisage a majority in favour of unity ever developing in the future. The anti-Agreement DUP was more pessimistic, arguing that consent made territorial claims equivalent, and the Union a hostage to demographics. But later, the DUP accepted consent as

[36] Norman Porter, *The Elusive Quest: Reconciliation in Northern Ireland* (Belfast: Blackstaff, 2003), pp. 218–9; Joseph Ruane and Jennifer Todd, 'The Belfast Agreement: context, content, consequences', in Joseph Ruane and Jennifer Todd (eds.), *After the Good Friday Agreement: Analysing Political Change in Northern Ireland* (Dublin: University College Dublin Press, 1999), pp. 20–1.
[37] David Mitchell, *Politics and Peace in Northern Ireland: Political Parties and the Implementation of the 1998 Agreement* (Manchester: Manchester University Press, 2015).
[38] Adrian Guelke, 'Northern Ireland, Brexit, and the Interpretation of Self-Determination' (2019) 25:4 *Nationalism and Ethnic Politics* 383–99.

a major gain.³⁹ In sum, despite conflicts over how sovereignty should be manifested, the 1998 Agreement's popularly endorsed constitutional arrangements did succeed in their intentions to a great extent: removing the national issue from everyday political argument.

At the same time, the principle of cross-community consent was also increasingly embedded, becoming a taken-for-granted feature of governance in the north. The DUP, which had previously opposed power-sharing, entered government with Sinn Féin in 1998. While the DUP showed little warmth for its partners in government, the principle of partnership was nonetheless accepted. The party became a frequent user of the 'petition of concern' – the mechanism designed to ensure that decisions had the support of both unionists and nationalists. Even the anti-peace process Traditional Unionist Voice (TUV) accepted the need for government to have cross-community composition, showing the degree to which the principle had been widely accepted and internalised.

Into this context, governed by these notions of consent, came Brexit. The challenges posed by the Brexit vote may be demonstrated by testing it according to the two standards of legitimacy within the 1998 Agreement. It fails on both counts. First, the vote did not have majority legitimacy in that 56 per cent of voters in Northern Ireland opposed leaving the EU. Brexit, of course, was a UK-wide vote which did not require majority support in Northern Ireland or the other devolved regions. This was established in early 2017 when, in response to legal challenges, UK Supreme Court judges ruled that Brexit did not need the consent of the Scottish Parliament and Welsh and Northern Ireland assemblies, and furthermore, that while the 1998 Agreement's principle of consent gave people in Northern Ireland the right to determine whether Northern Ireland remained in the United Kingdom, it did not give them the power to determine whether Northern Ireland remained in the EU.⁴⁰ The DUP, responding to the charge that Brexit, and DUP policy, lacked democratic legitimacy, repeated simply that the referendum was held on an all-UK basis. Since the party had supported, and welcomed, Brexit as a reassertion of UK sovereignty, this was a comfortable argument to make, even if it flew somewhat in the face of the ethos of partnership and consensus which was meant to govern the political arrangements in which the DUP had taken part for the previous decade. The imagined community of the Remain

---

[39] Peter Robinson praised how 'the right of self-determination for the people of Northern Ireland is a fundamental cornerstone of the political process'. Peter Robinson, 'Reflections on Irish unionism', Speech in Iveagh House, Dublin, 29 March 2012, CAIN web service, http://cain.ulst.ac.uk/issues/politics/docs/dup/pr290312.htm.

[40] R (Miller) v. Secretary of State for Exiting the European Union [2017] UKSC 5.

unionists also comprised the peoples of the United Kingdom, so it was ideologically and emotionally possible for them to acquiesce to the result. This was the approach taken by the UUP.[41]

But for nationalists, most of whom were Remainers, the UK-wide vote had a different meaning. They cared considerably less about the views of voters in Britain and faced the prospect of being cut off from their co-nationals in the Republic by a hard border. The territorial hue of the referendum results also drew a sharp contrast between Ireland, whose people both north and south were markedly pro-European, and England and Wales, whose people were much less so, thus arguably highlighting divergent political cultures on the two islands and playing into separatist Irish nationalist assumptions and arguments that English power in Ireland was not only historically unfortunate but actually incongruent with the sensibilities of the people in Ireland.

On the second standard of legitimacy – cross-community – the Brexit vote also failed. Brexit did not have cross-community consent. Unfortunately for community relations, it did not have the shared opposition of unionists and nationalists either – it was mostly supported by unionists. Again, Brexit did not require cross-community consent and it did not purport to directly impede on the region's internal arrangements. Yet this was little comfort to Remainers in the north, given fears that, by reintroducing a hard border, Brexit would affect the social and economic existence of thousands of people. Brexiteers argued that Europe was largely irrelevant to the 1998 Agreement and that the accord could not be altered by leaving the EU. But the 1998 Agreement said little about the EU and, indeed, the border, because in the climate in which the deal was concluded, it did not need to. The thrust of the accord was to bring each of the estranged partners in John Hume's three 'strands' – unionists and nationalists, north and south, United Kingdom and Ireland – into closer fellowship through new institutions. It was assumed in 1998 that all those institutions and each of the three dyads of cooperation would enjoy the canopy of Europe.

Thus, the EU would ease unionist-nationalist reconciliation through providing an overarching identity, facilitate north-south cooperation through

---

[41] However, unionists later became much more concerned about the consent of people in Northern Ireland. When the backstop and subsequently Johnson's withdrawal deal appeared to edge Northern Ireland away from Westminster and closer to Europe, the unionist parties opposed these arrangements on the grounds that they would supposedly breach the 1998 Agreement's principle of majority consent to change in the status of Northern Ireland. See Katy Hayward and David Phinnemore, 'Breached or protected? The "principle" of consent in Northern Ireland and the UK government's Brexit proposals', LSE Brexit Blog, 9 January 2019. https://blogs.lse.ac.uk/brexit/2019/01/09/breached-or-protected-the-principle-of-consent-in-northern-ireland-and-the-uk-governments-brexit-proposals/.

obviating the need for border checks and harmonising policy, and sustain British-Irish connections through shared membership of, and interests in, European institutions. The removal of Europe from the equation posed significant threats to all three relationships; hence the seriousness with which nationalists and others took the fact that they had not consented to that removal. Moreover, cross-community power-sharing had been welcomed in 1998 by nationalists as a bulwark against Westminster influence in northern Irish affairs. The fact of the Union had been made much more palatable by the presence of locally responsive and locally accountable government, linked of course, to north-south institutions. In this context, an encroachment by Westminster, of the magnitude of Brexit, was anathema.

At bottom, regardless of whether it was technically or legally defensible, Brexit demonstrated to people in Northern Ireland that a major change in the governance of the region could occur without their consent, either majoritarian or parallel. In a cohesive society, such a scenario may not have proved to be problematic. But in a region with fresh memories of misrule permitted and propagated by the national government, and that possessed, in the principle of consent's option of a border poll, a mechanism to change which state ruled, the lack of consent was extremely destabilising. The uncertainty created by Brexit, combined with the suspension of 'normal' political discourse due to the collapse of the power-sharing institutions, opened the space for a new phase of fundamental, existential questioning in and about Northern Ireland.

### THE EMERGENCE OF A NEW CONSTITUTIONAL DEBATE

At the outset, the emerging public discussion on Irish unity post-Brexit should be placed in the context of that discussion's near total absence pre-Brexit. This absence was surprising given the extent to which the support of pro-Agreement republicans was predicated upon the 1998 Agreement creating a transitional dispensation leading to the longstanding republican goal of a thirty-two-county Irish state. Sinn Féin argued in 1998 that the 'dynamic operation of all-Ireland structures', combined with all-island economic integration, the empowerment of nationalist culture and identity through the equality agenda, and demographic change in the north, would erode the Irish border and detach the six counties from the United Kingdom.[42] However, in the period

---

[42] Martin McGuinness, 'Leadership address by Gerry Adams MP and Martin McGuinness MP', Sinn Féin Ard Fheis, Dublin, 18 April 1998, Northern Ireland Political Collection, Linenhall Library, Belfast, p. 14.

1998 to 2016, it is hard to identify any unequivocal supporting evidence for Sinn Féin's transitional interpretation.

Indeed, observers highlighted that none of Sinn Féin's purported island-unifying processes would necessarily lead in that direction. The institutions comprising the 1998 Agreement's all-Ireland dimension were limited in scope and possessed no 'dynamic' of expansion. Cross-border social and economic cooperation would increase but were not necessarily a channel to political union. The equality agenda would make Catholic-nationalist identity more visible, but it would do so within Northern Ireland. Sinn Féin did argue that the transition would require its own political growth on both sides of the border, and this was a realistic prospect. But the level of that electoral success and how exactly political strength would catalyse constitutional change in Ireland were again unclear.[43]

On the unionist side, there did exist a widespread post-Agreement perception that they were the losers in the peace process and that their culture and the British character of Northern Ireland were under continuous republican assault.[44] Yet objectively, on the constitutional question, unionists appeared to be successful. While the northern Catholic population was growing, the number of people desiring a united Ireland remained small. Indeed, in the 2015 Northern Ireland Life and Times Survey, only 14 per cent of respondents thought a united Ireland to be the 'best long term policy' for the north, and just 32 per cent of Catholics.[45] Accordingly, between 1998 and 2016, Irish unity, if not quite mythical, was a largely academic and abstract concept.

The public discourse around Irish unity that began in 2016 was, first and foremost, initiated by the Brexit referendum result. But the way in which the Brexit process unfolded, as well as several other subsequent developments in politics and society in United Kingdom and Ireland, reinforced and invigorated discussion. As noted, Sinn Féin called, as it had pledged to, for a border poll immediately after the referendum. However, given the considerable uncertainty surrounding the if, how, and when of leaving the EU, plus the tumult caused in British politics, the possibility of constitutional change did

---

[43] Norman Porter, *The Elusive Quest: Reconciliation in Northern Ireland* (Belfast: Blackstaff, 2003), pp. 237–40; Kevin Bean, *The New Politics of Sinn Féin* (Liverpool: Liverpool University Press, 2007), pp. 174–216.

[44] On declining unionist support for the peace process see Bernadette C. Hayes and Ian McAllister, *Conflict to Peace: Politics and Society in Northern Ireland Over Half a Century* (Manchester: Manchester University Press, 2013).

[45] ARK Northern Ireland Life and Times Survey, 2015 [computer file]. ARK, 2016 [distributor] www.ark.ac.uk/nilt.

not immediately take root in the public consciousness. The issue grew gradually.

An early indicator of potentially shifting attitudes at a grassroots level was the sharp increase in applications for Irish (i.e. EU) passports in the north, including among people of a Protestant background who tended to hold British passports. In fact, Ian Paisley Jnr, avowed unionist Brexiteer, encouraged people to get an Irish passport for pragmatic reasons.[46] This interest did not necessarily indicate that unionists were transformed by Brexit into nationalists in large – or even any – numbers. Yet it did show that many people of a Protestant-unionist background recognised the practical benefits of EU citizenship and did not want them removed, and that such people had no political or emotional aversion to possessing the passport of the Irish Republic, a state which had traditionally been an enemy to many northern unionists.

A more tangible boost for the Irish unity debate came in April 2017. While the end of partition presented itself to nationalists in the north as a potential solution to being taken, against their will, out of EU, it was not in fact certain that in the event of unification that the entire island of Ireland would automatically be inside the EU. Clarity came, however, when the EU declared, as part of its Brexit negotiation guidelines, that the north would indeed become part of the EU if Ireland was unified.[47] This commitment, in combination with Brexit, represented the greatest leap forward for the project of Irish unity in decades. Henceforth, a border poll would not simply be about the attractiveness or otherwise of all-Ireland state, but membership of the EU.

Political events in Belfast also contributed to discussion regarding constitutional change. The failure of power-sharing in early 2017 and the prolonged political vacuum that followed was open to the interpretation that Northern Ireland, as constituted, was ungovernable. Specifically, nationalists could argue that unionists were incapable of affording equality to all in the north, and that the DUP in particular – despite ten years of power-sharing with Sinn Féin – was still unreconciled to the principle of partnership government. This was the crux of Deputy First Minister Martin McGuinness's resignation letter which triggered what turned out to be a three-year suspension of government at Stormont. While Arlene Foster's refusal to step down as First Minister for an

---

[46] 'Apply for Irish passport if you can, advises DUP MP Ian Paisley', *Belfast Telegraph*, 27 June 2016, www.belfasttelegraph.co.uk/news/northern-ireland/apply-for-irish-passport-if-you-can-advises-dup-mp-ian-paisley-34835231.html.

[47] Denis Staunton and Pat Leahy, 'Brexit summit: EU accepts united Ireland declaration', *Irish Times*, 29 April 2017, www.irishtimes.com/news/world/europe/brexit-summit-eu-accepts-united-ireland-declaration-1.3066569.

inquiry into the Renewable Heat Incentive (RHI) scandal[48] was the immediate cause of the crisis, McGuinness made clear that this was, for his party, the final straw after numerous episodes which he claimed showed that 'The equality, mutual respect and all-Ireland approaches enshrined in the Good Friday Agreement have never been fully embraced by the DUP.'[49]

As the suspension continued, and especially after what appeared to be the final failure of talks to restore power-sharing in February 2018, the 1998 Agreement's partnership model appeared to be in unprecedented jeopardy. Meanwhile, campaigners, and most non-unionist parties, pressed for reform of abortion and same sex marriage laws, which were more conservative than those in Britain and Ireland. Yet Northern Ireland politics was unable to deliver change; reform of these issues was eventually enacted through Westminster in late 2019.[50] Indeed, it was not in fact clear that, despite stated positions, the central political protagonists wanted Stormont to operate. The DUP was occupied with its newfound influence in London, while Sinn Féin was waiting for the constitutional implications of Brexit to become clear.

At the same time as politics was stagnating in Northern Ireland, the Republic of Ireland underwent dramatic political and social change. The 2015 referendum on same sex marriage was followed in 2018 by a plebiscite which supported the removal of the constitutional ban on abortion. These moves arguably signalled the end of the south's historic, Roman Catholic-influenced social conservativism, and with it, one of unionism's central tenets. No longer could northerners argue that the Union offered a distinctly liberal and progressive context, in contrast to the Republic. Moreover, the economy south of the border was continuing a marked, post-financial crisis (and pre-coronavirus crisis) recovery, placing in doubt unionism's longstanding contention that a united Ireland was not economically viable. An innovative Citizens' Assembly was also established in the Republic in 2016 to deliberate on key public issues. The solidarity between Ireland and the rest of the EU-27 during the Brexit process enhanced the image of Ireland as an esteemed, cooperative, and outward-looking country. In 2020, Sinn Féin won the highest number of first preference votes in the Republic's general election. While the party campaigned mainly on socio-economic, rather than national/constitutional issues, this electoral breakthrough for the republican party naturally led

---

[48] Sam McBride, *Burned: The Inside Story of the Cash for Ash Scandal and Northern Ireland's Secretive New Elite* (Dublin: Merrion, 2019).
[49] Martin McGuinness, 'Full text of Martin McGuinness resignation letter', *Irish Times*, 9 January 2017, www.irishtimes.com/news/politics/full-text-of-martin-mcguinness-s-resignation-letter-1.2930429.
[50] Northern Ireland (Executive Formation etc.) Act 2019, ss. 8 and 9.

to another fevered round of speechifying and media commentary that a united Ireland had come one step closer.[51]

Throughout the period following the Brexit referendum, the media naturally took a strong interest in opinion polls on Irish unity. The extent of attitudinal change varied depending on the methodologies of polls, with online surveys recording much greater change in favour of Irish unity than face-to-face interviews.[52] One survey commissioned by academics showed that support among moderate nationalists for constitutional change would rise in the event of a hard Brexit: 'UKexit and the DUP's tactical and strategic response to it are sending liberal, bourgeois, educated Catholics toward the conviction that a reunified Ireland will better reflect their values, and their interests'.[53] Nevertheless, according to the 2019 Northern Ireland Life and Times Survey results released in June 2020, the overall proportion of people desiring Irish unity as the best long term policy for Northern Ireland was still just 22 per cent.[54]

POLITICAL PERSPECTIVES

All these developments stimulated an ever-growing constitutional discussion within countless fora – academic conferences, research reports, traditional and social media, and community debates. The discussions focused on several recurring questions. What would be unionists' reaction to a vote for Irish unity? What should be the required threshold for a border poll, a simple majority or weighted majority? What indicator should trigger a border poll? What form would a united Ireland take? Would a united Ireland be economically sustainable? What would be the effect of a vote for Scottish independence on Ireland? Are attitudes on unity changing? Are identities changing? In the wake of the Brexit vote, these questions were a novelty. By 2020, if not earlier, they were fixtures in political discourse. For the Northern Ireland political parties, this debate crystallised specific intra-bloc dilemmas.

[51] For instance, the cover story in *The Economist*, 'Irish unification is becoming likelier', 13 February 2020, www.economist.com/leaders/2020/02/13/irish-unification-is-becoming-likelier.
[52] Ann Marie Gray, Jennifer Hamilton, Gráinne Kelly, Brendan Lynn, Martin Melaugh and Gillian Robinson, *Northern Ireland Peace Monitoring Report, Number 5* (Belfast, Community Relations Council, 2019).
[53] John Garry, Brendan O'Leary, Kevin McNicholl and James Pow, 'The future of Northern Ireland: border anxieties and support for Irish reunification under varieties of UKexit', *Regional Studies* (2020) 1-11, p. 9.
[54] ARK Northern Ireland Life and Times Survey, 2020 [computer file]. ARK June 2020 [distributor] www.ark.ac.uk/nilt/.

Nationalism's main question was not in fact the nature of the possible 'new Ireland', something which all nationalists would have conceded had not even begun to take shape in public discussion and understanding. Rather, the question was the appropriate timing of a border poll. As noted, Sinn Féin was broadly more impatient than the SDLP, although in what circumstances, and with what degree of preparation, republicans wanted such a poll was not always clear.[55] A further issue for nationalism, which links with the discussion above on models of consent, was raised by the late Séamus Mallon in his 2019 autobiography.[56] He proposed that for the sake of relationships in a united Ireland, the poll had to be run on a basis other than a simple majority, perhaps with some form of parallel consent. Leo Varadkar, the Taoiseach, made a similar comment on the undesirability of a narrow victory in a referendum.[57] This view attracted derision from republicans, who pointed out that if a simple majority had been enough to prevent a united Ireland, then it should be enough to establish one. But regardless of the technical issues surrounding a border referendum, it was evident that there was some recognition within nationalism that constitutional change was not without risks.

By contrast, the debate within unionism centred on whether to participate – as nationalists invited them to participate – in debates on Irish unity. The commentary of key unionist figures provoked intense media interest and discussion. For instance, in the summer of 2018, the now former DUP leader Peter Robinson argued that unionism would be wise to engage in debates on Irish unity: 'I don't expect my own house to burn down but I still insure it because it could happen'. His colleague, Sammy Wilson, rejected the comments, retorting that 'Preparing for a possible united Ireland is not an insurance policy against something unpleasant happening, it is an invitation to republican arsonists to come in and burn our house down.'[58] Robinson was, indeed, asking a lot from unionists; as journalist Sam McBride pointed out, 'it would be profoundly illogical for unionists to help with something which would make the end of the Union easier – unless they believed that they would inevitably lose such

---

[55] Mark Devenport, 'Is Sinn Féin changing its view on a border poll?', BBC News website, 31 July 2018, www.bbc.co.uk/news/uk-northern-ireland-45020294.
[56] Seamus Mallon with Andy Pollak, *A Shared Home Place* (Dublin: Lilliput, 2019).
[57] 'Poll: Varadkar says more than 50% plus one needed in united Ireland poll – what do you think?', *Belfast Telegraph*, 17 October 2017, www.belfasttelegraph.co.uk/news/northern-ireland/poll-varadkar-says-more-than-50-plus-one-needed-in-united-ireland-poll-what-do-you-think-36235839.html.
[58] Gerry Moriarty, 'Peter Robinson has delivered a "wake-up call" for unionism', *Irish Times*, 31 July 2018, www.irishtimes.com/news/ireland/irish-news/peter-robinson-has-delivered-a-wake-up-call-for-unionism-1.3581228.

a plebiscite, which is not a commonly held view'.[59] Some unionists were, however, concerned to at least put the unionist case in Irish unity discussions. On this, Mike Nesbitt, former UUP leader, was vocal, warning unionists repeatedly using the analogy of a frog in boiling water, unaware of the danger as the temperature gradually rises.

This kind of strategic debate was a perennial theme in unionism – should it engage with opponents, or isolate itself? But talk of Irish unity also raised deeper questions about unionist identity. This came to the fore in April 2018 when, in an interview with the comedian Patrick Kielty as part of a documentary marking the twentieth anniversary of the 1998 Agreement, Arlene Foster said that if Ireland was united, she would probably leave the country.[60] This provoked much public discussion and the question was put to other unionist figures. Notably, Sylvia Hermon, the independent (and, incidentally, the only pro-Remain unionist) MP, answered it with some emotion that, whatever happened, she was going nowhere. Like her family, 'I'll be buried in the land that I love'.[61]

Foster's attitude expressed the fact that for many unionists, their unionism required the privilege of living under British institutions and thus assisting in the ending of those institutions' sovereignty in Northern Ireland would be nonsensical. Unionism, without the Union, was inconceivable. However, her remark also played into a longstanding image of unionists as somewhat unrooted, 'an unsettled people',[62] 'under siege'[63] with 'a precarious belonging',[64] an image which Hermon appeared to wish to reject. In sum, as well as the more tangible matter of whether and how to take part in discussions on Irish unity, the prospect of constitutional change also asked unionists to consider the fundamentals of their identity and how these related to the circumstances around them, circumstances which were in flux.

---

[59] Sam McBride, 'If Sinn Féin waits for unionists to help plan Irish unity, it may wait a long time', 29 February 2020, www.newsletter.co.uk/news/politics/sam-mcbride-if-sinn-Féin-waits-unionists-help-plan-irish-unity-it-may-wait-long-time-2004670.
[60] 'Arlene Foster says 'I would probably move' if there was united Ireland', *Irish News*, 5 April 2018, www.irishnews.com/news/brexit/2018/04/05/news/arlene-foster-says-i-would-probably-move-if-there-was-united-ireland-1297022/.
[61] Interviewed on *The View*, BBC, 4 May 2018, www.bbc.co.uk/programmes/p066805x.
[62] Susan McKay, *Northern Protestants: An Unsettled People* (Belfast: Blackstaff, 2000).
[63] Arthur Aughey, *Under Siege: Ulster Unionism and the Anglo-Irish Agreement* (London: Hurst, 1989).
[64] John Dunlop, *Presbyterians and the Conflict in Ireland: A Precarious Belonging* (Belfast: Blackstaff, 1995).

## CONCLUSION

The constitutional debate will continue for the foreseeable future, but its strength and progress depend on a number of factors. The first is whether the Irish government commences the 'preparations' for Irish unity that republicans wish to see. Despite some expectations, the programme for government agreed by the new Fianna Fáil/Fine Gael/Green Party coalition in June 2020 did not propose major initiatives in this area. Second is the unfolding of Brexit, which, with Boris Johnson's agreement with the EU in October 2019, entered a new phase. For the United Kingdom, the price of that accord was to allow a border in the Irish Sea, the precise nature of which is still to be determined. This avoids a hardening of the border in Ireland and thus to some extent assuages the nationalist anger which had been the dominant theme since 2016. A third factor is the performance of the Northern Ireland Executive, reformed in January 2020. If it remains stable and governs effectively, interest in constitutional change could wane. Fourth, the coronavirus crisis may have an impact. Notwithstanding Sinn Féin's argument that the virus proves the illogic of partition on a small island,[65] in fact, the shutdown may stall the momentum of the unity discussion, especially given the financial pressures it will impose into the future.

There has clearly been growth in support for Irish unity, but not enough to cause the British Secretary of State for Northern Ireland to call a border poll, the only legal mechanism through which one can be held. Given the demographic balance, a border poll will be decided by the non-unionist and non-nationalist bloc, a constituency which, as shown by election successes by the Alliance Party and Greens in 2019, is growing. Alliance continues to reject defining itself by the constitutional question, pledging to take part in debates on constitutional change, and stating that it will decide whether to take a position, and what position, if and when a border poll is called.[66] This 'other' bloc will not be influenced by cultural and historical arguments but evidence of the socio-economic implications of constitutional arrangements. In theory, this should prompt the unionist and nationalist parties to finally demonstrate the spirit of persuasion and reassurance called for by the 1998 Agreement, and actually make the case for the Union and unity respectively, while simultaneously ensuring that

---

[65] Jayne McCormack, 'Coronavirus: Foster criticises Irish unity claim by Sinn Féin', BBC News website, 27 April 2020, www.bbc.co.uk/news/uk-northern-ireland-52445887.

[66] C. McCurry, 'Stephen Farry: Alliance will engage in discussions around border poll', *Belfast Telegraph*, 7 March 2020, www.belfasttelegraph.co.uk/news/northern-ireland/stephen-farry-alliance-will-engage-in-discussions-around-border-poll-39023549.html.

these circumstances can accommodate and welcome all traditions and backgrounds. It remains to be seen whether unionists and nationalists are capable of such genuine outreach, rather than relying on demographic change and/or partisan political appeals, in pursuit of their constitutional ideals.

# 5

# The Constitutional Significance of the People of Northern Ireland

## C. R. G. Murray

### INTRODUCTION

Northern Ireland's 'constitutional question' is, in essence, about constituent power. The Belfast/Good Friday Agreement (the 1998 Agreement) established that the people of Northern Ireland have the ability to determine whether Northern Ireland remains part of the United Kingdom,[1] and the UK Parliament accepted this state of affairs in the Northern Ireland Act 1998.[2] This makes Northern Ireland unique within the United Kingdom; Parliament's role is (supposedly) constrained when it comes to maintaining the United Kingdom's statehood over Northern Ireland.[3]

This contribution traces the ambiguities which continue to bedevil these arrangements to their genesis. It begins by tracking the concept of 'the people of Northern Ireland' through the constitutional thought of John Hume, the dominant figure in constitutional nationalism in Northern Ireland in the latter part of the twentieth century, exploring his efforts to simultaneously clarify the constitutional question and remove the issue from Northern Ireland's day-to-day politics. This account does not attempt a holistic reappraisal of Hume's role during Northern Ireland's conflict and peace process,[4] but explores how his

---

[1] Agreement between the Government of the United Kingdom of Great Britain and Northern Ireland and the Government of Ireland (with annexes) (1998) 2114 UNTS 473.

[2] Northern Ireland Act 1998, s. 1.

[3] Whether this constraint is symbolic or practical in its significance is dependent on the account of parliamentary sovereignty to which one subscribes; see Sylvia de Mars, Colin Murray, Aoife O'Donoghue and Ben Warwick, *Bordering Two Unions: Northern Ireland and Brexit* (Bristol: Policy Press, 2018), pp. 129–30.

[4] Considered as a whole, the 1998 Agreement's tripartite structure, for example, mirrors Hume's longstanding attention towards the 'totality' of relationships across the Atlantic archipelago. For a thorough contextualisation of Hume's constitutional thought, see P. J. McLoughlin, *John Hume and the Revision of Irish Nationalism* (Manchester: Manchester University Press, 2010).

constitutional thinking shaped this element of the 1998 settlement. It then considers how the operation of the constituent power held by this group is constrained under the Northern Ireland Act, focusing upon the debates which did (and did not) happen at the time of the legislation's enactment. This reevaluation of the enactment of the legislation facilitates an assessment of how the United Kingdom's strained relationship with the European Union has bought questions about the status, composition, and rights of the people of Northern Ireland to the fore.

## TWO PEOPLES OR ONE?

Those who have a say in choosing the form and character of the system by which they are governed are said to hold constituent power. In a liberal democratic constitutional order, the assumption is that this power is invested in the people of a polity.[5] The people create, and by their will maintain (or change) a constitutional order, quite apart from the question of who governs under that order (the constituted power holders).[6] The concept of constituent power is, however, often easier to articulate in theory than put into practice. In the context of the partition of Ireland, the key question became how to define the group of constituent power holders and whether, put simply, the island played host to 'one nation or two'.[7] This question defines the relationship between the nation state of Ireland and its relationship with the island of Ireland.[8]

Most of twentieth-century Irish nationalist thinking treated partition as illegitimate; constituent power was possessed by the people of Ireland as a whole, and because the majority supported independence from the United Kingdom, the entirety of Ireland should therefore be a unified and independent state.[9] Even as it became apparent that all of Ireland could not be kept in the Union against its will, however, unionists insisted that 'the north-east of Ireland', where they

---

[5] See Dieter Grimm, 'Does Europe Need a Constitution?' (1995) 1 European Law Journal 282–302, p. 289.
[6] See Aoife O'Donoghue, *Constitutionalism in Global Constitutionalism* (Cambridge: Cambridge University Press, 2014), p. 56.
[7] See Nicholas Mansergh, *The Unresolved Question: The Anglo-Irish Settlement and Its Undoing 1912–72* (New Haven: Yale University Press, 1991), pp. 43–5.
[8] For an account of the legal shaping of the identity of the Irish people, see Oran Doyle, 'Populist Constitutionalism and Constituent Power' (2019) 20 German Law Journal 161–80, p. 176.
[9] See John Hutchinson, *Dynamics of Cultural Nationalism: The Gaelic Revival and the Creation of the Irish Nation State* (London: Allen and Unwin, 1987) p. 304. For an account of revisionist debates over Irish nationalism, see Richard Kearney, *Postnationalist Ireland: Politics, Culture Philosophy* (Abingdon: Routledge, 1997), p. 5.

predominated, 'had come to acquire a claim to entitlement to be treated as a separate polity'.[10] After Northern Ireland gained autonomous status within the United Kingdom under the Government of Ireland Act 1920, unionists sought to cement this position. In the Ireland Act 1949 they gained recognition that Northern Ireland's place in the United Kingdom would not be changed without the support of the Parliament of Northern Ireland.[11] This safeguard was partly about deep-seated concerns that the UK and Irish governments might negotiate about the status of Northern Ireland over the head of Stormont.[12] But it was also about asserting the dominance of unionism through Stormont, rather than through direct democracy, because of the success of gerrymandering at marginalising Irish nationalism within the devolved legislature. For Northern Ireland's prime minister, Viscount Brookeborough, partition rested upon 'the declared will of the Northern Ireland people, expressed through their elected Parliament'.[13]

When John Hume was elected to the Parliament of Northern Ireland in 1969, he found that any effort to advance the civil rights movement's aims in Stormont was met with 'incessant invocation of the constitutional question'.[14] Many unionist politicians refused to engage with anyone who challenged Northern Ireland's status as part of the United Kingdom, and the Special Powers Acts criminalised membership of groups espousing republican aims.[15] Although Hume maintained that it was entirely legitimate to advocate for a united Ireland by democratic means, he nonetheless accepted that Northern Ireland's status depended upon the will of the majority of its people.[16] His attempts to ringfence the constitutional question coalesced in a submission to the Royal Commission on the Constitution in 1970 in which he not only accepted that the right to self-determination applied to Northern Ireland but mooted the possibility of periodic referendums on

---

[10] Harry Calvert, *Constitutional Law in Northern Ireland: A Study in Regional Government* (Belfast: Stevens, 1968) p. 36.

[11] Ireland Act 1949 (UK), s. 1(2).

[12] See Conor Cruise O'Brien, *States of Ireland* (London: Hutchinson, 1972), pp. 138–9 and Mansergh, *The Unresolved Question*, p. 341.

[13] B. Brooke, 'Ulster's best interests lie with the United Kingdom' in *Why the Border Must Be: The Northern Ireland Case in Brief* (Belfast: Northern Ireland Government, 1956).

[14] McLoughlin, *John Hume*, p. 26. On contemporary unionist accounts, nationalism's hostility to Northern Ireland's existence provoked the measures which the civil rights movement was challenging; 'The measures provoked by their own intransigence gave them ample ground for complaint'. R. J. Lawrence, *The Government of Northern Ireland* (Oxford: Oxford University Press, 1965), p. 36.

[15] Regulation 24A, promulgated under the Civil Authorities (Special Powers) Acts (Northern Ireland) 1922–1943. See *McEldowney v. Forde* [1971] AC 632.

[16] *Hansard*, HC (Northern Ireland) Debs., vol. 74, col. 140–1, 1 October 1969.

Northern Ireland's constitutional status.[17] His submission recognised that the border had created two blocks of constituent power holders on the island of Ireland, based not on nationality, but on their location.

There is no straight line in Hume's thinking on this point; he was a politician obliged to adjust to circumstances.[18] As P. J. McLoughlin highlights, when the Social Democratic and Labour Party (SDLP) subsequently abstained from Stormont in 1971, Hume justified this by 'falling back on a more traditional nationalist critique of Stormont'.[19] And, thereafter, the SDLP would boycott the 1973 border poll, in spite of the prominent part that periodic referendums had hitherto played in Hume's thinking on the issue. This was in part because, as demonstrated in the previous year's SDLP policy paper, *Towards a New Ireland*, Hume's thinking had pivoted towards a solution to the escalating conflict based around joint sovereignty, as the SDLP desperately sought to reinforce constitutional nationalism (even if doing so risked 'a corruption of … [its] founding philosophy'[20] as a reforming party without sectarian alignment). This was not, however, to say that this paper was not innovative, for it also advocated an international agreement between the United Kingdom and Ireland which would 'recognise the right of inhabitants of Northern Ireland to claim either Irish or British citizenship, to hold either a British or Irish passport' and make it 'unlawful to discriminate against a person who holds a particular citizenship'.[21] Hume was beginning to tie protections for identity together with his thinking on constituent power.

In 1973, Hume's account of the people of Northern Ireland's constituent power found a place in the Sunningdale Communiqué, which rested upon 'parallel declarations by the British and Irish Governments that the status of Northern Ireland cannot be changed until a majority of the people of Northern Ireland so desire'.[22] The principle of consent, which he had done so much to develop, had become the 'fundamental axiom of revisionist nationalism'.[23] Its success was such that, in spite of its origins in Hume's thought, the 'constitutional guarantee' that the principle afforded became 'the minimum

---

[17] UK National Archives (UKNA), HO 221/114 John Hume, *Evidence submitted to Royal Commission on the Constitution* (Mar. 1970) 1–2.
[18] One biographer has lamented the tendency of many commentators to treat Hume as an 'honest broker' in the Northern Ireland conflict, rather than 'the Nationalist politician he really is'; George Drower, *John Hume: Peacemaker* (London: Victor Gollancz, 1995), p. 17.
[19] McLoughlin, *John Hume*, p. 34.
[20] Ibid., p. 43.
[21] SDLP, *Towards a New Ireland: Proposals by the Social Democratic and Labour Party* (1972) Appendix, para. 10.
[22] *Hansard*, Edward Heath MP, HC Deb., vol. 866, col. 29, 10 December 1973.
[23] McLoughlin, *John Hume*, p. 59.

requirement, a *sine qua non*, of Unionist participation in any scheme for government'.[24] And yet, the more that Hume promoted Sunningdale (with its elements of north-south cooperation[25]) as providing a route towards reunification, the more unionist support for the power-sharing Executive, led by Brian Faulkner, dissipated. Even as the Sunningdale consensus was fragmenting in early May 1974, Hume continued to badger the leading civil servant Kenneth Bloomfield about the Communiqué being given formal treaty status.[26] By this point, after the Irish Supreme Court's *Boland* judgment,[27] which was widely interpreted as downplaying Ireland's commitments under the Communiqué,[28] Hume must have appreciated that Irish governments could not enter into a treaty which recognised Northern Ireland's status for as long as Arts. 2 and 3 of the 1937 Constitution made legally binding claims over Northern Ireland.[29] Yet his continued pressure for an international agreement demonstrated a more dogmatic side to Hume's constitutionalism. Such a treaty would indeed come into place in 1998 but, given the instability in Faulkner's position as Northern Ireland's Chief Minister, and the lack of impetus for constitutional change in Ireland at the time, such efforts were a distraction.[30]

Into the 1980s, Hume saw the European Economic Community as a means to enhance cross-border cooperation on the island of Ireland and, through

---

[24] John Morison and Stephen Livingstone, *Reshaping Public Power: Northern Ireland and the British Constitutional Crisis* (London: Sweet and Maxwell, 1995), p. 105.

[25] The introduction of an 'Irish dimension' into Northern Ireland's governance had been mooted by the Heath government's White Paper ahead of Sunningdale, and was enthusiastically coopted by Hume; UK Government, *The Future of Northern Ireland: A Paper for Discussion* (London: HMSO, 1972), para. 76–8.

[26] UKNA, CJ 4/470, Kenneth Bloomfield (Permanent Secretary, Office of the Executive) to Brian Faulkner (Chief Minister) (3 May 1974) para. 1.

[27] *Boland v. an Taoiseach* [1974] IR 338.

[28] The court's observations that Ireland's commitments in the Communiqué merely reflected the reality of Northern Ireland's existence at that time, at 362–363 (Fitzgerald CJ), prevented Faulkner from presenting the deal as qualifying Ireland's territorial claims over Northern Ireland. In discussion with the Northern Ireland Secretary, Merlyn Rees, Faulkner lamented that the Communiqué's declaration upon Northern Ireland's status 'had been eroded by the protracted Boland case'; UKNA, CJ 4/471, Martin Reid (Principal Private Secretary, NIO), 'Talk with Mr Faulkner: Sunningdale' (9 April 1974), para. 1.

[29] See Brendan O'Leary, *A Treatise on Northern Ireland: Volume 3 Consociation and Confederation* (Oxford: Oxford University Press, 2019), p. 61.

[30] When Hume and other SDLP leaders dined with the Northern Ireland Secretary on 11 April 1974, the Northern Ireland Office notes of the meeting recount their dismissiveness towards Faulkner's difficulties; 'The SDLP leaders said that "wee Brian" was losing his nerve; that he was exaggerating his difficulties with his own party … '. UKNA, CJ 4/471, Martin Reid (Principal Private Secretary, NIO), 'Discussion with the SDLP: Sunningdale' (16 April 1974), para. 2.

pooling sovereignty in European institutions, an opportunity to defuse some of the tensions around Northern Ireland's constitutional status.[31] The more complex Ireland and the United Kingdom's partnership in Europe became, the more there would be for north-south bodies to address in any settlement. Hume's attraction to a post-nation-state 'Europe of the regions' was precisely because it offered a way out of zero-sum questions about sovereignty over Northern Ireland, and counterbalanced Ireland's 'oppressive and obsessive relationship with Britain'.[32] This was a controversial stance for many nationalists, exemplified by Bernadette McAliskey's famous retort that for all Hume's talk of the nation state being dead-and-gone, she hadn't had hers yet.[33] Hume's enthusiastic Europeanism showcased his ability to reconceptualise Northern Ireland's status, but also demonstrated how his constitutional thinking could outrun the realities on the ground; the EU remains to this day an organisation of member states.[34] Even Hume's deputy, Seamus Mallon, would despair that this complex constitutional message, delivered in what he called 'Humespeak',[35] occluded the SDLP's commitment to unity and risked pushing support towards Sinn Féin. For many unionists, the more Hume enthused about Europe, the more they smelled a rat. Even more positive unionist statements on Europe had a distinctly transactional quality, which did not dwell upon its implications for UK sovereignty.[36]

Hume's thinking on Northern Ireland's constitutional status continued to evolve through the New Ireland Forum in the 1980s. The creation of the Forum, fulfilling a 1982 SDLP manifesto pledge, demonstrated Hume's influence over Irish government policy, an influence which would grow during the Forum's proceedings.[37] His explicit commitment to the legitimacy of unionist aspirations, made at the Forum, was adopted into its final report.[38] Just as this

---

[31] See Martin Loughlin and Stephen Tierney, 'The Shibboleth of Sovereignty' (2018) 81 *Modern Law Review* 989–1016, p. 1011.

[32] John Hume, 'Europe of the Regions', in Richard Kearney (ed.), *Across the Frontiers: Ireland in the 1990s* (Dublin: Wolfhound, 1988), pp. 45, 56. See also Gerard Delanty, 'Northern Ireland in a Europe of the Regions' (1996) 67 *Political Quarterly* 127–34.

[33] See James Anderson, 'Territorial Sovereignty and Political Identity' in Brian Graham (ed.), *In search of Ireland: A Cultural Geography* (Abingdon: Routledge, 1997), pp. 215, 222.

[34] See Michael Cunningham, 'The political language of John Hume' (1997) 12 *Irish Political Studies* 13–22, p. 16–17.

[35] Seamus Mallon with Andy Pollak, *A Shared Home Place* (Dublin: Lilliput Press, 2019), p. 69.

[36] See David Trimble, 'Focusing on the Future', in David Trimble, *To Raise Up a New Northern Ireland: Articles and Speeches 1998–2000* (Belfast: Belfast Press, 2001), pp. 105–110.

[37] See Brian Girvin, 'Constitutional nationalism and Northern Ireland' in Brian Barton and Patrick J. Roche (eds.), *The Northern Ireland Question: Perspectives and Policies* (Beatty, Nevada: Avebury, 1994), p. 5.

[38] See New Ireland Forum, *Report* (Belfast: TSO, 1984), paras. 4.8–4.10 and 5.2(4). McLoughlin, *John Hume*, p. 120.

part of his agenda was falling into place, however, Hume saw other parts slipping. The Forum's report, in trying to establish a position around which the SDLP, Fianna Fáil, Fine Gael, and the Irish Labour Party could coalesce, adopted a fudged form of wording on the principle of consent, and criticised the relevant parts of the Northern Ireland Constitution Act 1973.[39] Fianna Fáil's leader, Charles Haughey, moreover, promptly captured the post-Forum headlines by abandoning 'any semblance of unity with the other participants in the Forum' in asserting that Irish unity was a matter for the people of Ireland as a whole.[40] Unionists retorted that the report provided unacceptable evidence that the nationalist parties 'have dragged their feet on conceding to unionists the right to refuse consent'[41] and underlined that '[t]he affairs of Northern Ireland are for the people of the North'.[42]

For Hume, one benefit of giving form to the principle of consent was that it allowed its ambit to be restricted to the question of Northern Ireland's place in the United Kingdom. This was vital because, since Sunningdale, the 'orange card' had been used by unionists to stifle constitutional innovation. The Northern Ireland Office (NIO) was unimpressed with the unionist rebuttal of the Forum, which it saw as an effort to steel the UK government against negotiating with their Irish counterparts.[43] The Forum's overtures might have been brusquely rejected by Margaret Thatcher,[44] but her Northern Ireland Secretary, James Prior, was notably more conciliatory in Commons debate, accepting that the principle of consent 'does not necessarily mean that the Province will be governed in exactly the same way as other parts of the United Kingdom or that it must be governed exactly as the majority wish'.[45] The groundwork for the Anglo-Irish Agreement was falling into place, and even if it would do little more than stoke unionist outrage and provide a new basis for political stalemate in the late 1980s, most Northern Ireland parties would eventually seek to negotiate a more durable alternative.

The 1998 Agreement finally combined these disparate strands of Hume's thinking into the treaty between the United Kingdom and Ireland that he had so long sought, with Art. 1 of the UK-Ireland Agreement aligning with

[39] New Ireland Forum, Report, para. 5.1(4).
[40] UKNA, CJ 4/5101, UK Embassy Telegram, 'Fianna Fáil and the Forum' (29 June 1984) para. 4.
[41] Peter Smith, *Opportunity Lost: A Unionist View of the Report of the Forum for a New Ireland* (Belfast: Ulster Unionist Council Publications, 1984), 3.
[42] UKNA, CJ 4/6632, Jim Allister (DUP Chief Whip), quoted in A. J. Merrifield (NIO) Memorandum, 'Further DUP Comment on Forum Debate' (4 July 1984), para. 2.
[43] UKNA, CJ 4/6632, S. G. Hewitt (NIO, Political Affairs Division) Memorandum, 'Opportunity Lost' (13 November 1984), para. 6.
[44] See O'Leary, *A Treatise*, pp. 82–3.
[45] *Hansard*, HC Deb., vol. 63, col. 27, 2 July 1984.

paragraph 1 of the Constitutional Issues section of the multi-party deal. These provisions mention 'traditionalist'[46] Irish nationalism's contention that 'it is for the people of the island of Ireland alone ... to exercise their right of self-determination', but package this with a recognition that 'this right must be achieved and exercised with and subject to the agreement and consent of a majority of the people of Northern Ireland'.[47] Both constitutional visions were accepted as 'legitimate' within Northern Ireland.[48] Protections for the identity of the people of Northern Ireland were grafted onto these principle of consent provisions, recognising their 'birthright' to 'identify themselves and be accepted as Irish or British, or both, as they may so choose.[49] In this regard, at least, the 1998 Agreement was thus not, as Mallon's arch summary would have it, 'Sunningdale for slow learners'.[50] Its commitments regarding constituent power were more refined than those of 1973, and its identity provisions offered protections which would apply to both Northern Ireland as part of the United Kingdom and under any future united Ireland.[51] These commitments concerning the people of Northern Ireland were, in large part, the culmination of Hume's constitutional thinking.

## THE PATH TOWARDS REUNIFICATION?

Months after the 1998 Agreement was agreed and subsequently accepted in referendums in Northern Ireland and Ireland, a month after the first Northern Ireland Assembly elections and weeks after its first sitting, Westminster finally got round to incorporating elements of the 1998 Agreement into domestic law in July 1998. The status of Northern Ireland as part of the United Kingdom, and the circumstances under which this status could be changed, were front-and-centre in Clause 1 and Schedule 1 of the Northern Ireland Bill. The night of 22 July was one of unionist unity, with luminaries from the Democratic Unionist Party (DUP), the UK Unionist Party (UKUP), and the Ulster Unionist Party (UUP) urging amendments to the Bill's terms relating to a referendum on changing Northern Ireland's status. The Reverend Ian Paisley, the DUP leader, proposed adding a requirement of a cross-community vote in support of a reunification

---

[46] Cunningham, 'Political Language', p. 15.
[47] Belfast Agreement, UK-Ireland Agreement, Art. 1(ii).
[48] Ibid., Art. 1(iii).
[49] Ibid., Art. 1(vi).
[50] Jonathan Tonge, 'From Sunningdale to the Good Friday Agreement: Creating devolved government in Northern Ireland' (2000) 14 *Contemporary British History* 39–60, p. 39.
[51] See Paul Arthur, *Special Relationships: Britain, Ireland and the Northern Ireland Problem* (Belfast: Blackstaff, 2000), pp. 247–9.

referendum before it could be triggered.⁵² Ever the barrister, UKUP leader Robert McCartney fulminated about the 'unbridled power' that the legislation would hand to the Northern Ireland Secretary with regard to holding a -referendum.⁵³ They sought an amendment requiring a majority of all registered voters in Northern Ireland to support reunification, not a majority of those voting.

On the issue of a (re)unification referendum, not even David Trimble was a pro-Agreement unionist. He could not resist tabling an amendment which proposed hollowing out the Secretary of State's duty to give effect to a majority vote in favour of a united Ireland unless it was favoured by more than 60 per cent of those voting.⁵⁴ The 1998 Agreement contains some notably open-textured provisions, so-called 'constructive ambiguities' which allowed its proponents to sell its terms their constituents.⁵⁵ The meaning of majority in the provisions relating to the principle of consent, however, was not amongst them. Although, as Unionist politicians lined up to insist, the term is not explained in the 1998 Agreement's 'Constitutional Issues' section, the terms of the UK's incorporating legislation were explicitly agreed in Annex A to this section. This Annex settled, word for word, what was being debated that night; a majority meant a simple majority of those voting in a referendum. The Unionist amendments were defeated by overwhelming majorities. Under the Northern Ireland Act 1998 a referendum on (re)unification must therefore be conducted on this basis, and the UK Government is obliged to give effect to an outcome which favours a united Ireland. This provides the *lex specialis* of how self-determination functions in Northern Ireland.

Amid the commotion over the meaning of the majority, however, the parliamentary debate offered little clarification about important elements of a referendum process. One such area of uncertainty relates to how the 1998 Agreements's principle that Northern Ireland remained part of the United Kingdom by the consent of its people is to be tested. The Northern Ireland Bill would give the Secretary of State a power to make arrangements for a referendum on Northern Ireland's status as part of the United Kingdom,⁵⁶ and also impose a duty to institute a referendum if at any time it appears likely 'that a majority of those voting would express a wish that Northern Ireland should cease to be part of the United Kingdom and form part of a united Ireland'.⁵⁷ As Parliament was

---

52 *Hansard*, HC Deb., vol. 316, col. 1188, 22 July 1998.
53 *Hansard*, HC Deb., vol. 316, col. 1193, 22 July 1998.
54 *Hansard*, HC Deb, vol. 316, col. 1203, 22 July 1998.
55 See David Mitchell, 'Cooking the Fudge: Constructive Ambiguity and the Implementation of the Northern Ireland Agreement, 1998–2007' (2009) 24 *Irish Political Studies* 321–36, p. 322.
56 Northern Ireland Act 1998, Schedule 1(4).
57 Northern Ireland Act 1998, Schedule 1(2).

heading towards recess, the UK government did not call upon its heavy hitters in this legislative debate. Mo Mowlam, as Secretary of State for Northern Ireland, was not present. One of her junior ministers, Paul Murphy, deputised. Under sustained questioning, he advanced that the 'spirit of the agreement is that the Secretary of State should, when she or he thinks fit – this is reproduced in schedule 1 – hold a border poll'.[58]

Neither the 1998 Agreement, nor the enacted Northern Ireland Act, detail how the Secretary of State should assess whether there is a likelihood of a majority in favour of reunification. Therefore, although the Act imposes a duty on the UK government to act in the event of that condition being reached, it appears to hand unrestricted discretion to ministers over how to gauge the opinion of the people of Northern Ireland. Ian Paisley, ever alive to a potential opportunity for UK government ministers to betray unionism, pocketed Murphy's 'when she or he thinks fit' response for future use, stating his concern that on this reading if the Secretary of State came before Parliament with regard to a referendum she 'does so of her own volition'[59] and 'elected representatives will have no say about when it should be held'.[60] Alarmed at how his account of the bill was being spun, Murphy was obliged to make a clarification:

> In order for the mechanics of that poll to be agreed by Parliament, there would be an opportunity ... for both Houses to review the Secretary of State's decision if it were judged rash and ill-defined and if it was believed that a border poll was being held without basis in reason or common sense. I have not the slightest doubt that hon. Members in this and the other place would point that out during such a debate.[61]

In other words, Murphy was asserting that the UK Parliament could reject the statutory instruments that would be needed to organise a referendum if it was unhappy with the prospect. There is, by contrast, no parliamentary mechanism (short of a private member's bill) to push the Secretary of State into triggering a referendum if the UK government is recalcitrant towards evidence of a shift in opinion in Northern Ireland towards favouring reunification. There is also the Northern Ireland Act's haziness regarding a referendum outcome favouring reunification; the legislation merely requires the UK government to 'lay before Parliament ... proposals to give effect to that wish'.[62] For all that the 1998 Agreement imposes a 'binding obligation' upon the UK government to respect

---

[58] *Hansard*, HC Deb., vol. 316, col. 1197, 22 July 1998.
[59] *Hansard*, HC Deb., vol. 316, col. 1198, 22 July 1998.
[60] *Hansard*, vol. 316, col. 1215, 22 July 1998.
[61] *Hansard*, HC Deb., vol. 316, col. 1215, 22 July 1998.
[62] Northern Ireland Act 1998, s. 1(2).

the outcome of a reunification referendum as a matter of international law,[63] this statutory pledge falls short of obliging the UK Parliament to give effect to such a referendum outcome (even if the notion of a substantive 'obligation' makes any sense in a constitutional order which prioritises the sovereignty of the sitting Parliament).[64] The statutory language exactly reflects the wording required of the UK government by the 1998 Agreement, and should therefore be interpreted by the courts in line with the overarching international obligation,[65] but in over three hours of parliamentary debate the ambiguity of 'lay before' was never probed.

Sinn Féin can pledge, in its manifesto for Ireland's 2020 general election to '[s]ecure a referendum, north and south, on Irish Unity', but delivering upon this promise is not within the Irish government's power under the 1998 settlement.[66] If the Northern Ireland Secretary does not accept that there could be majority support for a united Ireland, the duty to call a referendum is not triggered. Moreover, all of the debate invested in the issue of what was meant by a majority meant that there was almost no substantive discussion of what was meant by 'the people of Northern Ireland', with only the DUP's Peter Robinson making substantive suggestions over giving that term meaning in the context of a referendum vote.[67] These shortcomings mean that nationalist politicians should have had as many questions over the working of a referendum on unity as their unionist counterparts. But the 22 July 1998 debate saw no interventions from John Hume or Seamus Mallon. Eddie McGrady was left to spend the evening needling his Unionist counterparts about the meaning of a majority, rather than asking substantive questions about Schedule 1's operation.

This debate, in short, manifested unionist anxieties and nationalist hubris with regard to reunification. As Hume confidently insisted, given a couple of generations of dealing with the legacy of the conflict, north-south co-operation and power sharing in Northern Ireland's own institutions, 'a new Ireland will evolve'.[68] His goal (for all that he had muddied the waters at times in the interest of protecting his base of political support) had, for decades, been to restrict the pervasive encroachment of the constitutional question into all aspects of politics in Northern Ireland. By 1998, his party was at ease with

---

[63] Belfast Agreement, UK-Ireland Agreement, Art. 1(iv).
[64] Morison and Livingstone, *Reshaping Public Power*, p. 105.
[65] See *Garland v. British Rail Engineering Ltd* [1983] 2 AC 751, 771 (Lord Diplock). See also below, n. 79.
[66] *Giving Workers and Families a Break: A Manifesto for Change*, Sinn Féin, 2020, p. 5.
[67] Hansard, HC Deb., vol. 316, col. 1206, 22 July 1998.
[68] John Hume, *A New Ireland: Politics, Peace and Reconciliation* (Boulder: Roberts Rinehart Press, 1997), p. 125.

the issue being moved off the table for some decades (Sinn Féin, which was not, had excluded itself from Westminster's debates). The SDLP's leadership was also at ease with entrusting broad discretion to the UK government, a mark of its comfortable relations with New Labour.[69] It was confident that the 1998 Agreement provided a bedrock for reform and reconciliation, and that the third arm of this strategy, reunification, would come to fruition in the fulness of time. The unionist parties, as the Commons debate illustrated, remained committed to thwarting this arc. More than that, Hume's promotion of this roadmap gave many unionists explicit reason not to buy into its first two elements, or to pursue minimal compliance with the 1998 settlement.

## THE 1998 SETTLEMENT UPON THE ANVIL OF BREXIT

In the decades which have followed, many of Hume's confident expectations regarding the 1998 settlement went unfulfilled. A truth and reconciliation process is still being debated, a Bill of Rights for Northern Ireland has not been delivered, and Northern Ireland's institutions have lurched between crises. Reform stalled, reconciliation measures were shelved, but reunification shot to prominence following the United Kingdom's 2016 referendum on EU membership. The July 1998 debate should have been a warning that, for all of the importance Hume had long invested in having the terms of a settlement embodied in an international treaty, they remained contested, and its implementation within domestic law would assume increasing significance in making this new constitutional dispensation work.

Domestic courts addressing the 1998 settlement found that, no matter the 1998 Agreement's terms, they could not 'overlook the importance of the terms in which the 1998 Act are cast'.[70] Over time, the consequences of the failure to translate some of Hume's most significant innovations in constitutional thought into domestic law would become ever more apparent, as showcased in litigation over the birthright of the people of Northern Ireland. Alongside this litigation, the negotiations over Brexit would expose tensions inherent between the concepts of protecting rights in Northern Ireland against diminution and parity of esteem between Northern Ireland's communities. Concerns over the implications of Brexit for Northern Ireland, moreover, brought unresolved questions over the process of reunification to a head.

---

[69] Nick Randall, 'New Labour and Northern Ireland' in David Coates and Peter Lawler (eds.), *New Labour in Power* (Manchester: Manchester University Press, 2000), pp. 92–107.
[70] *In re McCord* [2016] NIQB 85, at para. 154 (Maguire J).

## BIRTHRIGHT LITIGATION

Under the terms of the British Nationality Act 1981, which was not altered after the 1998 Agreement, members of the people of Northern Ireland automatically become British citizens upon birth in Northern Ireland.[71] This underlying, and sometimes unwanted, imposition of British citizenship is difficult to square with the 1998 Agreement's articulation of the 'birthright' of the people of Northern Ireland 'to identify themselves and be accepted as Irish or British, or both, as they may so choose'.[72] For many years, however, this apparent disconnect between UK nationality law and the 1998 agreement was of limited practical importance, until the Home Office, at the height of Theresa May's 'hostile environment' drive to reduce net migration, seized upon a judgment of the Court of Justice of the EU[73] to prevent all dual nationals with UK citizenship from exercising family reunification rights under the Free Movement Directive.[74] This change had distinct legal implications for some of the people of Northern Ireland, including Emma De Souza. The blanket imposition of this rule, without exception being made for cases involving the people of Northern Ireland who had acquired dual citizenship by exercising their 1998 Agreement birthright, prevented her from exercising her EU law rights to maintain family life in Northern Ireland with her husband Jake (a US citizen).[75] The UK government's position was that this was a 'purely internal situation',[76] and that it could impose domestic law requirements upon Jake's residency in the United Kingdom.[77] De Souza was insistent that she identified solely as Irish, and challenged the automatic application of British citizenship as a breach of the United Kingdom's 1998 Agreement obligation to accept her as such.

In the First Tier Tribunal, Judge Gillespie found for the De Souzas, asserting that '[t]he constitutional changes effected by the Good Friday Agreement with its annexed British-Irish Agreement, the latter amounting to an international treaty between sovereign governments, supersede the British Nationality Act 1981 in so far as the people of Northern Ireland are concerned'.[78] This is quite a startling proposition in light of the orthodox dualist account of

---

[71] British Nationality Act 1981 (UK), s. 1.
[72] Belfast Agreement, UK-Ireland Agreement, Art. 1(vi).
[73] Case C-434/09 *McCarthy* v. *Secretary of State for the Home Department* (2011) ECLI:EU: C:2011:277.
[74] Directive 2004/38/EC, OJ 2004 L 158, 77, Art. 3(1).
[75] The Immigration (European Economic Area) Regulations 2016, reg. 2(1) (SI 2016/1052) (UK).
[76] *McCarthy*, at paras. 46 and 54.
[77] See Sylvia de Mars and Colin Murray, 'With or Without EU? The Common Travel Area after Brexit' (2020) 21 *German Law Journal* 815–37, pp. 823–24.
[78] *De Souza* v. *Home Office* (2017) First Tier Tribunal (unreported).

the United Kingdom's constitutional order. Judge Gillespie leapt over the possibility of the 1998 Agreement influencing the interpretation of the 1981 Act,[79] which might in itself have been a stretch given that this statute long predated the treaty, and straight into the territory in which unincorporated elements of a treaty 'supersede' a statute. The subsequent Upper Tribunal decision pulled hard in the opposite direction, finding that the 1998 Agreement did not condition the application of the 1981 Act,[80] and furthermore disputing whether it even had any clear implications for UK nationality law:

> If the parties to the multi-party agreement and the governments of Ireland and the United Kingdom had intended the concept of self-identification necessarily to include a person's ability to reject his or her Irish or British citizenship, it is inconceivable that the provisions would not have dealt with this expressly.[81]

Any lack of specificity in these terms, say by comparison to the genesis of the identity proposal in *Towards a New Ireland*,[82] is part and parcel with the nature of negotiating a peace agreement. The Upper Tribunal's decision, moreover, overstated the supposed ambiguity by not addressing the scope of the 1998 Agreement's notion of birthright being 'to identify ... *and be accepted*' (Alison Harvey's emphasis).[83]

*De Souza* demonstrates how judges steeped in the 'constitutionalism of Dicey, Bagehot and their natural successors'[84] have struggled to accommodate the novel constitutional elements of the 1998 settlement. Even if they accepted that the Northern Ireland Act provided 'in effect a constitution' for Northern Ireland, what that meant in practice was shrouded in uncertainty.[85] In fairness to these judges, unlike the Human Rights Act, which provides parliamentary authority for them to depart from Diceyan orthodoxy on their interpretive role in human rights cases, the 1998 settlement provides no such cover.[86] Hume's ideas on identity might have provided the basis for the relevant provisions in

---

[79] See, regarding the 1998 Agreement, *Re McComb's Application for Judicial Review* [2003] NIQB 47, at para. 31.
[80] *Secretary of State for the Home Department v Jake Parker De Souza* [2019] UKUT 355, at para. 28.
[81] Ibid., at para. 39.
[82] See SDLP, *Towards a New Ireland*.
[83] See Alison Harvey, *A Legal Analysis of Incorporating into UK Law the Birthright Commitment under the Belfast (Good Friday) Agreement 1998* (Belfast/Dublin: Joint Committee of the Irish Human Rights and Equality Commission and the Northern Ireland Human Rights Commission, 2020), p. 4.
[84] Morison and Livingstone, *Reshaping Public Power*, p. 88.
[85] *Robinson v Secretary of State for Northern Ireland* [2002] UKHL 32, at para. 11 (Lord Bingham).
[86] Indeed, the courts only feel secure in their role with regard to legislation under the Human Rights Act because it amounts to 'a duty imposed upon the court by Parliament'; *Re MB* [2006] EWHC 1000 (Admin), at para. 103 (Sullivan J).

the Agreement, but enough ambiguity had been introduced into their terms during negotiations for the Upper Tribunal in *De Souza* to feel confident in brushing off these commitments. Because they were not articulated in the subsequent Northern Ireland Act, judges have, moreover, felt constrained in applying treaty commitments within the United Kingdom's dualist order. As Christopher McCrudden forewarned, the United Kingdom's constitutional orthodoxies 'are likely over time to reassert themselves, submerging the *sui generis* aspects of the Northern Ireland Constitution unless the latter are continually safeguarded and reinforced'.[87]

The need to reinforce the birthright commitment had indeed been recognised in 1998. If a right to 'identify and be accepted' had been built into a Northern Ireland Bill of Rights, with equivalent status and powers to the UK-wide Human Rights Act, the courts would have had the authority to raise issues with, or reinterpret, the British Nationality Act 1981 as it applied in Northern Ireland.[88] The 1998 Agreement had specifically highlighted the potential need for such a statute, passed by Westminster, to provide for 'additional rights to reflect the principles of mutual respect for the identity and ethos of both communities and parity of esteem'.[89] Progress towards a Northern Ireland Bill of Rights had, however, stalled over a lack of consensus around the proposals presented by the Northern Ireland Human Rights Commission (NIHRC) in 2008.[90] The promise of the 1998 settlement's identity provisions would thus appear to have been thwarted in their implementation.

Or its promise would have been thwarted, had the UK government not been obliged to amend the application of the EU Settlement Scheme for the people of Northern Ireland, notwithstanding the outcome of the *De Souza* litigation. It came under concerted pressure, including from Ireland, the NIHRC and various parties in Northern Ireland to address the *De Souza* complaint, and Theresa May was obliged 'to review these issues urgently'.[91] Her successor eventually acted as part of the *New Decade, New Approach* agreement which

---

[87] Christopher McCrudden, 'Northern Ireland, the Belfast Agreement, and the British Constitution' in Jeffrey Jowell and Dawn Oliver (eds.), *The Changing Constitution* (Oxford: Oxford University Press, 5th edn., 2004), pp. 195–236.

[88] Northern Ireland Act 1998, s. 69(7).

[89] Belfast Agreement, Multi-Party Agreement, Rights, Safeguards and Equality of Opportunity, para. 4.

[90] *A Bill of Rights for Northern Ireland: Advice to the Secretary of State for Northern Ireland*, NIHRC, 10 December 2008, www.nihrc.org/uploads/publications/bill-of-rights-for-northern-ireland-advice-to-secretary-of-state-2008.pdf. See Colin Murray, Aoife O'Donoghue and Ben Warwick, 'The Implications of the Good Friday Agreement for UK Human-Rights Reform' (2016–2017) 11–12 *Irish Yearbook of International Law* 71–96, p. 90.

[91] Theresa May, 'PM speech in Belfast', gov.uk, 5 February 2019, www.gov.uk/government/speeches/pm-speech-in-belfast-5-february-2019.

restored power sharing to Northern Ireland in January 2020, announcing that the people of Northern Ireland would be able to assert EU law family rights regarding family.[92] The Northern Ireland Secretary informed Parliament that this reform was necessary because 'there should never be an incentive to renounce British citizenship'.[93] In some cases, however, renunciation has not affected the outcome of efforts to assert EU family rights.[94] That the translation of this commitment into law did not require someone to have activated their entitlement to Irish citizenship, illustrates instead the impact of the 1998 Agreement's principle of parity of esteem; a special dispensation has to apply generally to the people of Northern Ireland, not to those who identify as Irish or British.[95] This response is nonetheless a short-term fix; it creates a new arrangement for the people of Northern Ireland which will only operate until the EU Settlement Scheme elapses in the summer of 2021.[96] This addresses the symptom (the loss of family reunification rights for the people of Northern Ireland), rather than the underlying causes (the automatic imposition of British citizenship and the refusal to recognise EU citizenship rights for dual nationals).[97]

## BREXIT AND THE PEOPLE OF NORTHERN IRELAND

Cases like *De Souza* raise a disconnect. Although judges maintain the precepts of parliamentary sovereignty and deny that the 1998 settlement in reality provides what Wade described as the 'ultimate political fact' of Northern Ireland's governance order,[98] the UK government can find itself compelled to adapt to the 1998 Agreement's precepts (even when they are supposedly unclear or have not been incorporated into domestic law). Judges might struggle draw upon such elements of the Agreement, but as Galileo is said to have responded to denials of the earth moving around the sun, *e pur si muove*. In the course of the negotiations on the United Kingdom's withdrawal from the EU, successive UK prime ministers found the 1998 Agreement's constitutional force to be undeniable, and were obliged to maintain the United Kingdom's commitment to its 'letter and spirit'.[99]

[92] *New Decade, New Approach* (January 2020), Annex A, paras. 13–15, https://assets.publishing.service.gov.uk/government/uploads/system/uploads/attachment_data/file/856998/2020-01-08_a_new_decade__a_new_approach.pdf.
[93] *Hansard*, Julian Smith MP, HC Deb., vol. 669, col. 1168, 16 January 2020.
[94] See *Capparrelli* v. *Home Office* [2017] UKUT 162.
[95] Belfast Agreement, UK-Ireland Agreement, Art. 1(v).
[96] Statement of Changes in Immigration Rules (14 May 2020) CP 232, para. 7.2.
[97] It is notable that the 2020 agreement also put the Northern Ireland Bill of Rights back onto the agenda; *New Decade, New Approach*, Part 2, para. 28.
[98] H. W. R. Wade, 'The Basis of Legal Sovereignty' (1955) 13 *Cambridge Law Journal* 172–97, p. 188.
[99] May, 'PM speech in Belfast'.

This is most evident in terms of the 1998 Agreement's Strand Two commitments, which prompted the UK government's commitment 'to protect North-South cooperation and its guarantee of avoiding a hard border'.[100] Special arrangements covering Northern Ireland were concluded in October 2019 notwithstanding the Northern Ireland Court of Appeal acknowledging that they had no power to intervene to enforce treaty obligations which would be breached by a no-deal Brexit (as there were no relevant statutory restrictions on the conduct of Brexit negotiations).[101] But the 1998 Agreement requirement of equality of treatment between the people of Northern Ireland, however they identify, has also shaped the negotiations. In 2017 the UK committed, in light of the 1998 Agreement's requirements, to '[n]o diminution of rights' as a result of Brexit.[102] The EU and United Kingdom also emphasised that Irish citizens living in Northern Ireland 'will continue to enjoy rights as EU citizens'.[103] Although the preamble of the Withdrawal Agreement's Protocol on Ireland and Northern Ireland reaffirms these commitments, the operative provisions suggest that the legal guarantees might be less substantive in practice. Art. 2 of the Protocol maintains EU law against discrimination within Northern Ireland's law, rather than explicit rights protections. These commitments are not insignificant, but a gap is potentially emerging between what people assume the Withdrawal Agreement's protections to be and their actual scope.[104]

This shortfall is sure to produce more flashpoint cases concerning EU law rights. The problem which confronted both the United Kingdom and the EU was that as soon as the Brexit negotiations edged towards extending some rights and entitlements to the people of Northern Ireland who maintained their EU citizenship rights by virtue of holding Irish citizenship, and not those who identified solely as British, this outcome clashed with the 1998 Agreement's commitment to

---

[100] Agreement on the Withdrawal of the United Kingdom of Great Britain and Northern Ireland from the European Union and the European Atomic Energy Community (17 October 2019) Protocol on Ireland/Northern Ireland, Preamble. See also Stephen Weatherill, 'The Protocol on Ireland/Northern Ireland: Protecting the EU's Internal Market at the Expense of the UK's' (2020) 45 European Law Review 222–36.

[101] *McCord (Raymond), JR 83 and Jamie Waring's Applications* v. *The Prime Minister* [2019] NICA 49, at para. 111. (Morgan LCJ).

[102] Joint Report from the negotiators of the European Union and the United Kingdom Government on progress during phase 1 of negotiations under Art. 50 TEU on the United Kingdom's orderly withdrawal from the European Union (TF50 2017, 19) 8 December 2017, para. 53.

[103] Ibid., para. 52.

[104] See Sylvia de Mars, Colin Murray, Aoife O'Donoghue and Ben Warwick, *Continuing EU Citizenship "Rights, Opportunities and Benefits" in Northern Ireland after Brexit* (Joint Committee of the Irish Human Rights and Equality Commission and the Northern Ireland Human Rights Commission, 2020), p. 42.

'parity of esteem'.[105] And for so long as EU citizenship is parasitic upon member state citizenship, the EU is unable to extend its protections to the people of Northern Ireland who have not exercised their entitlement to claim Irish citizenship.[106] As a result of this irreducible conundrum, it has proven impossible to provide a full expression of its rights protections once the United Kingdom left the shared framework provided by EU law.

## THE CONSTITUTIONAL QUESTION

Brexit, in Northern Ireland politics, is inextricably connected to the constitutional question. For the DUP, Brexit held out an opportunity to thwart movement towards a Europe of the regions and any further dilution of the United Kingdom's sovereignty over Northern Ireland. The United Kingdom's clean break from the EU would, it was hoped, create new differences between Northern Ireland and Ireland (which remains in alignment with Brussels) and would thereby make the reunification of Ireland more difficult to achieve. That Northern Ireland's majority support for continued EU membership in the June 2016 referendum was an irrelevance to these aims, is evidenced in the DUP's reaction to the UK Supreme Court's 2017 decision, in *Miller*,[107] that the 1998 Agreement's principle of consent did not extend beyond the question of Northern Ireland's status as part of the United Kingdom.[108] The party's Brexit spokesperson, Sammy Wilson, enthused that this decision had prioritised the 'clear and decisive' UK-wide vote.[109]

Such are the ironies of the principle of consent that Wilson, a politician who rose to prominence opposing the Anglo-Irish Agreement's imposition of governance arrangements against the wishes of the majority of the people of Northern Ireland, now delighted in the principle's confinement to the strict question of Northern Ireland's place in the United Kingdom. Brexit, however, has inspired many unexpected cross-overs in constitutional thought. Peter Robinson resurrected Hume's idea of periodic referendums on reunification.[110] Seamus Mallon suggested a cross-community requirement in referendums very much in keeping with Ian Paisley Senior's contributions to the July 1998 debate. The leaders of

---

[105] Belfast Agreement, UK-Ireland Agreement, Art. 1(v).
[106] *Continuing EU Citizenship*, pp. 43–4.
[107] *R (Miller) v Secretary of State for Exiting the European Union* [2017] UKSC 5; [2018] AC 61.
[108] Ibid., at para. 135.
[109] 'Reaction to Supreme Court Northern Ireland Brexit ruling', BBC News website, 24 January 2017, www.bbc.co.uk/news/uk-northern-ireland-38728434.
[110] 'Peter Robinson warns of border poll chaos', BBC News website, 8 June 2018, www.bbc.co.uk/news/av/uk-northern-ireland-44412855/peter-robinson-warns-of-border-poll-chaos.

Fianna Fáil and Fine Gael have suggested a functioning Assembly as a prerequisite for such a vote[111] and questioned whether its simple-majority requirement is a 'good thing'.[112] The authors of the 1998 settlement believed that they had punted such a referendum far enough into the future that society in Northern Ireland would have had sufficient opportunity to make the transition necessary to address the constitutional question through democratic politics. Amid the Brexit debate, these actors were no longer so sure, and their suggestions all involve restraining moves towards a referendum on Northern Ireland's status or ringfencing such a vote from everyday politics. Under this pressure, the orthodox account of the 1998 Agreement's principle of consent seemed to waiver.

Even as this confusion has mounted, the UK government has repeatedly refused to be drawn upon how it assesses public opinion in Northern Ireland (the weight, for example, it gives to opinion polls or election results). Parliamentary questions have been dismissed on the basis that the Secretary of State does not believe that the conditions triggering the duty to hold a referendum have been met.[113] Given the febrile debate over Brexit's potential impact upon Northern Ireland, it was therefore almost inevitable that there would be a turn to law to clarify the UK government's apparently unconstrained discretion over operation of the principle of consent. This was particularly the case after *Miller*, in which the majority's reasoning was so terse that it avoided any discussion of how Brexit could be accommodated with the United Kingdom's 1998 Agreement commitments.[114] Raymond McCord, who had been a party to *Miller*, followed up this case with challenge against the Northern Ireland Secretary's refusal to make public the grounds under which the UK government determined whether public opinion in Northern Ireland necessitated a reunification referendum.

Girvan LJ, in the Northern Ireland High Court, began his judgment with an important clarification of the law. In keeping with the July 1998 parliamentary debate, he reaffirmed that the 1998 Agreement required 'majority votes north and south in favour of unification'.[115] This plain assertion is an antidote to some of the wilder speculation as to whether a majority really means a simple majority. As for constraining the Secretary of State's discretion, administrative

---

[111] Stephen O'Brien, 'Forget about border poll for now, says Micheál Martin', *Sunday Times*, 22 December 2019, www.thetimes.co.uk/article/forget-about-border-poll-for-now-says-micheal-martin-k25rhbrns.

[112] 'Irish unity poll a "bad idea", warns Varadkar', BBC News website, 8 June 2018, www.bbc.co.uk/news/uk-northern-ireland-44406029.

[113] See *Hansard*, Karen Bradley, HC Deb., WA 230086 13 March 2019 and Julian Smith, HC Deb., WA 281830 3 September 2019.

[114] See Christopher McCrudden and Daniel Halberstam, '*Miller* and Northern Ireland: A critical constitutional response' (2017) 8 *UK Supreme Court Yearbook* 299–343, p. 343.

[115] *In re McCord* [2018] NIQB 106 at para. 5.

law in the United Kingdom has increasingly turned towards obliging public bodies to set out policy positions, particularly in cases where broadly framed discretionary powers produce uncertainties which have serious implications for affected individuals.[116] But *In re McCord* involved an open-ended discretion with serious implications for society as a whole, not for a particular individual's ordering of their affairs. Girvan LJ swiftly dismissed this challenge, concluding that '[t]he overall evidential context on how it should be analysed and viewed is a matter for the Secretary of State'.[117] It was always going to be a struggle to convince the courts to tie the hands of ministers over such a decision, but Girvan LJ's brusque tone illustrated his reluctance to address the interpretation of fundamental aspects of the 1998 Agreement's incorporation into domestic law. Even if the obligation to trigger a reunification referendum is based upon the Secretary of State's political assessment of the state of public opinion amongst Northern Ireland's voters, that assessment must be conducted in accordance with public law principles.[118] At the very least, this requires what Paul Murphy described, during the July 1998 Commons debate, as '*a proper assessment* of the political circumstances at the time'.[119]

Although the Northern Ireland Court of Appeal did not overturn Girvan LJ's decision on appeal, Stephen LJ's judgment did make more of this opportunity to clarify the boundaries of the UK government's role. The duty to call a referendum, arising in circumstances in which a majority of the people of Northern Ireland could favour reunification, did not simply require an honest assessment of popular opinion in Northern Ireland, as Girvan LJ had acknowledged.[120] For the Court of Appeal, the Secretary of State 'must also act with rigorous impartiality' with regard to this assessment.[121] The 1998 Agreement's rigorous impartiality duty applies to government decisions by whichever country has statehood over Northern Ireland.[122] The Northern Ireland Court of Appeal is thereby using the 1998 Agreement to interpret how the Northern Ireland Secretary's Northern Ireland Act duty to call a referendum operates.[123] This extension upon Girvan LJ's position, however, might appear further reaching than it will be in practice. Without parameters by which to assess the UK

---

[116] See, for example, *R (Purdy)* v. *Director of Public Prosecutions* [2009] UKHL 45, [16] (Lord Phillips).
[117] *In re McCord* [2018] NIQB 106 at para. 20.
[118] See Colin Murray and Aoife O'Donoghue, 'Life after Brexit: Operationalising the Belfast/Good Friday Agreement's Principle of Consent' (2020) 42 *Dublin University Law Journal* 147–189, p. 169.
[119] *Hansard*, HC Deb., vol. 316, col. 1198, 22 July 1998, emphasis added.
[120] *In re McCord* [2018] NIQB 106 at para 20.
[121] *In re McCord* [2020] NICA 23 at para. 82.
[122] Belfast Agreement, UK-Ireland Agreement, Art. 1(v).
[123] *In re McCord* [2020] NICA 23 at para. 50.

government's approach, a departure from rigorous impartiality is difficult to challenge.[124] The crunch test of the judiciary's safeguarding over the principle of consent is thus deferred until the Secretary of State is called upon to act on evidence of shifting majority sentiment.

CONCLUSION

John Hume's ideas regarding the special status of the people of Northern Ireland might have been front-and-centre in the 1998 treaty between the United Kingdom and Ireland, but the significance of his contribution to constitutional thought regarding to Northern Ireland has hardly registered in wider UK discourse. Northern Ireland's governance has long been difficult to fit within UK constitutional thought, and even before 1998 the suspicion was that few writers made an effort to do so.[125] The recent awkward attempts to accommodate the 1998 Agreement's birthright and parity-of-esteem commitments illustrate the shallow roots of these concepts within public law theory. The Brexit negotiations, moreover, have seen the United Kingdom and the EU struggle to deal with the overarching requirements of the 1998 Agreement, even as they wrapped themselves in its letter and spirit.

Instead, sticking plaster solutions have been reluctantly applied to the most pressing tears in the 1998 settlement. This is, in itself, significant. The emergence of *sui generis* arrangements for Northern Ireland in the Brexit negotiations, and special family reunification rights for the people of Northern Ireland in response to *De Souza*, illustrate how policy makers have found themselves obliged to accept the particularities of Northern Ireland's constitutional order. The 1998 settlement, as a centre, might well hold, at least for now. The latest surveys of public opinion in Northern Ireland point to enduring faith in that settlement.[126] But it could also prove unsustainable, particularly as the impact of Brexit is felt and more modifications become necessary. These piecemeal adjustments are contributing to a rolling crisis in Northern Ireland's governance, as one cause célèbre gives way to the next and everything seems to remain in flux. It remains to be seen how much of this buffeting Northern Ireland's unique (and fragile) constitutional order can sustain.

[124] Ibid., at para. 66, provides an illustration of one way in which this requirement could be breached.
[125] Morrison and Livingstone, *Reshaping Public Power*, pp. 111–115.
[126] The latest comprehensive survey sees only 10 per cent of respondents assert that the 1998 Agreement either is not, or never has been, 'a good basis for governing Northern Ireland'; Northern Ireland Life and Times Survey 2019, www.ark.ac.uk/nilt/2019/Political_Attitudes/VIEWGFA2.html.

# 6

## The Constitutional Politics of a United Ireland

Oran Doyle, David Kenny and Christopher McCrudden

INTRODUCTION

The United Kingdom's withdrawal from the European Union renders a united Ireland more likely than before. Estimates of its likelihood radically diverge,[1] but unification is now a subject of political discussion. Unification would likely be accompanied by significant constitutional change or even a new constitution. In this chapter, we explore the modalities and implications of amending Ireland's constitution to make a newly unified state more sensitive to the concerns and aspirations of those from the Ulster Scots and Ulster British traditions. Human rights would, no doubt, contribute to this, with specific legal and constitutional protections for minorities.[2] Our focus in this chapter lies elsewhere, however, upon what we term the 'constitutional politics' of a united Ireland. We do not advocate a united Ireland. Nor do we advocate any particular constitutional provisions save those we identify as required by the Belfast/Good Friday Agreement (the 1998 Agreement), should a united Ireland come about. Rather, we seek to draw attention to the complexities involved in the constitutional design of a united Ireland.

James Bryce, the nineteenth century constitutionalist and member of Gladstone's Home Rule Cabinet, noted that political constitutions are exposed to centripetal forces which 'draw ... men or groups of men together into one organized community', and centrifugal forces which 'make ... men,

---

[1] Unification would require approval in referendums concurrently held north and south. An opinion poll in the south in May 2019 suggests support of 65%. See www.rte.ie/news/elections-2019/2019/0525/1051603-rte-tg4-exit-poll/. But opinion polls in the north over 2019 and 2020 show support ranging between 25 and 46%. '51% of people in Northern Ireland support Irish unification, new poll finds', thejournal.ie, 11 September 2019; ARK Northern Ireland Life and Times Survey: www.ark.ac.uk/nilt/2019/Political_Attitudes/REFUNIFY.html.

[2] For analysis of some of these issues, see James Rooney, 'The Minority Rights Implications of Irish Unification' in this volume.

or groups, break away and disperse'. Bryce argued that four factors determine whether a polity will keep together or fall apart: obedience, individualism, interest and sympathy. Whether these four forces are centripetal or centrifugal in any given state 'depends upon whether they are at the moment giving their support to, or are enlisted in the service of, the State as a whole, or are strengthening the group or groups inside the State which are seeking to assert either their rights within the State or their independence of it'.[3] We adopt this framework to explore a tension within constitutional adaptations to the concerns of those from the Ulster Scots and Ulster British traditions. These adaptations may simultaneously exert centripetal and centrifugal forces: the constitutional challenge of accommodating different identities and interests is a complex one.

We first consider how devolved, consociational government for Northern Ireland could continue within a united Ireland, politically empowering those from the Ulster Scots and Ulster British traditions given that they are likely to be approximately 50 per cent of the population in Northern Ireland, but only 15 per cent of the newly unified state's population. This might increase the sympathy of individuals from that tradition for the new state – a centripetal force. But the operation of devolution could presage a divergence of interests that leads to significant tensions between the national institutions and the devolved institutions, and within the national institutions themselves – a centrifugal force. We then identify the many provisions of the current Irish Constitution that posit a notion of Irish identity exclusionary of those from the Ulster Scots and Ulster British traditions. Amendment of these constitutional provisions would reduce the risk of alienation from the unified state. Many of these provisions, however, manifest and reflect indicia of Irish identity dearly held by many if not most citizens of the current Irish state. Their removal – at least without detailed consideration of how the constitution might be amended to respect multiple identities – risks reducing the sympathy of existing citizens for the unified state. Whatever approach is taken, these challenges would continue long past the moment of unification. We therefore conclude by exploring how the various constitutional changes considered would be interpreted and amendable after unification.

---

[3] The essay 'The Action of Centripetal and Centrifugal Forces on Political Constitutions' was composed in 1885, but not published until 1901 in James Bryce, *Studies in History and Jurisprudence*, vol. 1 (Oxford: Clarendon Press, 1901). For an application of Bryce to the analysis of devolution in the United Kingdom, see Christopher McCrudden, 'State architecture: subsidiarity, devolution, federalism and independence', in Mark Elliott and David Feldman (eds.), *The Cambridge Companion to Public Law* (Cambridge: Cambridge University Press, 2015), pp. 193–214.

The problem of terminology haunts political discourse on the island of Ireland. We have generally adopted conventional usage of contested terms, whilst distancing ourselves from accepting the political implications that some would place on such use. Thus, for example, we refer to the 'unification' of Ireland, rather than 're-unification', whether or not the latter term may be historically justified. There is one area, however, where no clear conventional usage has yet emerged: what are we to call those who were 'unionists' and self-identified as 'British' in Northern Ireland pre-unification, but would – in the possible future that this chapter explores – find themselves in a united Ireland? We should not make assumptions about how that community may come to self-identify, nor should we assume that it will not change its identity over time. 'Unionists' suggests that they remain committed to a 'union' that would no longer exist. 'British' assumes a loyalty they may no longer have. 'Protestants' over-emphasises the religious dimension and insufficiently distinguishes them from co-religionists in the south. Moreover, this community's identity is likely to affect, and be affected by, the issues that we discuss in this chapter. For want of anything better, and in the knowledge that unionist representatives themselves accepted the designation in *New Decade, New Approach*, the document which re-established devolved government in Northern Ireland,[4] we shall continue to refer to 'those from the Ulster Scots and Ulster British traditions'. We apologise in advance to anyone offended by this usage. One final comment on terminology is necessary. We later explore the possibility that the Irish-language titles of state institutions might be altered in a united Ireland: however, we largely adopt the current terminology for our analysis, even when discussing possible post-unification institutions: Oireachtas (parliament), Dáil (Lower House), TD (member of the Lower House), Seanad (Upper House) and Taoiseach (prime minister).

Finally, we should outline our understanding of how unification might take place.[5] Under the 1998 Agreement and the Constitution of Ireland, unification requires a referendum in the north and a concurrent expression of democratic consent in the south. If unification were accompanied by the sort of constitutional changes explored in this chapter, the democratic expression of consent in the south would have to involve or be accompanied by a referendum. Concurrence does not require simultaneity but does require that the two

---

[4] *New Decade, New Approach*, January 2020, https://assets.publishing.service.gov.uk/government/uploads/system/uploads/attachment_data/file/856998/2020-01-08_a_new_decade__a_new_approach.pdf.

[5] C. R. G. Murray and Aoife O'Donoghue, 'Life after Brexit: Operationalising the Belfast/Good Friday Agreement's Principle of Consent' (2019) 42:1 *Dublin University Law Journal* 147.

electorates approve substantively the same proposal. This leaves open a wide range of options, the key variable being the extent to which the unification terms are resolved *before* or *after* the referendums. We do not address those questions here, but our discussion is framed by this understanding.[6] We take the current Irish Constitution as the baseline of analysis, but do not differentiate between constitutional amendment and constitutional replacement as mechanisms of constitutional change.

## DEVOLUTION AND CONSOCIATIONALISM IN NORTHERN IRELAND

### *The Belfast/Good Friday Agreement*

The 1998 Agreement involves two connected and cross-referring agreements: an international agreement between the British and Irish Governments; and a multi-party agreement between the parties in Northern Ireland and the two governments.[7] The 1998 Agreement was brought into UK law primarily by the Northern Ireland Act 1998 (UK) (NIA 1998). Although the institutions established have been frequently suspended when the political parties failed to agree, and the details of how the institutions were to operate have been amended in subsequent agreements, the basic structure of the 1998 Agreement has remained. The 1998 Agreement consists of three strands: relationships within Northern Ireland; relationships between Northern Ireland and the south; and relationships between Britain and Ireland. Institutions were developed under each of the strands, reflecting these interlinking relationships, considered further below. The 1998 Agreement crucially includes other provisions dealing with the constitutional status of Northern Ireland, the decommissioning of paramilitary weapons, the release of paramilitary prisoners, and human rights and equality.

---

[6] See generally Alan Renwick et al., *Interim Report of Working Group on Unification Referendums on the Island of Ireland*, Constitution Unit, UCL (London: UCL Constitution Unit, 26 November 2020).

[7] Where appropriate, we refer to the terms of the Agreement as subsequently adapted by the St Andrew's Agreement. This section draws on more detailed analysis in Christopher McCrudden, 'Northern Ireland and the British Constitution since the Belfast Agreement', in Jeffrey Jowell and Dawn Oliver (eds.), *The Changing Constitution* (Oxford: Oxford University Press, 6th edn., 2007), pp. 227–70.

## Devolution

The 1998 Agreement was concluded, and the NIA 1998 (devolving powers from Westminster to Belfast) passed, at the same time as the devolution of powers to Wales and Scotland.[8] The Northern Ireland arrangements are similar to devolution in Scotland and Wales – as they have developed – with devolved assemblies and executives, exercising powers over a relatively similar set of issues, with a relatively similar set of other issues reserved to Westminster. The NIA 1998 identifies three categories of functions: 'excepted', 'reserved', and 'transferred', and only in the latter two instances has the Assembly any powers to legislate.[9] Only in the case of transferred functions does the Assembly have full authority to pass primary legislation for Northern Ireland, subject to the European Convention on Human Rights and the provisions of the Ireland-Northern Ireland Protocol to the Withdrawal Agreement between the EU and the United Kingdom. The operation of these devolved powers is governed by UK law, as ultimately interpreted by the UK Supreme Court.

Notwithstanding the considerable similarities between the devolved administrations, the 1998 Agreement broke new institutional and constitutional ground in British constitutional terms, setting Northern Ireland apart from Wales and Scotland. First, Northern Ireland's system of government is based on a model of cross-community power-sharing termed 'consociationalism'. Second, it is connected to a broader set of institutions and embedded in an international agreement between Ireland and the United Kingdom. Third, the 1998 Agreement provides for Northern Ireland to leave the United Kingdom if the majority of its people vote at a referendum for unification with the south. The devolutionary arrangements, therefore, anticipate a possible change of constitutional status; as discussed later, devolved institutions might even persist post-unification.

Brexit has foregrounded a tension between British constitutional practice and the constitutional arrangements for Northern Ireland envisaged by the 1998 Agreement. In Britain, or at least in England, the constitution is the outward manifestation of a substantial degree of consent, or at least acquiescence. Traditionally, constitutional procedures in Britain derive from that consent or acquiescence to the legitimacy of the state.[10] In Northern Ireland, given the absence of consent from a significant proportion of the population in

---

[8] Government of Wales Act 1998; Scotland Act 1998.
[9] NIA 1998, s. 4.
[10] See further, McCrudden, 'Northern Ireland'. See also Martin Loughlin, 'In Search of the Constitution' in the current volume.

the recent past, there have been attempts to construct consent in part on the basis of constitutional guarantees. Brexit threatens that agreed status quo. In particular, the power of Westminster to alter the precise contours of the devolution settlement in Northern Ireland might be exercised in a way that undermines the consent to the state that devolution was intended to construct.[11] Similar issues might arise in reverse in a united Ireland, as we shall see below.

The 'domestic' Northern Ireland institutional structures exist in a broader framework. North-south governmental activity was formalised in three ways: the North-South Ministerial Council; cross-border 'implementation bodies' for specified issues; and a looser arrangement for agreed cooperation between bodies with jurisdiction over designated functions in the two jurisdictions. There would be little reason for these north-south institutions to continue in the event of unification, so we do not consider them further here.

East-west cooperation, however, potentially retains significance post-unification. Two institutions were established: a British-Irish Council (BIC) and a British-Irish Intergovernmental Conference (BIIC). The BIC was established 'to promote the harmonious and mutually beneficial development of the totality of relationships among the peoples of these islands'. Membership of the BIC comprised representatives of the United Kingdom and Irish governments, representatives of devolved institutions in Northern Ireland, Scotland, and Wales, and representatives of the Isle of Man and the Channel Islands. Of considerably greater practical importance, however, a standing British-Irish Intergovernmental Conference was also established, subsuming institutions established under the earlier 1985 Anglo-Irish Agreement. The BIIC is a forum in which the British and Irish governments formally discuss Northern Ireland. We consider the relevance of the BIIC in a united Ireland below.

## Consociationalism

At the risk of oversimplification,[12] there are two broad options for democratic states that incorporate a multi-ethnic or multi-national population: the state may choose either to *eliminate* or to *manage* the differences in ethnic or national identity. Elimination may involve policies of assimilation, or liberal

---

[11] Christopher McCrudden and Daniel Halberstam, '*Miller* and Northern Ireland: A Critical Constitutional Response' (2016) 8 *The UK Supreme Court Yearbook* 299–343, p. 31.

[12] This section draws on Christopher McCrudden and Brendan O'Leary, *Courts and Consociations: Human Rights versus Power-Sharing* (Oxford: Oxford University Press, 2013).

integrationist approaches: majority rule accompanied by minority rights protections. Management can involve geographically based confederal or federal arrangements. Two other approaches, however, have attracted significant scholarly and political attention: the first, associated with Horowitz, encourages the different ethnic or national groups to cross their tribal boundaries;[13] the second, associated with Lijphart, encourages power-sharing through the adoption of what has been termed 'consociationalism'.[14]

Consociations are commonly thought to contain four key elements:[15] parity of the contending groups through cross-community power-sharing (shared-government); community autonomy over some decision-making (self-government); proportional representation in shared institutions; and veto rights on vital issues. Northern Ireland has embedded consociationalism across these four dimensions: parity through cross-community power-sharing is evident in executive formation which requires cross-community government; community autonomy over some decision-making is provided especially on issues of primary and secondary education; proportional representation in shared institutions is seen in the composition of the police and the civil service; and veto rights on vital issues are possible through the 'petition of concern' mechanism.

Elections to the Assembly are by the single transferable vote system of proportional representation (PR-STV). In these elections, the Democratic Unionist Party (DUP) and Sinn Féin have emerged as the largest unionist and nationalist parties respectively. Together with the Ulster Unionist Party (UUP), the Social Democratic and Labour Party (SDLP), and Alliance, these comprise the five largest parties. In these results, we can identify another important feature of Northern Ireland that stands in marked contrast to politics in the rest of the United Kingdom and in Ireland: the virtual absence of UK-wide and (with the exceptions of Sinn Féin and the Green Party) Ireland-wide political parties in Northern Ireland.[16]

Safeguards require both parts of the community to participate and work together in the operation of the Assembly. Members of the Assembly are, controversially, required to register a designation of identity (nationalist, unionist, or other) for the purposes of measuring cross-community support in Assembly votes. Key decisions are taken on a cross-community basis. This involves either 'parallel consent' – that is, a majority of those members present

---

[13] Donald Horowitz, *Ethnic Groups in Conflict* (Berkeley: University of California Press, 1985).
[14] Arend Lijphart, *Democracy in Plural Societies: A Comparative Exploration* (New Haven: Yale University Press, 1977).
[15] McCrudden and O'Leary, *Courts and Consociations*.
[16] See David Mitchell, 'Political Parties in Northern Ireland and the Post-Brexit Constitutional Debate' in this volume.

and voting, including a majority of both the unionist and the nationalist designations present and voting – or a weighted majority (60 per cent) of members present and voting, including at least 40 per cent of each of the nationalist and unionist designations present and voting.[17]

Key decisions in the Assembly requiring cross-community and concurrent majority support include the election of the presiding officer of the Assembly (equivalent to the Speaker at Westminster or the Ceann Comhairle in the Dáil); the election of the First Minister and Deputy First Minister; the adoption of standing orders; the exclusion of a person or party from ministerial office; and budget allocations. In other cases, a 'petition of concern' brought by at least thirty Assembly members triggers decisions requiring cross-community support. The chairs and deputy chairs of the Assembly committees, shadowing the main executive functions, are allocated proportionally, using the d'Hondt system. Membership of the committees is in broad proportion to party strengths in the Assembly. These requirements are intended to ensure that both communities in Northern Ireland support Assembly decisions and prevent the simple majoritarianism that operated in Northern Ireland prior to 1972.

The Northern Ireland Executive consists of a First Minister and a Deputy First Minister and up to ten ministers with departmental responsibilities (with additional junior ministers who can be appointed). The First Minister and Deputy First Minister are jointly elected into office by the Assembly voting on a cross-community basis according to the 'parallel consent' method discussed above. The posts of ministers are then allocated, in sequential order, to parties on the basis of the d'Hondt system, by reference to the number of seats each party has in the Assembly. The Executive is convened, and presided over jointly, by the First Minister and Deputy First Minister, whose functions include dealing with and coordinating the work of the Executive and how the Northern Ireland administration manages its relationships with other actors.[18]

Consociationalism also has considerable reach into other dimensions of life in Northern Ireland. An important aspect of 'normalisation' involved the creation of a police force which all sections of the population could recognise as legitimate, and to which they could give their consent and support. Central to encouraging cross-community support for these arrangements was a system of recruitment (now discontinued) to ensure that the new police service would be more representative of the community as a whole.[19]

[17] NIA 1998, s. 4.
[18] NIA 1998, Pt. III.
[19] *A New Beginning: Policing in Northern Ireland: The Report of the Independent Commission on Policing for Northern Ireland*, September 1999 (the 'Patten Report').

## Devolution and Consociationalism Post-Unification

How might Northern Ireland's current governmental structures continue, if at all, in a united Ireland? One approach would be for the new Irish state to operate as a single entity, without special arrangements for Northern Ireland. Another would be national consociationalism for a unified, unitary Irish state, with a new Irish parliament and government composed on the same basis as the existing Northern Ireland Assembly and Executive. Operationalising this option would raise significant questions, and (so far as we are aware) is not strongly advocated in any of the present debates.

A third approach, and the focus of this chapter, would continue consociational arrangements in a Northern Ireland Assembly and Executive in a similar manner as currently operating, but with sovereignty shifting from London to Dublin. Whether as a requirement of the 1998 Agreement or not, this is considered by some to be the most appropriate way of recognizing the values embedded in the 1998 Agreement.[20] If even greater autonomy were given to the region in a unified Ireland, this would cease to look like devolution and would become a federal, or even a confederal model. Such a possibility merits consideration in more detail than we can provide here.[21] In the next section, we explore the implementation of devolution and consociationalism in a united Ireland broadly similar to the current arrangements under the 1998 Agreement.

## CONSTITUTIONAL CHANGES NECESSARY TO ACCOMMODATE DEVOLUTION AND CONSOCIATIONALISM

### Devolved Legislative and Executive Powers

The current Irish state is unitary, highly centralised, and executive-dominated.[22] Local government is weak, both as a matter of constitutional principle and in practice.[23] There is no tradition of, or experience with, regional government.

---

[20] Richard Humphreys, *Beyond the Border* (Dublin: Merrion Press, 2018), p. 117, argues that this is a requirement. Others see it as a prudential judgment to be made, as aspects of the agreement may be difficult to resile from, e.g. Sylvia de Mars, Colin Murray, AoifeO'Donoghue and Ben Warwick, *Bordering Two Unions: Northern Ireland and Brexit* (Bristol: Policy Press, 2018), p. 88.

[21] See Brendan O'Leary, 'The Choices on the Future Menu', IACL-IADC Blog, 25 February 2020, https://blog-iacl-aidc.org/irish-unification/2020/2/25/the-choices-on-the-future-menu.

[22] See John Coakley and Michael Gallagher (eds.), *Politics in the Republic of Ireland* (London: Routledge, 6th edn., 2018). See also David Kenny and Conor Casey, 'The Resilience of Executive Dominance in Westminster Systems: Ireland 2016–2019' (2021) *Public Law* (forthcoming).

[23] Art. 28A provides constitutional recognition for local government, but the Oireachtas has granted only limited powers.

Existing constitutional provisions might allow the integration of some devolved institutions, but probably not the continuation of the devolved institutions that currently exist in Northern Ireland. Article 15.2 of the Irish Constitution vests the legislative power exclusively in the Oireachtas, while allowing the Oireachtas to create or recognise subordinate legislatures, as well as specifying their powers and functions. A unified Ireland could, therefore, accommodate a devolved legislature in Belfast, but the extent of the powers that could be granted to that legislature is unclear.[24]

The possibility of subordinate legislatures is a limited qualification to the emphatic statement that the Oireachtas holds sole and exclusive legislative authority. Without invoking this provision, the courts have allowed the delegation of law-making power to other entities, such as government ministers, subject to limits that might not fully apply in constitutionally authorised 'subordinate legislatures'.[25] But 'subordinate' implies limitations on any devolved legislature in Belfast that are probably broadly equivalent to those that currently pertain in the United Kingdom, considered above. The Oireachtas could not alienate power *permanently* to a devolved legislature; in other words, the Oireachtas could always revoke devolution or alter its scope in the future; and the Oireachtas could – if it wished – legislate in respect of a matter on which competence had been devolved to the subordinate legislature.

It is also unclear whether executive powers could be devolved at all. Article 6 provides that the powers of government, including the executive power, shall be exercisable only by or on the authority of the organs of state established by the constitution. There is no provision – parallel to that in Art 15.2 – allowing the creation or recognition of a subordinate executive, still less to provide for its powers or functions. Moreover, the courts have held, in the context of foreign affairs, that the government cannot delegate its own executive power.[26] The courts have recognised, in the immigration context, the power of the Oireachtas to legislate in a way that removes an aspect of the executive power and assigns it to an administrative agency.[27] But it would be a step further to create a *separate* executive to execute the laws of a *different* legislature. It could be argued that the authorisation of devolved legislatures implies the

---

[24] Gerard Hogan, Gerry Whyte, David Kenny and Rachael Walsh, *Kelly: the Irish Constitution* (Dublin: Bloomsbury, 5th edn., 2018), para. 4.2.94.

[25] Ibid., para. 4.2.09–93. Moreover, this jurisprudence is not particularly strict in terms of its judicial application, and some have called for the test to be reformulated. See ibid., para. 4.2.50–1.

[26] *Crotty v. An Taoiseach* [1987] IR 713.

[27] *Laurentiu v. Minister for Justice* [1994] 4 IR 26.

permissibility of a devolved executive, but this is highly contestable, given the constitutional silence on the issue and the general insistence that the executive power be exercised only by the government created by the constitution. Article 3 allows for the establishment of north-south bodies with executive powers and functions, but this appears limited to the pre-unification institutions envisaged by Strand Two of the 1998 Agreement.

Even if executive power could be devolved, the financial competences of devolved institutions in Belfast would remain limited; the Irish Constitution provides for a budgetary system for taxation and expenditure.[28] These lie entirely in the bailiwick of the government and the Dáil and could not be devolved to any subordinate legislatures and executive that might be created.[29] The Northern Ireland institutions could probably hold the same limited financial competence as is currently the case, but the devolution of any wider financial competence would likely be unconstitutional. More generally, the state would remain bound by the Treaty on Stability, Coordination and Governance in the Economic and Monetary Union (the Fiscal Compact Treaty), effected in Irish law by the Fiscal Responsibility Act 2012. The obligations of debt and deficit control under this treaty would likely reduce the national government's willingness to concede greater financial autonomy to Northern Ireland than the UK government currently has.[30]

In short, while there are possible constitutional bases for the continuation of Northern Ireland's devolved institutions in the event of unification, such an approach is fraught with constitutional risk; even on the most permissive of interpretations, the devolution of some further competences is likely to be stymied.

### Consociationalism

The consociational arrangements required by the 1998 Agreement for Northern Ireland's devolved institutions could not – without constitutional change – be replicated at the national level in a united Ireland. The constitution provides that all questions in each House of the Oireachtas must be determined by a majority vote.[31] This requirement for majority voting might, by implication,

---

[28] Arts. 11, 17, 21 and 22.
[29] See Hogan et al., *Kelly*, paras. 3.4.27–50, 4.5.08–17.
[30] There are constitutional issues around the economics of unification that need to be considered, from institutional divergence between the economies of the south and north that would need to be bridged (intensified by Ireland's Eurozone membership) to broader questions about the economic constitution of a united Ireland. These must await another occasion.
[31] Art. 15.11.

extend to subordinate legislatures also, given that they exercise – albeit in a delegated manner – the same legislative power as the Oireachtas.

The problems with the constitutionality of a devolved executive, discussed above, are exacerbated in the context of a consociational/power-sharing executive. There being no equivalent to this in the Irish constitutional order, it is not clear whether it is permissible to divide executive power or compose an executive in this way, as the constitution offers no guide as to how executive power can be delegated to regional executives. If a devolved executive in Northern Ireland is conceived not as a delegate of delegated executive power, but rather as an assignee of powers removed from the national government by the Oireachtas, then this might quell constitutional objections.

More broadly, consociationalism as practised in Northern Ireland requires cross-community representation in various aspects of governance, notably in Northern Ireland policing and to some extent the staffing of the civil service. Even if consociational requirements in these contexts were seen as prima facie unequal, the risk of judicial invalidation is low. The constitution guarantees equality before the law, but allows for due regard to differences of capacity, physical and moral, and of social function.[32] Moreover, the courts have – to say the least – enforced the equality guarantee in a highly deferential manner.[33]

### Constitutional Amendments Required to Allow for Devolution and Consociationalism

There are, therefore, significant constitutional doubts as to whether the current devolution and consociational aspects of Northern Ireland governance could continue in a united Ireland without constitutional amendment. It would be prudent, if it were desired to continue these institutional arrangements, to provide a complete constitutional basis rather than simply attempt to plug the constitutional gaps identified above. The following issues would need to be addressed:

- The establishment of devolved legislatures and executives, with some indication as to their range of competences;
- The establishment of new financial arrangements that provide devolved institutions with financial competence while ensuring that Ireland continues to meet its obligations under the Fiscal Compact Treaty;

---

[32] Art. 40.1.
[33] See Hogan et al., *Kelly*, paras. 7.2.01–157.

- The authorisation of consociational features for the devolved institutions, including parallel consent, weighted majority voting, petitions of concern, and executive formation;
- The authorisation of consociational features in other domains, such as policing.

The basic design choice is whether to empower the Oireachtas to create the relevant institutions or to establish those institutions in the constitution itself. If the former, the Oireachtas would retain a relationship of superiority over the devolved institutions similar to that currently enjoyed by Westminster – arguably greater if Strand One of the 1998 Agreement is superseded by unification, since then there would be no obligation in international law to preserve the devolved institutions in Northern Ireland. If the latter, the issues regulated in the constitution could only be changed by further constitutional amendment, thereby rendering devolution more rigid, and enhancing the power of the Irish Supreme Court as interpreter of these provisions. In either scenario, there would be continuing issues about the day-to-day management of relations between the national parliament and government and the devolved institutions in Belfast, to which we now turn.

## THE POLITICAL CHALLENGES OF MANAGING DEVOLUTION AND CONSOCIATIONALISM

Devolution within the United Kingdom contributes to constitutional tension in two respects, each of which could be replicated in a united Ireland if devolution in Northern Ireland were to continue. First, the devolution of powers to Scotland, Wales, and Northern Ireland is – as a matter of UK law – subject to being overridden by the Westminster Parliament, simply by repealing the devolution statutes. Of greater practical importance is the way in which Westminster can adjust the practice of devolution, whether by altering the scope of competences devolved or by choosing to legislate in respect of a particular issue notwithstanding that competence has been devolved. Constitutional conventions and understandings have developed that regulate the relationship between Westminster and the devolved assemblies. In particular, the so-called Sewel Convention provides that Westminster will not normally legislate in devolved areas without the consent of the devolved assembly. But these operate in the political rather than the legal domain, and thus remain legally unenforceable, even though incorporated into Scottish and Welsh devolution statutes.³⁴ Brexit has strained the Sewel Convention to breaking point, with the UK Parliament overriding decisions of the Scottish Parliament, Welsh Assembly (now Parliament), and the Northern Ireland Assembly refusing consent to legislation at Westminster and thus affecting the operation of devolved powers.³⁵

If the Irish Constitution were amended to provide a clear legal power for the Dublin Parliament to create devolved institutions in Belfast broadly similar to those that currently operate, devolution would be subject to the same constitutional insecurities as devolution in the United Kingdom. Constitutional conventions have not been entirely successful at mediating these conflicts in the United Kingdom, but would hold even less purchase in an Irish state, where there is no tradition of constitutional actors explicitly constraining their own actions with reference to conventions. These insecurities might undermine one of the core reasons for continuing devolution in the first place: to assuage the concerns of those from the Ulster Scots and Ulster British traditions.

Specifying the devolution of competences in the constitution itself might provide reassurance to voters in the north, but it would reduce the flexibility of the devolution settlement. A constitutional amendment would therefore be required for any change to the terms of devolution. This is not a far-fetched scenario: devolution and power sharing are highly complex, and their implementation in a united Ireland would bring new and unexpected challenges. Given that amendments were made to the functioning of the 1998 Agreement institutions in the St Andrews Agreement within a decade of its signing, it is entirely possible that significant changes might also be required in a united Ireland. Constitutional entrenchment, particularly assuming the continuation of a referendum requirement for amendment, could impede swift and necessary reform. Moreover, the Stormont institutions have been suspended on a number of occasions when consociational governing arrangements have broken down. In such cases, it was a relatively straightforward matter – under the UK constitutional system – for the UK government to step in to secure continuity. This would not be possible for an Irish government in Dublin if the terms of devolution were entrenched in the constitution. Of course, provision could be made to allow for Dublin to suspend devolution in certain circumstances, but the very existence of such a unilateral power could

---

³⁴ *R (Miller)* v. *Secretary of State for Exiting the European Union* [2017] UKSC 5.
³⁵ See Elisenda Casanas Adam, 'Brexit and the Mechanisms for the Resolution of Conflicts in the Context of Devolution: Do We Need a New Model?' in the current volume.

recreate the distrust that the continuation of devolution and its protection in the constitution were supposed to address.

The second constitutional tension within UK devolution is the response to the so-called 'West Lothian' question. In the absence of devolution for England, why should MPs from Scotland, Wales, and Northern Ireland be permitted to vote on specifically English issues, while English MPs may not vote on those issues devolved to Scotland, Wales, and Northern Ireland? The current 'solution' to this problem is known as 'English Votes for English Laws' (EVEL), whereby MPs from the devolved nations and regions have agreed not to participate in some votes on English issues. A new stage is added to the usual law-making process at Westminster allowing MPs for English constituencies to vote on issues that only affect England.[36] These English MPs are able to veto the legislation before it comes before all MPs in the final stage.[37] EVEL is potentially a source of constitutional instability at Westminster, as the UK government must maintain a dual legislative majority if it is to govern effectively: one for the United Kingdom and one for England. The risk of constitutional instability is reduced, however, by English MPs making up 82 per cent of the membership of the House of Commons, and by the UK electoral system providing a significant seat-bonus to the winning party.[38]

The risk of constitutional instability associated with this question would be far higher in a united Ireland, given the higher proportion of northern TDs in the national parliament (30 per cent) and the PR-STV electoral system. It is readily conceivable that an Irish government in a unified state could be elected with the support of Northern TDs but lack a majority among TDs from the south. This could be problematic if the Oireachtas were to enact laws for the south that were opposed by a majority of TDs from the south. Political controversy would surely arise if northern TDs supported less generous public spending arrangements for the south than those which their parties supported for the north, whether through the devolved institutions or financial negotiations with the national government.

The United Kingdom's EVEL 'solution' would be more difficult to implement in a united Ireland, for the same reasons as make the West Lothian question itself a greater source of instability. With each passing election, the

---

[36] Introduced by changes to the House of Commons' Standing Orders on 22 October 2015.
[37] For a detailed explanation of the procedure, see 'English votes for English laws: House of Commons bill procedure', UK Parliament, www.parliament.uk/about/how/laws/bills/public/english-votes-for-english-laws/.
[38] Daniel Gover and Michael Kenny, Answering the West Lothian Question? A Critical Assessment of 'English Votes for English Laws' in the UK Parliament, *Parliamentary Affairs*, 71:4 2018, 760–82.

PR-STV electoral system produces an increasingly fragmented party system in the south, making government formation more difficult. With 30 per cent of TDs drawn from Northern Ireland, it would be even more challenging to form a government with a legislative majority both for the state as a whole and for the south. While it is difficult to predict how an electoral system in a united Ireland would play out in practice, the implementation of an EVEL-variant in a united Ireland would likely be problematic.

Consociationalism within the devolved northern institutions, in contrast, poses few direct challenges to day-to-day relationships with the institutions of the broader, unified state. Indeed, a consociational executive in Belfast might be better placed to manage good relations with the Dublin government, since the devolved administration in Belfast could not be dominated by parties opposed to the government in Dublin. The continuation of consociationalism in the Police Service of Northern Ireland (PSNI) would, however, imply the continuation of two discrete police services. The relationships between these services would need to be clarified.

## CONSTITUTIONAL ACCOMMODATION OF ULSTER-SCOTS AND ULSTER-BRITISH IDENTITY

### Overview

A crucial aspect of any constitutional settlement in a united Ireland is how it would accommodate and provide for the identity of those from the Ulster Scots and Ulster British traditions.[39] This is not only highly desirable to enable people from those traditions to feel sympathy for the new state; it is also essential to honour the commitments in the 1998 Agreement,[40] where there are several seemingly enduring commitments to respect the identities of groups in Northern Ireland. Whatever choice is made by the people of Northern Ireland, the 1998 Agreement states:

> the power of the sovereign government with jurisdiction there shall be exercised with rigorous impartiality on behalf of all the people in the diversity of their identities and traditions and shall be founded on the principles of . . .

---

[39] For a more detailed account, see David Kenny, 'The Irish Constitution, a United Ireland, and the Ship of Theseus: Radical Constitutional Change as Constitutional Replacement' SSRN, 30 April 2019, https://papers.ssrn.com/sol3/papers.cfm?abstract_id=3399054.

[40] Brice Dickson, 'Unionist fears in a United Ireland' IACL-IADC Blog, 27 February 2020, https://blog-iacl-aidc.org/irish-unification/2020/2/27/unionist-fears-in-a-united-ireland.

parity of esteem and of just and equal treatment for the identity, ethos, and aspirations of both communities.[41]

The parties further 'recognise the birthright of all the people of Northern Ireland to identify themselves and be accepted as Irish or British, or both, as they may so choose'.[42] These commitments explicitly apply in a united Ireland. Respecting them requires the accommodation of the identity and ethos of those from the Ulster Scots and Ulster British traditions, and this should be reflected at the constitutional level, where the most fundamental commitments to values are enumerated.

In this section, we explore several provisions of the current constitution that might be thought to exclude those from the Ulster Scots and Ulster British traditions. Many of these provisions, however, manifest and reflect indicia of Irish identity dearly held by many, if not most, citizens of the current Irish state. Simply amending provisions to reduce the alienation of new citizens might also reduce the sympathy of existing citizens for the unified state. Indeed, it might amount to a converse breach of the sovereign government's obligation to respect the identity and tradition of northern nationalists. What would be required – we suggest – is an inclusive process directed to the agreement of a more accommodating account of Irish identity. We confine ourselves here to identifying what may be the most problematic provisions from the perspective of those from an Ulster Scots and Ulster British tradition, along with possible responses.

### Symbols

Symbolic accommodation of these traditions in the Irish Constitution would have two elements: what should be removed, and what should be added. Parts of the Preamble to the Irish Constitution are not only religiously sectarian (reflecting Catholic political theology) but also politically sectarian (reflecting Irish nationalist tropes).[43] Those from non-Catholic or non-nationalist traditions may consider themselves excluded from the Preamble's 'We, the people … '.[44] A new Preamble, based perhaps on values in the 1998 Agreement, and specifically acknowledging the Ulster Scots and Ulster British traditions, would be needed.

---

[41] Belfast/Good Friday Agreement, Constitutional Issues, para. 1(v).
[42] Belfast/Good Friday Agreement, Constitutional Issues, para. 1(vi).
[43] It speaks of 'our fathers' enduring 'centuries of trial' in a 'heroic and unremitting struggle' to obtain independence.
[44] Oran Doyle, *The Irish Constitution: A Contextual Analysis* (Oxford: Hart, 2018), p. 14.

Article 2 of the constitution outlines the concept of an 'Irish nation', one which 'cherishes its special affinity with people of Irish ancestry living abroad *who share its cultural identity and heritage*' (emphasis added). This could be redrafted in order to acknowledge that a new national identity centrally includes the Ulster Scots and Ulster British traditions. Article 7 dictates that the national flag be the tricolour of green, white and orange, a flag with long and controversial associations with the conflict in Northern Ireland.[45] If a unified Ireland is to have a flag with which all citizens can identify, including those from the Ulster Scots and Ulster British traditions, Art 7 would require amendment.

Perhaps the most challenging accommodation of the Ulster Scots and Ulster British traditions would be acknowledgement or recognition of the British monarch. Various commentators have suggested that a united Ireland could rejoin the Commonwealth of Nations, of which it was a member until 1949,[46] and the constitution was clearly drafted to permit Commonwealth membership.[47] For as long as the British monarch remains Head of the Commonwealth, Irish membership would imply some recognition of that monarch, notwithstanding Ireland's status as a republic. Indeed, the majority of Commonwealth countries at present are republics.

Beyond this, the British monarch could be acknowledged in the Irish Constitution in some more specific form. Any such option would require constitutional changes. The British monarch could, for example, be recognised as a joint head of state alongside the Irish President. Such a constitutional amendment would likely precipitate repeal of the Republic of Ireland Act 1948 – a state could scarcely describe itself as a republic if its head of state is a monarch. More modestly, the British monarch could be recognised as an important figurehead for a substantial portion of the population, affording constitutional recognition without any formal legal powers.

## Languages and Terminology

The Irish language has been a flashpoint between the communities in Northern Ireland in recent years.[48] The Irish Constitution provides that Irish

---

[45] The orange in the Irish tricolour was intended as a gesture of inclusion towards the Protestant community, but this gesture has not ingratiated the flag to that community in Northern Ireland.
[46] See for one of many examples, Hugh O'Connell, 'FF TD: United Ireland could celebrate The Twelfth and rejoin Commonwealth' *Irish Independent*, 18 December 2019.
[47] See Art. 29.4.2; Hogan et al., *Kelly*, paras. 5.3.34–7.
[48] See generally, Daithí Mac Síthigh, 'Official status of languages in the UK and Ireland' (2018) 47:1 *Common Law World Review* 77–102, p. 77.

is the national and 'first official' language of the state, with English given the status of second official language.[49] Moreover, most of the institutions of the state are given their Irish titles even in the English text of the constitution.[50] There might need to be some changes in this respect, using English names for these offices; making the two languages joint and equal first languages; and/or some guarantee of not having to use the language in any official context for non-Irish speakers.

## Citizenship

Allowing those from the Ulster Scots and Ulster British traditions to maintain their identity through retaining British citizenship is a crucial guarantee of the 1998 Agreement. The two states confirmed that those born in Northern Ireland had the 'right to hold both British and Irish citizenship' and that this would 'not be affected by any future change in the status of Northern Ireland'.[51] No Irish constitutional settlement could guarantee British citizenship to people in Northern Ireland; this would have to be done by the British state. However, if this were done, the Irish Constitution would have to ensure there were no barriers to its residents maintaining such citizenship. Moreover, full rights of political participation,[52] and other rights, should be given to those who wished to accept *only* British citizenship, and not legally become citizens of a united Ireland. This would respect the duty in the 1998 Agreement to allow people in Northern Ireland to identify as British or Irish or both. Recent litigation has highlighted that this is a problem the British government did not fully address after the 1998 Agreement.[53] After Brexit, the problem is even more stark as Irish citizens will enjoy EU citizenship and British citizens will not.[54] There are no obvious or easy solutions to these quandaries.

---

[49] Art. 8. The Irish text is the authoritative version of the constitution in case of conflict; see Hogan et al., *Kelly*, para. 1.1.16; Mark de Blacam, 'Official Language and Constitutional Interpretation' (2014) 52:2 *Irish Jurist* 90–114, p. 90.
[50] See Doyle, *Contextual Analysis*, p. 15. The Oireachtas, Dáil, Seanad, and Taoiseach are called by their Irish titles within the English text of the constitution, though their English translations are provided. Art. 4 says the state's name is 'Éire, or, in the English language, Ireland'.
[51] Belfast/Good Friday Agreement, Constitutional Issues, para. 1(vi).
[52] At present British citizens may vote in Dáil elections but not, unless they are also Irish citizens, at presidential elections or referendums. Only Irish citizens may be elected as President, TDs, or senators.
[53] See *Secretary of State for the Home Department v. Parker De Souza* [2019] UKUT 355. For analysis, see Colin Murray, 'The Constitutional Significance of the People of Northern Ireland' in this volume.
[54] See de Mars et al., *Bordering Two Unions*, pp. 60–5.

## PROTECTION OF POLITICAL ACCOMMODATIONS

The purpose of this chapter has been to explore how a united Ireland might be constitutionally designed in a way that strengthens centripetal forces in respect of those from the Ulster Scots and Ulster British traditions. We have considered constitutional amendments that would clarify the constitutional status of devolved institutions in Northern Ireland, organised on a consociational basis. Such measures would minimise the amount of change experienced at the moment of unification and might provide reassurance that those from the Ulster Scots and Ulster British traditions would have the power to protect their interests in the new state, thereby reducing alienation from that state. We have also explored constitutional provisions that would require change to recognise multiple identities or construct a more expansive notion of Irish identity. Underlying this analysis – and indeed all discussion of unification – is a move to legal constitutionalism, in contradistinction to the political constitutionalism that currently predominates in the United Kingdom. This distinction can sometimes be overstated; all legal systems in truth show a mix of legal and political constitutionalism.[55] Nevertheless, unification in any form would involve a constitutional culture shock for Northern Ireland. The terms of unification will be expressed legally rather than primarily through political practice, and given their final authoritative interpretation by judges rather than by politicians.

If the measures considered in this chapter were to reassure those from the Ulster Scots and Ulster British traditions, we must also consider safeguards about how such measures would be interpreted and amended. As noted above, the Irish Constitution is ultimately interpreted by the Irish Supreme Court. Some concerns could arise – particularly but not only for those from an Ulster Scots or Ulster British background – that the unification terms might be interpreted by judges trained in only one particular legal system. The composition of the courts raises issues that go beyond this chapter, including the protection of fundamental rights and the more quotidian challenges associated with merging two legal systems. The membership of the Supreme Court would, at the very least, have to expand to include members of the Northern Ireland judiciary to provide expertise on the law of Northern Ireland. This would not be *guaranteed* within the framework of the existing Irish Constitution, which currently gives sole discretion on the selection of judges to the government. Appointments might, perhaps, be dealt with informally as

---

[55] Aileen Kavanagh, 'Recasting the Political Constitution: From Rivals to Relationships' (2019) 39 *King's Law Journal* 43–73, p. 46.

a convention, but we have noted the relative weakness of constitutional conventions in the Irish system.[56] Should a more far-reaching change be adopted? For example, should the constitutional unification terms, implicitly endorsed in two separate referendums in previously separated jurisdictions, be interpreted by a special court composed of equal numbers from each jurisdiction, with an independent chair? These questions all warrant more detailed consideration.

The possibility of later constitutional amendment, as opposed to interpretation, raises different concerns. Any reassurance provided by the political accommodations explored in the previous sections would be weakened if they could be undone using the current constitutional amendment procedure – a majority vote in both houses of the Dublin Parliament, followed by a simple majority in a referendum. As we noted in the Introduction, there are two broad models of unification referendums: settling the terms of unification either before or after the referendums. If the constitutional configuration of a united Ireland were unknown before the unification referendums, then the problem of subsequent amendment is not so acute: voters in Northern Ireland would have given their consent to unification without knowing the terms and therefore could expect no special role in protecting those terms. In contrast, however, if the constitutional terms of unification were settled before the unification referendums, then voters in the north might approve unification on a certain basis and find themselves in a unified state wherein those terms could be reversed by simple majorities in parliament and at referendum. Such a risk might not materialise, but the very possibility could be destabilising.

At present, the Irish Constitution, unlike many others, imposes no substantive restrictions on the power of constitutional amendment. We see three broad possibilities for protecting the constitutional terms of unification by limiting amendability.[57] The most extreme approach would be eternal entrenchment of the terms of the unification settlement. But eternal and absolute entrenchment is problematic: subsequent generations should seldom be absolutely bound by the choices of the current generation, and certainly not in relation to detailed arrangements for government, as distinct from universal values.[58] A second approach would be to make the unification provisions

---

[56] Such a system operates in Canada with respect to representation on the Supreme Court. In the early years of the Irish state, a convention operated in respect of the appointment of Protestant judges to the Supreme Court.

[57] This speaks only to amendment. Constitutional replacement could legally circumvent any limitations on amendment. However, the conditions for amendment are likely to influence the perceived political legitimacy of any proposal for constitutional replacement.

[58] See German Constitution, Art. 1 (on human dignity).

subject to a heightened or double-majority requirement. While it is difficult to identify what level of heightened majority requirement should apply, a dual-majority requirement that mirrored the unification referendums themselves might be attractive. Such an approach would cohere with the constitutional entrenchment of devolution for Northern Ireland, but might seem out of place if devolution did not continue. Over time, however, it might be perceived as incongruous for 15 per cent of the population to retain a veto on certain constitutional changes.

A third approach would be to deploy what Albert terms a safe harbour clause.[59] This would protect the unification terms from amendment for a period of time, thereafter opening them up to constitutional amendment in the usual way. This would amount to a quasi-transition period: the unification terms would be guaranteed for, say, ten years but would not necessarily be replaced after that time. In particular, if devolution and consociationalism were to continue in a united Ireland, this would provide a means of testing different solutions to the West Lothian question before any decision could be made to discontinue devolution. This would provide an element of certainty for a period after unification, but it would not bind the state indefinitely to structures that proved difficult to operate in practice. Finally, one could combine the last two approaches, so that the unification terms are protected for a specified period unless a double-majority, north and south, votes in a referendum to amend them.

Might the prospect of amendment after the 'safe harbour' period be problematic for those from the Ulster Scots and Ulster British traditions? Potentially, but it is important not to overstate how easy it is to amend the Irish Constitution currently. The people have repeatedly rejected amendments that would have removed constraints on the government or dominant political parties; and no amendment has ever been approved that was opposed by the main opposition party.[60] Those from the Ulster Scots and Ulster British traditions may, therefore, have relatively little to fear from the capacity of nationalist parties to build a consensus in favour of amending the constitution to alter the unification terms.

We have seen that the Irish government is, under the existing arrangements, a political co-guarantor of the 1998 Agreement. What role, if any, should the British government play vis-à-vis those from the Ulster Scots and Ulster British traditions in a united Ireland? In particular, should it play an equivalent role

---

[59] Richard Albert, 'The Structure of Constitutional Amendment Rules' (2014) 49 *Wake Forest Law Review* 913–75, pp. 952–4.

[60] See Doyle, *Contextual Analysis*, chap. 10.

regarding those communities to that currently played by the Irish government in informally reflecting the views of, and seeking to protect, the ethno-religious minority in the north? It is not uncommon in comparative constitutional practice to have arrangements where a state with close ties of kinship with a minority in another state has a role as an external guarantor for that minority.[61] We consider that such a role might well be appropriate, not least as a potentially important confidence-building measure for those from the Ulster Scots and Ulster British traditions, although we do not underestimate the political tensions to which such an arrangement might give rise. Provided such a role were exercised through the existing 1998 Agreement institutions, authorised by the Constitution,[62] no constitutional amendment would be required.

## CONCLUSION

In this chapter, we have identified ways in which centripetal forces could be encouraged in a united Ireland, with a particular focus on the likely concerns of those from Ulster Scots and Ulster British traditions. As we have seen, the continuation of devolution and consociationalism could have a centripetal effect in terms of sympathy while – for the very same reason – unleashing centrifugal forces if a divergence of interests between the north and the rest of the state becomes embedded. In addition, the practical problems it poses for national government might cost so much in terms of state capacity that it offsets the gain of greater sympathy for the state from those of Ulster Scots and Ulster British traditions. When we turned to the identitarian aspects of unification, we saw how core indicia of current Irish constitutional identity could tend to alienate those from Ulster Scots and Ulster British traditions. It is imperative to reconsider these constitutional provisions, not least because of the enduring obligations in the 1998 Agreement. But this must be done in a sensitive way if it is not to alienate existing citizens from any unified Ireland. Balancing these centripetal and centrifugal forces is a complex and multifaceted task, but not an impossible one. The main risk, we suggest, is that insufficient time is given to consider these questions. One consequence of the radically different assessments of the likelihood of a united Ireland is that some of its advocates press on enthusiastically, talking largely to themselves, while

---

[61] Discussed in Venice Commission, Report on the Preferential Treatment of National Minorities by Their Kin-State, adopted October 19–20 2001, https://www.venice.coe.int/web forms/documents/?pdf=CDL-INF(2001)019-e.
[62] Art. 29.7.

those opposed or indifferent to unification opt out of the discussion. This latter course is, in our view, unwise. Recent years have shown how quickly politics can change in both the United Kingdom and Ireland. Time is required to tease out the constitutional compromises that could underpin the success of a united Ireland, should the people of Ireland – north and south – ultimately so choose. The analysis in this chapter will, we hope, inform that debate.

# 7

# The Minority Rights Implications of Irish Unification

James Rooney

INTRODUCTION

Following the vote of the majority of the British (but not Northern Irish) electorate to exit the European Union, the prospect of Irish unification is being considered with increasing urgency. The sense that a border poll could come sooner than previously anticipated has been increased by the unexpected boost in support for Sinn Féin in the 2020 Irish general election. For the first time since the foundation of the state, neither Fianna Fáil nor Fine Gael won the most votes in a national poll. Whilst the election was largely fought on social issues such as housing and healthcare, the success of a party whose dominant political objective is the ending of partition makes considering how unification may occur even more pertinent.[1]

This chapter considers the effect unification may have on minority rights protection. As Doyle has noted, since independence, Ireland has established 'a stable democratic system of government that respects minority rights and personal freedoms'.[2] On current rankings, Ireland is the sixth most democratic country in the world according to the EUI's Democracy Index,[3] the seventh freest country in regards to civil or political rights according to Freedom

---

[1] This point is made while aware that calling a border poll is a decision for the Secretary of State for Northern Ireland and thus need not be directly affected by the composition of the Government of Ireland. See Colin Murray, 'The Constitutional Significance of the People of Northern Ireland' in this volume.

[2] Oran Doyle, *The Constitution of Ireland: A Contextual Analysis* (Oxford: Hart, 2018), p. 2. For the avoidance of doubt, 'Ireland' will here be used to refer to the twenty-six counties of the island of Ireland currently governed by the Constitution of Ireland.

[3] 'Democracy Index 2019', Economist Intelligence Unit, www.eiu.com/public/topical_report.aspx?campaignid=democracyindex2019.

House,[4] and according to Reporters Without Borders Ireland has the thirteenth freest press in the world.[5]

It has recently been suggested that the successful emergence of a democratic rights-protecting culture in Ireland may be attributable in part to the relative cultural and demographic homogeneity of the Irish state.[6] With unification, a large and politically significant minority – the Ulster Scots/Ulster British population of Northern Ireland – will be incorporated into the Irish constitutional order.[7] If Ireland's high international rankings for civil and minority rights protection *is* partially due to its general homogeneity, then unification – the creation of a pluri-national state order governing both the Irish and Ulster Scots/Ulster British peoples of the island – would change this characteristic.

In Ireland, the judiciary are responsible for ensuring that the fundamental rights in the Constitution of Ireland (also known as 'Bunreacht na hÉireann) are protected.[8] So far, the judiciary have not developed an understanding that their constitutional function includes a particular role in ensuring the rights of minority groups are protected against attack. That is, while racial, religious, and sexual minorities, and people with disabilities, have challenged discrimination and social exclusion within the Irish courts since independence, in adjudicating these disputes, the court has not factored into its reasoning the minority status of these groups. Nor has the Irish judiciary understood their function as including a role for supporting the interests of underrepresented minority groups who are obstructed by their minority status from participating in the democratic decision-making process.[9]

The judiciary in a united Ireland may respond to minority rights claims brought by members of the Ulster Scots/Ulster British population in one of two ways. The court may respond with the same lack of regard for their

---

[4] 'Global Freedom Scores 2020', Freedom House, https://freedomhouse.org/countries/freedom-world/scores.

[5] 'World Press Freedom Index 2020', Reporters Without Borders, https://rsf.org/en/ranking_table.

[6] See Oran Doyle and Rachael Walsh, 'Deliberative mini-publics as a response to populist backsliding', in Maria Cahill, Colm O'Cinneide, Seán Ó Conaill, and Conor O'Mahony (eds.), *Constitutional Change and Popular Sovereignty: Populism, Politics, and the Law in Ireland* (Abingdon on Thames: Routledge, *forthcoming*).

[7] Consistent with the contribution to this volume by Oran Doyle, David Kenny, and Christopher McCrudden, I use the term 'Ulster Scots/Ulster British' per the *New Decade, New Approach* document that re-established devolution in January 2020. Oran Doyle, David Kenny, and Christopher McCrudden, 'The Constitutional Politics of a United Ireland'.

[8] Arts. 34.3, 34.4, and 34.5 of the Constitution of Ireland 1937.

[9] John Hart Ely, *Democracy and Distrust: A Theory of Judicial Review* (Cambridge: Harvard University Press, 1980).

membership of a minority group as the Irish courts have with other groups in the past. Alternatively, a 'minority rights protecting' conception of the judicial role may emerge in response to engagement with the rights interests of this particular minority. If the latter eventuality were to occur, it could potentially increase the chances of protecting the interests of minority groups more generally through the judicial process.

This latter possibility is supported by comparative experience. In this chapter I examine the minority rights reasoning of Canada and the United States, two common law jurisdictions which also have judicially enforceable bills of rights. A minority rights protecting conception of the judicial role developed in those jurisdictions in cases where the judiciary engaged with the rights claims of minority groups whose relationship to the majority population was the site of intense and enduring political controversy.[10] Reflecting on their jurisprudence, a similar shift in judicial attitude to minority rights could occur in Ireland upon the incorporation of the Ulster Scots/Ulster British minority into a unified legal system.

As the contribution of Doyle et al. in this volume notes, considering how Irish unification might take place or what a unified Ireland might look like is a dauntingly complex exercise.[11] In this chapter, save for in the final section, I make only three assumptions about unification, all of which I consider to be uncontroversial. By limiting the variables in this way, I hope my analysis will retain relevance in a broad spectrum of unification scenarios.

First, I assume the unified constitutional order includes judicial rights review, at minimum approximating that currently provided under Bunreacht na hÉireann.[12] In uniting Ireland, either Ireland would adopt the political constitutionalist model of Northern Ireland, or Northern Ireland the legal constitutionalist model of Ireland. The latter seems more likely, given both the contemporary dominance of legal constitutionalism in the common

---

[10] Sujit Choudhry, 'Does the world need more Canada? The politics of the Canadian model in constitutional politics and theory', in Sujit Choudhry (ed.), *Constitutional Design for Divided Societies: Integration or Accommodation* (Oxford: Oxford University Press, 2008), p. 141. Michael Klarman, *From Jim Crow to Civil Rights: The Supreme Court and the Struggle for Racial Equality* (Oxford: Oxford University Press, 2004); Michael J. Perry, *We the People: The Fourteenth Amendment and the Supreme Court* (Oxford: Oxford University Press, 1999).

[11] See also Richard Humphreys, *Beyond the Border: The Good Friday Agreement and Irish Unity after Brexit* (Dublin: Merrion Press, 2018).

[12] While there may well also be a bill of rights for the devolved region corresponding to Northern Ireland, I am assuming here that at the legal apex there will be a bill of rights in an Irish constitution, whose rights provisions will be authoritatively interpreted by the Supreme Court of the united Ireland.

law world,¹³ and because, as suggested in the previous chapter, Northern Ireland already places more emphasis on written constitutionalism in building state support than does the rest of the United Kingdom.¹⁴

Second, I assume the judiciary in the unified legal system would be constructed from members of the pre-existing Irish and Northern Irish legal communities, most likely from senior judges of both jurisdictions. Their understanding of what is judicially possible in the unified constitutional order would then be informed by their prior experiences of judging within these two jurisdictions. Given the population differences between Ireland and Northern Ireland, and the experience of strong-form judicial rights review amongst the Irish judiciary, I assume both more Irish than Northern Irish judges would be on the bench, and that the experience of rights adjudication under Bunreacht na hÉireann would be the primary influence upon the courts' rights reasoning.¹⁵

Third, were unification to occur, I assume at the time of unification there would still be a large population in Ulster whose Ulster Scots/Ulster British identity would be a socially salient distinction from the majority Irish population.¹⁶ If these three premises are accepted, it is highly likely that a bench of judges predominantly made up of Irish lawyers would end up adjudicating upon rights-based controversies between the Irish and Ulster Scots/Ulster British populations of the island. A minority rights protecting

---

13  See Ran Hirschl, *Towards Juristocracy: The Origins and Consequences of the New Constitutionalism* (Cambridge: Harvard University Press, 2004); Stephen Gardbaum, *The New Commonwealth Model of Constitutionalism: Theory and Practice* (Cambridge: Cambridge University Press, 2012).

14  As Doyle et al. noted, in contrast to the rest of the United Kingdom, 'given the absence of consent from a significant proportion of the population [of Northern Ireland] in the recent past, there have been attempts to construct consent in part on the basis of constitutional guarantees'. Doyle et al. 'Constitutional Politics'.

15  This assumption follows from the prevailing trend of constituting the bench of a new legal order from incumbent judges. In the last 100 years, there have been three transitions between legal systems in Ireland: from the British to Northern Irish legal system; from the British to Free State legal system; and from the Free State legal system to the legal system under Bunreacht na hÉireann. In all transitions save the British-Northern Irish transition, the judiciary of the incipient legal order has been predominantly populated by the senior judiciary of the prior legal order. For a study of the first Northern Irish judiciary see, Lord Carswell, 'Founding a legal system: the early judiciary of Northern Ireland', in Felix M. Larkin and N. M. Dawson (eds.), *Lawyers, the Law and History: Irish Legal History Society Discourses and other papers 2005 – 2011* (Dublin: Four Courts Press, 2013), p. 15; For commentary on the Free State judiciary see Anon. , 'The Judiciary' (1922) 56 *Irish Law Times Reports* 15–16.

16  This is presumed even noting comments by senior Unionist figures such as current First Minister Arlene Foster that she would leave the island were unification to occur. See Arlene Foster's comments to Patrick Kielty for his television programme, 'My Dad, the Peace Deal and Me,' BBC One, 4 April 2018.

role conception may emerge amongst the judiciary in response to such politically controversial adjudication; with potential knock-on effects for the court's treatment of rights claims by minority groups in Ireland more generally.

First, I examine minority rights protection under the Bunreacht na hÉireann. I show how the Irish court presently does not place any determinative weight on the fact that a rights claimant is a member of a minority group. I then explain why unification may cause the court's attitude towards minority rights adjudication to change. In the final section, I engage with the contribution of Doyle et al. in their chapter in this volume. I consider how maintaining consociationalism for what is presently Northern Ireland upon unification may also inform the judiciary's understanding of their role in adjudicating upon minority rights claims.

## MINORITY RIGHTS PROTECTION UNDER BUNREACHT NA HÉIREANN

In considering how a unified Supreme Court, predominantly populated by Irish judges, may deal with cases pertaining to the discrete interests of the Ulster Scots/Ulster British population, the closest analogue may be the Irish court's earlier engagement with rights claims made by the Protestant community. In two early cases, the Supreme Court considered issues that bore directly on the interests of the Protestant minority, but, informatively, the fact that these cases affected this community is not made clear on the surface of either judgment.

First, in the *School Attendance Bill case*, the Supreme Court considered the constitutionality of legislation that would create an offence where parents failed or neglected to cause their children to attend school without a prescribed excuse.[17] However as O'Rahilly noted, 'one of the purposes of the School Attendance Bill was to enable the Minister to prevent parents from sending their children to schools in England'.[18] In this objective, the bill directly affected the interests of the Anglo-Irish population, who were almost uniformly Protestants. This motivation for the bill is not mentioned anywhere in the court's judgment. Whilst the bill was ultimately declared unconstitutional, thereby securing the interests of the Anglo-Irish/Protestant population, that this context was not raised in the court's deliberations reflects a judiciary that was not factoring such minority considerations into its reasoning.

---

[17] Re Article 26 and the School Attendance Bill 1942 [1943] IR 334 at 339.
[18] Arthur O'Rahilly, *The Constitutional Position of Education in Ireland* (Cork: Cork University Press, 1952), p. 9.

The absence of a minority rights protecting dimension to the court's reasoning in the *School Attendance Bill case* may at first be attributed to the fact that this case was a pre-enactment review and so there were no directly affected parties in court. However, in *Tilson's case* the court maintained a similar silence as to the impact of the impugned law on the interests of Ireland's Protestant minority.[19] *Tilson's case* was an action by a Protestant father who sought to raise his children in his faith, contrary to the desires of his Catholic spouse, and the prenuptial agreement he signed affirming their children would be raised Catholic. The signing of the prenuptial agreement resulted from the papal Ne Temere decree requiring non-Catholics marrying Catholics to promise that any children born of the marriage would be raised in the Catholic faith.

In *Tilson's case*, the Supreme Court held both that the common law rule of paternal supremacy in determining a child's faith was unconstitutional, and that the prenuptial agreement between the spouses should be respected. Whilst on the one hand, this judgment was a victory for the principle of equality; in finding that the prenuptial agreement was binding, the Supreme Court also 'invaded one of the most sensitive areas of interdenominational relations in Ireland', without adverting to this context at all.[20]

As Ferriter has written, 'between 1946 and 1961, the Protestant population [of Ireland] fell almost five times faster than the overall population'.[21] By ensuring the children of mixed marriages were raised as Catholics, the Ne Temere decree played a significant role in the decline of Ireland's Protestant population. With *Tilson's case*, 'in a religiously homogeneous State where the Protestant population was relatively small and scattered, the indirect enforcement of the Ne Temere rule by the courts inevitably served to erode that minority population still further'.[22]

Whilst the effect of these judgments on the interests of the Protestant minority varied, a commonality between the two cases is that in neither was the minority status of the parties considered when assessing the constitutionality of the impugned law. In this early period, the Irish courts cleaved to a model of parliamentary supremacy similar to the British system that had

---

[19] *In re Tilson* [1950] IR 1.
[20] Gerard Hogan and Gerry Whyte, *Kelly: The Irish Constitution* (Dublin: Bloomsbury, 3rd edn., 1994), p. xci.
[21] Diarmuid Ferriter, *The Transformation of Ireland: 1900 – 2000* (London: Profile Books 2004), p. 582.
[22] Gerard Hogan, 'A Fresh Look at 'Tilson's' Case' (1998) 33 *Irish Jurist* 311–32, p. 311. Later the same decade, the boycotting of Protestant business in Fethard-on-Sea because the Protestant spouse in a mixed marriage refused to comply with the Ne Temere decree, shows the highly controversial nature of this decision. Ferriter, *Transformation of Ireland*, p. 582.

preceded independence, and the judiciary were, by and large, reluctant to engage in novel rights adjudication. As Hamilton CJ wrote extra-judicially:

> 'The first generation of Irish judges had spent their working lives in a pure common law environment, where Parliament reigned supreme. Old habits die hard, and it is not surprising if a certain wariness and timidity coloured judgments in the first few decades of the constitutional era.'[23]

That the judiciary in this period understood their rights protection function in a minimalist way that excluded any particular responsibility in protecting the rights of minorities is therefore not peculiar. However, the absence of this conception of the role becomes more notable with the explosion of judicial power in Ireland in the second half of the twentieth century.

From the mid 1960s to mid 1990s, influenced heavily by American jurisprudence,[24] 'a veritable revolution occurred in the legal system',[25] as the Irish judiciary began engaging innovatively with the constitution's rights provisions for the first time. At the height of the judiciary's confidence in their capacity for rights adjudication, the Supreme Court not only engaged substantively with the constitution's enumerated rights, but developed an expansive doctrine of unenumerated rights protection – declaring that additional unenumerated rights, latent within the Irish constitutional order, existed and could be discerned by the courts.

Notably, throughout this period, the express constitutional guarantee against discrimination – the constitutional right with the most direct implications for the protection of minority groups – 'remained a constitutional backwater'.[26] As O'Cinneide has noted:

---

[23] Liam Hamilton, 'Matters of Life and Death' (1996) 65 *Fordham Law Review* 543–59, p. 544. See also Macdara Ó Drisceoil, 'Catholicism and the Judiciary in Ireland, 1922–1960' (2019) 4 *Judicial Studies Institute Journal* 1–24, p. 13.

[24] '[Taoiseach] Seán Lemass consciously initiated the era of judicial activism as part of his project of modernising Ireland, by his selection of Ó Dálaigh CJ and Walsh J and by his private admonition to each of them on appointment . . . that he 'would like to see the Supreme Court behave more like the United States Supreme Court'. David Gwynn Morgan, *A Judgment Too Far: Judicial Activism and the Constitution* (Cork: Cork University Press, 2001), p. 12. Donal Coffey makes a similar claim about Éamon de Valera (quoting *The Irish Press*, 14 October 1982), see Donal K. Coffey, *Constitutionalism in Ireland 1932 – 1938: National, Commonwealth, and International Perspectives* (London: Palgrave Modern Legal History, 2018), p. 157.

[25] Bryan McMahon, 'A sense of identity in the Irish legal system', in Joseph Lee (ed.), *Ireland: Towards a Sense of Place: The UCC- RTÉ Lectures* (Cork: Cork University Press, 1985), pp. 34–5.

[26] Oran Doyle, *Constitutional Equality Law* (Dublin: Thomson Round Hall, 2004), p. viii.

'Given the range and development of other areas of constitutional rights in Irish law, in particular the personal rights protected under Article 40.3 of the Constitution, the restraint of the Court in interpreting and applying Article 40.1 is all the more striking.'[27]

Whilst the Supreme Court did not deal in this period with further rights claims from the Protestant minority, other minority groups challenged the discrimination and social exclusion they faced in the courts. In their treatment of rights claims raised by racial minorities, sexual minorities, and people with disabilities, the Irish court continued to eschew placing determinative weight on the fact that the parties before them were members of disadvantaged minority groups.

During this period, the court struck down a law that effectively prohibited mixed-faith couples adopting,[28] and upheld a statute that disenfranchised people with disabilities by not allowing postal voting.[29] The court also rejected the claim that Travellers had constitutional rights to furnished halting sites,[30] and upheld legislation on naturalisation that treated foreign spouses differently on the basis of their sex.[31] In their unenumerated rights jurisprudence the court also adjudicated upon the rights of minorities, most notoriously in *Norris v. Attorney General*.[32] In *Norris*, the Supreme Court upheld the legal prohibition of sodomy and gross indecency between men, a law that specifically affected the sex lives of gay men. While the dissents in *Norris* places *some* onus on the minority status of the plaintiff,[33] the Supreme Court ultimately did not see it as part of their judicial function to provide

---

[27] Colm O'Cinneide, 'Aspirations Unfulfilled: The Equality Right in Irish Law'; (2010) 1 *Irish Human Rights Law Review* 41–82, p. 56.

[28] *M v. An Bord Uchtála* [1975] IR 81. It was also during this period that the court imposed strict maternal consent rules on unmarried mothers whose children were put up for adoption. That the people directly affected by these rules were unmarried, often economically disadvantaged, women – amongst the most oppressed and socially disadvantaged groups in Irish society at the time – was not a consideration that factored into the court's reasoning. See *G v. An Bord Uchtála* [1980] IR 32. (Legalisation of adoption of marital children did not occur until passage of the Adoption Act 1988.)

[29] *Draper v. Attorney General* [1983] IR 277.

[30] *O'Reilly v. Limerick Corporation* [1989] ILRM 181.

[31] *Somjee v. Minister for Justice* [1981] ILRM 324.

[32] *Norris v. Attorney General* [1984] IR 36.

[33] Even noting this, in his dissent, Henchy J commented how Norris' 'public espousal of the cause of male homosexuals in this state may be thought to be tinged with a degree of that affected braggadocio which is said by some to distinguish a 'gay' from a mere homosexual'. After this, Henchy J stridently rejected that criminalising gross indecency between men contravened the guarantee of non-discrimination – the right which most easily could be used to advance minority rights interests. Ibid. [1984] IR 36 at 70.

a platform from which underrepresented minorities could advocate for their rights.[34]

In all these cases, the rights claim directly engaged with an aspect of a person's status that distinguished them as members of a minority group, whether it be religion, disability, Traveller culture, gay sex, or the intersection of ethnicity and sex. In all, the court did not place any weight on the fact that the laws were having a discrete impact upon the interests of a minority group.

From the mid-1990s to the mid-2010s, the court adopted a noticeably cooler attitude towards rights adjudication. The court stopped finding unenumerated rights,[35] and developed a greater cognisance of the importance of policing the separation of powers.[36] This decline in judicial fervour for rights adjudication naturally meant the court was less inclined to develop a proactive minority rights protecting understanding of its judicial function. During this period, the court considered the education rights of disabled children,[37] the language rights of Gaeilgeoirs (Irish language speakers),[38] the marriage rights of homosexuals,[39] and the gender recognition rights of trans people.[40] Again, while some of these actions were successful, the court continued to adjudicate without placing any determinative weight on the minority group status of the parties involved.[41]

---

[34] As O'Higgins CJ argued, the state has 'an interest in the general moral wellbeing of the community and as being entitled, where it is practicable to do so, to discourage conduct which is morally wrong and harmful to a way of life and to values which the State wishes to protect'. Ibid. [1984] IR 36 at 64.

[35] As O'Donnell J recently noted extrajudicially, 'the development of unenumerated rights, which had after all been the distinctive engine which had driven activism in the 1960s and early 1970s has in recent decades simply petered out'. O'Donnell, 'The Sleep of Reason' (2017) 40 *Dublin University Law Journal* 191–214, p. 200.

[36] See David Gwynn Morgan, '"Judicial-o-centric" Separation of Powers on the Wane?' (2004) 39:1 *Irish Jurist* 142.

[37] *O'Donoghue v. Minister for Health* [1996] 2 IR 20; *Sinnott v. Minister for Education* [2001] 2 IR 545; *T.D. v. Minister for Education* [2001] 4 IR 259.

[38] *Ó Beoláin v. Fahy* [2001] 2 IR 279; *Ó Gríbín v. An Chomhairle Mhúinteoireachta* [2005] 3 IR 28.

[39] *Zappone v. Revenue Commissioners* [2006] IEHC 404. See also *McD. v. L.* [2009] IESC 81, where the Supreme Court adjudicated upon the guardianship rights of a sperm donor against the lesbian parents of the child.

[40] *Foy v. An t-Ard Chláraitheoir* [2007] IEHC 470.

[41] There is one arguable exception to this trend in this period. In *Re Article 26 and the Health (Amendment) (No 2) Bill 2004*, a case concerning the state attempting to avoid compensation to the elderly, a group to whose interests the judiciary appeared particularly receptive. In the case, the court stated: 'The Constitution, in protecting property rights, does not encompass only property rights which are of great value. It protects such rights even when they are of modest value and *in particular*, as in this case, where the persons affected are *among the more vulnerable sections of society* and might more readily be exposed to the risk of unjust attack.'

In recent years, 'some signs of renewed engagement with Article 40.1 [the guarantee of protection against discrimination]',[42] have been noted. For instance, the test for unconstitutional discrimination has become more pro-applicant, as the burden of proof has been placed on the state to prove discrimination on protected grounds, where it is established, was not unconstitutional.[43] Further, in recent years the court has: imposed novel duties upon local authorities where halting site accommodation was found to be unsuitable;[44] required access to the workforce for asylum seekers;[45] and has departed from its reasoning in the earlier cases, such as *Norris*.[46]

In 2019, the Supreme Court made its strongest suggestion that the judicial function *may* include a minority rights protecting role. In *O v. Minister for Social Protection*, a case concerning the social welfare rights of ethnic minority Irish children born to non-national parents, O'Donnell J stated:

> Fundamental rights perform an important part of the constitutional balance in the State *precisely because they are guarantees designed to protect the minority (whether temporary or permanent) from certain decisions of the majority. There is an inbuilt risk, which entrenched fundamental rights are meant to counter, that a majority will, whether intentionally or unwittingly, tend to favour itself at the expense of a minority.* This is a consideration which is certainly capable of application when legislation distinguishes between citizens and non-citizens, especially when the legislation bears more heavily upon non-citizens. Any such provision would therefore fall to be scrutinised carefully under Article 40.1 [the guarantee of protection from discrimination].[47]

This suggests the judiciary's conception of its role *may* be shifting towards an understanding that the judicial function includes a duty to ensure the rights of minority groups are not maligned by policies passed by the majority. However, as Doyle and Hickey recently noted, 'the court's strongest rhetoric on [equality] is reserved for the weakest cases. Where difficult and challenging issues

---

However, this case did not signal a change in the court's rights reasoning as initially appeared. *Re Article 26 and the Health (Amendment) (No 2) Bill 2004* [2005] 1 IR 105 at 208, emphasis added. See also Eoin O'Dell and Gerry Whyte, 'Is This a Country for Old Men and Women? In Re Article 26 and the Health (Amendment) (No 2) Bill 2004' (2009) 27:1 *Dublin University Law Journal* 368–92.

[42] Gerard Hogan, Gerry Whyte, David Kenny and Rachael Walsh, *JM Kelly: The Irish Constitution* (Dublin: Bloomsbury Professional, 5th edn., 2018) p. 1563.

[43] *D.X. v. Buttimer* [2012] IEHC 175; *Murphy v. Ireland* [2014] IESC 19.

[44] *O'Donnell v. South Dublin County Council* [2015] IESC 28.

[45] *N.H.V. v. Minister for Justice and Equality* [2017] IESC 35.

[46] *P. v. Judges of the Circuit Court* [2019] IESC 26.

[47] *O. v. Minister for Social Protection* [2019] IESC 82 at [21], emphasis added.

arise, there is a move to extreme deference'.[48] Indeed, in O, notwithstanding the passage quoted above, the court ultimately found against the children. It may then only be when the court strikes down a popular legislation due to its adverse effect on a minority that a substantive change in the court's attitude can be affirmatively shown.

What this overview of Ireland's minority rights case law shows is that claims from minority groups have not garnered any additional scrutiny because of the fact that they related directly to an aspect of the claimant's minority status. Given this precedent, it is entirely foreseeable that upon unification, the Ulster Scots/Ulster British minority would be treated by the court in a similar manner. Some cases may succeed on technical grounds, but without any judicial consideration of the fact that the rights claim relates to their identity as members of the Ulster Scots/ Ulster British minority. As I explain in the next section however, there is an alternative possibility. It is possible that unification will see the courts *change* their perception of their minority rights protecting role.

## MINORITY RIGHTS PROTECTION IN A UNITED IRELAND

The absence of a minority rights protecting dimension to the Irish judiciary's understanding of their role is notable because it stands in contrast to the experience of the judiciaries in comparable jurisdictions. In the USA and Canada, the two jurisdictions to which the Irish judiciary refer most often in their rights reasoning,[49] an understanding has developed that the courts *can* act as a forum where otherwise under-represented minority groups can advocate for their rights. A similar conception has emerged in other comparable common law states with entrenched bills of rights, such as India and South Africa. Like the curious incident of the dog in the

---

[48] Oran Doyle and Tom Hickey, *Constitutional Law: Text, Cases and Materials* (Dublin: Clarus Press, 2nd edn., 2019) p. 356. For a critique of the incrementalism of the Irish judiciary, see Gerard Hogan, 'Harkening to the Tristan Chords' (2017) 40 *Dublin University Law Journal* 71–83.

[49] In 1988, Barrington J commented that 'nowadays a barrister arguing a point of constitutional law in the High or Supreme Courts will, as a matter of course, refer to the decisions of the American Federal Supreme Court as persuasive authority. If, by chance, he does not, the trial judge will, as likely as not, ask him if the American Federal Supreme Court ever had to consider this point.' Donal Barrington, 'The Constitution in the Courts' in Frank Litton (ed.), *The Constitution of Ireland 1937 – 1987* (Dublin: Institute of Public Administration, 1988), p. 115. As noted in *Kelly*, the proportionality test in *Heaney v. Ireland* [1994] 3 IR 593 was 'imported verbatim from the Canadian formulation of proportionality' in *R v. Chaulk* [1990] 3 SCR 1303'. Hogan et al., *Kelly*, p. 1479. See also O'Donnell, 'Sleep of Reason', p. 201.

night-time in Sherlock Holmes, it is the fact that Ireland *hasn't* developed this dimension which makes it curious, and which makes the absence notable.

John Hart Ely developed his focus on the minority rights protecting role of courts from studying the US Supreme Court's jurisprudence on racial discrimination in the first half of the twentieth century.[50] Beginning with the Supreme Court's *obiter* citation of the need to subject laws affecting discrete and insular minorities to heightened scrutiny,[51] Ely theorised a 'representation-reinforcement' conception of the judicial role which highlighted the ability of the court to amplify the rights concerns of minorities obstructed from advocating for their interests effectively through the democratic process due to their minority status. Whilst the court first applied this only to racial discrimination:

> 'During the Warren era, the Supreme Court was quite adventurous in expanding the set of suspect classifications beyond the core case of race. Laws classifying to the comparative disadvantage of aliens, persons of 'illegitimate' birth, even poor people, were all at one time or another approached as suspect.'[52]

Later, 'in the 1970s, the Supreme Court moved beyond racially discriminatory laws (and kindred laws discriminating on the basis of ethnicity or nationality) and began to outlaw some laws, policies, and other government action that discriminated on the basis of sex'.[53] In this way, 'expansions into other grounds has taken place primarily by way of extrapolation of principles developed for race', enabling the court to engage with rights challenges by other minority groups.[54]

The Canadian judiciary has also developed a capacious understanding of its role as a forum for mediating the interests of minority groups otherwise marginalised by democratic processes.[55] In Canada, the development of a robust minority rights protecting jurisprudence under the Charter of

---

[50] Ely, *Democracy and Distrust*; *Korematsu v. United States* 323 US 214 (1944); *Sweatt v. Painter* 339 US 629 (1950); *Brown v. Board of Education* 347 US 483 (1954); *Loving v. Virginia* 188 US 1 (1967); *Griggs v. Duke Power* 401 US 424 (1971).
[51] *United States v. Carolene Products* 304 US 144 (1938).
[52] Ely, *Democracy and Distrust*, p. 148.
[53] Perry, *We the People*, p. 117. See *Reed v. Reed* 404 US 71 (1971); *United States v. Virginia* 515 US 515 (1996).
[54] Sandra Fredman, *Discrimination Law* (Oxford: Clarendon Press, 2nd edn., 2011), p. 110.
[55] *Andrews v. Law Society of British Columbia* [1989] 1 SCR 143; *Ontario Human Rights Commission v. Simpsons-Sears* [1985] 2 SCR 536; *Eldridge v. British Columbia* [1997] 3 SCR 624; *Vriend v. Alberta* [1998] 1 SCR 493; *Reference re Same-Sex Marriage* [2004] 3 SCR 698.

Fundamental Rights and Freedoms coincided with 'the most significant issue in Canada's constitutional debates of the last two decades, [the question of] whether or not Canada [was] prepared to accept symbolically the national status of Quebec'.[56] In both America and Canada, then, the relationship of the majority with the most politically salient minority group was the foundation upon which a broader minority rights protecting conception of the judicial function has developed. In Canada, the relationship between Anglophones and Francophones, in the United States between white and Black Americans.

That the treatment of Black Americans has been the paradigmatic social and political issue throughout American history does not need substantive defending. Further, as Choudhry noted of Canada, 'it is the question of language that is truly central to making sense of the Canadian constitutional project'.[57] Without dismissing the salience of the relationship between the hegemonic majority groups in these jurisdictions and other minority groups (particularly indigenous populations),[58] the exceptionally high political and social salience of these national minority/majority interactions distinguishes these relationships.

Of course, as the decisions of the US Supreme Court in *Dred Scott*[59] and *Plessy v. Ferguson*[60] starkly illustrate, a court's engagement with the rights disputes of the most salient minority within their jurisdiction will not always cause a minority rights protecting conception to emerge.[61] Rather, as Klarman noted:

> Courts are likely to protect only those minorities that are favourably regarded by majority opinion. Ironically, when a minority group suffering from oppression is most in need of judicial protection, it is least likely to receive it. *Groups must command significant social, political, and economic power before they become attractive candidates for judicial solitude.*[62]

The unique social, political, and economic salience of particular group identities therefore can lead a court to develop a minority rights protecting

---

[56] Stephen Tierney, *Constitutional Law and National Pluralism* (Oxford: Oxford University Press, 2006), p. 235.
[57] Choudhry, 'Does the world need more Canada?', p. 150.
[58] See Maggie Blackhawk, 'Federal Indian Law as Paradigm within Public Law' (2019) 132 *Harvard Law Review* 1787–1877. Professor Blackhawk argues for a comprehensive reassessment of public law which includes the centrality of federal Indian law and the USA's tragic history with colonialism to its development. In Canada see *R v. Kapp* (2008) SCC 41.
[59] *Dred Scott v. Sandford* 60 US 393 (1857).
[60] *Plessy v. Ferguson* 163 US 537 (1896).
[61] See Paul Yowell, *Constitutional Rights and Constitutional Design: Moral and Empirical Reasoning in Judicial Review* (London: Bloomsbury Professional, 2018).
[62] Klarman, *From Jim Crow to Civil Rights*, p. 450, (emphasis added).

conception of the judicial function in cases where the rights of these particular groups are engaged. The Irish judiciary may not have developed a similarly minority-regarding conception of their function as the courts in these jurisdictions because the minority groups who have sought to have their rights protected through the courts have lacked the 'significant social, political, and economic power' needed 'for judicial solicitude'.[63]

This brings me to unification. If my analysis is correct that the understanding among American and Canadian judiciaries that their role included a duty to protect the interests of minorities arose out of their engagements with the rights interests of large discrete minorities with especially high political saliences, unification may be the prompt for a similar change of mind on the part of the Irish courts. Indeed, this possibility is further supported by the aforementioned trend whereby the Irish courts frequently consider the jurisprudence of American and Canadian courts when adjudicating upon a previously under-explored area.

Currently, Ulster Scots/Ulster British make up roughly 50 per cent of the population of Northern Ireland; about 900,000 people.[64] The population of the island of Ireland is approximately 6.6 million.[65] On these current figures, roughly 15 per cent of the population of a unified Ireland are likely to identify as Ulster Scots/ Ulster British. Not only is this demographically a sizeable minority group, the relationship of this group to the majority population of the island is – notoriously – highly politically charged.

As with the racial, sexual, religious, and disabled groups noted in the previous section, there are discrete cultural practices and beliefs associated with (at least some) Ulster Scots/Ulster British which a bill of rights similar to that currently existing in Ireland would protect.[66] For instance, consider a case

---

[63] Ibid.
[64] This figure is reached through the addition of the population in the 2011 Northern Irish census who identified as British only (39.89%), the population who identified as British and Northern Irish only (6.17%), and the expectation that a large proportion, perhaps a majority, of the 20.94% who identified as Northern Irish only would also consider themselves unionists. The total population of Northern Ireland in 2011 was 1,810,863. Thus, I reason around 900,000 of those – half the population – identify as unionist. '2011 Census: Key Statistics for Northern Ireland', Northern Ireland Statistics and Research Agency, www.nisra.gov.uk/sites/nisra.gov.uk/files/publications/2011-census-results-key-statistics-northern-ireland-report-11-december-2012.pdf.
[65] This figure is reached through adding the 1,810,863 from the 2011 Northern Ireland Census, with the 2016 Ireland Census, which recorded 4,761,865 living in Ireland, creating a total of 6,572,728 people living on the island. 'Census 2016 Summary Results – Part 1', Central Statistics Office, https://static.rasset.ie/documents/news/census-2016-summary-results-part-1-full.pdf.
[66] Former UUP Councilor Christopher McGimpsey described the task of defining Irish identity as being as simple as 'nailing jelly to a wall', a simile that also lends itself to the task of defining

which almost inevitably will arise before the courts if the three assumptions I have made hold. It concerns one of the most routinely controversial cultural practices associated with the Ulster Scots/Ulster British population: parading. Marching season in Ulster has been the volatile period of most years on the island for over a century.[67] In recent years, the regulation of parades in Northern Ireland through restrictions on passing through 'interface zones' has been a particularly controversial means of managing unrest.

Assume the constitution of a unified Ireland, like Bunreacht na hÉireann, includes the right to peaceful assembly subject to public order and morality.[68] A parade through a predominantly Irish area is banned by the authorities. The participants parade anyway. The participants are prosecuted for breaking the law. They allege their right to peaceful assembly (a right which has produced negligible jurisprudence from the Irish courts) has been infringed.[69] A court composed of former members of the benches of the two partitioned jurisdictions must resolve the case. How will they adjudicate upon this highly politically controversial rights dispute?

The political costs of a decision on the constitutionality of such a parade – either for or against – will be profound. Not having the choice to reject the case, the court must attempt to resolve one of the most sensitive aspects of the most intractable inter-community dispute in Ireland. Experience from the USA and Canada suggests that is in cases such as this that courts develop at least a conception that the presence of minority interests is relevant to deciding the case; and perhaps even an understanding that they have a particular responsibility to *protect* those interests.

If this were to be borne out in Ireland, then, as with these other common law judiciaries, we might see the court assert that it is a forum for protecting and representing minority group interests against the influences of unmoved majorities. With the heightened political salience of this dispute, the importance of making such assertions would be understood to be higher than instances where the rights of other minority groups were engaged.[70]

---

an Ulster Scots/Ulster British identity. James Loone (ed.), *The British-Irish Connection* (Social Study, 1985), p. 39.

[67] Tony Gray, *The Orange Order* (London: Bodley Head, 1972); Eric Kaufmann, *The Orange Order: A Contemporary Northern Irish History* (Oxford: Oxford University Press, 2007).

[68] Art. 40.6.1.ii of the Constitution of Ireland.

[69] Hogan et al. note only three cases concerning the guarantee of freedom of assembly: *Brendan Dunne v. Fitzpatrick* [1958] IR 29; *DPP v. Kehoe* [1983] IR 136; and *Hyland v. Dundalk Racing* [2014] IEHC 60. Hogan et al., *Kelly*, p. 2122.

[70] Having Northern Irish judges with experience of living within a divided society on the bench may increase the likelihood that this court would feel the need to expressively affirm the place of the Ulster Scots/Ulster British identity within the unified legal system.

Whichever side the court favours, by adopting this approach to resolving this highly politically and socially divisive rights dispute, the court may rhetorically base its institutional legitimacy in part upon its ability to act as a forum for minority social groups to challenge state actions encroaching on their group interests.

Turning back to comparative analysis, the path to minority rights protecting conceptions of judicial power predictably begin with a paradigm minority group within that society – Black Americans or Francophone Canadians – and then expands to include other groups: other sexual, ethnic, or religious minorities, and people with disabilities etc. A form of mission creep within judicial rights protection thereby occurs. Under these conditions a similar shift may occur in Ireland, which may increase the viability of minority interest groups seeking to protect group interests through litigation.[71]

Consider, under these conditions, a rerunning of the case in which the courts upheld a statutory refusal to make postal voting available to people with disabilities.[72] The applicant was thereby precluded from voting, and so was obstructed from being able to democratically have her specific interests heard. A judiciary with a minority rights protecting conception may understand their constitutional function as including the need to ensure that the courts act as a forum for members of minority groups, so that such interests could be addressed in court when they could not through conventional democratic means. This illustration shows how developing a minority rights protecting function may change the prospect of adjudication brought by minority groups across the board who are seeking to protect their rights through the courts.

## THE COURT, CONSOCIATIONALISM, AND MINORITY RIGHTS PROTECTION

So far, I have relied on just three uncontroversial assumptions in my analysis. In this final section, informed by the chapter in this volume by Doyle et al.,

---

[71] There are also strategic reasons why the court may expand its role as minority rights protector under unification. Hirschl has suggested that the international expansion of strong judicial review over the last century has been partially driven by judges seeking to garner praise and legitimacy from popular acts of judicial activism. As well as acting in this capacity as a centripetal force, to use the language of the previous chapter, by rhetorically validating practices discrete to members of the Ulster Unionist community, the court may be able to arrogate to itself a degree of legitimacy from this constituency which was previously absent. See Ran Hirschl, 'The Strategic Foundations of Constitutions' in Denis Galligan (ed.), *Social and Political Foundations of Constitutions* (Cambridge: Cambridge University Press, 2013), p. 157.

[72] *Draper v. Attorney General* [1983] IR 277.

I add the further consideration. How would continuing the consociational arrangements in a Northern Ireland Assembly and Executive in a similar manner as currently operating, but with sovereignty shifting from London to Dublin, affect the court's minority rights reasoning?[73]

I do not here discuss the many novel legal controversies which may arise from balancing the powers of a devolved administration against the national government.[74] My focus instead is on the *form* of devolution proposed – consociationalism – and how the presence of a consociational system may support the emergence of a minority rights focus within the united Irish court.

Bunreacht na hÉireann currently implicitly recognises that multiple national populations exist on the island of Ireland.[75] In the past, it has also made explicit reference to religious minority groups.[76] However, as my overview of minority rights protection showed, the inclusion of these provisions has not led the Irish judiciary to develop a minority rights protecting conception of the judicial role. The legal regulation of consociationalism would also see the unified state textually recognising the interests of a minority group.[77] However, this time, recognition would not simply be expressive. Instead, recognition would be a component of a legally prescribed mechanism of power-sharing.

Doyle et al. suggested that 'the terms of unification [and, therefore, devolution] will be expressed legally rather than primarily through political practice and given their final authoritative interpretation by judges rather than by

---

[73] Doyle et al. 'Constitutional Politics'. There are various means by which a devolved consociational government could be incorporated into the Irish constitutional order. My analysis here applies irrespective of whether this is done with or without further constitutional amendments.

[74] Per Doyle et al, 'there is no experience with regional government in Ireland'. Consequently, the Irish judiciary, with no experience resolving a devolutionary dispute, would have to devise a means of resolving such legal disputes. This issue would present itself to the court both if prescribed in primary legislation or if it was entrenched within the text of the constitution. Doyle et al., 'Constitutional Politics'. See also Tierney, *Constitutional Law*, p. 282.

[75] Per Art. 3.1 of the Constitution of Ireland: 'It is the firm wish of the Irish nation, in harmony and friendship to unite *all the people* who share the territory of the island of Ireland, in all the diversity of their identities and traditions . . . .' Emphasis added.

[76] Until 1972, Art. 44.1.3° of the Constitution of Ireland stated: 'The State also recognises the Church of Ireland, the Presbyterian Church in Ireland, the Methodist Church in Ireland, the Religious Society of Friends in Ireland, as well as the Jewish Congregations and the other religious denominations existing in Ireland at the date of the coming into operation of this Constitution.'

[77] Further, if unification comes about under the terms of the 1998 Agreement, Art. 1(v) of the Agreement would require the unified Irish state to exercise 'rigorous impartiality on behalf of all the people in the diversity of their identities'. Whilst the Agreement may not be domestically justiciable, this may further inform how the unified court may interpret justiciable constitutional provisions.

politicians'.[78] If so, adjudicating upon disputes arising from the regulation of consociationalism in the devolved region (for instance, a dispute over the appointment of one official over another, contrary to the principle of cross-community representation) would present a legal controversy in which the unified court would engage with the state's obligations to its Ulster Scots/Ulster British population on account of their group status. Whilst this dispute may not directly engage with fundamental rights, it may cause the court to consider its role in ensuring that the Ulster Scots/Ulster British minority are sufficiently represented within the body politic.[79]

Thus, by precipitating further judicial engagement with the state's duties to its Ulster Scots/Ulster British minority, consociationalism may indirectly increase the likelihood of the Irish judiciary developing a minority rights protecting frame of reference when dealing with the rights claims from minority groups. Inasmuch as this frame of reference may spill over to the court's rights reasoning, then, the installation of consociationalism may increase the likelihood that a representation-reinforcement approach to minority rights adjudication may emerge.

## CONCLUSION

The unification of Ireland would – self evidently – be a constitutional event of the highest significance. If successful, unification has the potential to resolve a centuries-long dispute between the two main population groups on this island. If unsuccessful, unification has the potential to result in a state where a numerically significant but politically marginalised minority are resentful and possibly resistant members of a unified state.

To date, the literature on unification has focused on *how* unification may occur, and what constitutional structures – federal, unitary, or devolutionary – might operate within a united Ireland. I believe this chapter is the first to examine the implications of unification for rights jurisprudence. The courts, given their influence within contemporary constitutionalism, would be likely to play a consequential role in determining whether unification was a success. While the Irish court has adjudicated upon the rights interests of minority

---

[78] Doyle et al., 'Constitutional Politics'.
[79] That the Irish court might examine the purpose of cross-community representation and engage on that basis with an understanding of how judicial function includes a duty to ensure Ulster Scots/ Ulster British are represented under devolution may be foreseeable given the purposive approach to interpretation frequently adopted by the Irish judiciary. See Finn Keyes, 'Our Herculean Judiciary: Interpretivism and the Unenumerated Rights Doctrine' (2020) 4:1 *Irish Judicial Studies Journal* 45–61, p. 59.

groups in the past; in size, and in political salience, the adjudication of rights claims pertaining to the Ulster Scots/Ulster British population would be a novel challenge.

There are two possible approaches a unified court could take. It could maintain the status quo of the Irish approach, and not place any weight on the minority group status of applicants when adjudicating upon their rights. Alternatively, the unified court could adopt the minority rights protecting approach I have described in this chapter. The former approach, by eliding the minority group dimension of rights claims raised by Ulster Scots/Ulster British parties, may prove problematic for unification. The latter approach, meanwhile, has the potential to provide greater legal protection for minorities, including but not limited to the Ulster Scots/ Ulster British population. Inasmuch as the rights protection for this community would be greater under the latter approach, the likelihood of buy-in from this community to the unification settlement likely would be greater too.

Which approach is adopted is a choice that will be made by the Irish judiciary. It is impossible to predict whether unification will happen, or when; but as Doyle et al. noted, 'recent years have shown how quickly politics can change in both the United Kingdom and Ireland'.[80] As discussions of unification grow, perhaps it is time the Irish judiciary started considering what role the court ought to have should unification occur, as it may do, sooner than expected.

[80] Doyle et al., 'Constitutional Politics'.

# PART II

# INSTITUTIONAL PRESSURES AND CONTESTED LEGITIMACY

# 8

# Populism and Popular Sovereignty in the UK and Irish Constitutional Orders

## Eoin Daly

### INTRODUCTION

One of the major uncertainties highlighted by the Brexit referendum is the ambiguous status of the 'people' within the UK constitutional order. Since the referendum verdict was recognised as politically but not legally binding, this suggests that referendums offer a potent source of political authority or political legitimation – but without any constitutional framework to meaningfully regulate or limit their use. In turn, it is possible to understand this ad hoc constitutional framework as facilitating or encouraging a 'populist' style of referendum use, with recourse to referendums being highly discretionary and potentially opportunistic, bypassing and undermining the standard procedures of deliberation and representation. In this constitutional structure, the 'people' potentially become a discretionary resource of symbolic legitimation for political elites, rather than a formally and procedurally constituted agent within the constitutional structure.

By contrast, Ireland seems to follow a radically different approach in having enshrined in constitutional law, as distinct from convention, the sovereignty of the people as expressed in the referendum process. Ostensibly at least, referendums are used only as part of a codified constitutional amendment procedure, based on amendments approved by both houses of parliament, thus limiting political discretion as to their use. Accordingly, it appears that by giving constitutional structure and form to popular sovereignty and to its expression in referendums, the Irish framework better safeguards against 'populist' or opportunistic appeals to the authority of popular sovereignty – of the kind that the United Kingdom's more ad hoc framework has arguably permitted. However, I will argue that the Irish experience suggests we should not overstate the capacity of constitutional law to safeguard against populism in the referendum process, or indeed, simply to stem the political logic of referendum use. Despite the codification and proceduralisation of referendum use, referendums continue to offer a potentially potent source of political legitimation and symbolic power, in ways that constitutional law cannot easily contain. Notwithstanding dramatically opposite styles of referendum regulation, in both jurisdictions, the logic of referendum use has been intractably political.

### THE AD HOC UK FRAMEWORK FOR REFERENDUMS – CONSTITUTIONAL UNDER-REGULATION?

One of the commonplace complaints arising from the Brexit vote has been that the ad hoc and uncertain constitutional framework for referendums helped to aggravate the confusion and political crisis that arose in the aftermath of June 2016. Indeed, while referendums offer a potent political resource and a powerful reservoir of moral and political legitimacy, they are not given a consistent or principled framework by British constitutional law. In this analysis, accordingly, the mismatch between the political and legal status of the referendum outcome results in a free-floating, chaotic, popular sovereignty that intervenes (or is deployed) in potentially destructive ways. This constitutional under-regulation applies in two distinct dimensions – both in relation to the *use* of referendums and separately, their *authority*.

Firstly, the considerable political authority of the referendum verdict is neither recognised nor regulated by constitutional law. The referendum was widely seen as politically binding – and in this sense, a 'sovereign' exercise – but without sufficient legal structure or recognition, with 'key issues, including the … consequences of the vote, [being] left to be determined on a case-by-case basis … '.[1] Thus in the Brexit scenario, most political actors recognised the referendum outcome had to be heeded, at least unless reversed in a subsequent referendum, to the point that Phillipson concludes there is now a constitutional convention stipulating that referendums are upheld.[2] Tuck goes as far as to suggest that while 'technically they are merely consultative … the idea that [referendums] could be disregarded seems to most people about as fanciful as the idea that the Queen could actually use the

---

[1] Aileen McHarg, 'Navigating without Maps: Constitutional Silence and the Management of the Brexit Crisis (2018) 16 *International Journal of Constitutional Law* 952–68, p. 956.

[2] Gavin Phillipson, 'Brexit, Prerogative and the Courts: Why Did Political Constitutionalists Support the Government Side in *Miller*?' (2017) 36:2 *University of Queensland Law Journal* 311–31.

power ... to veto a Parliamentary statute'.³ As Matthews puts it: 'to describe referendums as merely advisory therefore neglects how their prevalence has fuelled public expectations regarding the way in which governments should respond to the popular will ... any attempt to overrule 'the people' is politically untenable'.⁴

This *political* or conventional understanding of the referendum's authority – what has been described as 'the de facto paramountcy of popular sovereignty'⁵ – is out of kilter, however, with legal-constitutional doctrine. The Supreme Court, in *Miller (1)*, reaffirmed the orthodox view that the referendum result was purely advisory, partly because the sovereign parliament did not ascribe it binding status.⁶ Its 'popular' credentials are therefore legally meaningless. Green, in this light, describes as 'breathtaking' the idea that 'any popular vote is of zero legal relevance until parliament expressly chooses otherwise'.⁷

Accordingly, then, taking sovereignty in the very wide sense of ultimate or unaccountable power, we might say that the British people are conventionally recognised as 'sovereign' in that their decision is widely, if not unanimously, understood as binding, at least politically speaking, on all state organs.⁸ Such a political expectation, whether or not it should be framed as a 'constitutional convention', is hardly surprising in a democratic state, especially where political actors commit to upholding referendum results. And yet, this understanding is not captured or reflected in any formal constitutional doctrines. As Greene puts it, the courts have 'ignored' the 'emergence of the People as a constitutional agent'.⁹ And this appears, to say the least, somewhat anomalous. It is this inchoate, judicially unrecognised 'sovereignty' that, in effect, prevented Parliament from ignoring or legislating against the referendum outcome, despite the legal-constitutional doctrine of parliamentary

---

³ Richard Tuck, 'Brexit: A prize in reach for the left', Policy Exchange, 17 July 2017, https://policyexchange.org.uk/pxevents/brexit-a-prize-in-reach-for-the-left/.
⁴ Felicity Matthews, 'Whose Mandate is it Anyway? Brexit, the Constitution and the Contestation of Authority' (2017) 88 *Political Quarterly* 603–11, p. 607. It might be added, however, that this view could be qualified and challenged based on the growing political support for a 'People's Vote' and indeed, the repeated defeat of May's proposed Withdrawal Agreement across 2019 in particular.
⁵ Ibid.
⁶ *R (Miller)* v. *Secretary of State for Exiting the European Union* [2017] 1 All ER 158.
⁷ Les Green, 'Should parliamentary sovereignty trump popular sovereignty?', Semper Viridis Blog, https://ljmgreen.com/2016/11/03/should-parliamentary-sovereignty-trump-popular-sovereignty/.
⁸ The government explicitly acknowledged 'a democratic duty to give effect to the electorate's decision' by triggering Art. 50. McHarg, 'Navigating without Maps', p. 956.
⁹ Alan Greene, 'Parliamentary Sovereignty and the Locus of Constituent Power in the United Kingdom', SSRN, 11 September 2018, http://dx.doi.org/10.2139/ssrn.3247758, p. 6.

sovereignty. Taking the UK 'constitution' in the widest sense, we might say that the people are recognised as sovereign, albeit in an amorphous and undefined sense, but that this sovereignty lacks legal structure.[10]

In turn, this unstructured popular sovereignty has the potential to generate political crisis. McHarg argues, accordingly, that 'the lack of clear understanding of the constitutional authority of the referendum [created] a potential conflict between parliamentary democracy and popular democracy, [because] it risked exposing the gulf between Parliament's claim to constitutional authority as a representative institution and the weakness of its democratic credentials in practice'.[11] Thus, she argues these constitutional uncertainties '[contained] the seeds ... of a severe crisis of democratic legitimacy'.[12] Furthermore, McHarg argues that 'it is hard to avoid the conclusion' that this 'constitutional silence' – silence as to the referendum's authority as well as the territorial constitution and executive power – have been partly 'responsible for the Brexit crisis'.[13]

Secondly, UK constitutional law does not regulate the subject matter of referendums, thus allowing wide discretion and uncertainty as to their use. Thus, the question of whether referendums are held on particular issues in the United Kingdom 'is determined ad hoc, and has been entirely driven by party political considerations rather than constitutional principle'.[14] Infamously, this allowed an open-ended question, with unclear consequences, to be submitted to the people in June 2016. The House of Lords Select Committee on the Constitution regretted 'the ad hoc manner in which referendums have been used, often as a tactical device, by the government of the day'.[15] Similarly, Tierney argues that referendums have been deployed based on party-political reasons rather than any constitutional principle.[16] Thus the question of which categories of constitutional change require

---

[10] This must be set in the context of a wider set of uncertainties in the uncodified British constitutional structure, including the territorial constitution as well as the tension between the Westminster and Whitehall views of the constitution. The effect of Brexit on the latter question is explored by David Howarth, 'Westminster Versus Whitehall: What the Brexit Debate Revealed About an Unresolved Conflict at the Heart of the British Constitution' in this volume.

[11] McHarg, 'Navigating without Maps'.

[12] Ibid.

[13] Ibid., p. 967.

[14] Ibid., p. 959.

[15] Peter Leyland, 'Referendums, popular sovereignty and the territorial constitution' in Richard Rawlings, Peter Leyland, and Alison Young (eds.), *Sovereignty and the Law: Domestic, European and International Perspectives* (Oxford: Oxford University Press, 2013), p. 141. House of Lords Select Committee on the Constitution, 'Referendums in the United Kingdom' (12th Report of Session 2009–10), para. 62.

[16] Stephen Tierney, 'Direct Democracy in the United Kingdom: Reflections from the Scottish Independence Referendum' (2015) *Public Law* 633–51.

referendums, or whether referendums are even confined to purely constitutional questions, apparently depends on an entirely political logic.

Relatedly, it has been argued that it was the United Kingdom's constitutional flexibility that allowed the Brexit referendum to assume an open-ended, and a pre-legislative rather than post-legislative form, failing – dangerously – to define the subject being voted on through specific legislative proposals. This constitutional adhocracy allowed the people to be invited to vote on an uncertain abstraction, helping to cause years of political turmoil and instability. As Trueblood puts it, 'using referendums to ratify rather than initiate constitutional change would go a long way to creating constitutional and political stability'.[17]

## 'POPULIST' REFERENDUMS UNDER CONSTITUTIONAL ADHOCRACY?

So far, I have described an emergent understanding of the UK constitution as being somewhat anomalous or deficient in its failure to give legal structure or recognition to a nascent principle of popular sovereignty, as expressed in referendums. In particular, it has been criticised for failing to provide a clear conceptual and procedural framework for constitutional referendums and criteria for their use.

On the one hand, this failure of constitutional regulation has been blamed, in a general sense, for provoking or aggravating instability and chaos after the Brexit vote. The failure to properly institutionalise popular sovereignty seems, then, to give it an uncertain, slightly free-floating, and *lurking* nature, with significant capacity to provoke and inflame political crisis. According to this narrative, popular sovereignty – occupying a kind of constitutional shadow-world – is potentially disruptive and chaotic because its interventions assume a highly irregular, undefined form; undisciplined and uncontained by constitutional law and driven instead by political expediency and realpolitik. Without a proper legal-constitutional framework, then, the nascent popular 'sovereign' remains unpredictable and unwieldy.

On the other hand, this ad hoc constitutional framework may be understood, in a more specific sense, as encouraging or facilitating a peculiarly *populist* style of referendum use. This populist interpretation is not one which has explicitly been made by any of the legal-academic critics of the UK constitutional adhocracy whose views I discussed above. However, if the essence of their critique is

---

[17] Leah Trueblood, 'Referendums, Compromise and Ratification', UK Constitutional Law Blog, 5 July 2016, https://ukconstitutionallaw.org/2016/07/05/leah-trueblood-referendums-compromise-and-ratification/.

that popular sovereignty remains dangerously unstructured in UK constitutional law, this can naturally be extrapolated as having a populist potential – because consensually, one of the characteristic features of populism is a propensity for the 'people' (however constructed) to supervene in highly spontaneous ways that cannot be confined to those channels authorised by a mediating constitutional structure.

Leaving aside the constitutional framework, the Brexit referendum itself had, of course, a markedly 'populist' flavour, not only because of its focus on immigration, expertise, and elites, but also in its invocation of peoplehood ('will of the people') and popular control ('take back control'). Indeed the 'people', reflecting a common populist theme, was frequently invoked as a virtuous and undifferentiated agent both by politicians and media. Indeed, arguably, it is the very model of an advisory referendum, with the 'people' giving a simple acclamation ('yes' or 'no') to a simplified abstraction, which possibly invites such populist conceptualisations of popular agency. And this can be juxtaposed with the mediated, deliberative, and representative traits of parliamentary decision-making. In this light, Freeden identifies these familiar features of populism – undifferentiation, depluralisation, and bypassing of institutions – in the Brexit referendum campaign:

> Most populist references relating the people to democracy have a manipulative rhetorical effect, in which democracy is the abstract rule of the people en masse, without the liberal and intricate constitutional trappings that have come to be associated with European and North American democracies. . . . Demoting the accoutrements of constitutionalism, it is precisely the de-pluralized, unreal and powerful word 'people', employed as a weapon of argument, [that] rid[es] roughshod over diversity counter-claims located in public political discourse . . . Populism thus processes and ideologizes the 'people' as a stylized entity . . . . Brexiters, too, invoke the referendum as the 'will of the people', a phrase understood as a singular homogeneous monolith . . . Brexiters, however, fall into line with other European populists – a subtle irony here – by papering over normal pluralities and presenting themselves as articulating the true, real or unitary popular voice.[18]

In addition to substantively populist themes like immigration, the Brexit referendum tended to promote a more populist conception of political and constitutional structures. And specifically, the referendum and exit process are notable for having shifted the locus of political legitimacy away from constituted political organs, especially Parliament, and towards an abstract undifferentiated 'people',

---

[18] Michael Freeden, 'After the Brexit Referendum: Revisiting Populism as an Ideology' (2017) 22 *Journal of Political Ideologies* 1–11, pp. 2–3.

both as sovereign agent and source of political legitimacy.[19] In this light, McHarg notes 'an extraordinary outpouring of criticism – from politicians, journalists, lawyers, academics, and ordinary citizens – of the legitimacy of the referendum process, the quality of the referendum debate, and indeed of the compatibility of referendums with the UK's tradition of representative democracy'.[20]

Moreover, as I have described, it is arguably the United Kingdom's quite unstructured constitutional provision for referendums, which might facilitate this populist dynamic of referendum use, partly because this framework allows huge political discretion as to such use. If the critics are correct about this political discretion being problematic, such discretion inevitably lends itself to, or potentially encourages the populist style, partly because of the ways in which such discretion allows popular authority to be conceptualised, framed or invoked. In particular, this legal discretion allows for a politically *opportunistic* dynamic of referendum use, with political actors able to deploy referendums as a potentially significant source of political leverage, or perhaps, of political legitimation and symbolic power. Douglas-Scott argues that referendums 'have been used instrumentally by governments',[21] and similarly Leyland refers to the 'unprincipled' use of referendums in the British context.[22] In relation to Brexit, McHarg observes: 'there was no constitutional imperative to hold the referendum. Rather, the motivation was political: an attempt to resolve long-standing divisions in the Conservative party over the merits of EU membership, and to respond to the increasing electoral popularity of ... UKIP.'[23] In a similar vein, Delaney suggests that 'referendum politics have been marked by expediency and manipulation, tied to obtaining contingent electoral benefits or avoiding party fracture. ... Brexit is the apotheosis of this trend: a high-stakes example of short-term political maneuvering.'[24][25] While none of the legal-academic critics link their analysis to populism specifically, all of this post-

---

[19] See Margaret Canovan, 'Trust the People! Populism and the Two Faces of Democracy' (1999) 47 *Political Studies* 2–16, p. 2.

[20] McHarg, 'Navigating without Maps', p. 957.

[21] Sionaidh Douglas-Scott, 'Britain voted merely to leave the EU. We can't assume voters want a hard Brexit', LSE Brexit Blog, 5 September 2016, https://blogs.lse.ac.uk/brexit/2016/09/05/britain-voted-merely-to-leave-the-eu-we-cant-assume-voters-want-a-hard-brexit/.

[22] Peter Leyland. 'Referendums, Constitutional Reform and the Perils of Popular Sovereignty' (2017) 3 *Italian Law Journal* 121–31, p. 123.

[23] Ibid.

[24] Erin F. Delaney, 'Brexit optimism and British constitutional renewal' in Mark A. Graber, Sanford Levinson, Mark Tushnet (eds.), *Constitutional Democracy in Crisis?* (Oxford: Oxford University Press, 2018), p. 192.

[25] Erin F. Delaney, 'Brexit optimism and British constitutional renewal' in Mark A. Graber, Sanford Levinson, Mark Tushnet (eds.), *Constitutional Democracy in Crisis?* (Oxford: Oxford University Press, 2018), p. 192.

referendum analysis nonetheless maps onto a key populist theme; charismatic leadership claiming abstract, democratic authority against constituted state structures.

On the surface, it may seem as though the unstructured or elusive nature of popular sovereignty in the UK constitutional order allows for insurgent interventions of popular sovereignty from *below*, with the people asserting themselves over and outside the normal representative framework. It might seem like a democratic populist dynamic. Alternatively, however, it can be argued that this flexible or unstructured constitutional framework allows popular sovereignty to be instrumentalised from *above*, as a resource for political elites, whether in partisan power struggles or as a source of personal and symbolic legitimation. And this top-down dynamic more comfortably fits a populist logic, with political leaders invoking a unitary or constructed people as a political authority that supersedes both the pluralist public sphere and the representative political structure centred on Parliament. In this elite-led populist model, the free-floating or unstructured popular sovereignty I have described represents a resource for instrumentalisation – and indeed manipulation – by political actors. Because the abstract principle of popular sovereignty can never be fully realised in any specific institutional mechanism, whether representative or 'direct', this democratic gap gives a considerable disruptive power not only to the people themselves, who lack direct voice, but to political actors who may invoke it on their behalf.

We might say that all claims or expressions of popular sovereignty are mediated, orchestrated or represented in some form – because of the impossibility of spontaneous or unmediated popular expression – such that all claims that are ostensibly claims *of* popular sovereignty are in fact claims made *on its behalf*. It is the amorphous or diffuse nature of popular sovereignty; its lack of a clear independent structure or agency, which means it is more likely to be *instrumentalised* or *invoked*, than it is ever *exercised* in a truly autonomous or independent sense. Indeed for McCormick, this is the context and source of populism itself – the necessity of somehow giving representation to the 'people' in response to the absence of any full-blown democracy in the sense of direct popular rule.[26] Interestingly in this light, Matthews – pointing to a wider crisis of the British constitution preceding Brexit – refers to the emergence of 'discretionary spaces' that have created 'opportunities for competing claims to legitimacy to be advanced'.[27] The populist claim, then, is

---

[26] John McCormick, 'Democracy, plutocracy and the populist cry of pain', in Giuseppe Ballacci and Rob Goodman (eds.), *Populism, Demagoguery, and Rhetoric in Historical Perspective* (forthcoming 2021).

[27] Matthews, 'Mandate', p. 608.

a claim of representation, a claim advanced in competition with, or as an alternative to, more structured or 'constitutionalised' forms of representation.

In summary then, popular sovereignty in the Brexit scenario is more plausibly mobilised by, rather than against, elites. Moreover, this instrumentalisation or invocation of popular sovereignty can be interpreted as being facilitated by those features of the UK constitution that, as various commentators outline, enable highly discretionary recourse to referendum use.

## THE LIMITS OF CONSTITUTIONAL REGULATION: THE IRISH COMPARISON

While the United Kingdom's ad hoc constitutional framework for referendums has been blamed for political instability and crisis, and may, furthermore, be associated with a populist style of referendum use, I have argued elsewhere that we should not overestimate the capacity of constitutional law to contain referendum politics, and especially the political logic of referendum use.[28] Even where the principle of popular sovereignty is constitutionally structured and enshrined, it retains a potentially disruptive dimension that cannot be fully exhausted or absorbed by constitutional recognition.

It is true, on the one hand, that the UK constitution fails to structure the principle of popular sovereignty or regulate its exercise, thus giving it a potentially potent capacity for disruption. However, this elusive and disorderly character of popular sovereignty is arguably unremarkable; a feature of every democratic constitutional order – simply because any contingent institutional structure for popular sovereignty, any attempt to institutionally enshrine or absorb the idea, is constantly subject to disputation and challenge. As Frank argues, the 'people are at once enacted through representational claims and forever escaping the political and legal boundaries inscribed by those claims'.[29] Möllers similarly argues: 'democratic government always leaves room for a supplement, a surplus of democratic practice that cannot be fully included into formal constitutional procedure'.[30] By the same measure, the formal and procedural constraints imposed by constitutional mechanisms of popular sovereignty create a 'gap' between principle and

---

[28] Eoin Daly, 'Constitutionalism and Crisis Narratives in Post-Brexit Politics' (2020) *Political Studies*, 1–21.

[29] Jason Frank *Constituent Moments: Enacting the People in Post-Revolutionary America* (Durham: Duke University Press, 2010), p. 3.

[30] Christoph Möllers, 'We are (afraid of) the people': Constituent power in German constitutionalism', in Martin Loughlin and Neil Walker (eds.), *The Paradox of Constitutionalism* (Oxford: Oxford University Press, 2007), p. 87.

effectuation, that permanently leaves open a possibility of what might reasonably be described as populist egression. The 'sovereign' claim, by its nature, cannot be fully exhausted or absorbed by constitutional recognition, partly because of the limits that any procedural form must impose on 'sovereign' power. Thus, no *constituted* expression of popular sovereignty can ever fully satisfy its *supraconstitutional* dimension – that is, the people's claim that lies outside the juristic domain and necessarily exceeds it. It is the inevitable gap between the idea, or the *claim* of popular sovereignty, on the one hand, and its institutional expressions, on the other, which means that popular sovereignty as an abstraction so easily slips towards populism in practice. A populist constitutional intervention, then, might simply be one responding to the limits imposed by contingent constitutional mechanisms for concretising popular sovereignty.

In turn, it is this inexhaustibility of popular sovereignty that undermines the possibility of effective constitutional safeguards against populist styles of referendum use – that is, against the discretionary, opportunistic, performative or symbolic use of referendums. Following the Brexit referendum, much of the liberal and constitutionalist criticism of the UK constitutional framework has focused on the absence of legal-constitutional criteria specifying the proper subject matter of referendums and criteria for their use. The implication is that such rules should stem the purely political logic of referendum use. Leyland, for example, argues that 'to prevent abuse by government, clear rules need to be formulated to determine when constitutional referendums can be held'.[31] Yet experience from elsewhere undermines the idea that constitutional regulation can effectively stem opportunistic or discretionary invocations of popular sovereignty via referendum.

Ireland is probably the most useful comparator for the United Kingdom's constitutional adhocracy, mainly because its very different constitutional framework ostensibly allows for no political discretion as to referendum use. In Ireland, referendums are used as a mandatory component of the constitutional amendment process; they must be used for all amendments to the 1937 Constitution that are passed first by the Houses of the Oireachtas (parliament). The referendum serves only to ratify a legal text, an Act first passed by the Oireachtas. While popular sovereignty itself is alluded to as a foundational principle in the constitutional text – and while it has, furthermore, been

---

[31] Leyland, 'Referendums', p. 141. The House of Lords Constitution committee also stated: 'we regret the ad hoc manner in which referendums have been used, often as a tactical device, by the government of the day'. House of Lords Select Committee on the Constitution, 'Referendums in the United Kingdom', para. 62.

recognised as an overarching principle in the case law on referendums – it is also enshrined in concrete institutional form under the 1937 Constitution through this requirement of mandatory referendums for all constitutional amendments. In contrast with systems such as that used by the French, which uses alternatives of referendums and special parliamentary majorities, there is no political discretion as to the use of referendums in the constitutional amendment process. Thus, the Irish comparison allows us to test the hypothesis that constitutional under-regulation facilitates, or even encourages, an unprincipled and more specifically, a 'populist' style of referendum use.

Popular sovereignty is, in effect, recognised as a general principle in Art. 6 of the Irish Constitution which states: 'All powers of government ... derive, under God, from the people, whose right it is to designate the rulers of the State and, in final appeal, to decide all questions of national policy, according to the requirements of the common good.' However, this is given concrete expression in the constitutional-amendment process governed by Arts. 46 and 47 of the constitution which – unusually in European terms – require that every constitutional amendment be approved by both Houses of the Oireachtas before being submitted to a 'decision of the people' in a referendum. This link between popular sovereignty and constitutional amendment referendums has been cemented by constitutional case law, which has conceptualised the amendment process as the primary expression of the abstract principle of popular sovereignty enshrined in Art. 6 of the constitution. In particular, the Supreme Court has invoked popular sovereignty to assert a principle of substantively unfettered constitutional amendability, rejecting all challenges to the validity of proposed amendment or referendum verdicts. The constitution, the Supreme Court has said, 'was enacted by the people and ... can be amended by the people only [as] the sovereign authority',[32] while ruling in a separate case that 'the people *intended to give themselves full power to amend any provision of the Constitution*'.[33]

In this light, the Brexit referendum and its aftermath help to illustrate a marked contrast between the way popular sovereignty is conceptualised in the Irish and UK constitutional orders. Whereas Irish constitutional doctrine explicitly recognises the people's sovereignty and concretises this as a substantively unfettered power of constitutional amendment via referendum, the traditional Diceyan doctrines in the United Kingdom have continued to recognize only Parliament as the 'legal' sovereign, while, at most, recognising the people as sovereign only in a separate 'political' domain that is

---

[32] *Byrne v. Ireland* [1972] IR 241 at 262. Emphasis added
[33] *Finn v. Attorney General* [1983] IR 154 at 163. Emphasis added.

not legally cognisable.[34] At most, popular sovereignty might now be recognised through constitutional conventions that require both that referendums be held on certain issues, and that the people's verdict be upheld.[35] In Ireland, because it is legally recognised, the people's authority is also legally defined and thus – paradoxically – legally limited; it is limited to a power of participation in the formal constitutional amendment process. In the United Kingdom, however, the lack of constitutional recognition or structure for popular sovereignty has apparently given constitutional referendums – or at least the Brexit referendum – a seemingly chaotic, disruptive capacity, primarily because the 'sovereign' people's authority is extra-legal, uncertain, and indefinite.

In the United Kingdom, then, popular sovereignty probably exists only as an inchoate political principle that has not been meaningfully structured or ordered by or within the constitution itself. By way of contrast, popular sovereignty in Ireland at least appears to be wholly *absorbed* within the legal-constitutional order. It is, first, explicitly recognised, and second, given specific institutional mechanisms, mostly notably referendums, that assign it a definite (and regulated) form, within the constitutional structure. And this constitutional absorption of the principle might be understood as giving or appearing to give it both structure and limits. Whereas popular sovereignty in the United Kingdom *eludes* constitutional recognition and regulation, popular sovereignty in Ireland is – ostensibly at least – *exhausted* by its constitutionally assigned form. Or, at least, the structuring of popular sovereignty in this way may be seen to discourage alternative or irregular manifestations of it outside the recognised framework. The Irish Constitution seems to fully absorb, or profess to fully absorb, the claims of popular sovereignty within its normative and institutional structure, and while the constitution cannot preclude different or unexpected manifestations of or claims on the idea, the structure it gives the principle seems to lean against such a possibility.

On the one hand, this seems like a distinct advantage compared to the ad hoc, elusive form that popular sovereignty has assumed in the more organic UK constitution. Since popular sovereignty receives a definite constitutional structure, it seems to be less prone to opportunistic instrumentalisation by political elites, particularly in the guise of unregulated, ad hoc referendums that appeal to the people – or invoke their authority – outside an established constitutional structure. It has been argued that it was this lack of

---

[34] For analysis of Dicey's views on popular sovereignty, see James Kirby, 'A.V. Dicey and English Constitutionalism (2019) 45:1 *History of European Ideas* 33–46.
[35] Vernon Bogdanor, 'Brexit, the Constitution and the alternatives' (2016) 27 *King's Law Journal* 314–322.

constitutional structure for referendums, or indeed the failure of the constitutional order to absorb popular sovereignty, that allowed David Cameron to appeal to the people in an ad hoc, opportunistic way, with such disruptive consequences. One might argue that by absorbing the claims of popular sovereignty within a definite constitutional procedure – and by requiring that referendums confirm a legislative text decided through the parliamentary process[36] – the Irish Constitution precludes any such populis' instrumentalisation of constitutional referendums. The absorption of popular sovereignty within constitutional structures potentially seems to domesticate it, which may have the effect not simply of foreclosing any superventions of popular 'will' into the constituted political order – but more importantly perhaps, of foreclosing any top-down invocations of popular sovereignty by political leaders, acting through a populist logic that bypasses intermediary institutions.

There is some support for such a view, indeed, in the history of referendum use in Ireland. Partly because the procedure and subject-matter of referendums are constitutionally defined, some commentators have interpreted the constitutional referendum as a stabilising device – as a part of a system of checks and balances through which governmental power over constitutional change is contested and braked – rather than as a majoritarian or populist practice.[37] The main contrast with the UK framework, as I have said, lies in the fact that referendums are used essentially in a ratificatory way; only for confirming legislative provisions for constitutional amendment.

On the other hand, however, this apparent contrast with the United Kingdom should not be overstated. While the Irish Constitution appears to recognise and thus to absorb the claims of popular sovereignty, this cannot easily preclude popular sovereignty from supervening, or from being invoked, in potentially disruptive and unprincipled ways. Whereas the Irish Constitution gives popular sovereignty definite structures, it makes little explicit allowance for disruptive interventions by the sovereign people outside of the relatively reactive role it enjoys in the constitutional amendment process. Notwithstanding the recent innovation of Citizens Assemblies, popular involvement in the constitutional revision process is nonetheless left at the

---

[36] This argument is succinctly put by Simon Hix: 'in Ireland, referendums are systematically linked up to political processes both inside and outside parliament before a referendum takes place . . . referendums that amend the constitution must be approved by both the Dáil and the Seanad, which is a significant constraint on the proliferation of referendums and on the ability of powerful interests to mobilise and capture a particular initiative'. Simon Hix, 'Remaking Democracy: Ireland as a Role-Model, the 2019 Peter Mair Lecture' (2020) *Irish Political Studies* 1–16.

[37] See Bill Kissane, 'Is the Irish referendum majoritarian?' In W. Marxer (ed.), *Direct Democracy and Minorities* (New York: Springer, 2012), p. 152.

discretion of the Oireachtas, or effectively the government, as the institutions that enjoy a monopoly on the formal initiation of constitutional amendments. It is true that, in recent years especially, grassroots campaigns, such as the campaign to repeal the Eighth amendment (the 'pro-life' amendment), have occasionally succeeded in forcing the Oireachtas to propose certain constitutional amendments. However, there is no apparent mechanism by which the people may occasionally egress within the constitutional order other than through a passive, reactive capacity that takes the form of a mere veto over amendments passed by the parliament.[38] And to say the least, this sits uneasily with the very concept of sovereignty, whose very nature suggests it cannot be fully exhausted or absorbed by legal-constitutional recognition. Indeed, as Colón-Ríos argues, democratic constitutions might need to leave scope for the constituent power to egress periodically from outside to disrupt the constituted order, regardless of whatever specific form popular sovereignty might have already have been given within the formalised constitutional amendment process.[39]

On the other hand, however, this apparent domestication of popular sovereignty should not be overstated, largely because the referendum mechanism itself, despite its highly structured nature, allows popular sovereignty to be deployed and invoked in highly flexible ways. In one sense, the Irish people remain sovereign outside of any proceduralised capacity ascribed to them in Arts. 46 and 47 of the constitution, and perhaps this is a deep, originative sense of sovereignty that might be usefully disaggregated from a 'constituted', proceduralised version of the concept. Indeed Walker has argued that 'much of the contemporary confusion ... over sovereignty' stems from 'a failure to distinguish between sovereignty as a deep framing device for making sense of the modern legal and political world ... and the particular claims which are made on behalf of particular institutions, agencies, rules, or other entities to possess sovereignty'.[40] In this sense, accordingly, we might do well to distinguish separate capacities of sovereignty within or indeed, adjacent to the constitutional order, and the different kinds of juristic and normative claims they generate. In another sense, however, the existing referendum mechanism appears, despite its comparatively structured nature, to leave ample scope for disruptive or flexible invocations of, and interventions by, popular sovereignty within the political and constitutional order. Thus, we should not observe too

---

[38] Joel Colón-Ríos, 'The Legitimacy of the Juridical: Constituent Power, Democracy, and the Limits of Constitutional Reform' (2010) 48 *Osgoode Hall Law Journal* 199–245.
[39] Ibid.
[40] Neil Walker, 'Sovereignty Frames and Sovereignty Claims', in Rawlings, Leyland, and Young (eds.), *Sovereignty*, p. 27.

firm a distinction between a 'constituted', constitutionally recognised sovereignty, on the one hand, and one that interlopes from outside, on the other.

In light of this analysis, the Irish constitutional order is perhaps not all that different from the United Kingdom's more organic framework. In fact, the unabsorbed, residual, and extra-constitutional sovereignty that I have described – the sovereignty that is not fully captured by the referendum provisions – is in fact already alluded to in the constitutional text. While Art. 6 of the Irish Constitution refers to the people as 'deciding all matters of national policy ... *in final appeal*'(emphasis added) – that is, as a constituted political power – the same provision affirms that all powers of government 'derive ... from the people'. The people might both be a constituted sovereign through their referendum and electoral role, while also retaining their status as an originative, constitutive authority that is never fully captured in constituted power, or in any definite legal mechanism or procedure.

Curiously, this disaggregation of separate, or adjacent sovereign claims, has already occurred, or is occurring, in UK constitutional discourse. As explained, the traditional Diceyan theories conceptualise Parliament as a legal, and thus a constituted sovereign, but the people as sovereign in a separate political domain that is not legally cognisable – or which today might be recognised at most through constitutional convention.[41] Thus after the Brexit referendum, Green drew a distinction between parliamentary sovereignty as an 'institutional device', on the one hand, and the foundational 'moral ideal' that popular sovereignty represents, on the other.[42] Recently, Loughlin and Tierney similarly refer to the 'power-generative' dimension of sovereignty that standard theories of parliamentary sovereignty are lacking.[43] These might well be labelled as 'procedural' and 'legitimating' concepts of sovereignty. In the United Kingdom, these have been distinguished because they vest in separate entities, Parliament and people. In Ireland, they have not been disaggregated, I suggest, partly because they vest in what is ostensibly the same entity, the 'people'. But it might bring greater conceptual clarity to disaggregate the different, perhaps even separate senses in which the Irish people are 'sovereign'. There might be different 'peoples' for different constitutional purposes; the 'people' that amend the constitution, as a 'sovereign', might be different to the 'people' alluded to as an originative authority in Art. 6. As Frank notes:

---

[41] For analysis of Dicey's views on popular sovereignty, see Kirby, 'Dicey'.
[42] Green, 'Parliamentary Sovereignty'.
[43] Martin Loughlin and Stephen Tierney, 'The Shibboleth of Sovereignty' (2018) 81 *Modern Law Review* 989–1016.

> Both democratic history and democratic theory demonstrate that the people are a political claim ... not a pregiven, unified, or naturally bounded empirical entity ... In the United States the power of claims to speak in the people's name derives in part from a constitutive surplus inherited from the revolutionary era, from the fact that since the Revolution the people have been at once enacted through representation – how could it be otherwise? – and in excess of any particular representation.[44]

In more practical terms, and in light of the above analysis, it seems the constitutional 'absorption' of popular sovereignty in Ireland may do little to firmly safeguard against populist uses of the referendum device. While the referendum mechanism fails to exhaust the claims of popular sovereignty even on the terms of the principle that is constitutionally recognised, the incorporation of the referendum mechanism within a codified constitutional amendment process fails, on the other hand, to prevent referendums being used to instrumentalise the symbolic power of the popular voice in a recognisably populist style. While the constitutionalised 'people' is given a formalised, limited role in ratifying constitutional amendments proposed by the parliament, the extra-constitutional 'people' remain a potent source of political capital and symbolic power, and a potentially significant resource for political actors to instrumentalise notwithstanding the formal constitutional structure and constraints.

And this is arguably borne out, at least to some degree, in the history of referendum use in Ireland. Some analysis has suggested the referendum is essentially a stabilising or even a conservative device, possibly deterring or checking the dynamics of constitutional amendment – and in particular, slowing or disincentivising radical institutional changes.[45] And indeed, a significant proportion of referendums have related to rather technical legal reforms, such as the court structure or the legal status of the adoption board, rather than socially or culturally contentious issues.[46] However, there have equally been many instances where referendums have been initiated not simply as a means to an end of achieving a given constitutional or legal change, but rather as a powerful political and symbolic resource in their own right. Recourse to the people has a powerful expressive and symbolic function that makes the constitutional referendum irreducible to any neutral procedural device.

---

[44] Frank, *Constituent Moments*, p. 17.
[45] See Kissane, 'Irish referendum'.
[46] Ibid.

There are many instances where having recourse to referendum is not a means to an end, but rather, at least partly, an end in itself. The best example of this in Irish referendum history, is arguably the referendum on the Twenty-seventh Amendment in 2004, which aimed to end *jus soli* citizenship in the context of widespread anti-immigration discourse, and was held on the same day as local and European elections.[47] In such instances, an appeal to the 'people' is not merely a procedural hurdle imposed by the constitution in order to achieve a given constitutional-legal change, but rather constitutes a political resource in its own right – thus opening the possibility of a 'populist' dynamic of referendum use notwithstanding the highly proceduralised and structured status of the referendum within the constitutional system. The main apparent safeguard in Ireland against unprincipled or populist referendums, compared with the UK advocacy, is the requirement that referendums can be used only to approve a legal text, an Act of the Oireachtas that contains a proposed constitutional amendment, rather than an open-ended or abstract question (like Brexit) that appears to have more symbolic than legal import. However, this advantage should not be exaggerated, chiefly because there is no formal limit on what the text of a constitutional amendment can contain. And it is entirely possible to adopt constitutional amendments that effect little or no legal change, and whose purpose is mostly or entirely symbolic or expressive.[48] This formal flexibility further enhances the populist potential of referendum use even in a constitutional structure that is more structured and codified than the UK equivalent.

Ultimately, there is little that constitutional codification of referendum use can do to safeguard against politically opportunistic invocations of the constitutional amendment process – invocations whose purpose is so often to appeal to an amorphous 'people'. It has been stated that, in the United Kingdom, much of the uncertainty and opportunism around referendum use is due to the lack of any definition of their proper subject matter, constitutional or otherwise. However, based on the discussion above – and based on the flexibility as to what a constitutional amendment can contain or what it can do – it seems that confining referendum use to a defined, constitutional subject matter does little to stem this dynamic of political and symbolic

---

[47] See Siobhán Mullally, 'Citizenship and Family Life in Ireland: Asking the Question "Who Belongs"?' (2005) 25 *Legal Studies* 578–600, p. 578.

[48] A good example of this is Ireland's 'children's rights' referendum of 2012 which, according to Doyle and Kenny, 'made minimal change and largely reproduced what [civil society] groups had claimed to be a constitutional malaise'. See Oran Doyle and David Kenny, 'Constitutional change and interest group politics: Ireland's children's rights referendum', in Richard Albert, Xenophon Contiades, and Alkmene Fotiadou (eds.), *The Foundations and Traditions of Constitutional Amendment* (Oxford: Hart Publishing, 2017), p. 200.

instrumentalisation. For example, in the Italian referendum of 2017, Prime Minister Renzi 'deliberately turned a technical question of constitutional reform requiring formal approval, into a plebiscite for himself, and his Government, by promising to resign if he failed to achieve the desired outcome'.[49] Like Cameron in 2016, Renzi was 'seeking voter endorsement to consolidate [his] own political standing'.[50] It is for much the same reason that it difficult to confine referendums to a purely ratificatory or post-legislative role, simply because the amendment to be voted upon will inevitably be drafted in light of the logic and dynamics of referendum politics itself, rather than the net legislative issue that is ostensibly being decided. Amendments may be framed abstractly or symbolically, for expressive political purposes rather than technically focused reform goals, and it is difficult to envisage how constitutional regulation can stem this dynamic.

Irish referendums offer plenty of examples of the flexible form and purpose of referendums within what is ostensibly a highly structured and proceduralised system when compared with the UK version. Despite the fact that in Ireland, referendums are used only to ratify parliamentary bills containing constitutional amendments, this does not necessarily preclude the problems of uncertainty and opportunism that have been highlighted within the United Kingdom's more ad hoc framework. The Supreme Court has affirmed that there can be no judicial review of amendment proposals for clarity or coherence (or any substantive grounds, for that matter).[51] This principle of substantively unfettered amendability is comparatively unusual in codified constitutional systems, and in principle there is nothing to prevent judicial review for such desiderata of clarity, coherence and so on, that many identified as lacking in the Brexit referendum. However, many of the same problems that Tierney identifies in the attempt to define properly 'constitutional' issues would similarly arise, while the desire for clarity or precision seems to elide the intractably political nature of referendum processes, and the inevitability, in democratic debate, of contested and necessarily vague concepts.[52] In this light, indeed, Rocher and Lecours argue that unrealistic requirements of clarity in referendum proposals are not only counter-productive, but undemocratic.[53]

---

[49] Leyland, 'Referendums', p. 121.
[50] Ibid.
[51] *Finn v. Attorney General* [1983] IR 154.
[52] Daly, 'Constitutionalism'.
[53] François Rocher and André Lecours, 'The correct expression of popular will: does the wording of a referendum question matter?' in Laurence Morel and Matt Qvortrup (eds.), *The Routledge Handbook to Referendums and Direct Democracy* (London: Routledge, 2012), p. 207.

Equally, while some of the commentators mentioned earlier argue that a purely ratificatory, as distinct from advisory, referendum model would avoid many of the problems of the Brexit debacle, the Irish experience shows that the formal constraints imposed by such a model should not be overstated. The requirement that a referendum ratify a legal text does not ultimately mean very much when the content of that text is, by necessity, politically driven, symbolically charged, and unamenable to judicial direction or constraint. The profusion of deliberately vague and abstract language in the constitutional text – of symbolic or performative affirmations and so on – shows that this model cannot secure certainty, clarity or principled-ness, the desiderata thought to be missing in the UK adhocracy. Moreover, this ratificatory model cannot preclude the problems of contingency that are associated with Brexit - the problem, in particular, of an advisory vote giving overwhelming legitimacy to an ill-defined abstract whose precise contours politicians are empowered to later decide. Of course, there has never been an Irish referendum to compare with the Brexit referendum, and the various structural, constitutional flaws it has been associated with. But this can be regarded more as a result of historical and political happenstance than of constitutional design. The relevant case law suggests that the codified ratificatory model I have described lacks constraints, in terms of the form of constitutional amendments, of the sort that would prevent the kind of flexibility and contingency that are criticised in the UK adhocracy. This is in evidence, for example, in *Riordan v. An Taoiseach (no. 2)*, which related to the amendment providing for the ratification of the Belfast/Good Friday Agreement, and which accordingly proposed to alter the old Arts. 2 and 3 that had effectively laid claim to Northern Ireland. The court rejected the application despite the fact that the bill containing the Nineteenth Amendment provided for the constitutional changes to take place only if and when the government were to 'declare that the State has become obliged, pursuant to the [Belfast] Agreement, to give effect to the amendment of this Constitution referred to [within the bill]'[54] – in other words, when the other components of the Belfast Agreement had been approved. Effectively, then, the lack of scope to review constitutional amendment bills led the court to uphold a referendum whose textual subject matter was contingent on the occurrence of future events, giving discretion to the government to decide whether such events occurred, thus implying much of the formal flexibility – understood as a negative – that has been associated with the UK adhocracy.

---

[54] Nineteenth Amendment of the Constitution Act 1998, Schedule 7.

Similarly, the Supreme Court approved a similar flexibility of form in constitutional amendments, in upholding another proposed amendment bill, relating to abortion, which claimed to constitutionally incorporate an extraneous statute.[55] This does not mean the Irish framework is the same, or as flexible as the UK equivalent, but from the discussion above, it can nonetheless be surmised that the specificity of the UK adhocracy can easily be overstated, in terms of its capacity for, or encouragement of, dangerously open-ended or contingent referendums.

In principle, constitutional regulation – particularly regulation of the initiation power – might at least limit the power of elites to instrumentalise popular sovereignty. As we see in Ireland, whatever the formal role of referendums within the constitutional structure, it is difficult to meaningfully normativise the dynamics of referendum use, which retains an inherently political logic. In Ireland, constitutional referendums have not been a neutral procedural device; instead they have often been used expressively, on issues of cultural and social identity as much as constitutional structure or even policy. And the expressive capacity of referendums itself possesses a political significance that inevitably exceeds the formal constitutional issue that is ostensibly being voted upon. Inevitably, this offers a significant political resource whose populist potential is obvious, and is not easily regulated by constitutional law.

## CONCLUSION

In light of what I have argued, the political logic of referendum is probably intractable, and the populist style of referendum use is not easily regulated by constitutional safeguards. Therefore, various complaints as to the excessively political character of the referendum process in the United Kingdom, particularly after Brexit, appear somewhat unrealistic. The constitutional recognition and proceduralisation of popular sovereignty in the Irish Constitution leaves open the possibility of a populist dynamic of referendum use. The contrasting practice of referendum use in both countries may be as much to do with political and historical happenstance as with constitutional structure.

---

[55] *Morris v. Minister for the Environment* [2001] 3 IR 326.

# 9

## Party, Democracy, and Representation

### The Political Consequences of Brexit

Malcolm Petrie

The political impact of the 2016 referendum on the United Kingdom's membership of the European Union (EU) remains difficult to assess; for every set of political questions generated by the poll that have been resolved, further ambiguities have come into view. That the victory of the Leave campaign by the narrow margin of 52 to 48 per cent introduced a new divide into British politics is clear enough. Equally clear was the effect of the result upon the political career of David Cameron, who, as prime minister, had held the referendum in an attempt to unite a Conservative Party long divided on the issue of Europe, and to prevent a further rise in support for the Eurosceptic United Kingdom Independence Party (UKIP), led by the ubiquitous Nigel Farage.[1] Cameron, who campaigned for the United Kingdom to remain within the EU, resigned the morning after the vote.[2] Yet the wider significance of the referendum has proved harder to determine. The binary identities that emerged following the poll – Brexiters or Leavers vs. Remainers – initially overlapped only imprecisely with existing political loyalties. Brexit plainly had the potential to upend electoral politics, yet the probable shape of the post-referendum realignment shifted constantly. At the 2019 general election, the Conservative Party secured its largest parliamentary majority since the 1980s, and its highest share of the vote since 1979, arguably by appealing almost exclusively to Brexit supporters, but this outcome was not always predictable.

The recourse to a referendum provided a further complication. There were, of course, precedents, not least the 1975 European referendum, and other constitutional matters had been subject to popular votes in the intervening

---

[1] UKIP returned one MP at the 2015 general election, but received 3.8 million votes, almost 13 per cent of the total. See: Philip Cowley and Dennis Kavanagh, *The British General Election of 2015* (Basingstoke: Palgrave, 2016), pp. 49–56 and 372–4.
[2] Tim Shipman, *All Out War: The Full Story of Brexit* (London: Collins, 2017), pp. 451–3.

years.³ Nevertheless, the 2016 poll differed from previous referendums in three key aspects. First, in contrast to the devolution referendums of 1979 and 1997, no detailed alternative to the status quo was offered. Second, the referendum produced conflicting verdicts in the constituent nations of the United Kingdom, with Scotland and Northern Ireland voting to Remain while England and Wales returned majorities for Leave, an outcome that cemented existing constitutional divisions. Third, the result created a conflict between the authority of a putatively sovereign parliament and the popular, if slender, mandate of the referendum.⁴ Unlike in 1975, when parliamentary and public opinion had been in alignment, the 2016 referendum left a gulf between the electorate and their representatives, with the latter overwhelmingly in favour of continued EU membership.

Brexit's political impact was, then, not just electoral; rather, it brought into focus issues of representation, sovereignty, and national identity, which had longer lineages than suggested by a consideration of the European referendum alone. The relationship between these questions provides the focus of this chapter. The analysis concentrates first upon the consequences of Brexit for 'high' politics, focussing on the key developments at a parliamentary level after 2016. The constitutional challenges raised by Brexit in a Scottish context are then explored.⁵ The final section assesses the wider political context of the referendum, and the degree to which Brexit was an example of a broader trend towards forms of political 'populism'.

## THE ELECTORAL POLITICS OF BREXIT

Upon resigning, David Cameron declared that he would remain in office until the autumn to allow adequate time for a leadership contest; he was, however, replaced within weeks, as the selection of his successor descended into farce. The implosion of the candidacies of Boris Johnson, the former Mayor of London and a leading figure in the Vote Leave campaign, and Andrea Leadsom, a junior minister and another key Brexit supporter, allowed Theresa May, the former Home Secretary, to win by default; May entered office on 13 July 2016, less than three weeks after the

---

3   Robert Saunders, *Yes to Europe! The 1975 Referendum and Seventies Britain* (Cambridge: Cambridge University Press, 2018); Vernon Bogdanor, *The New British Constitution* (Oxford: Oxford University Press, 2009), pp. 173–96.
4   Martin Loughlin and Stephen Tierney, 'The Shibboleth of Sovereignty' (2018) 81:6 *Modern Law Review* 989–1016.
5   The impact of Brexit in Wales and Northern Ireland is addressed in separate chapters.

referendum.⁶ In retrospect, after her shortcomings as prime minister became obvious, May's avoidance of the scrutiny of a leadership contest assumed a certain significance. Yet it is easily forgotten how popular May was in the early months of her premiership, and not just with Conservatives. Having quietly supported Remain, May pivoted swiftly, appointing hardened Brexiteers to key cabinet positions: Boris Johnson became Foreign Secretary; Liam Fox received the International Trade portfolio; and David Davis headed the new Department for Exiting the EU (DexEU). Supported by her longstanding advisors Fiona Hill and Nick Timothy, May also began to outline a new Conservative ethos that repudiated the economic austerity and social liberalism of the Cameron era. In her inaugural speech as prime minister, May announced her desire to tackle inequality in all its forms; she would, she declared, always prioritise the interests of the 'just managing' over the 'privileged few', an obvious criticism of the atmosphere of easy elitism that had surrounded her predecessor.⁷

May's appeal to working-class and lower-middle-class voters was a response to the political divisions revealed by the referendum. In both England and Wales, a majority had backed leaving the EU, with the referendum prompting a higher than usual turnout. There were, however, striking geographical disparities in the result, with the Leave vote higher in the English regions.⁸ Support for Brexit also correlated closely with age, income, educational background, and ethnicity; Leave voters were, overall, likely to be older, white, less wealthy, and not to have attended university.⁹ While such generalisations obscured the substantial middle-class Leave vote, for May and her team, Brexit pointed nonetheless to a fundamental political realignment that would allow the Conservatives to construct a genuine mass appeal. The influence of Nick Timothy was important: he felt the Conservatives should seek to foreground patriotism and social conservatism and reject an unthinking celebration of the free market in favour of intervening to protect workers and consumers.

---

⁶ Nicholas Allen, 'Gambling with the Electorate: The Conservatives in Government' in Nicholas Allen and John Bartle (eds.), *None Past the Post: Britain at the Polls, 2017* (Manchester: Manchester University Press, 2017), pp. 14–16.
⁷ Statement from Theresa May, gov.uk, 13 July 2016, www.gov.uk/government/speeches/statement-from-the-new-prime-minister-theresa-may.
⁸ Will Jennings and Gerry Stoker, 'The Divergent Dynamics of Cities and Towns: Geographical Politics and Brexit' (2019) 90:S2 *Political Quarterly* 155–66.
⁹ Matthew Goodwin and Oliver Heath, 'The 2016 Referendum, Brexit and the Left Behind: An Aggregate-Level Analysis of the Result' (2016) 87:3 *Political Quarterly* 323–32.

This interpretation of Brexit was evident in the speeches May delivered at her first conference as Conservative leader. The first affirmed her commitment to delivering Brexit: she announced that she would invoke Art. 50 of the Lisbon Treaty by 31 March 2017, starting the two-year process of leaving the EU. May also declared that Brexit would require the United Kingdom to enjoy full control over immigration policy, and to no longer be subject to the jurisdiction of the European Court of Justice. Although left unstated, in practice these changes would mean leaving the single market.[10] May's second speech was an attempt to situate Brexit within her broader domestic political vision, and the diplomatic and constitutional implications scarcely featured. For May, the referendum had uncovered a feeling that society was run in the interests of the 'privileged few'; support for Brexit 'was a vote not just to change Britain's relationship with the European Union, but to ... change ... the way our country works – and the people for whom it works – forever'. Those in 'positions of power' who identified more 'with international elites than with people down the road', who found 'patriotism distasteful' and 'concerns about immigration parochial', were criticised; to hold such views, May claimed in a soon infamous line, was to be a 'citizen of nowhere'.[11] This analysis was, in some respects, perceptive. Likewise, prioritising the end of free movement was, given the prominence of immigration in the Leave campaign, at least comprehensible, whatever its moral or economic merit. Certainly, the political coherence of May's position was irrefutable: Brexit would provide the impetus for a wider renewal of Conservatism, easing the return of former supporters lost to UKIP, while appealing to traditional Labour voters in the English regions.

The politics were, though, impeded by legal and constitutional complexities. In November 2016, the English High Court ruled on a case brought by the activist Gina Miller, declaring that a parliamentary vote would be required to trigger Art. 50 and rejecting the government's position that the executive's prerogative powers were sufficient; the decision was endorsed by the Supreme Court in January 2017. Politically, the case was a charade: the government expected to lose, but persisted since doing so mollified Eurosceptic opinion within the Conservative Party and the media.[12] Further, the ruling was, in the short term, not significant: the necessary legislation was passed within weeks,

[10] Kate Allen, Alex Barker and George Parker, 'Theresa May sets Brexit course away from EU single market', *Financial Times*, 2 October 2016, www.ft.com/content/dea04ec2-8881-11e6-8aa5-f79f5696c731.

[11] Jim Pickard and Kate Allen, 'Theresa May sets out post-Brexit vision for a fairer Britain', *Financial Times*, 5 October 2016, www.ft.com/content/d38287f4-8afb-11e6-8cb7-e7ada1d123b1.

[12] Tim Shipman, *Fall Out: A Year of Political Mayhem* (London: Collins, 2017), pp. 114–17.

meeting the government's self-imposed deadline. Nonetheless, the case did hint at the difficulties ahead. While May continued to interpret Brexit in a manner that would preclude membership of the single market or customs union, the controversy regarding Art. 50 had confirmed the presence of a group of influential Conservative MPs who wished the United Kingdom to retain these affiliations as part of a so-called 'soft' Brexit. Having inherited a majority of just twelve, May was faced with the possibility that her Brexit proposals might fail in the Commons. If such concerns provided one incentive for May to call an election, straightforward partisan interest offered another. Since the referendum, opinion polls had consistently given the Conservatives a comfortable lead over the Labour Party; May's personal ratings were even stronger. Further encouragement came with the Conservative victory at the February 2017 Copeland by-election, the first mid-term gain by a governing party since 1982.[13] Unsurprisingly, in April 2017 May announced that she intended to call an election. The 2011 Fixed-Term Parliaments Act, a relic of the coalition era that required a two-thirds Commons majority for an early dissolution, proved no obstacle.

From a constitutional perspective, the 2017 election reversed previous custom: voters were effectively being asked to endorse, via a general election, a specific interpretation of a referendum result. Politically, the scale of the Conservative lead in the polls encouraged a belief too that the election would enable a lasting political reorientation. The election result, which saw the Conservatives lose their majority, and continue in office only with the support of the Democratic Unionist Party, the dominant political representatives of Northern Ireland's unionist community, was therefore a bitter disappointment. Further, the importance of the border between the United Kingdom and the Republic of Ireland in negotiations with the EU made an explicit alliance with Ulster unionism deeply controversial. May's standing within her party never recovered; her key aides, Hill and Timothy, already disliked by many within the party for their abrasive style, were forced to resign; and the belief that Brexit was an opportunity to craft a more interventionist Conservatism left with them.

The Conservative failure in 2017 was, at a basic level, May's responsibility. The campaign exposed weaknesses in her judgement, most obviously in relation to the proposed changes to the funding of elderly care, a policy abandoned mid-campaign in a humiliating U-turn. Indeed, May's limitations as a leader defined the campaign, at least for the press. While never a charismatic performer, prior to the election her diligent and modest public

---

[13] Allen, 'Gambling with the Electorate', pp. 22–3.

persona seemed well-suited to the prevailing political mood. During the election, however, May appeared increasingly ill at ease in public; her refusal to participate in the leaders' debates was telling. Certainly, the decision to build the Conservative appeal around her alleged attributes was mistaken.[14] But the media obsession with May's flaws reflected a tendency, visible throughout the post-referendum period, to overstate the role of party leaders, and to neglect deeper political changes.[15] May's belief that Brexit could be used to reunite the political right was borne out: UKIP's support vanished, while the Conservatives polled over 42 per cent nationally, the party's highest share of the vote since 1983; in England, that figure reached almost 46 per cent. The issue was the failure to translate this support into seats: the Conservative vote rose in many Labour-held constituencies, but not by enough to oust the incumbent. This was accentuated by the surprisingly robust performance of the Labour Party; one unexpected consequence of Brexit was a short-lived revival of two-party politics, in England at least.

After defeat at the 2015 election, which prompted the resignation of Ed Miliband as leader, the Labour Party was in seeming disarray. Despite his popularity with party members and activists, Miliband's successor, the veteran left-wing MP Jeremy Corbyn, enjoyed little support from a Parliamentary Labour Party (PLP) deeply suspicious of his stance on defence and foreign policy. Brexit only exacerbated these rifts. Although he had, like the majority of the PLP, publicly supported Remain, Corbyn was accused of having failed to campaign with sufficient enthusiasm. Corbyn's history as a left-wing critic of the EU hardened such doubts, as did his call for Art. 50 to be activated immediately. There followed a coordinated series of shadow cabinet resignations, and a vote of no confidence in Corbyn's leadership by the PLP passed by a margin of four to one. Nevertheless, Corbyn, sure his mandate came from the membership rather than MPs, refused to resign, and easily fended off a subsequent leadership challenge.[16]

Where Brexit had offered Conservatives an opportunity, for Labour it appeared as a threat to party unity. While most Labour voters had supported Remain, a minority had backed Leave; the electoral significance of the latter group blurred existing internal divisions. While some on the left were critical of the EU, the firmest believers in honouring the referendum result were MPs on the right of the PLP, unsympathetic to Corbyn, but who represented

---

[14] Shipman, *Fall Out*, pp. 241–6.
[15] See the post-election commentary in *The Economist*, 10 June 2017 and *The Observer*, 11 June 2017.
[16] Thomas Quinn, 'Revolt on the Left', in Allen and Bartie (eds.), *None Past the Post*, pp. 34–53.

constituencies where a majority had voted for Brexit. Conversely, the left-wing members committed to Corbynism defended the principle of free movement, and tended to advocate softening, or even reversing, Brexit. The leadership's downplaying of the European question in favour of economic issues indicated, perhaps, a rarely credited degree of political wisdom, since it diminished internal tensions while blunting Conservative attempts to poach pro-Brexit Labour voters. It echoed, too, May's sense that the Brexit vote was driven by domestic discontents. Corbyn, and the astute shadow chancellor John McDonnell, opted to portray Brexit as a rejection of the austerity programme imposed by the Conservative-Liberal Democrat coalition between 2010 and 2015.

Labour's electoral prospects in 2017 appeared bleak: dire opinion poll forecasts were seemingly confirmed by the disastrous results of the May 2017 local elections. Yet at the general election Labour polled 40 per cent of the vote, up 10 points on 2015, gaining thirty seats and preventing a Conservative majority. The result partly reflected the campaign, where Corbyn, unlike May, had thrived. Labour's unabashedly left-wing manifesto, which promised the abolition of university tuition fees, investment in public services, and large-scale nationalisations, proved popular with younger voters and those weary of austerity. But a studied vagueness on Brexit helped too, checking Conservative progress in the north of England while, at the same time, allowing Labour to benefit from tactical voting by opponents of Brexit. In urban and southern England, former Liberal Democrat and Green supporters backed Labour on this basis, delivering surprise victories in seats such as Canterbury, and Kensington and Chelsea. Indeed, the failure of the Liberal Democrats to become the party of Remain, despite calling for a confirmatory referendum on the final Brexit deal, proved crucial, with progressive voters unwilling to overlook the party's record in office during the coalition years. The election also entrenched the generational gulf present during the referendum: exit polls revealed that voters under the age of forty-five overwhelmingly backed Labour over the Conservatives; the picture was reversed for those over forty-five.[17]

For Conservatives, although still in office, the election resembled a defeat; for the left, meanwhile, it felt something like a victory. In the summer of 2017, it was Labour that enjoyed a sense of momentum, with the party having mobilised a new electoral alliance. Certainly, it seemed implausible that May could continue as prime minister, especially following the tragic fire at

---

[17] Peter Dorey, 'Jeremy Corbyn Confounds his Critics: Explaining the Labour Party's remarkable resurgence in the 2017 election' (2017) 17:3 *British Politics* 308–34.

Grenfell Tower, a residential tower block in Kensington, a week after the election, that resulted in seventy-two deaths. May's inept response to the disaster reinforced the perception that she was ill-suited to the role of prime minister. May would, however, survive in office for a further two years, and the Conservatives, led by her successor, Boris Johnson, would win a comfortable majority at the December 2019 general election. The ability of the Conservatives to retain power rested, paradoxically, upon an inability to secure a Brexit deal that could command parliamentary support. The negotiating position adopted by Theresa May, elaborated in July 2018, was rejected by pro-Brexit Conservatives, who objected to the proposed 'common rulebook' for goods, which would have required key sectors of the UK economy to remain in close regulatory alignment with the EU. Unwilling to support May's proposals, David Davis and Boris Johnson resigned from the cabinet.[18] The Withdrawal Agreement eventually concluded with the EU in November 2018 faced similar opposition, and prompted the resignation of Dominic Raab, Davis's successor at DexEU.[19] The following month, the government suffered a series of humiliating parliamentary defeats as MPs demanded more influence over the final Brexit deal; May survived an internal confidence vote only after promising that she would not contest another election.[20] By March 2019, with the Commons having repeatedly rejected both the deal negotiated by May and the possibility of a no-deal Brexit, the government was forced to seek an extension to the deadline for negotiations imposed by Art. 50, due to expire at the end of March 2019.

Unable to deliver Brexit, May's humiliation was complete; she announced her departure in May 2019. The delays provided the basis for the eventual electoral victory enjoyed by Boris Johnson, who replaced May in July 2019. Between 2017 and 2019, the debate over Brexit became increasingly polarised. For many Brexit supporters, the lack of progress was evidence of the

[18] HM Government, The Future Relationship between the United Kingdom and the European Union, Cm 9593 (2018).
[19] Heather Stewart, Pippa Crerar and Dan Sabbagh, 'May's plan "sticks in the throat", says Boris Johnson as he resigns over Brexit', *Guardian*, 9 July 2018, www.theguardian.com/politics/2018/jul/09/boris-johnson-resigns-as-foreign-secretary-brexit; Pippa Crerar and Matthew Weaver, 'McVey and Raab quit as May addresses MPs over Brexit deal', *Guardian*, 15 November 2018, www.theguardian.com/politics/2018/nov/15/dominic-raab-quits-as-brexit-secretary-over-eu-witi hdrawal-deal.
[20] Heather Stewart, Jessica Elgot and Rajeev Syal, 'Theresa May staggers on after three Brexit defeats in single day', *Guardian*, 5 December 2018, www.theguardian.com/politics/2018/dec/04/theresa-may-staggers-on-after-three-brexit-defeats-in-single-day; Heather Stewart, 'Theresa May defeats Tory coup over Brexit deal but is left damaged', *Guardian*, 13 December 2018, www.theguardian.com/politics/2018/dec/12/theresa-may-defeats-leadership-challenge-by-83-votes.

recalcitrance of an establishment that had, from the outset, refused to accept the referendum result, and the performance of the Brexit Party, Nigel Farage's post-UKIP vehicle, at the 2019 European elections demonstrated the potency of such sentiments. Similarly, by 2019, opponents of Brexit had become more confident of revisiting the decision: the early concern with ensuring parliamentary oversight of the negotiations was replaced by calls for a second referendum, notably with the launch of the People's Vote campaign in early 2018. Such developments shielded the Conservatives from the consequences of their own failures; instead, any setbacks could be attributed to alleged efforts to frustrate Brexit. May had flirted with this narrative, but with the arrival of Johnson and his chief advisor, the former Vote Leave strategist Dominic Cummings, it became the basis of government policy.[21] A series of confrontations with Parliament were contrived, with the aim of hardening public perceptions that the political establishment was blocking Brexit; the whip was removed from twenty-one Conservative MPs who voted against the government and an attempt was made to prorogue Parliament, although this was ultimately overturned by the Supreme Court. Johnson eventually goaded his opponents into granting him the election he wanted. It was contested by the Conservatives on the brutally simple promise that they would 'Get Brexit Done', and there was little sense of any broader political vision. While the Conservative vote increased only marginally, Johnson, aided by the decision of the Brexit Party not to contest Conservative-held seats, achieved the electoral breakthrough that eluded May, winning a swathe of traditional Labour seats in the north of England and securing a majority of eighty.[22] A revised version of the Withdrawal Agreement was passed, and the United Kingdom formally left the EU on 31 January 2020.

Critics of Brexit were hampered by an inability to agree on an alternative. Instead, positions and alliances constantly shifted; there was even the launch of a short-lived new party, Change UK, established in early 2019 by disillusioned pro-Remain Labour and Conservative MPs.[23] By the 2019 election, the Liberal Democrats had abandoned calls for a second referendum in favour of claiming that they would simply revoke Art. 50.[24] The Liberal Democrat stance was, despite the ambitious claims of the party's leader, Jo Swinson,

---

[21] Meg Russell, 'Brexit and Parliament: The Anatomy of a Perfect Storm' (2020) *Parliamentary Affairs*. Published online 11 June 2020.

[22] David Cutts et al., 'Brexit, the 2019 General Election and the realignment of British Politics' (2020) 91:1 *Political Quarterly* 7–23.

[23] Change UK dissolved after the 2019 election.

[24] *Stop Brexit, Build a Brighter Future: Liberal Democrat Manifesto 2019*, www.libdems.org.uk/liberal-democrats-2019-manifesto.

irrelevant. Nevertheless, the policy shift was indicative of a wider rejection of compromise. This absolutism was most challenging for the Labour Party, which needed both Leave and Remain voters. For Labour it would have been preferable had May been able to pass her deal, removing the need to engage with the debate over a second referendum; being forced to fight another election while Brexit remained unresolved was an unwelcome outcome. The artful ambiguities of 2017 could not be reprised; with pro-Remain voices gaining ground in the party – especially the shadow Brexit secretary Keir Starmer, and the shadow foreign secretary, Emily Thornberry – Labour contested the election committed to an impenetrable policy that involved negotiating a new Brexit deal, which would then be put to a referendum alongside a Remain option.[25] The coalition assembled in 2017 dissolved; Labour's vote share fell to 32 per cent, and the party's parliamentary representation slumped to its lowest level since the 1930s.

Brexit dominated UK politics after 2016, but, in the aftermath of the 2019 election, it was striking just how ephemeral much of the debate proved to be. For all the tumult, politics evolved in a direction that was, in hindsight, discernible before the referendum. The exception was the disappearance of UKIP, left purposeless once Leave had won; the Conservatives are now the party of Brexit, and have absorbed much of UKIP's former base. For Labour, the 2017 result looks now to have been an anomaly, one reliant upon too many contingencies to be easily replicated. The party struggles to contest the dominance of the Conservative Party in England and has done for half a century: since 1970, Labour has polled above 40 per cent of the vote in England at only three general elections: 1997, 2001, and 2017. The confusion over the party's Brexit position; Corbyn's unpopularity with large parts of the electorate; the controversy surrounding allegations of anti-Semitism within the party: all were, no doubt, damaging. But the 34 per cent polled by Labour in England in 2019 was just below the 2005 result, when Tony Blair had been returned for a third term, and higher than was accomplished by either Gordon Brown in 2010 or Ed Miliband in 2015. Shifting demographics have accentuated this long-term weakness by concentrating Labour voters in fewer, predominantly urban, seats. It is not just that Labour voters have become younger or more likely to have attended university; there are now fewer Labour voters in the seats the party needs to win. In the northern English constituencies targeted successfully by the Conservatives in 2019, for example,

[25] *It's Time for Real Change: The Labour Party Manifesto 2019*, https://labour.org.uk/manifesto-2019/.

the electorate has become markedly older since the late 1990s.[26] Labour's English problems were, of course, compounded by the party's collapse in Scotland; this too, however, predates Brexit.

Brexit highlighted the divergent political cultures across the nations of the United Kingdom, but it did not create them. An English identity which was anti-metropolitan, Eurosceptic, and anti-immigration in inclination had been gaining in political influence since the 1990s; especially following the extension of free movement of labour to the new eastern European EU member states in 2004, a key moment in the rise of UKIP.[27] Once the referendum had been held, Conservatives were always going to be more comfortable with the sentiments underlying the Leave vote, and better placed to appeal to an explicitly English identity.[28] Of course, by confirming the reality, and the power, of a distinctive English politics, Brexit posed a serious challenge to the constitutional integrity of the United Kingdom.

## BREXIT AND THE ANGLO-SCOTTISH UNION

In Scotland, the debate over the United Kingdom's relationship with the EU landed in a political landscape where, following the 2014 referendum on Scottish independence, constitutional questions were already central to politics. Although in 2014 a majority had voted to remain part of the United Kingdom, the 'Yes' campaign had polled 45 per cent, creating a substantial pro-independence constituency inclined towards the Scottish National Party (SNP). At the 2015 general election, the SNP gained almost half the popular vote in Scotland, winning an extraordinary fifty-six of Scotland's fifty-nine Westminster seats; Labour's long era of dominance in Scotland was over. The SNP had also retained a leading position at the Scottish Parliament, where it had held power since 2007; although the May 2016 Scottish parliamentary elections saw the SNP lose the outright majority gained in 2011, there was still, with the support of the Scottish Greens, a pro-independence majority at Holyrood.[29]

---

[26] *2019 Election Review* (London: Labour Together, 2020), p. 55, https://www.labourtogether.uk/review.

[27] Michael Kenny, 'The Return of "Englishness" in British Political Culture: The End of the Unions?' (2015) 53:1 *Journal of Common Market Studies* 35–51; Ailsa Henderson et al., 'England, Englishness and Brexit' (2016) 87:2 *Political Quarterly* 187–99; Helen Thompson, 'Inevitability and Contingency: The Political Economy of Brexit' (2017) 19:3 *British Journal of Politics and International Relations* 434–49.

[28] Andrew Gamble, 'The Conservatives and the Union: The "New English Toryism" and the Origins of Anglo-Britishness' (2016) 14:3 *Political Studies Review* 359–67.

[29] Paul Cairney, 'The Scottish Parliament Election 2016: another momentous event but dull campaign' (2016) 25:3 *Scottish Affairs* 277–93.

At the 2016 election, the SNP had pledged to demand a second independence referendum if there was a 'material change in the circumstances that prevailed in 2014'.[30] The result of the EU referendum surely met this criterion: Scots supported EU membership by a margin of 62 per cent to 38, but faced being forced to leave on the basis of the results in England and Wales. A further irony was that the prospect of a newly independent Scotland being required to reapply for EU membership had been an important plank in the pro-Union campaign in 2014. But the way in which Brexit interacted with the debate over Scottish independence was complex, and, at times, counter-intuitive. Outwardly, the divergent verdicts recorded across the United Kingdom in 2016, and the SNP's official commitment to EU membership, vindicated assertions that Scottish interests were not adequately represented at Westminster. But if Brexit unquestionably deepened the constitutional conflicts left unresolved after 2014, it would, nevertheless, be wrong to straightforwardly equate support for independence with a belief in European integration. While the overlap between these stances was significant, it was not total; further, Brexit complicated as much as strengthened the case for Scottish independence.[31]

From the outset, Nicola Sturgeon, the First Minister of Scotland and leader of the SNP, insisted that the 'stark divergence in democratic will between the different nations of the United Kingdom' had to be recognised and called for Scotland to at least be allowed to remain within the European single market, even if England and Wales exited.[32] Yet this position concealed important divisions within the pro-independence movement. Although precise assessments were difficult, polling suggested that as many as one in three SNP supporters had voted to leave the EU.[33] A concern for sovereignty and a desire to be free from the influence of both London and Brussels may well offer some explanation, but the SNP's history, and its traditional sources of support, were also relevant. Until the late 1980s, the SNP had instinctively mistrusted European integration, fearing its implications for smaller nations.[34] Traces of this scepticism were clearly still present within sections of the party's base. Further, prior to the early twenty-first century, the SNP had enjoyed greatest

[30] *Re-Elect: SNP Manifesto 2016*, p. 2, https://d3n8a8pro7vhmx.cloudfront.net/thesnp/pages/5540/attachments/original/1461753756/SNP_Manifesto2016-accesible.pdf?1461753756.
[31] Nicola McEwen, 'Brexit and Scotland: Between Two Unions' (2018) 13:1 *British Politics* 65–78.
[32] *Scotland's Place in Europe* (Edinburgh: Scottish Government, 2016), p. vi.
[33] Michael Settle, '36% of SNP and Labour supporters backed Brexit, finds survey', *Glasgow Herald*, 7 December 2016, https://www.heraldscotland.com/news/14950013.36-of-snp-and-labour-supporters-backed-brexit-finds-survey/.
[34] Andrew D. Devenney, 'Regional Resistance to European Integration: The Case of the Scottish National Party' (2008) 33:3 *Historical Social Research* 319–45.

success in the largely rural constituencies of central and eastern Scotland. Although no Scottish constituency recorded a majority in favour of Brexit, it was in the SNP's north-east heartlands that the Leave campaign performed best: in Moray, then represented by the SNP's Commons leader Angus Robertson, Leave polled 49.9 per cent. In such constituencies, it was by no means evident that voting for the SNP signified agreement with the party's policy on Europe, or even on Scottish independence.

More than this, in Scotland, Brexit was a secondary issue, one viewed in terms of its relationship to the debate over Scotland's constitutional status, a hierarchy confirmed by the 2017 election. What might have been understood as the centre-ground of Scottish politics – pro-UK and pro-EU – was embodied best by the Liberal Democrats, and the party's vote flatlined as it finished in fourth place. Instead, the election was dominated by the question of how many seats the SNP would hold, and whether Labour or the Conservatives would become the principal voice of pro-Union Scots. On the latter issue, it was the Conservatives who performed better, returning thirteen MPs after two decades in which the election of a single Scottish representative was considered a success, a result that proved vital to the party remaining in government. Admittedly, the Scottish Conservatives were, under the leadership of Ruth Davidson, more pro-European than their English and Welsh colleagues. It was, though, perhaps telling that their most notable successes came in the north-east, where Conservative candidates ousted both Angus Robertson, defeated in Moray, and Alex Salmond, Sturgeon's predecessor as SNP leader and the architect of the 2014 referendum, who lost in Gordon. Here a rejection of Scottish independence possibly blended with a traditional Euroscepticism.

For the SNP, while Brexit allowed the argument for a second independence referendum to be advanced in some respects, it also presented significant challenges. The 2017 election made clear that opposition to Brexit simply did not inspire the same level of popular enthusiasm as independence. The party's representation at Westminster fell from fifty-six to thirty-five, in part as a result of tactical voting by opponents who had learned the lessons of 2015, but principally due to a sharp fall in turnout. Between 2015 and 2017, the SNP shed almost half a million votes, and overall turnout in Scotland fell from 71 per cent to 66 per cent, in contrast to the increased participation witnessed in England and Wales. The political impact of Brexit was thus uneven across the United Kingdom; for a Scottish electorate already realigning around poles generated by a constitutional referendum, the question of Europe was subordinate.[35]

---

[35] Gerry Hassan, 'After the Landslide: Scotland still Marches to a Different Politics, Only Slightly Less So' (2017) 88:3 *Political Quarterly* 375–81.

Nonetheless, Brexit did affect political and constitutional debates in Scotland in two important ways. First, Brexit effectively ended the viability of the independent Scotland envisioned by the SNP in 2014. The SNP had portrayed independence as transformative yet strangely undisruptive: common membership of the EU was a vital part of this prospectus, suggesting that political independence could be achieved without any interruption to flows of goods, services, or people. The White Paper produced by the Scottish government prior to the referendum argued that while independence would end the 'parliamentary union', it would 'not affect the many other ties that bind Scotland to the other nations of the UK'; an independent Scotland would remain part of 'five continuing unions': the EU; the Union of the Crowns; a currency union, in which Scotland would continue to use sterling; NATO; and a social union 'made up of connections of family, history, culture and language'.[36] Brexit obviously threatened the first of these unions, suggesting that an independent Scotland might face similar border issues to the ones created by Brexit on the island of Ireland. Similarly, the notion of a currency union, already a critical weakness in the SNP's case in 2014, looked even more implausible after Brexit, since it was hardly compatible with the ambition that an independent Scotland would seek to rejoin the EU.

Second, and perhaps most significantly, Brexit raised questions about the stability of the devolved constitutional settlement. The Scottish Parliament was, in one sense, a legislative creation of the UK Parliament, which, while it enjoyed competence over all matters not explicitly reserved, remained formally subordinate to the still sovereign Westminster Parliament.[37] The authority of the devolved Parliament had, however, been buttressed by the overwhelming endorsement that the devolution proposals received in the 1997 referendum. The decision to hold a referendum reflected the Parliament's roots in the cross-party Campaign for a Scottish Assembly (CSA), formed following the failed 1979 devolution referendum. In 1988, as part of the creation of the Constitutional Convention that would eventually produce the blueprint for the devolved Parliament, the CSA published the Claim of Right, a forthright assertion, or invention, of a Scottish tradition of popular sovereignty.[38] Devolution's mandate was thus twofold, part-legislative, part-popular, and, after an unsteady start, the Parliament was recognised as

---

[36] *Scotland's Future: your guide to an independent Scotland* (Edinburgh: Scottish Government, 2013), pp. 214–15.

[37] Scotland Act 1998, s. 28(7).

[38] Roger Levy, 'The Scottish Constitutional Convention: Nationalism and the Union' (1992) 27 *Government and Opposition*, 222–34; James Mitchell, *The Scottish Question* (Oxford: Oxford University Press, 2014), chap. 10.

Scotland's principal representative institution. It was, then, with some justification that the Scottish government demanded it be granted a formal role in the Brexit negotiations as the voice of a distinctive Scottish polity.

Devolution had, however, arrived at a time when EU membership was assumed to be a permanent part of the constitutional backdrop. The Scottish Parliament's legislative competence was circumscribed by a requirement to comply with EU law, a measure that limited divergence between UK jurisdictions; Brexit threatened to remove this guard rail.[39] There was, in addition, ambiguity over how competences that had resided at the European level would be distributed after Brexit; the stated desire of the UK government to ensure that a UK 'internal market' operates post-Brexit promises to be a continued source of constitutional tension.[40] The manner of the Conservative government's pursuit of Brexit created further concerns regarding the status of the Scottish Parliament. Following the 2014 independence referendum, the UK government had established the Smith Commission to examine the case for devolving further powers to Holyrood. The commission's recommendations, which centred upon extending the Parliament's fiscal powers, formed the basis of the Scotland Act 2016, passed three months prior to the EU referendum.[41] The legislation began with an assertion that the devolved Parliament was 'a permanent part of the United Kingdom's constitutional arrangements', and could not be 'abolished except on the basis of a decision of the people of Scotland voting in a referendum'. This was followed by statutory recognition of the Sewel Convention, under which the UK Parliament agreed to 'not normally legislate with regard to devolved matters without the consent of the Scottish Parliament'.[42]

Ostensibly, the 2016 Act placed the devolved institutions beyond the reach of partisan politics, and, indeed, of the sovereign authority of Westminster: the Parliament's popular mandate trumped its statutory basis. Brexit, however, posed an immediate challenge to any such assumptions. The *Miller* case, although principally concerned with whether parliamentary approval was required to trigger Art. 50, had seen contributions from the devolved administrations, who argued that the Sewel Convention applied to the process of

[39] Scotland Act 1998, s. 29(2)(d).
[40] Editorial, 'Boris Johnson risks a disunited UK over state aid clash', *Financial Times*, 13 July 2020, https://www.ft.com/content/ocdf860e-c50d-11ea-9d81-eb7f2a294c50.
[41] *Report of the Smith Commission for Further Devolution of Powers to the Scottish Parliament* (London: The Smith Commission, 2014).
[42] Scotland Act 2016, s. 1 and s. 2. See: Chris Himsworth, 'Legislating for Permanence and a Statutory Footing' (2016) 20:3 *Edinburgh Law Review* 361–7; Aileen McHarg and James Mitchell, 'Brexit and Scotland' (2017) 19:3 *British Journal of Politics and International Relations* 512–36.

leaving the EU, since this would affect devolved matters. The Supreme Court ruled that this was not the case: leaving the EU was a reserved matter, and Sewel did not apply. Nevertheless, the court's ruling, while ambiguous, suggested that it viewed Sewel as a political convention that was not justiciable.[43] There remained, then, questions over the true value of the 2016 Act. If the guarantees offered to the Scottish Parliament were political rather than legal, they depended upon the UK government recognising such limits. The post-referendum conduct of the Conservative government provided few assurances.

At a UK level, Brexit had accelerated existing political trends rather than diverting them; yet in Scotland the European referendum functioned, in effect, as a constraint on political progress. Conducted in the shadow of 2014 and interpreted in that context, Brexit still precluded any attempt to move beyond the constitutional stalemate that followed the independence referendum. Scottish politics remains in the mould set prior to 2016: the SNP's dominance was reasserted at the 2019 election, with the party's Westminster representation increasing from thirty-five to forty-eight; while the SNP's share of the Scottish vote rose from 37 to 45 per cent. Likewise, while the number of Scottish Conservative MPs fell from thirteen to seven, the party is still the principal opposition to the SNP, with the Labour Party continuing to struggle in Scotland.[44] Only a second independence referendum can alter that picture, but with the shape of the final post-Brexit relationship between the United Kingdom and EU still to be settled and the UK government refusing to consider the Scottish government's calls for a further independence poll, this seems unlikely to take place until after the 2021 Holyrood elections. So much happened in Scottish politics between 2016 and 2019, yet so little changed.

## BREXIT, POPULISM, AND THE PEOPLE

The electoral and constitutional impact of Brexit was principally to reinforce tendencies apparent prior to 2016; still, the broader consequences for political culture and understandings of representation were significant, chiefly since the victory of the Leave campaign was such a shock to the political establishment. While there had, since the 1990s, been a significant Eurosceptic

---

[43] Tom Mullen, 'The Brexit Case and Constitutional Conventions' (2017) 21:3 *Edinburgh Law Review* 442–7.
[44] Malcolm Harvey, 'A Dominant SNP in a Unionist Scotland? The 2019 General Election in Scotland' (2020) 91:1 *Political Quarterly* 56–60; Ailsa Henderson, Rob Johns, Jac Larner and Chris Carman , 'Scottish Labour as a case study in party failure: Evidence from the 2019 UK General Election in Scotland' (2020) 29:2 *Scottish Affairs* 127–40.

element in British politics, particularly among Conservative politicians and their allies in the print media, there was little expectation that these voices would be able to overcome the consensus in favour of continued EU membership that prevailed among the leadership of all the major parties, and, indeed, among most of the key institutions of British public life. Brexit thus produced a sense of political dislocation, of vertigo, and in the summer of 2016 it felt, especially for those on the losing side, that British politics had been shunted abruptly onto a different, unrecognisable, path. As one prominent liberal commentator wrote on the morning after the referendum, Britons had 'woken up in different country... This is not the country it was yesterday. That place has gone for ever.'[45]

For those occupying the centre of British politics, there was a persistent sense of regret that David Cameron had allowed the United Kingdom's position in the EU to be risked in such a manner. Underlying such judgements was a dislike of the mechanism of the referendum, considered a blunt constitutional instrument ill-suited to settling complex issues that could not be reduced to a binary proposition. It was felt that direct democracy, used in such a manner, encouraged the polarisation of the electorate.[46] This analysis, alongside the closeness of the 2016 result, encouraged portrayals of Britain as a deeply divided society, with Leave and Remain signifying competing and incompatible worldviews. The suggested alternative labels varied – 'Brexitland' versus 'Londonia'; 'Closed' versus 'Open'; 'Somewheres' versus 'Nowheres' – but the premise was consistent. Brexit had revealed the divisions between the beneficiaries of globalisation, who tended to be middle class, university-educated, and reside in major cities, and the economically left behind, located predominantly in declining provincial towns and rural areas, who experienced open markets and immigration as threats to stability and employment, and who held more conservative social views.[47]

Brexit, in consequence, came to be read as a British example of the populist politics believed to be gaining influence in many democracies: according to *The Economist* 'chunks of the British electorate' were 'now in thrall to an angry

---

[45] Jonathan Freedland, 'We have woken up in a different country', *Guardian*, 24 June 2016, www.theguardian.com/commentisfree/2016/jun/24/eu-referendum-britain-different-country.

[46] See the revealing article by Peter Mandelson, a key Labour figure in the Blair era and prominent supporter of Remain: 'How the struggle for Europe was lost', *Financial Times*, 2 July 2016, www.ft.com/content/98619c5c-3f70-11e6-8716-a4a71e8140bo.

[47] Bagehot, 'Brexitland versus Londonia', *Economist*, 2 July 2016, www.economist.com/britain/2016/06/30/brexitland-versus-londonia; Leader, 'The New Political Divide', *Economist*, 30 July 2016, www.economist.com/leaders/2016/07/30/the-new-political-divide; David Goodhart, *The Road to Somewhere: The Populist Revolt and the Future of Politics* (London: C. Hurst & Co., 2017).

populism'.[48] Anti-elitist, anti-immigration, nationalist, and protectionist in its rhetoric, this populism rested upon a claim to speak for the people, an ability to channel the voice of the 'true' nation, alleged to have been ignored by an aloof and self-serving establishment. While there were other, and perhaps better, comparisons available, the most frequent analogy for British commentators was with Donald Trump's unexpected political rise in the United States; Trump seized the Republican presidential nomination in the month before Brexit, going on to win a shock election victory in November 2016 on an aggressively chauvinistic and anti free-trade platform. This wider context heightened fears that Brexit might curdle into something more openly xenophobic and authoritarian.[49]

There was, to be sure, some substance to these fears. Although similarities between the United Kingdom and United States can be exaggerated, there were commonalities. Perhaps most striking was the growing centrality of social media in political campaigning. It was evident that, like Trump, the Leave campaign had exploited Facebook and Twitter, and there was unease that claims made on these platforms were not subject to the same regulation and accountability as traditional methods of political advertising, amid allegations of illegality and Russian interference in both the United Kingdom and the United States.[50] There were anxieties, too, that the rise of online campaigns was creating a more emotive, volatile, even nihilistic political culture, one in which anonymous abuse was commonplace, and the adoption of extreme viewpoints was rewarded.[51] The appalling murder of the Labour MP Jo Cox during the referendum campaign by Thomas Mair, a far-right extremist,

---

[48] Leader, 'A Tragic Split', *Economist*, 25 June 2016, www.economist.com/leaders/2016/06/24/a-tragic-split.

[49] Studies of populism flourished after 2016. See, for example: Roger Eatwell and Matthew Goodwin, *National Populism: The Revolt Against Liberal Democracy* (London: Pelican, 2018); Jan-Werner Muller, *What is Populism?* (Philadelphia, PA: University of Pennsylvania, 2017); Cas Mudde, *Populism: A Very Short Introduction* (Oxford: Oxford University Press, 2017); Pippa Norris and Ronald Inglehart, *Cultural Backlash: Trump, Brexit and Authoritarian Populism* (Cambridge: Cambridge University Press, 2019); Ivor Crewe and David Sanders (eds.), *Authoritarian Populism and Liberal Democracy* (Cham: Palgrave Macmillan, 2020).

[50] The allegations focus on the role of Cambridge Analytica. Carol Cadwalladr, '"I made Steve Bannon's psychological warfare tool": meet the data war whistleblower', *Observer*, 18 March 2018, www.theguardian.com/news/2018/mar/17/data-war-whistleblower-christopher-wylie-faceook-nix-bannon-trump and Carol Cadwalladr, 'The Great Hack: the film that goes behind the scenes of the Facebook scandal', *Observer*, 21 July 2019, www.theguardian.com/uk-news/2019/jul/20/the-great-hack-cambridge-analytica-scandal-facebook-netflix.

[51] For a discussion of this phenomenon, see, Richard Seymour, *The Twittering Machine* (London: The Indigo Press, 2019).

suggested that concerns over the impact of the campaign were not without foundation.

It is, though, important to recognise that Brexit represented a fruition of domestic political trends. The notion that referendums were inherently divisive, that populism was foreign to British politics, or even a consequence of social media's influence, suggests a curious myopia about British political history. For Nick Clegg, the pro-Remain former Liberal Democrat leader who had been deputy prime minister between 2010 and 2015, the referendum had seen 'the political stability, legal reliability and economic openness which have marked out Britain as a global leader ... casually cast aside'.[52] But this represents only a different version of the exceptionalism that was considered so characteristic of the Leave campaign, often accused of pedalling various myths regarding the Second World War and the Empire.[53] To see the United Kingdom as having been uniquely stable, its politics measured and rational, is to accept uncritically a version of British history that is hardly unpolitical; it exposes, too, a certain naïveté, not least in regard to Northern Ireland, which, as Brexit has confirmed, remains an eternal learning curve for British politicians.[54]

Constitutional referendums do reduce complex issues to binary choices; they can, as Tierney has recognised, lead to the creation of political identities, a 'framing of the collective self'.[55] And in the case of Brexit, the narrowness of the result produced two competing political identities. Even so, the 2016 referendum did not mark the introduction of a new populism in which the mandate of the majority would be pitted against a pro-Remain parliament. The divergence in opinion between the electorate and their representatives was a notable difference from previous referendums held in the United Kingdom. But populist rhetoric and the attempt by politicians, often themselves from elite backgrounds, to claim that they represented the people against an establishment conspiring against the true interests of the nation was scarcely unknown in British politics. Certainly, in the late 1960s and 1970s,

---

[52] Nick Clegg, 'Brexit: Cameron and Osborne are to blame for this sorry pass', *Financial Times*, 24 June 2016, www.ft.com/content/6044d4c8-3a03-11e6-a780-b48ed7b6126f. After losing his seat in 2017, Clegg joined Facebook as head of Global Affairs and Communication.

[53] Fintan O'Toole, *Heroic Failure: Brexit and the Politics of Pain* (London: Head of Zeus, 2018); Danny Dorling and Sally Tomlinson, *Rule Britannia: Brexit and the End of Empire* (London: Biteback, 2019).

[54] On the creation of these stereotypes, see, Jon Lawrence, 'Forging a Peaceable Kingdom: War, Violence, and Fear of Brutalization in Post-First World War Britain' (2003) 75:3 *The Journal of Modern History* 557–89.

[55] Stephen Tierney, *Constitutional Referendums: The Theory and Practice of Republican Deliberation* (Oxford: Oxford University Press, 2012), p. 16.

the anti-immigration rhetoric of Enoch Powell rested upon a powerful sense that the people had been betrayed by their representatives.[56] Similarly, the turn to the right by the Conservatives in the late 1970s under the leadership of Margaret Thatcher evinced certain populist elements.[57] The referendum gave political authority to a tendency long latent within British politics.

The true significance of the referendum lay in two other areas. First, as with the 2014 poll on Scottish independence and Jeremy Corbyn's election as Labour leader a year later, it signalled a reversal of decades of declining political engagement, as indicated by falling levels of turnout and party membership.[58] However uncomfortable aspects of the referendum campaign were, it clearly represented a significant moment of re-politicisation, drawing formerly disengaged voters back into politics. Just as the events of 2014 had created a new Scottish politics orientated around the constitution, 2016 reshaped English (and, to a lesser extent, Welsh) politics. Brexit, in this regard, was never simply about the United Kingdom's relationship with Europe; rather, it has come to represent a certain outlook on a range of social, economic, and cultural questions. The degree of change in an English context may seem less dramatic, since the Conservatives have remained in office throughout this period. Nevertheless, beneath party labels, there has been an important shift. Brexit has allowed the Conservative Party to reassert its leadership of the political right, at the cost of marginalising pro-European, socially liberal opinion within the party. From the perspective of the right, Brexit was a way of resolving extant tensions: it did not create them.

Second, Brexit gave political expression to increasingly important social divisions. Between 2016 and 2019, it appeared that the British electorate was fractured along generational lines, with younger, Labour-leaning, pro-EU voters being outvoted by older, more Conservative, pro-Brexit electors. Various explanations can be posited: the rise of university attendance among recent generations; changing social attitudes; falling rates of home ownership. One of the more suggestive analyses has been offered by Runciman, who has argued that in recent decades electorates in established democracies have come increasingly to resemble their elected representatives. For the majority of the twentieth century politicians were older than their electorates, and far more likely to have attended university: this is no

---

[56] Bill Schwarz, *The White Man's World* (Oxford: Oxford University Press, 2011); Camilla Schofield, *Enoch Powell and the Making of Postcolonial Britain* (Cambridge: Cambridge University Press, 2013).

[57] Stuart Hall, 'The Great Moving Right Show' (January 1979) *Marxism Today*, 14–18.

[58] Peter Mair, *Ruling the Void: The Hollowing of Western Democracy* (London: Verso, 2013).

longer the case.⁵⁹ The result has been a growing rejection of the very principle of representation, and a growth in support for direct forms of popular political participation such as referendums. Representation, paradoxically, might require that representatives and their constituents be unalike: if politicians were no longer more experienced, or more educated, than the wider public, then their legitimacy is open to question. Indeed, one way of understanding Brexit might be as part of a broader collapse of political authority: if the public was less willing to respect the wisdom of elected politicians, then the course of Labour and Conservative politics in this period would suggest that the same could be said for party members and even backbench parliamentarians. Between 2016 and 2019, the deference traditionally accorded to party bureaucracies and leaderships was barely visible; the notable exception in this regard was within the SNP, where, for all the party's commitment to constitutional change, the old tenets of party discipline still held.

## CONCLUSION

Despite the profound constitutional consequences of the referendum result, Brexit was, at root, primarily a political event, a high political effort to resolve tensions formed by social and economic changes that had taken place over decades. This is not to suggest that Brexit was inevitable: the decision to hold a referendum, the context in which it was held, and the weakness of the Remain campaign were all necessary contingencies. But underlying economic and political shifts created an environment in which those short-term factors mattered. Most obviously, the financial crash of 2008–9 left a legacy of stagnant wages and precarious employment that eroded faith in the political establishment and ensured that the Remain campaign's warnings regarding the likely economic impact of Brexit lacked credibility with much of the public.⁶⁰ Further, as Edgerton has contended, the transformation of the Conservatives into the party of Brexit, in opposition to the wishes of much of the business community, reflected the fact that key sectors of the British economy, particularly financial services, were, since the 1980s, increasingly

---

[59] For various versions of the argument, see, David Runciman, *How Democracy Ends* (London: Profile, 2018) and ' Why is democracy so surprising?' (2019) 90:S1 *Political Quarterly* 36–46. A clear exposition is available as a short lecture at: www.talkingpoliticspodcast.com/blog/2018/129-democracy-for-young-people.

[60] Thompson, 'Inevitability and Contingency'; Matthew Watson, 'Brexit, the left behind and the let down: the political abstraction of "the economy" and the UK's EU referendum' (2018) 13:1 *British Politics* 17–30.

international in focus and under foreign ownership.[61] This created a disconnect between the political and economic spheres, while simultaneously contributing to the popular desire to 'take back control' that was central to the Leave victory in 2016.

Equally, in political terms, Brexit reflected the growth of a right-leaning English political identity, the strength of which had been obscured by divisions over Europe. The triumph of the Leave campaign allowed those splits to be resolved, and for the arrival of a new Conservative ascendancy in England. It is the dominant position of the Conservatives in England that provides the most striking political legacy of Brexit: at the 2019 election, the party polled 47 per cent in England, a figure that rises to 49 per cent outside London. In a functional, political sense, then, Brexit is over; it may have happened in a different way from that intended by David Cameron, but the referendum still achieved its primary purpose of ending the threat posed by UKIP to the Conservative Party. This could be detected in the Conservative Party's 2019 slogan, 'Get Brexit Done': while in one sense this expressed a continued commitment to implementing the referendum result, it also spoke to a desire to move on, for politics to be about something else. The constitutional and economic consequences of Brexit are likely to make such a desire impossible to realise anytime soon.

[61] David Edgerton, 'How Britain was sold', *New Statesman*, 13 November 2019, www.newstatesman.com/politics/uk/2019/11/how-britain-was-sold.

# 10

## Westminster versus Whitehall: What the Brexit Debate Revealed About an Unresolved Conflict at the Heart of the British Constitution

### David Howarth

In *Representative and Responsible Government: An Essay on the British Constitution* A. H. Birch observed: 'there are two languages in which the relations between Parliament and the executive are described'.[1] One talks 'of Parliamentary sovereignty, of the responsibility of ministers to Parliament ... of the defence of the people's rights through the vigilance of the "Parliamentary watchdog", of the democratic advantages of a system in which there is no separation of powers between legislature and executive'.[2] The other talks 'of the responsibility of Her Majesty's Government for the administration of the country, ... of Parliament's function as a debating chamber in airing public opinion, ... [of] "the Crown as the embodiment of the unity and continuity of our national life" ... [of] the Government['s] mandate to put its policies into effect and [that it] is ultimately answerable to the electorate (not Parliament) for their success'.[3] Birch continued:

> In these two languages, Parliament appears in two guises. In [the former] Parliament is a corporate entity wielding power. ... . In [the latter] Parliament is not a corporate entity so much as an arena or forum. In this forum individual Members air grievances and groups of Members carry on the party struggle.[4]

Birch called the latter the 'Whitehall language', since it emanated from the street that houses many government departments. He called the former the 'Liberal language', although that makes it more politically partisan than necessary – it is better called the 'Westminster language', since its home is

---

[1] A.H. Birch, *Representative and Responsible Government: An Essay on the British Constitution* (London: Allen & Unwin, 1964), p. 165.
[2] Ibid.
[3] Ibid.
[4] Ibid., p. 166.

on the floor of the House of Commons and in the corridors of the Palace of Westminster.

## TWO VIEWS OF THE CONSTITUTION

Birch remarked that the conflict between these two views caused confusion in debates about the British constitution. The conflict continues, as does the confusion. The Westminster view of the relationship between Parliament and government sees governments as completely dependent upon the House of Commons. The Commons lies at the heart of British democracy not only formally, through its legislative supremacy, but also in terms of political attention – the 'cockpit of the nation'.[5] The Whitehall view sees the government as the central institution of the constitution with the Commons' only effective role in a 'fused' system as providing governments with the resources, financial and legal, they need to govern. Beyond that, its functions are rhetorical. To echo the words of Mario Cuomo, the Commons campaigns in poetry while ministers govern in prose.[6]

Birch saw the Westminster view as an 'ideal' rather than a 'description' and the Whitehall view as a description rather than an ideal.[7] But since his time, the Whitehall view has developed into an ideal in its own right.[8] The idea is that British democracy consists of the process whereby the electorate at general elections chooses between competing party manifestoes. The winning party is not merely entitled to implement its manifesto (to exercise its 'mandate') but obligated to do so. Consequently, parliamentary activity that tends to obstruct the implementation of the winning party's manifesto should be regarded as anti-democratic. It is a form of Schumpeterian plebiscitary democracy,[9] but with the added non-Schumpeterian moral element of binding party manifestos. But the Westminster view is a description not just an ideal. It sees Britain as a representative democracy in which members of parliament exercise their own judgment, in the tradition of Edmund Burke, and do not automatically

---

[5] See David Howarth, 'Westminster versus Whitehall: Two Incompatible Views of the Constitution', UK Constitutional Law Blog, 10th April 2019, https://ukconstitutionallaw.org/.
[6] Fred Barnes, 'Meet Mario the Moderate', *New Republic*, 8 April 1985, p. 17.
[7] Birch, p. 167–8.
[8] See David Howarth, 'The Backbench Business Committee of the House of Commons' (2011) *Public Law* 490–98 (where the Westminster view is described as the 'Hilary Armstrong theory of the constitution', in honour of the former Labour chief whip who expounded it to the Wright Committee).
[9] Joseph Schumpeter, *Capitalism, Socialism and Democracy* (London: Taylor & Francis, 2010), especially chap. 22.

follow the views of their party. The choice of government lies, actually and not just ideally, with the electorate's representatives in the Commons.

The purpose of this chapter is to assess how the Brexit debate has altered the balance between the two views, both as descriptions and as ideals. The chapter first lays out the strengths and weaknesses of the two views as they appeared before the referendum and then turns to the events of 2017–19.

## The Two Views as Descriptions

The two views would not have survived unless they had some factual basis. Birch emphasises the realism of the Whitehall view – ministers, not the Commons, decide policy and modern British politics is a contest between parties and their leaders, not between individual candidates in parliamentary constituencies. But the Westminster view also reflects several straightforward legal and historical facts: British voters elect individual members of parliament, not a president or executive; since the Great Reform Act, prime ministers have quite often resigned as a result of losing votes in the Commons; few voters read party manifestos;[10] and political debate often concerns issues, such as how to react to a pandemic, about which no party or leader can claim a 'mandate'.

Similarly, although, as the Whitehall view requires, the British electoral system usually conjures single-party majority governments from minority popular support, nothing prevents results in which no single party wins an overall majority. Over the last 135 years, single party majority government has existed for only about three quarters of the time. Strong, geographically based parties, like the Irish Parliamentary Party and the Scottish National Party, have frustrated the creation of majority governments. And when the parties are in flux, as in the 1920s and 30s, single-party majorities become less common even without strong geographical parties. And so general elections are not guaranteed to decide which party takes power. Even the often-heard claim that the electoral system allows the electorate to throw governments out is not borne out historically: a majority of electors often vote for a party other than the governing party and yet the governing party returns to office, a phenomenon that in the last fifty years has occurred more often than not.

Moreover, when a prime minister resigns or dies, the decision about who becomes the next prime minister does not revert to the electorate, as the

---

[10] Thomas Däubler, 'What the UK General Elections of 2005/10 Tell Us about the Demand for Manifestos (and the Other Way Round)' (2015) 68:2 *Parliamentary Affairs* 401–22.

Whitehall view might predict. Incoming prime ministers are often urged to call an election to establish their own mandate, but almost equally often they decline. Furthermore, incoming prime ministers see themselves as unhindered by their predecessor's mandate. Gordon Brown, for example, immediately announced a programme of constitutional reforms no sign of which appeared in Labour's 2005 manifesto.[11]

Conversely, contrary to the Westminster view, both the biggest parties and the media, especially broadcasters, increasingly present elections in a Whitehall fashion, as contests between potential prime ministers.[12] And even technically, the Commons does not choose governments. It has never voted to appoint a prime minister, let alone other ministers. The monarch takes a view about whether a specific person could win the confidence of the House, but any votes of confidence that might take place, and there might be none, happen after governments are formed, not before.[13]

The balance between the views can change over time. If one traces, for example, the degree of control governments have exercised over the agenda of the Commons, the situation has shifted over the past two centuries from one in which ministers struggled to get their business discussed, to one during the World Wars in which the government took all the time of the House.[14] Since 1945, the government has controlled most if not all the time of the House; voting has been largely along party lines;[15] and control over future policy, for example through the financial procedures authorising expenditure, has become almost entirely formal or rhetorical.[16] That looks largely Whitehallist. But from the later years of the Blair government, MPs became more rebellious,[17] and some reforms look Westminster-inspired, most prominently the Wright Committee reforms of 2009–10, which introduced, for

---

[11] For Brown's constitutional reform programme, see Ministry of Justice, *The Governance of Britain*, Cm 7170 (2007); cf. Labour Party, *Britain Forward, Not Back: 2005 Manifesto* (London: Labour Party, 2005), pp. 102–12.

[12] Especially televised debates, which both BBC and ITV insist should include 'head-to-head' debates between the leaders of the two largest parties: *R (Liberal Democrats and Scottish National Party) v. ITV Broadcasting Ltd* [2019] EWHC 3282 (Admin); [2020] 4 WLR 4.

[13] *The Cabinet Manual* (London: Cabinet Office, 2011), chap. 2.

[14] Howarth, 'The Backbench Business Committee of the House of Commons'.

[15] Philip Cowley and Mark Stuart, 'Rates of Rebellion 1945–2014', https://web.archive.org/web/20150815124520/http://revolts.co.uk/?p=711.

[16] See John McEldowney and Colin Lee, 'Parliament and Public Money' in Philip Giddings (ed), *The Future of Parliament* (London: Palgrave, 2005) 88–97; Tony Prosser, *The Economic Constitution* (Oxford: OUP, 2014), pp. 111–115.

[17] Philip Cowley, 'The Most Rebellious Parliament of the Post-War Era', Political Studies Association Blog, 28 March 2015, www.psa.ac.uk/insight-plus/blog/most-rebellious-parliament-post-war-era.

example, the election of select committee chairs by secret ballot. The Wright Committee expressly sought to expand the role of the Commons beyond the party struggle.[18] Nevertheless there were limits: the most radically Westminster-oriented of the Wright Committee's proposals, that governments should cede the power to set the Commons' agenda to a committee of the House and ultimately to the House itself, was never implemented, despite reaching the 2010 Coalition Agreement.[19]

Historical change can reduce the accuracy of both theories. The clearest example is the rise of referendums, which, as Eoin Daly points out in Chapter 8 of this volume, have no clearly defined formal role in the UK system, but have significant disruptive capacity. From a Westminster point of view, referendums displace Parliament from the centre of politics and undermine representative democracy. But referendums also pose problems for the Whitehall point of view: they create two potentially contradictory plebiscitary events, a referendum and a general election. If the two are politically aligned, no problem arises. But what if they are not? Which takes precedence? And what about changes through time? Do subsequent elections supplant referendums, or can only a new referendum have that effect? The answer before the 2016 Brexit referendum was unclear. The only UK-wide referendums had been the 1975 referendum on continued membership of the European Community and the 2011 referendum on the alternative vote system for UK parliamentary elections. The former was treated as binding on Parliament by many who opposed its result, which is why they campaigned for another referendum. On the other hand, the only major party manifesto to commit to withdrawal before 2017, Labour's 1983 manifesto, promised withdrawal without a second referendum.[20] As for the voting system referendum, the losing side, the Liberal Democrats, proposed in their next manifesto to introduce a more radical reform without a further referendum.[21]

## The Two Views as Ideals

As ideal theories the two views have largely complementary strengths and weaknesses. The strength of the Westminster view is that it incorporates the

---

[18] House of Commons Reform Committee, 'Rebuilding the House' (1st Report of Session 2008–9), HC 1117, para. 24.

[19] HM Government, The Coalition: our programme for government', Cabinet Office, May 2010, p. 27, www.gov.uk/government/publications/the-coalition-documentation.

[20] *The New Hope for Britain: Labour's Manifesto 1983* (London: Labour Party, 1983), reproduced in Iain Dale, *Labour Party General Election Manifestos, 1900–1997* (London: Routledge, 2000), p. 281. Also available at www.labour-party.org.uk/manifestos/1983/1983-labour-manifesto.shtml.

[21] *Manifesto 2015: Stronger Economy, Fairer Society: Opportunity for Everyone* (London: Liberal Democrats, 2015), p. 132.

ideal of democracy as government by discussion (as conceived by Mill)[22] – perhaps not full-scale deliberative democracy,[23] since it is characterised by discussion *in* public rather than *by* the public, but open enough for the public to be able to hear and comment on the reasons being given for decisions. At the same time, it is flexible, able to meet new challenges and to 'adjust, adapt and find ways through'.[24]

The Whitehall critique of the Westminster view rests ultimately on the long-standing condemnation of government by large assemblies as ineffective, vacillating, and weak. It is perhaps best summarised in Hobbes' *Leviathan*: 'in assemblies . . . there ariseth an inconstancy from the number. For the absence of a few that would have the resolution, once taken, continue firm (which may happen by security, negligence, or private impediments), or the diligent appearance of a few of the contrary opinion, undoes today all that was concluded yesterday'.[25] Government by parliaments, Hobbes pointed out, is inconsistent, ruled by emotion, and given to bouts of vengeance or what is now called 'blame-storming'. Westminsterists might attempt to parry these criticisms by saying that the Commons authorises governments to act on its behalf and governments can govern consistently, rationally and calmly as long as they retain the confidence of the House. The Commons no longer seeks to govern,[26] merely to determine

---

[22] See William Selinger, *Parliamentarism: From Burke to Weber* (Cambridge: CUP, 2019), pp. 164–93. The phrase 'government by discussion' belongs to Bagehot in the introduction to the second edition of *The English Constitution*. See P. Smith (ed.), Bagehot: The English Constitution (Cambridge Texts in the History of Political Thought) (Cambridge: Cambridge University Press, 2001), pp. 193–229.

[23] Alison Young, 'Taking (Back) Control?', See P. Smith (ed.), Bagehot: The English Constitution (Cambridge Texts in the History of Political Thought) (Cambridge: Cambridge University Press, 2001), pp. 193–229. UK Constitutional Law Blog, 23 Apr. 2019, https://ukconstitutionallaw.org/. The Wright Committee included recommendations on public participation, which eventually produced a new petitions procedure (see e.g. Standing Order no. 145A), but a more traditional Westminsterist view would be that democratic election is crucial, rightly giving those who were elected more access than the self-appointed or those appointed by newspaper owners.

[24] David Runciman, *The Confidence Trap: A History of Democracy in Crisis from World War I to the Present* (Princeton: Princeton University Press, 2013), p. 293

[25] Thomas Hobbes, *Leviathan* (London: Andrew Crooke, 1651 (reprinted Oxford University Press, 1909) p. 96. Hobbes adds that, in assemblies, orators 'give their advice in long discourses which may, and do commonly, excite men to action, but not govern them in it. For the understanding is by the flame of the passions never enlightened, but dazzled'; and that 'orators, that is to say, favourites of sovereign assemblies, though they have great power to hurt, have little to save. For to accuse requires less eloquence (such is man's nature) than to excuse; and condemnation, than absolution, more resembles justice' (pp. 96–7).

[26] It did, however, arguably seek to govern in the eighteenth century, through detailed local and private Acts of Parliament. See F. W. Maitland, *The Constitutional History of England* (Cambridge: Cambridge University Press, 1908), pp. 383–4.

who does. But Whitehallists could respond that if one treats the Commons as having a corporate view of anything, as opposed to being merely a forum for the party battle, one concedes to it the power to govern.

The strength of the Whitehall view is that it reconciles strong decisive government, unhampered by obstructionism, with democracy, which it achieves through a direct link, unavailable in the Westminster view, between the electorate and the government's programme.

The Westminster critique of the Whitehall view is that the Whitehall view cannot cope with flux in political life – Macmillan's possibly apocryphal 'events dear boy, events'. Governments faced with problems not contemplated by their manifestos can choose to do nothing, or call for a general election, or do something which, according to the Whitehall view, is, because of the lack of a mandate, undemocratic. Usually, only the third is practical, but choosing it on Whitehallist terms forgoes drawing any distinction, outside periodic elections, between democracies and dictatorships.[27] The Westminster view insists that representative democracy is more democratic than dictatorship not only at elections but also between elections, through open debate in which arguments are fully tested, not just internal discussion in the closed world of Whitehall, where the notorious acronym DAD ('Decide, Announce, Defend') still rules.[28]

## POLITICAL INSTABILITY 2017–19 AND THE CONSTITUTION

The question this chapter poses is: how did the constitutional struggle around Brexit affect the balance, descriptive and ideal, between the two views? That struggle began long before the 2016 referendum. It began before the United Kingdom entered the European Community. But the conflicts following the referendum were particularly intense, calling into question not only the relationship between governments and the Commons, but also the relationship between both and the courts.

The constitutional struggle was related to and partly caused by a parallel period of political instability. For the whole period from the referendum until the election of December 2019, the government lacked a stable Commons majority, essentially because the Conservative Party could not agree internally on Brexit. Some

---

[27] This criticism is made of Schumpeter himself. See Gerry Mackie, 'Schumpeter's Leadership Democracy' (2009) 37:1 *Political Theory* 128–153.
[28] UK central government should now operate on the more inclusive 'EDD' (Engage, Deliberate, Decide) basis (see Clare Twigger-Ross and Lindsey Colbourne, *Improving institutional and social responses to flooding: Synthesis report* (Bristol: Environment Agency, 2009), but engagement, even on constitutional matters, is often perfunctory, especially on manifesto-mandated reforms proposed early in a government's term.

Conservative MPs believed that ministers were insufficiently committed to Brexit and were looking for ways out of it or at least of maintaining such close links with the EU that the situation would amount to Brexit in name only. Others, on the opposite wing, considering Brexit a political and economic disaster, were looking for ways to delay. These two groups combined to ensure that the government could not construct a majority for any version of its deal and it lost three successive motions to fulfil the requirement of s. 13 of the European Union (Withdrawal) Act 2018 that the Commons needed to approve any Withdrawal Agreement.[29] Even when it did eventually construct a majority for a deal, in October 2019,[30] it was only because it benefited from a counter-rebellion in the main opposition party. Both the governing and main opposition parties suffered defections and expulsions, leaving the party system in Autumn 2019 very different from that elected in 2017.[31] The situation was exacerbated between the elections of 2017 and 2019 by the Conservative Party's lack of an overall majority even if it could unite, causing vulnerability to procedural ambushes. It maintained a majority for formal confidence and supply purposes through an arrangement with the Democratic Unionist Party, an arrangement which itself complicated the search for an acceptable agreement, but in September 2019 lost even that through defections.

The instances of constitutional struggle were many, but one can identify five main themes: the extent to which governments can act without needing specific parliamentary authorisation; the power of governments to ignore the Commons or veto its proposals; control over the Commons' agenda; the identification and consequences of the Commons losing confidence in the government; and the constitutional status of the 2016 referendum.

## GOVERNMENTS' POWER TO ACT WITHOUT PARLIAMENTARY AUTHORISATION

The part of the struggle that has attracted most attention from lawyers, simply because it finished in the courts, is the issue of governmental ability to act without any form of parliamentary authorisation. In the jargon of UK constitutional law, the issue is one of the existence and scope of prerogative powers.

---

[29] House of Commons, Division 293 of 15 January 2019 (lost 432-202), Division 354 of 12 March 2019 (lost 391-242), and Division 395 of 29 March 2019 (lost 344-286).

[30] House of Commons, Division 4 of 22 October 2019. The government lost its majority in the following vote (Division 5 of 22 October 2019).

[31] The seats in the new 2017 Parliament: Conservative 317, Labour 262, SNP 35, Liberal Democrat 12, Democratic Unionist 10, Sinn Féin 7, Plaid Cymru 4, Green 1, Independent 1. At dissolution in 2019, the seats were approximately as follows: Conservative 298, Labour 242, SNP 35, Independents 25, Liberal Democrats 20, Democratic Unionist 10, Sinn Féin 7, ChangeUK 5, Plaid Cymru 4, Green 1.

But that language disguises the real issue, which is the extent to which some form of prior parliamentary authorisation, either statutory or by resolution, is required for a government to act. The issue came up in two instances, both of which ended in Supreme Court judgments. The first was whether ministers could invoke Art. 50 of the Treaty on European Union without prior statutory approval.[32] As is well known, the Supreme Court decided that statutory authority was required. The second was in 2019 when the government purported, again using the prerogative, to prorogue Parliament for five weeks, thereby precluding further parliamentary activity hostile to the government.[33] The Commons could have adjourned itself for that period but that proposition was not put to it. The issue was whether ministers could suspend Parliament without specific authorisation – this time a resolution – from Parliament. The Supreme Court decided that the prerogative power to prorogue did not cover situations in which suspension would, without good reason, preclude Parliament from carrying out its constitutional functions and that, because the government had offered no reasons, no such power existed.

In both cases, the two views gave clear answers. In *Miller 1*, the Whitehall view was that since foreign policy was the sole responsibility of ministers, with parliament confined to asking questions after the event or passing legislation so that ministers could fulfil their international obligations, unless legislation had specifically restricted its power, the government could invoke Art. 50 without recourse to Parliament. The Westminster view was that major decisions, especially ones involving economic, political, and constitutional risks, should only be taken after the Commons had blessed the proposed policy.

In *Miller 2/Cherry*, the division is even more stark. The Whitehall view was that Parliament's role is to accede to governmental demands to pass legislation. So, if the government needs no legislation to be passed, there is no need for Parliament to meet. As the formula used at the start of a new parliament puts it: 'My Lords and Members of the House of Commons, we have it in command from Her Majesty to let you know that, as soon as the Members of both Houses shall be sworn, the causes of Her Majesty calling this Parliament will be declared to you', and so it is Her Majesty, now in the form of her ministers, who determines whether any such causes exist and continue to

---

[32] *R (Miller)* v. *Secretary of State for Exiting the European Union* [hereinafter *Miller 1*] [2017] UKSC 5; [2018] AC 61.The government did obtain a Commons resolution (see House of Commons Votes and Proceedings, 7 December 2016, p. 2) but the Supreme Court held (at [123]) that a resolution was legally insufficient.

[33] *R (Miller)* v. *Prime Minister; Cherry* v. *Advocate General for Scotland* [hereinafter *Miller 2/Cherry*] [2019] UKSC 41; [2020] AC 373.

require Parliament to meet.³⁴ The Westminster view, in sharp contrast, was that since any government's authority to govern derives entirely from the confidence of the Commons, long prorogation without the Commons' consent is tantamount to a coup d'état.

The Supreme Court's judgments in the *Miller* cases endorse the Westminster view. In *Miller 1*, the majority held that major constitutional change needed a clear statutory basis, even though citizens' rights arising from EU membership had never been anything but conditional on the United Kingdom's international obligations flowing from its continued EU membership. In *Miller 2/Cherry*, the court was even clearer: the two basic principles of UK constitutional law are parliamentary sovereignty and parliamentary accountability and Parliament must have the opportunity to legislate and to hold ministers to account, regardless of whether ministers want it to have that opportunity.³⁵

### POWER OF GOVERNMENTS TO IGNORE OR VETO THE COMMONS' PROPOSALS

The second field of struggle goes beyond ministerial powers to act without parliamentary authorisation and into open conflict. What happens when the Commons acts contrary to government policy? Can the government ignore the Commons or even veto its decisions? Two striking examples occurred during the Brexit crisis: successful motions requiring ministers to reveal documents, and passage through all stages of two bills requiring the government to make moves it opposed in the Brexit negotiations, the Cooper-Letwin and Benn Bills (which became the European Union (Withdrawal) Act 2019 and the European Union (Withdrawal) (No. 2) Act 2019).

#### Humble Addresses

During the minority government of 2017–19 a peculiar practice developed in which the government would not oppose motions critical of it proposed by its opponents.³⁶ It claimed that Commons resolutions were not 'binding' on ministers – a position that was legally accurate since resolutions are not legislation,³⁷

---

[34] Clerk of the Parliaments, *Companion to the Standing Orders and guide to the Proceedings of the House of Lords* (London: House of Lords, 2017), Appendix F.
[35] *Miller 2/ Cherry* at paras. 41–7.
[36] Hansard, HC Deb., 6th series, vol. 628, cols. 849–946, 9 September 2017. For a full list see http://researchbriefings.files.parliament.uk/documents/SN06315/CBP06315_DATA.xlsx.
[37] *Miller 1* at para. 123 and *Bowles v. Bank of England* [1913] 1 Ch 57.

but the real issue was not legal. At stake was whether the government was the servant of the House or the House a servant of the government.

As the Brexit crisis developed, opposition members looking for ways of making Commons resolutions more effective alighted on the old procedure of a Humble Address, a motion communicating to the monarch the House's wish that she do something. The procedure had fallen into merely ceremonial or technical use but historically had facilitated more substantial demands, including the dismissal of the king's ministers,[38] and requests that ministerial papers be delivered to the House. The Opposition revived the mechanism of the Address to call for the delivery to the House of papers containing the government's analyses of the impact of Brexit.[39] The motion passed without a division. After some confusion, ministers partially complied, and a Commons committee resolved that they had done enough. Later, the process went one step further.[40] The Opposition proposed an Address instructing ministers to release the Attorney-General's legal advice on the latest iteration of the Withdrawal Agreement. The motion again passed without division, but this time the government refused to comply.[41] The Opposition complained to the Speaker that the government was in contempt. The Speaker, exercising his power to put privilege motions on the order paper,[42] allowed a contempt motion to proceed. The government divided the House but lost. The government complied the following day.[43]

The conflict about Humble Addresses shows the Westminster versus Whitehall debate in its starkest terms. The government's view that Commons resolutions are not binding upon it is pure Whitehall. The opposing view is pure Westminster. Westminster won.

### Reviving the Veto?

The story of the two bills passed in the teeth of government opposition encompasses aspects of two of the remaining categories: agenda control and confidence, but here we are concerned with the end of the legislative process.

---

[38] See Journal of the House of Commons, vol. 39 pp. 964–5, 1 March 1784.
[39] *Hansard*, HC Deb, 6th series, vol. 630, cols. 877–935, 1 November 2017.
[40] *Hansard*, HC Deb, 6th series, vol. 649, cols. 189–236, 13 November 2018.
[41] It instead issued *EU Exit: Legal Position on the Withdrawal Agreement*, Cm 9747 (December 2018).
[42] Erskine May, *Treatise on the Law, Privileges, Proceedings and Usage of Parliament* (25th edn., online 2019), para. 18.39.
[43] Subsequently, the government asked the Commons' Procedure Committee to examine the issue. It recommended change, see House of Commons Procedure Committee, 'The House's Power to call for papers: procedure and practice' (9th report of Session 2017–19), HC 1904, 20 May 2019.

Some commentators suggested that the government could stop these bills becoming law by advising the Queen to veto them.[44] No bill has been vetoed for more than 300 years, but some asserted that the formal power still exists and that the monarch must act on ministerial advice. Others said the power had fallen into desuetude and that the monarch must assent to bills passed by both Houses. Parliamentarians openly raised suspicions that the government intended to advise the Queen to veto the Benn Bill.[45] In the event, without conceding the principle, ministers promised that they would present the bill for assent if it passed, which they duly did.[46] The issue remains unresolved, although in *Miller 2/ Cherry* the Supreme Court said: 'The sovereignty of Parliament would ... be undermined as the foundational principle of our constitution if the executive could, through the use of the prerogative, prevent Parliament from exercising its legislative authority ... '.

The pro-veto view is another stereotypical Whitehall idea. Parliament's task is to assist government by passing legislation of which the government approves, and so legislation of which the government disapproves should not become law. The Whitehall view is often expressed in quasi-mystical terms about the Crown being part of Parliament but, more brutally, it holds that Parliament is largely decorative: democracy means electing a government to implement a programme unencumbered by parliamentary obstruction, so legislation the government opposes can only result from abuse of the constitution.[47] The anti-veto view is an equal and opposite stereotypical Westminster view, that the government's very existence as a creation of the Commons, means its legitimacy ends when it acts contrary to the will of the Commons.

### Control over the Commons' agenda

Governments exercise notoriously tight control over the Commons' agenda,[48] taking the form of a near monopoly on the allocation of the House's time,[49]

---

[44] See the views collected in R. Craig, 'Could the Government Advise the Queen to Refuse Royal Assent to a Backbench Bill?', UK Constitutional Law Blog, 22 January 2019, https://ukconstitutionallaw.org/.
[45] E.g. *Hansard*, Lord Kerr of Kinlochlard, HL, 5th series, vol. 799 col. 1190, 5 September 2019.
[46] *Hansard*, Lord Callanan, HL, 5th series, vol. 799 col. 1276, 6 September 2019.
[47] E.g. *Hansard*, Jacob Rees-Mogg MP, HC Deb, 6th series, vol. 666 col. 1144, 24 October 2019.
[48] Herbert Döring, 'Time as a scarce resource: Government Control of the agenda', in H. Döring, Parliaments and Majority Rule in Western Europe (Frankfurt and New York: Campus and St Martin's, 1995), chap.7, pp. 223–47.
[49] Standing Orders of the House of Commons for Public Business, SO no. 14

and a monopoly on proposals that spend public money or raise public revenue or affect the powers and interests of the Crown.[50]

## Time

Governmental control over time rests on Standing Order no. 14, which gives government business priority over all other business. That control is given to ministers as ministers. No vote is required. Some days, the leader of the Opposition or the Backbench Business Committee decides the agenda, but the government controls when those days happen, and so can usually parry dangerous proposals.[51] Other days are given to private members' bills, but time is allocated only to the bills themselves and not to the procedural motions, especially timetable motions, that sponsors of bills need to be able to frustrate opponents determined to obstruct their bills and 'talk them out'.[52]

Only two major exceptions exist, neither mentioned in Standing Order no. 14. First, the Speaker can make time for debates on motions relating to the privileges of the House.[53] Secondly, if a proposal is supported by forty members, Standing Order no. 24 allows the Speaker to make time for an emergency debate. Before the Brexit crisis, however, neither was thought important. Issues of privilege were related to misconduct by backbench MPs or by members of the public, and Standing Order no. 24 was thought to allow only general debates in neutral terms, an opportunity for MPs to let off steam but no threat to the government's programme.

These rules reflected the Whitehall view. The government controls the House's agenda, with opportunities for MPs to complain about but not change government policy. The Westminster explanation was that the House's sub-servience was voluntary, created by its own resolutions, and that it could take back control if it wanted, although it was difficult to see how it could in practice since opposition leaders aspire to reach office and, once there, exercise its privileges.

The Brexit debates utterly changed the position. Speaker Bercow used his power to put down for debate motions relating to privilege to allow the opposition successfully to accuse ministers of contempt,[54] and Standing Order no. 14 was suspended by a series of manoeuvres culminating in

---

[50] Standing Orders of the House of Commons for Public Business, SO no. 48.
[51] Howarth, 'The Backbench Business Committee', see note 8 above.
[52] House of Commons Procedure Committee, 'Private Members' Bills' (3rd Report of Session 2015–16), HC 684, 18 April 2016.
[53] See May, *Treatise on the Law*, para. 18.39.
[54] See above p 227.

a startlingly new interpretation of Standing Order no. 24, essentially destroying the government's monopoly on time.

The manoeuvres started with a successful amendment to a government bill, which would eventually become s. 13 of the European Union (Withdrawal) Act 2018, resulting in a legal obligation on ministers to move a series of motions in the House, which the Speaker proceeded, contrary to the government's expectation, to declare amendable. Members then successfully moved amendments, which the Speaker ruled in order, setting aside days for debates the government did not want,[55] including 'indicative votes' (a failed attempt to find a majority for a Brexit negotiating position),[56] and the Letwin-Cooper Bill.[57] The amendments allowed not only debates on resolutions and bills but also procedural motions ensuring proposals could not be talked out. The process worked by a daisy-chain: at each stage, a further motion was moved to set aside another day, so the sequence ended when the government defeated a proposed further day.[58] That was not, however, the end of suspending Standing Order no. 14. In a novel interpretation, albeit foreshadowed in Erskine May,[59] the Speaker allowed Standing Order no. 24 to be used for substantive purposes, including creating time for the Benn Bill.[60]

### Money and Crown Powers

The Brexit debates also threw into sharper relief two other rules that deny the House opportunities to decide matters of policy: the rule that excludes anyone except a minister from proposing additional expenditure or additional taxation ('Queen's Recommendation'),[61] and the rule that matters affecting the powers and interests of the Crown cannot be debated without the permission of the Crown ('Queen's Consent').[62] Both, however, turned out to be less useful for ministers than academic commentary had suggested.[63] Commentators

---

[55] *Hansard*, HC Deb, 6th series, vol. 657 col. 60, 25 March 2019.
[56] *Hansard*, HC Deb, 6th series, vol. 657 cols. 333–68, 27 March 2019.
[57] *Hansard*, HC Deb, 6th series, vol. 657 cols. 1128–51, 3 April 2019.
[58] *Hansard*, HC Deb, 6th series, vol. 657, cols. 1058–127, 3 April. The vote was tied (Division 42 at cols 1112-15), but Speaker Bercow, in accordance with precedent (and contrary to his enemies' expectations) then voted with the government.
[59] May, *Treatise on the Law*, para. 19.22, footnote 20.
[60] *Hansard*, HC Deb, 6th series, vol. 664 cols. 76–7 and 81–139, 3 September 2019.
[61] Standing Order no. 48
[62] May, *Treatise on the Law*, paras. 9.6 and 30.79.
[63] E.g. Robert Craig, 'Why Royal Consent Is Required for the Proposed Article 50 Extension Bill', UK Constitutional Law Blog, 25th February 2019, https://ukconstitutionallaw.org/; Stephen Laws, 'Why a Money Resolution with Queen's Recommendation Is Required for a Bill for the Postponing or Cancelling of "Exit Day"', UK Constitutional Law Blog, 29th January 2019, https://ukconstitutionallaw.org/.

asserted that the Cooper-Letwin Bill violated both rules: the money rule because any delay in implementing Brexit would result in additional public expenditure and the Crown powers rule because it fettered the exercise of prerogative powers over foreign policy. The Speaker decided otherwise.[64] The Speaker's explanation was brief, and rested on a rule that authorisation in relevant previous bills is enough. So, for example, the money resolution for the government's own European Union (Withdrawal) Act 2018 covered the financial consequences of any extension of the date the United Kingdom was to leave the EU.[65]

The time allocation and Crown powers stories reveal the Speaker's previously invisible powers. Unlike Speakers of the US House of Representatives, for example, Commons Speakers have no formal role in agenda setting, but shrewd use of powers to interpret the rules turned Speaker Bercow into a leading political figure. That development reinforces the Westminster view, since Speakers are elected by the Commons and hold office only if they retain its confidence.[66]

## Confidence

The most perplexing constitutional controversy to emerge concerned a fundamental but ill-defined principle of the British constitution: the doctrine of confidence. From the Westminster perspective, governments have no authority whatsoever without the confidence of the House. Although they need not win every vote, lack of confidence need not be expressed in specific words, but can be inferred from the subject matter of the government business rejected by the House.[67] Thus, defeat on the Queen's Speech, the government's legislative programme, implies withdrawal of permission to govern, as does defeat on authority to tax (Finance Bills) or to spend (Supply and Appropriation Bills) or to discipline the armed forces.[68] The most radical

---

[64] *Hansard*, HC Deb, 6th series, vol. 657 col. 1130, 3 April 2019.

[65] On Queen's Consent, the Speaker provided an additional justification, that the government had thought it unnecessary to obtain consent for its own European Union (Notification of Withdrawal) Bill 2017. Precisely why the 2017 bill needed no consent was unclear, but he was effectively saying that ministers were estopped. See May, *Treatise on the Law*, para. 30.79.

[66] The Speaker's appointment needs the monarch's 'approbation' (see May, *Treatise on the Law*, para. 8.20), but not even the most dedicated Whitehallists have suggested that ministers can veto a Speaker by 'advising' the monarch to refuse it.

[67] House of Commons Public Administration and Constitutional Affairs Committee, 'The Role of Parliament in the UK Constitution Interim Report: The Status and Effect of Confidence Motions and the Fixed-term Parliaments Act 2011' (14th Report of Session 2017–19), HC 1813, 11 December 2018, para. 8.

[68] Philip Norton, 'The Fixed-term Parliaments Act and Votes of Confidence' (2016) 69 Parliamentary Affairs 3–18.

version of the Westminster view holds that any defeat on a matter central to the government's programme counts as losing confidence, or even any vote on a three-line whip,[69] although this view allows the government to restore confidence by immediately holding and winning an affirmative vote of confidence.[70]

From the Whitehall perspective, however, confidence only matters because the monarch needs to be satisfied that the person she appoints as Prime Minister could command the confidence of the House, but no need exists for testing that proposition either then or later. The prime minister is presumed to retain confidence and may govern with full powers unless the House expressly declares that it has no confidence. In an extreme version of Whitehallism, the monarch can only know whether a person has the confidence of the House through the prime minister, and so the prime minister holds office with full powers until the prime minister personally accepts that she or he has lost the confidence of the House.

In 2017–19, the Commons repeatedly defeated the government on a central manifesto proposal – leaving the EU with a deal.[71] The government also lost procedural control and suffered the unique indignity of having two bills passed by Parliament it vehemently opposed. From a Westminster point of view, the government had lost the confidence of the House. The Westminster interpretation would suggest that the government was entitled to attempt to restore confidence, but instead of tabling and winning an affirmative vote of confidence (which, it presumably feared it would lose), the government tried repeating the vote on its deal and then marginally changing its position and holding a third vote, all of which failed. Whichever way the government turned it lost the votes of one faction or another.[72] Not even a change of prime minister and a renegotiated Irish backstop could do the trick.[73] At that point, without an affirmative vote of confidence, the Westminster view demanded that the government should either propose a general election or resign.

---

[69] This is true of any vote in which government MPs 'know perfectly well that this vote is a question of confidence on which the government will either win or go', P. de Zulueta, Letter, *Times*, 13 July 1971.

[70] For example, Harold Wilson's government lost a vote on its entire public expenditure policy (*Hansard*, HC Deb, 5th series, vol. 907 cols. 430–574, 10 March 1976) but responded the following day with another vote, technically on the adjournment but expressly stated by Wilson to be about confidence, which it won (*Hansard*, HC Deb, 5th series, vol. 907 cols. 634–758, 11 March 1976).

[71] *Forward, together: Our Plan for a Stronger Britain and a Prosperous Future* (London: Conservative Party, 2017) pp 6, 35–7.

[72] Division 293 of 15 January 2019 (lost 432–202), Division 354 of 12 March 2019 (lost 391–242) and Division 395 of 29 March 2019 (lost 344–286). One exception occurred: the Brady Amendment (Division 313 of 29 January 2019), but that was more about what the Commons did not want than what it did.

[73] Division 3 of 19 October 2019 (lost 322–306).

The law on the calling of elections was governed by the Fixed-term Parliaments Act 2011, which allowed general elections before the end of a parliament's five year term only if either two thirds of the House of Commons voted for an early election or the government lost a motion in the precise terms 'That this House has no confidence in Her Majesty's Government' and no government, either the old one or a new one, received the House's approval within fourteen days in the form of an equally precisely worded motion 'That this House has confidence in Her Majesty's Government'. The Act could be amended, but only by a new Act of Parliament, a majority for which at that point the government lacked. The government repeatedly tried to persuade the House to pass early election motions, but failed every time.[74] The express no confidence route was blocked by the reluctance of the leader of the official opposition, who alone, at least by convention, can require a no confidence motion to be debated,[75] to propose any such motion. In the background lay a serious political problem: MPs opposed to the government, although a majority, repeatedly failed to put together their own viable administration. The leader of the Opposition insisted that he should become prime minister in any new government, even though he was unacceptable to many of the government's opponents, but he had enough influence on his own side to deprive any other possible candidate of a majority.[76]

The result was impasse. The government had lost the confidence of the House, had failed to restore it, and failed to secure an election. According to the Westminster view, it should have resigned to facilitate the appointment of a new prime minister, but it refused to do that as well. Admittedly, it managed to gain approval for its Queen's Speech,[77] which might count as restoring confidence, but it still had no majority for its central policy and so could have lost confidence again at any time.

From the Whitehall perspective, however, the situation was much simpler. The government retained the confidence of the House because the House had not passed an express vote of no confidence.[78] Its inability to persuade the House to support its central policy was irrelevant. Westministerists might retort that the

---

[74] Division 443 of 4 September 2019 (286 votes for); Division 445 of 9 September 2019 (293 votes for); and Division 13 of 28 October 2019 (299 votes for).
[75] May, *Treatise on the Law*, para. 18.44. The government could, however, provide time for other party leaders' no confidence motions.
[76] See, 'Why governments of national unity are so hard to form', *Economist*, 29 August 2019, www.economist.com/britain/2019/08/29/why-governments-of-national-unity-are-so-hard-to-form.
[77] Division 12 of 24 October 2019.
[78] *Hansard*, J. Rees-Mogg MP, HC Deb, 6th series, vol. 664 cols. 97–98, 2 September 2019.

government told its backbenchers that support on opposing the emergency motion providing time for the Benn Bill was a matter of confidence[79] and proceeded to act on that view by expelling from the party the twenty-one Conservative MPs who voted for it. But in the extreme Whitehall view, what matters is what the prime minister believes, no matter how contradictory.

The situation was complicated by a common belief on the government benches that the Fixed-term Parliaments Act controlled not only when an early general election could be called but also when governments were obliged to resign. In the words of the then chair of the Public Administration and Constitutional Affairs Committee, 'The Prime Minister may no longer be able to call a general election, but he is no longer obliged to resign either—at least not for 14 days. That has the effect of strengthening the incumbency of a sitting Prime Minister.'[80] The prime minister accordingly announced that he would not resign even after an express vote of no confidence and that he would attempt to precipitate a general election by refusing to give way to any successor in the fourteen day period.[81] That interpretation effectively excluded the whole Westminster version of confidence, removing any continuing requirement for governments to maintain confidence and replacing it with the Act's mechanical device.

The Westminster interpretation of the 2011 Act was that it had no effect whatsoever on the doctrine of confidence.[82] On this view, the Act controlled nothing except election timing, but with the very important consequence that it had abolished the doctrine, sometimes traced to the struggle in 1784 between the Commons and Pitt the Younger, that a government faced by a hostile Commons was entitled to eradicate the Commons by precipitating a general

---

[79] Peter Walker, 'Tomorrow's vote will be treated as confidence matter, says No 10', *Guardian*, 2 September 2019. Walker cites 'a Number 10 source' as saying 'The view is that tomorrow's possible vote is an expression of confidence in the government's negotiating position to secure a deal and will be treated as such', www.theguardian.com/politics/2019/sep/02/brexit-no-10-boris-johnson-ignore-legislation-block-no-deal.

[80] *Hansard*, Sir Bernard Jenkin MP, HC Deb, 6th series, vol. 664 col. 119, 3 September 2019.

[81] See, S. Swinford and H. Zeffman, 'Boris Johnson to defy any vote of no confidence' *Times*, 6 August 2019, www.thetimes.co.uk/article/boris-johnson-to-defy-any-vote-of-no-confidence-s28ksnhzm. Whether he could have succeeded is unclear. *Miller 2/Cherry* probably means that governments cannot stop the Commons meeting during the fourteen-day period, but the issue was whether the House could pry the prime minister out. Suggestions included impeachment (too slow), expulsion from the House (would it persuade the monarch to dismiss?) and a statute declaring anyone held in contempt of the House ineligible for ministerial office.

[82] Also the view of the Public Administration and Constitutional Affairs Committee, as opposed to its chair: House of Commons Public Administration and Constitutional Affairs Committee, 'The Role of Parliament in the UK Constitution Interim Report: The Status and Effect of Confidence Motions and the Fixed-term Parliaments Act 2011', House of Commons Public Administration and Constitutional Affairs Committee, 14th Report of Session 2017–19), HC 1813, 11 December 2018, paras. 57–8.

election. Prime ministers were no longer entitled to a dissolution but had to ask the Commons' permission, fundamentally shifting the balance of power in the direction of the Commons.

In the event the government succeeded, as did Pitt, in dissolving the Commons. In late October 2019, it persuaded Parliament to pass a short bill temporarily overriding the effect of the 2011 Act.[83] Although the Commons' permission was sought and given, in an important sense the Whitehall view prevailed. As in 1784, the government avoided resignation despite losing vote after vote and then, again as in 1784, the government appealed from the Commons to the electorate, which gave its verdict resoundingly to the government.

Admittedly the result might have been different if the resolutions the Commons passed against Pitt had been passed in 2019 – a motion to delay supply, a motion to delay the Mutiny Bill, and a Humble Address asking the King to dismiss the ministry.[84] Could the view that governments need not resign even if defeated survive when the sinews of government, both financial and military were denied it and the Commons expressly called for its dismissal? That remains unclear.

### STATUS OF THE 2016 REFERENDUM

The 2016 referendum was, notoriously, not legally binding,[85] but as Eoin Daly points out in chapter 8 that fact has not limited its effects. It might not be surprising in the British context that explaining the constitution requires one to go beyond the law, but, again as Eoin Daly argues, referendums can break through all institutional boundaries, including the boundaries of the very institutions that create referendums themselves, and thereby reshape whole systems. The claim that referendums can come to represent an extra-institutional expression of popular sovereignty, like the constitutional amending 'conventions' that Art. V of the US Constitution attempts to corral,[86] has great emotional power, however unsustainable it looks if examined in detail.[87] One

---

[83] Early Parliamentary General Election Act 2019.
[84] John Cannon, *The Fox-North Coalition: Crisis of the Constitution 1782–4* (Cambridge: Cambridge University Press, 1970).
[85] *R (Miller) v. Secretary of State for Exiting the European Union* [*Miller 1*] [2017] UKSC 5; [2018] AC 61, at paras. 119–20.
[86] See Bruce Ackerman, *We, The People vol 2: Transformations* (Cambridge, MA, Harvard UP, 1998), pp. 70–95. See further, Bruce Ackerman, *Revolutionary Constitutions: Charismatic Leadership and the Rule of Law* (Cambridge, MA: Harvard University Press), pp. 370–4.
[87] To take one obvious example, s. 2 of the European Union Referendum Act 2015 did not include in the franchise for the Brexit referendum either EU citizens who were not British, Irish or Commonwealth citizens (who could vote in local elections) or sixteen and seventeen

illustration of that power appeared in 2017–19, when many Brexit supporters denied the legitimacy of a 'Remainer Parliament' that was 'blocking the result of the referendum' despite the fact that the Parliament in question had been elected after the referendum.[88] They also developed a doctrine, seemingly self-contradictory, that holding another referendum would be 'undemocratic' because it might overturn the 'will of the people'.[89] What explains these doctrines is a revolutionary view of the 2016 referendum as a constitutionally foundational moment in which the people spoke in an unprecedented way.[90] On this view, the legitimacy of institutions after 2016 depends on their acceptance of the referendum result. Others reject this position outright in favour of a straightforwardly Westminsterist view that referendums need have no lasting effects and can soon fade, or be made to fade, into the political background.[91] Others still reassert a Whitehallist theory of election mandates according to which outright general election victories can overturn referendums.[92] Another proposal, an old perennial of British constitutional debate, is that referendums need to be incorporated and domesticated into a formal codified constitution.[93]

Whether the 2016 referendum has a revolutionary effect, or any other effect for good or ill, is not yet clear. Referendums have no automatically better claim to count as 'the people' than elected assemblies. The open nature of the UK system allows such questions to be endlessly reopened. Direct democracy, once tasted, might well prove irresistible. But referendums might instead come to be widely regarded as nothing but exercises in elite manipulation and the institutional expression of ochlocracy. In the Netherlands, for example, all provision for national referendums has been

---

year-olds (who voted in the Scottish independence referendum), thus excluding more than 3 million voters. 'The People' defined differently might well have decided differently.

[88] See *Hansard*, Crispin Blunt MP, HC Deb, 6th series, vol. 657, col. 38, 25 March 2019; *Hansard*, Anne Main MP, HC Deb, 6th series, vol. 657 col. 758, 29 March 2018; Allison Pearson, 'Boris's win proves the soul of our nation is intact - I am so proud of what our country has done', *Daily Telegraph*, 14 December 2019, Factiva.

[89] See *Hansard*, Jacob Rees-Mogg MP, HC Deb, 6th series, vol. 651, col. 545, 17 December 2018; *Hansard*, Iain Duncan-Smith MP, HC Deb, 6th series, vol. 664, col. 270, 4 September 2019; R. Prince, 'The last thing we need at this point is a second referendum', *Daily Telegraph*, 17 October 2019, Factiva; The Sun Says (Editorial), 11 November 2019; A. Green 'Humphrys: Second Brexit Referendum undemocratic', *Western Mail*, 21 November 2019, Factiva.

[90] C.f. Les Green, 'Should parliamentary sovereignty trump popular sovereignty?', https://ljmgreen.com/2016/11/03/should-parliamentary-sovereignty-trump-popular-sovereignty/ and Eoin Daly, Chapter 8.

[91] *Hansard*, Kenneth Clarke MP, HC Deb, 6th series, vol. 651, cols. 91–2, 10 Dec. 2018.

[92] *Stop Brexit: Build a Brighter Future: Manifesto 2019* (London: Liberal Democrats, 2019), p. 1

[93] Vernon Bogdanor, *Beyond Brexit: Britain's Unprotected Constitution* (London: IB Tauris, 2019), pp. 261–5, 275–9 and Daly this volume, Chapter 8.

abolished,[94] having been characterised by the Council of State as a threat to representative democracy and the rule of law.[95] The Whitehall view has its own competing claim on the concept of direct democracy and the Westminster view might provide a refuge for those looking to protect government-by-discussion from the domination of politics by illicit political and economic forces. But the potential for further change that downgrades both the Westminster and Whitehall views undoubtedly exists.

## WHAT HAVE WE LEARNED?

To summarise: on governmental power to act without parliamentary approval and ability to ignore or veto parliamentary decisions, the Brexit debate has led to advances for the Westminster view, both in in the courts and in the Commons; and similarly for control of the Commons' agenda, at least where the Speaker supports the Westminster view. But on the fundamental matter of confidence and the ability of governments to appeal from the Commons to the electorate, although in theory the Westminster view held its own, in practice, in 2019 as in 1784, the Whitehall view triumphed. Meanwhile, in the background, the use of referendums continues to chip away at the descriptive power of both views.

What about the two views as ideals? The Brexit debate brings home the weaknesses of government by large assemblies, as Hobbes warned. The Commons knew what it was against but consistently failed to decide what it was for. The defence of the Westminster view that Parliament seeks not to govern but merely to insist on its own choice of government also failed to work because the Commons could not agree on an alternative administration. Effectively, the Commons created a situation for months in which the government failed to command its confidence, but no new government was created, and no general election was called. For the Westminster view to work, the Commons must take responsibility for creating a government in which it has confidence, either by installing a new government or by agreeing to an election. In 2017-19, the Commons signally failed to take responsibility. The question for Westminsterists is whether politics founded on confrontation and theatricality can produce parliamentarians capable of making the Westminster view work.

---

[94] 'Intrekkingswet Wet raadgevend Referendum 2018', https://wetten.overheid.nl/BWBR0041149/2018-07-12 .

[95] Council of State of the Kingdom of the Netherlands, Annual Report for 2016, p. 17, https://jaarverslag.raadvanstate.nl/2016/wp-content/uploads/sites/4/2017/03/PDF-Jaarverslag-2016-DEFINITIEF.pdf.

The Whitehall view, however, also proved inadequate. The government lacked any mandate from the 2015 election for any specific form of Brexit, and so could not reasonably expect to impose its choice on the Commons without challenge or debate. In the event it failed even to persuade its own side. Then it failed to obtain a mandate at the 2017 election. The idea that in those circumstances the Commons is a secondary appendage is hopelessly unrealistic. For the Whitehall view to work, it must somehow exclude the possibility of minority governments and even of divided majority parties. It is difficult to see how to achieve that without direct election of the prime minister and a switch to an openly presidential system.[96]

Also worrying is the gap between the Supreme Court's view of the constitution, which is very much Westminsterist, and the determinedly Whitehallist views of the government and other political actors. Mutual incomprehension between the organs of the British state is not new but this one is fundamental – ultimately it concerns the meaning of democracy. The customary British approach to fundamental theoretical differences is to ignore them, relying on moderation and mutual forbearance to produce practical if not entirely coherent answers. Perhaps we will find a way to replicate that approach. Or perhaps we will find a new democratic consensus that will supplant the whole British political tradition with something more inclusive and thoughtful.[97] The danger is that no solution will appear, with both theories challenged by national populist and illiberal theories that promote the supremacy of plebiscites and the easily manipulated steamroller myth of the 'will of the people'.[98] If that happens, Britain will lurch towards a very different type of system.

---

[96] See Graham Allen, *The Last Prime Minister: Being Honest About the UK Presidency* (London: Societas, 2nd edn., 2003).

[97] See Emma Vines and David Marsh, 'Anti-politics: beyond supply-side versus demand-side explanations' (2018) 13 *British Politics* 433–53.

[98] Albert Weale, *The Will of the People: a modern myth* (London: Polity, 2018).

# 11

# Brexit and the Problem with Delegated Legislation

Adam Tucker

INTRODUCTION

Brexit will have an impact on the United Kingdom constitution in myriad interconnected ways. Most prominently, the constitution will be substantively, or directly, changed as its institutions are disentangled from the institutions of the European project. New institutions will be created to perform functions previously performed by the European Union and existing institutions will change as they acquire new functions and competencies. There will also be indirect change, as constitutional and wider political practices develop independently of connected practices in the Union. Some domestic practices previously anchored – formally or informally – to connected or analogous practices in Europe will naturally drift over time – sometimes by design, sometimes not. Some of these changes are predictable, others are not. Some have already begun, others will take place in the future. Alongside these types of change, which flow from the *fact of* Brexit; the very *process of* Brexit will also leave its mark on the constitution. The way that institutions and political actors engage with the task of implementing the outcome of the 2016 referendum will leave its own impression. This is a chapter about one instance of this particular type of change. It examines the impact of the process of implementing Brexit on a pre-existing constitutional problem, that of delegated legislation. Its core argument is that one likely legacy of the Brexit process will be – and perhaps already is – the exacerbation of the already troubling constitutional position of delegated legislation. But the chapter also, albeit very tentatively, does highlight some indications that the Brexit process may yet lay the foundations for improving the position of delegated legislation in the United Kingdom's constitutional landscape.

The first part of the chapter provides a critical overview of the constitutional position of delegated legislation pre-Brexit and thereby sets out the context in which the heavy reliance on delegated legislation in the implementation of Brexit arose. The second part examines the place of delegated legislation in the legislative response to Brexit, focusing in particular, but not exclusively, on delegated legislation by the UK government under the European Union (Withdrawal) Act 2018. This leads to my pessimistic, core conclusions about the likely legacy of that period. The third part excavates the more positive elements of the story, a quest which has – alas – been made more difficult by the approach to delegated legislation adopted by Parliament in more recent statutes, in particular the European Union (Withdrawal Agreement) Act 2020.

## THE PROBLEM WITH DELEGATED LEGISLATION

The significance, especially the wider *constitutional* significance, of the role played by delegated legislation in the process of leaving the EU must be understood in the context of the pre-existing – and troublesome – constitutional position of the practice.[1]

Delegated legislation is legislation made by the executive, under the authority of an empowering piece of primary legislation (commonly referred to as a 'Parent Act'). There is no overarching constitutional framework for delegated legislative power. Rather, the boundaries of each delegation are individually set in each Parent Act. So, although delegations tend to follow the same basic structure, their details can vary widely: the holder or holders of the power, its breadth or scope, any restrictions on its exercise, its duration, any restrictions on the purposes for which it can (or cannot) be exercised, and so on are potentially different and individually specified each time Parliament delegates a power to legislate.

Delegated legislation is not merely a common practice in the contemporary constitution. In fact, in some senses, it is now the dominant form of law-making. A vastly greater volume of delegated than primary legislation is passed each year.[2] More importantly (and more interestingly), delegated legislation is now routinely the way in which decisions of fundamental national importance are made, and the route by which statutory instruments touch every area of national life. Policies which have been enacted by way of delegated legislation in recent years include: the so-called Bedroom Tax; eligibility changes radically restricting the availability of legal aid; bank nationalisations during the

---

[1] This part draws on Adam Tucker, 'Parliamentary Scrutiny of Delegated Legislation', in Alexander Horne and Gavin Drewey (eds.), *Parliament and the Law* (Oxford: Hart Publishing, 2018).

[2] In 2019, for example, Parliament passed thirty-one Acts whereas the UK government made 1410 Statutory Instruments.

financial crisis; the periodic extension of terrorism legislation under sunset clauses; and large numbers of new criminal offences. Statutes across all areas routinely delegate significant legislative power, and so-called 'skeleton statutes', which simply delegate wide authority across entire policy areas to the executive, are common.[3] The development of the resultant patchwork of delegated power, and of the legislation which emerges through its exercise, is haphazard. There is no real discrimination as to which policy areas are, and are not, suitable to be tackled in this way, nor as to which parts of individual policy areas are appropriately left to executive discretion. The relentless and routine delegation of legislative power is a core feature of primary legislation and, as a result, delegated legislating is now a core feature of law-making in the United Kingdom.

Delegated legislation – especially on this scale – is a constitutionally risky practice. Even the scrupulously lawful exercise of a power sensibly delegated by Parliament still has the constitutional flaw that it is legislation by the executive and is therefore a violation of the separation of powers. The executive lacks both the procedural and democratic virtues of Parliament, which are the foundation of the legitimacy of primary legislation. This risk is exacerbated in the case of so-called 'Henry VIII powers', which empower the executive to use delegated legislation to amend primary legislation. By permitting the executive to override primary legislation, these also undermine parliamentary sovereignty. These risks cannot be eliminated; they are inherent to the practice. But they can be managed, ideally by ensuring adequate scrutiny of delegated legislation, aimed at boosting its constitutional legitimacy. Accordingly, it is customary for delegations of legislative power to be accompanied by provisions requiring its exercise to be subject to parliamentary scrutiny, and Parliament has developed institutional features and a number of practices aimed at discharging this significant responsibility.

Despite the lack of an overarching framework, and the ad hoc way in which scrutiny requirements are imposed, certain forms of parliamentary scrutiny do tend to be required in parent Acts.[4] The most common involve what are usually called either affirmative or negative procedures. Under affirmative procedures, statutory instruments take effect only if they are approved by one or both Houses. Under negative procedures, instruments take effect unless they are voted down by one or both Houses. Different procedures are sometimes specified, in particular hybrid procedures where instruments are

---

[3] For a recent example, see the Space Industry Act 2018.
[4] For an overview of the core approaches, see Richard Kelly, *Statutory Instruments*, House of Commons Library Briefing Paper No. 06509 (15 December 2016), pp. 7–11.

vulnerable to annulment unless the government seeks prior approval. Variants on these procedures seem to have become more common in recent years.[5] In particular, some statutes require enhanced procedures. For example, some delegated legislation under the Legislative and Regulatory Reform Act 2006 is subject to a sixty-day consultation period and enhanced power (in both Houses) for committees to block the passage of instruments.[6]

Whilst the level of scrutiny applicable to each delegated power is determined in its primary, parent, legislation, its practical effectiveness ultimately depends on the internal rules and arrangements of the Houses which put those requirements into practice. Here, the House of Commons and House of Lords act not as legislators but as supervisors, charged with scrutinising an exercise of law-making power by the executive, and the level of supervision which they thereby subject government to depends on what they make of their role as supervisors. As the Delegated Powers and Regulatory Reform Committee put the point (in reference to the House of Lords, but equally true of both Houses):

> The existence of these scrutiny procedures in legislation does not in itself ensure that the House exercises its ... scrutiny role. Effective scrutiny in all cases relies on the House putting in place mechanisms (for example, nominating a committee) to undertake scrutiny and report its conclusions ...[7]

Unfortunately – and despite the dedication of substantial levels of parliamentary resources to the task – parliamentary scrutiny of delegated legislation is inadequate and fails to meet the demands of constitutional principle. There are two main dimensions to the problem. First, there is an overwhelming bias towards *technical* rather than *merit*-based scrutiny of proposed statutory instruments. Secondly, whatever level of scrutiny they are subject to, statutory instruments are essentially invulnerable to defeat in the scrutiny process.

The aversion to merit based scrutiny is exemplified by – but goes well beyond – the Joint Committee on Statutory Instruments, the main engine of parliamentary scrutiny of delegated legislation. Its terms of reference require statutory instruments to be assessed against a number of specified grounds (whether or not charges are imposed, any purported retrospective effect, doubts about vires and so on) but they expressly preclude assessment of 'its

---

[5] Ruth Fox and Joel Blackwell identified sixteenvariants in 2014, *The Devil is in the Detail: Parliament and Delegated Legislation* (London: Hansard Society, 2014).
[6] Legislative and Regulatory Reform Act 2006 s. 18.
[7] House of Lords Delegated Powers and Regulatory Reform Committee, *Special Report: Strengthened Statutory Procedures for the Scrutiny of Delegated Powers* (3rd Report of Session 2012–13), HL Paper 19, para. 27.

merits or the policy behind it'.[8] In other words, the main, most prestigious parliamentary committee for the scrutiny of delegated legislation is explicitly precluded by its own terms of reference from asking the most important question – whether or not the proposals before it are, or are not, desirable changes to the law. Other, lower profile, committees are at least able to engage in merit based scrutiny. In the House of Commons, delegated legislation committees are convened on an ad hoc basis whenever an instrument is referred for committee scrutiny. Their sessions are short (capped at ninety minutes) and involve small numbers of participants. And although they can – and do – engage with the merits of the instruments before them, they are convened at a frenetic pace (sometimes hundreds of sittings per session) and many do not engage even in the pretence of scrutiny.[9] The House of Lords has a more stable structure for scrutinising statutory instruments – in particular the Secondary Legislation Scrutiny Committee, which does engage with the merits of the instruments it examines.

In any event, and independent of whatever scrutiny they are subject to, proposed statutory instruments are effectively invulnerable to defeat. Committees have no power to reject instruments and cannot even recommend that the Houses do so. The Joint Committee on Statutory Instruments and the Secondary Legislation Scrutiny Committee can only 'draw [an instrument] to the special attention of the House' (which is not, to be clear, code for recommending a rejection). And Commons Delegated Legislation Committees vote (if at all) not on substantive motions, but that 'the Committee has considered' an instrument.[10] The power to reject motions is vested by legislation only in the Houses themselves. And it is a power that they do not exercise. The House of Commons – for obvious reasons – never votes against delegated legislation. In fact, it only votes *at all* on delegated legislation when absolutely necessary (because, for example, affirmative measures require its approval). And even these votes often take a list of multiple instruments at once and are carried without discussion or division (or indeed authentic attention or participation from MPs). 'Prayers' to annul instruments almost never make it to the floor as the Opposition have limited time and other priorities. The House of Lords never votes against negative instruments. Like

---

[8] *Standing Orders of the House of Commons – Public Business*, para. 151; *The Standing Orders of the House of Lords Relating to Public Business*, para. 73.
[9] Fox and Blackwell, *The Devil is in the Detail*, cite one debate which lasted only twenty-two seconds. See text accompanying n. 35 for an example of some recent, more typical, proceedings.
[10] The form of the motion is prescribed in House of Commons Standing Order 118(5). In 2015–16, only thirteen such meetings went to a division.

the Commons, it rarely even finds time to debate them. As a consequence, the only form of delegated legislation vulnerable in any sense to defeat in Parliament is that which requires approval in the Lords. In theory, the Lords retains the power to decline to pass the (necessary) motion which gives its authorisation to such instruments. But this power is basically never exercised, and the Lords is creative in finding ways to avoid rejecting even instruments it disapproves of, preferring to pass legally ineffective motions of regret; non-fatal motions which express but do not enforce disagreement. And even this, very hesitant, approach was put under pressure by the government-commissioned Strathclyde Review in 2015 which favoured the abolition of the Lords' power to veto delegated legislation.[11]

In summary, much delegated legislation is never scrutinised at all in Parliament; what scrutiny does take place happens against the backdrop of a deeply embedded tradition of avoiding merit-based scrutiny. Regardless of the outcome of that scrutiny, there is no real chance of Parliament rejecting any delegated legislation; and the government has recently proposed to relax rather than to tighten these already unsatisfactory constitutional arrangements.

Thus, immediately before the constitutional upheaval of Brexit, the constitution was teetering on the edge of what I have previously characterised as a 'legitimacy precipice'.[12] There was a pressing need to reassess the approach to delegated legislation in contemporary constitutional practice, in particular, the widespread extent of the use of delegations and their inadequate scrutiny by Parliament. At that point, a sensible and realistic ambition for this area of the constitution would have been movement towards less and better scrutinised delegated legislation.

Arising against this backdrop, Brexit imposed constitutional pressures which put that ambition on hold. It generated a period of widespread political upheaval in which longer-standing, principled issues of constitutional governance were subsumed by the more immediate need to interpret and implement the result of the 2016 referendum. And part of that pressure consisted of the need to actually legislate for Brexit. So, on one level, as we see across the other chapters in this volume, Brexit overwhelmed the capacity of the UK constitution to develop, to reform, and to incrementally adapt.[13] But Brexit also had to be dealt with within our existing institutions and constitutional practices. The

[11] Strathclyde Review: Secondary legislation and the primacy of the House of Commons, Cm 9177 (2015).
[12] Tucker, 'Parliamentary Scrutiny of Delegated Legislation', p. 370.
[13] On this, see also Michael Gordon, 'Constitutional Overload in a Constitutional Democracy: The UK and the Brexit Process' in Sacha Garben, Inge Govaere and Paul Nemitz (eds.),

legislative response to Brexit, then, was – naturally – developed within the existing practice, as described above, of over-delegating and under-scrutinised powers. So, to the extent that Brexit involved resort to delegated legislative power, it became an instance of those practices. On the one hand, the problem with delegated legislation is independent of, and indeed predates, the constitutional pressures of Brexit. But on the other hand, with that pressure on the constitution, the legislative response to Brexit became part of the story: an instance of those troublesome practices and an instantiation and reinforcement of the problem, as I will go on to explain.

### THE LEGISLATIVE RESPONSE TO BREXIT

Leaving the European Union entailed a massive legislative project. This need was partly 'merely' technical, preparing the UK institutional arrangements for disconnection from those of the Union. But the requirement for legislation also had inherently political elements because there is more than one vision of the institutional arrangements and constitutional culture needed to replace those which had prevailed under the EU constitutional architecture. Whilst this legislative process is still ongoing, its foundation was the European Union (Withdrawal) Act 2018 (EUWA).[14] Before its publication, the bill was, rather grandly, promoted as the 'Great Repeal Bill' by the government.[15] And in late 2016 the then Secretary of State for Exiting the European Union told the Exiting the EU Committee that it was 'going to be a simple Bill'.[16] In the end, it was neither 'great' nor 'simple'.

The EUWA provides for several dimensions of the post-EU membership legal order. Most famously, it provides for Parliament's involvement in the eventual approval, but not the negotiation, of a Withdrawal Agreement.[17] But this was an afterthought, added as the bill went through Parliament. The bill's foundation and starting point was the repeal of the European Communities

---

*Critical Reflections on Constitutional Democracy in the European Union* (Oxford: Hart Publishing, 2019).

[14] The boundaries of that process are vague, but it certainly also includes the European Union (Withdrawal Agreement) Act 2020 and, before Parliament at the time of writing, the Agriculture Bill, the Environment Bill, the Fisheries Bill, the Immigration and Social Security Co-ordination (EU Withdrawal) Bill, the Medicines and Medical Devices Bill, and the Trade Bill.

[15] Legislating for the United Kingdom's withdrawal from the European Union (The Repeal Bill White Paper), Cm 9446 (2016).

[16] Exiting the European Union Committee, Oral Evidence: The UK's negotiating objectives for its withdrawal from EU, 14th December 2016 (2016 HC 815), in response to Q481.

[17] European Union (Withdrawal) Act s. 13.

Act 1972.[18] But this was coupled with the immediate saving of, almost, the entire body of law that would otherwise have been severed from the domestic legal system by that repeal.[19] In the name of legal certainty, EUWA rescued much of the substance of the European-derived law applicable on exit day by creating a new category of UK law, 'retained EU law'. Whilst this remained valid for the time being, it was plainly anticipated (and inherent in the project itself) that it would be progressively eroded and replaced by domesticated regulation in the policy areas previously governed on a Europe-wide basis. Accordingly, the creation of this new category of law was accompanied by provisions intended to make it a static – or stable – body of law, severed from future EU development and with an attenuated hierarchy between different sources.[20]

The government readily acknowledged that a significant potential drawback to the approach of formally repealing but also immediately resuscitating EU law was that the resultant body of law would not be properly functional without further amendment.[21] Both retained EU law and domestic law more generally would continue to presuppose, in many different ways, the United Kingdom's membership of the European Union. For example, law might variously depend on or refer to now-disconnected European institutions or bodies left by the United Kingdom through Brexit, or be dependent on EU programmes or systems of which the United Kingdom is no longer part of, or be predicated on the implementation of EU policies in which the United Kingdom no longer participates, and so on. In other words, the repeal-yet-retain strategy bought legal continuity (and hence certainty) at the price of legal unintelligibility. As the government tended to put the point, without more the architecture of EUWA would have left the United Kingdom with a non-functioning statute book.[22] The government chose delegated legislative power as the solution to this important problem.

The most important delegation is made in s. 8 EUWA, under the subheading 'Dealing with deficiencies arising from withdrawal'. It gives the executive an extremely wide-ranging power to legislate. That power is triggered at a relatively low threshold – whenever the minister considers it 'appropriate'.

---

[18] European Union (Withdrawal) Act s. 1.
[19] European Union (Withdrawal) Act ss. 2–4. The parenthetical 'almost' is necessitated (mainly) by s. 5 which excludes (subss. 4–5) the principle of supremacy of EU law and the Charter of Fundamental Rights from the saving. 'Mainly' because Schedule 1 further excludes general principles of EU law and the rule in Francovich.
[20] European Union (Withdrawal) Act s. 6 and Schedule 1.
[21] The Repeal Bill White Paper. See also the secretary of state's explanation at second reading in the Commons, *Hansard*, HC, vol. 628, col. 349, 7 September 2017.
[22] The Repeal Bill White Paper, paras. 1.13–1.14.

This threshold survived attempts to amend it to the tighter standard of 'necessity' as the bill went through Parliament. It has a broadly defined purpose – it can be used 'to prevent, remedy or mitigate' legal deficiencies, a formula which gives ministers great flexibility over the intensity of their interventions in the statute book. And although some of the ways in which it defines the deficiencies to which it applies look narrowly technical,[23] others are drafted more widely – notably ss. 2(d) which brings within the ambit of this power any existing 'provision for, or in connection with, any ... arrangements ... which ... are no longer appropriate, as a result of the United Kingdom ceasing to be a party to any of the EU Treaties'. There are substantive limits to the exercise of this delegated power: it cannot be used to impose or increase taxes, for retrospective law making, to create more serious criminal offences and to establish public authorities, to implement the Withdrawal Agreement, or to amend the Human Rights Act and the Devolution settlements (although any other constitutional or similarly important statutes are not protected). There is also a time limit: initially two years after exit day.[24]

When the bill was originally published, this delegated power was to be underpinned by a wholly conventional approach to the scrutiny of legislation made under it, consistent with the problematic situation outlined above. A small list of triggers indicated which kinds of instruments would require affirmative procedures; all others would require negative procedures.[25] But this did not survive parliamentary scrutiny. Instead, the government accepted an amendment proposed by Charles Walker (the chair of the Procedure Committee) for the introduction of a *sifting* mechanism.[26] This supplemented the triggers for affirmative procedures with mechanisms to enhance Parliament's opportunity to scrutinise the remaining legislation otherwise destined for negative procedures. The statute empowered a committee in each House to make recommendations as to the appropriateness of the government's choice to use negative procedures. A new Commons committee, the European Statutory Instruments Committee was established. The existing Lords Secondary Legislation Scrutiny Committee added sifting to its existing responsibilities. These committees undertook the massive task of

---

[23] Subs. 2(a), for example, applies the power to 'anything which no longer has practical application ... or is otherwise ... substantially redundant' and subs. 2(d) relates to arrangements which 'no longer exist'.
[24] European Union (Withdrawal) Act 2018, ss. 8(7) and 8(8).
[25] Schedule 7 of the bill as originally introduced to Parliament.
[26] House of Commons Procedure Committee, *Scrutiny of delegated legislation under the European Union (Withdrawal) Bill: interim report* (1st Report of Session 2017–19), HC 386. See European Union (Withdrawal) Act 2018, Schedule 7.

evaluating whether or not every negative instrument ought really be subject to affirmative procedures. Whilst their recommendations are not mandatory, the statute creates a delay in which sifting can take place, and requires government to provide justificatory statements to facilitate the process, as well as obliging ministers to explain any failure to respect a committee recommendation. As the process of legislating under s. 8 EUWA unfolded, these mechanisms established themselves as institutionalised parts of the secondary legislative process, and are now part of the workflow of government and of Parliament as statutory instruments are made.

The constitutional legacy of s. 8 EUWA depends on the interplay between the two main elements of this story: on the one hand, the scale of the legislative project undertaken by the government under the section and on the other hand, the significance of the creation of the sifting procedure.

The scale of the body of law created by the government under s. 8 EUWA is, despite the apparent constraints on that power, enormous. The government initially estimated that it would require around 1000 statutory instruments and whilst that total has not yet been reached, the figure is still slowly growing and is likely to have been broadly accurate, perhaps even a slight underestimate. But this is not really a question of the quantity of legislation. It is substance that matters. And the gap between the government's characterisation of how the power was intended to be used and the ways in which it has actually been used is remarkable. In committee evidence, the secretary of state distinguished 'material' changes, which would be made in primary legislation, from 'technical' changes, which would be made using delegated legislation using the following example of an anticipated use of the provision: 'if it were a technical amendment, say, that we could no longer put something in the European Journal and that it had to be put on the British Government website'.[27] In the Delegated Powers Memorandum published alongside the bill, the government was reluctant to detail the way that s. 8 EUWA might be used, citing the 'need to protect the UK's negotiating position', but stressed that its aim was '[making] sure the UK's statute book functions on exit'; the examples that were given included the removal of (now redundant) references to European Parliamentary elections from statutes not otherwise repealed as part of the exit process and of repatriating functions to domestic bodies, such as ensuring that the Civil Aviation Authority acquired the necessary jurisdiction to regulate air safety or identifying alternatives to the European Chemicals Agency for the 'evaluation and authorisation of chemicals'. The government also

---

[27] Exiting the European Union Committee, Oral Evidence, in response to Q483.

anticipated using the power to 'resolve the imbalance' in the event of a lack of agreement on continued reciprocity.[28]

In practice, delegated legislation under s. 8 EUWA has been used to make substantive policy changes which go far beyond the merely 'technical'. For example, Sinclair and Tomlinson have highlighted that substantive changes to the immigration system – including the revocation of asylum procedures and return/transfer mechanisms and changes to deportation thresholds – were made in the Immigration, Nationality and Asylum (EU Exit) Regulations 2019, a piece of secondary legislation enacted under s. 8.[29] Introducing those regulations in committee debate, the minister made it clear that one purpose of the instrument was to align exit-day immigration law with the government's policy ('our intention, which the Home Secretary has already announced'), thus demonstrating the overtly political and partisan quality of the legislation.[30] A conflict between retained EU law and the government's preferred policy position is not at all the same thing as having a non-functional statute book. So, whilst many of the instruments enacted under s. 8 EUWA do make the kind of 'technical' change it was said to be designed for, many others are actually substantive policy changes with dramatic consequences for people's everyday lives. The body of law enacted under s. 8 EUWA, then, must be understood as the aggregation of all these individual policy interventions.

This gap between the way the power was characterised by the government and the way it has been used might be surprising. But it makes conceptual sense on the face of the provision, the characteristics of which explain the expansive use to which it has been put. Firstly, whilst it is explicitly aimed at rectifying deficiencies in *retained* law, it nevertheless empowers the government to amend *any* law rather than simply retained law in pursuit of that aim. That is, the entire body of domestic law (other than the limited exceptions explicitly protected in the statute) is vulnerable to change under the provision, including primary legislation, as it is a Henry VIII power. So, deficiencies can be rectified by remaking domestic law rather than simply bringing retained EU law into line, unconstrained even by primary legislation. Secondly, whilst the correction of deficiencies might look like a narrow foundation for

---

[28] European Union (Withdrawal Bill), Memorandum concerning the Delegated Powers in the Bill for the Delegated Powers and Regulatory Reform Committee, paras. 4, 19 and 20.

[29] Alexandra Sinclair and Joe Tomlinson, 'Brexit, Primary Legislation, and Statutory Instruments: Everything in Its Right Place?', UK Constitutional Law Association Blog, 25 March 2019, https://ukconstitutionallaw.org/2019/03/25/alexandra-sinclair-and-joe-tomlinson-brexit-primary-legislation-and-statutory-instruments-everything-in-its-right-place/.

[30] House of Commons Delegated Legislation Committee on the Draft Immigration, Nationality and Asylum (EU Exit) Regulations 2019, 18 March 2019, col. 4.

legislative activity, it gives ministers considerable leeway over the scope of their interventions: it is, in principle, possible to tackle a perceived deficiency in a policy not just by severing its newly redundant European connections, but by abandoning that policy altogether and revoking the legislation which enacts it or by replacing it with a new policy altogether, and legislating for a new policy in the field in question. And finally, s. 8 EUWA applies to the entire range of policy areas which previously came under, or, because undesirable interactions are themselves a 'deficiency', were somehow adjacent to EU competence. Hence the sheer variety of topics covered by the legislation made using this power.

So, on the one side of the balance – the substantive legal impact of legislation made under s. 8 EUWA – we have, in effect, a mini shadow legal system which makes a wide variety of substantive policy changes across the whole range of policy areas previously within the purview of the EU, as well as many adjacent policy areas. In contrast, the other side of the balance – the effectiveness and legacy of the sifting system under which these changes were scrutinised – is, unfortunately, less momentous. There is no doubt that the sifting procedures represent a step forward in the parliamentary scrutiny of delegated legislation. The considerable effort which went into their design, implementation and operation is a positive development in a problematic constitutional area. Nevertheless, it represents only a very modest change.

The key weakness of the sifting process is that it was superimposed on an underlying system of scrutiny which was itself inadequate. It can only redirect a proposed Statutory Instrument away from negative procedures and towards affirmative procedures. But, as we saw above, there is no practical difference between these two types of scrutiny. Neither track involves proper scrutiny of the merits of proposed legislation and neither exposes proposals to any real prospect of defeat. The sifting process essentially redirects instruments between existing and inadequate processes. It 'sifts' effectively in the sense of singling things out for scrutiny, of isolating particular pieces of legislation for different treatment, but it does not affect the underlying reality, which is that they still do not get the examination they need. The creation of the sifting system was not accompanied by further reform of those underlying processes. Furthermore, the sifting process is an inherently temporary innovation, that is, not only is it modest in effect, but it only applies to a subset of delegated legislation, that made under s. 8 EUWA. For a period, that subset has been a very significant and prominent subset of the government's legislative activity. And during that period, the prominence of that species of delegated legislation lent its significance to the sifting processes itself. But it is now fading, and will continue to fade. Eventually, there will be no more delegated legislation for the process to sift. And whilst the lifespan of s. 8 has been extended (its original expiry date, two years after exit day, was pushed back by EUWA s. 27(2)(d) until two years after IP completion day) it is an inherently time-limited power. Whatever progress the sifting processes represent, they are, in any event, destined for extinction when the power to which they apply expires. And in the meantime, there will be a steady increase in the significance and proportion of conventional delegated legislation, made under parent provisions under other Acts, and hence excluded from sifting altogether.

So, overall, constitutional practice under EUWA resulted in the entrenchment of the existing problem with delegated legislation through further normalisation of the practice of poorly scrutinised executive legislation. In this regard, one likely legacy of Brexit is that there will be more, and more inadequately scrutinised, delegated legislation than before. It is too early to tell how serious the impact of this legacy will be on our constitutional culture. But recent developments suggest pessimism.

The practical significance of s. 8 EUWA persists for now, but EUWA is no longer the main statute regulating the Brexit process. It has been superseded by the European Union (Withdrawal Agreement) Act 2020. And, like all statutes, the EUWAA itself delegates significant new legislative power to the government, in this instance powers connected with the implementation of the Withdrawal Agreement. Most significantly, it delegates extensive power to legislate for the domestic regulation of the implementation period, including the implementation of the Northern Ireland Protocol (the 'Implementation powers') and for the implementation of the citizens' rights provisions in the Withdrawal Agreement ('the Citizens' Rights powers').[31] The Implementation powers in particular have much in common with s. 8 EUWA. In form, they are even inserted into EUWA as supplements to that section, ss. 8A, 8B, and 8 C. Their nature is similarly consistent with the original s. 8: drafted and promoted as implements of technical change, they are nevertheless obviously capable of being used for significant policy interventions, simply because the way in which the implementation period is regulated is a matter of live political controversy rather than a set of neutral technical problems. Similarly, the Citizens' Rights powers present problems of acute political controversy such as citizens' rights to residency, employment rights, the

---

[31] 'Most significantly' for present purposes, that is. There are other delegations in EUWAA, and the ones that I do mention are significant in ways that I do not mention here. The labels for the powers I do discuss are originally from Adam Tucker, 'A First Critical Look at the Scrutiny of Delegated Legislation in the Withdrawal Agreement Bill', UK Constitutional Law Association Blog, 24 October 2019, https://ukconstitutionallaw.org/2019/10/24/adam-tucker-a-first-critical-look-at-the-scrutiny-of-delegated-legislation-in-the-withdrawal-agreement-bill/.

shape of appeals and review mechanisms and so on – some of the most sensitive and most important policy elements of the withdrawal process – as technical issues. In this way, in terms of its approach to delegated legislative power, EUWAA represents a kind of continuity with its predecessor EUWA. It too has the potential to ground its own mini legal order consisting entirely of delegated legislation. But this is coupled with a discontinuity of fundamental importance: the creation of these new, deceptively straightforward powers runs alongside a dilution of the scrutiny processes to which they will be subject. The legislation, including even that inserted into EUWA as ss. 8A, 8B and 8C, is not tied into the sifting process. Instead, EUWAA represents a retreat back to the more conventional approach initially drafted into the EU Withdrawal Bill, but rejected by Parliament in the amendments which created the sifting process. It adopts a short list of defined triggers for affirmative procedures, and leaves all exercises of the powers it delegates which do not engage those triggers to negative procedures. It does not institutionalise any way for instruments destined for negative procedures to be redirected to affirmative scrutiny; thus its trigger-based categorisation is effectively final.[32] Most delegated legislation made under these provisions in EUWAA will be subject only to negative scrutiny procedures. So the progress represented by the sifting process is now being abandoned, in favour of a return to the pre-existing and deeply problematic position described earlier in the chapter. Sifting had its weaknesses, but EUWAA does not even incorporate this small degree of scrutiny.

At the same time, as indicated above, substantive statutes on individual policy areas impacted by Brexit areas have also now started to go before Parliament.[33] Whilst these contain varied levels of delegation, they are uniformly consistent with the rowing back from procedures designed to enhance scrutiny which started with EUWAA. Each contains some powers subject to affirmative procedures, some triggered affirmative procedures, and lots of negative procedures (typically the default level of scrutiny) and it is likely that further legislation will also adopt this approach. There is no sign of a re-engagement with or continuation of the experiment with sifting. In fact, post EUWA statutes show no innovation at all in this regard. Sifting under EUWA might have held the potential for a change to constitutional practice in the scrutiny of delegated legislation, but that potential is now being diluted with

---

[32] The precise triggers vary slightly between the Implementation powers and the Citizens Rights' powers, and between different elements of the Citizens' Rights powers. The scrutiny requirements for the Implementation powers were inserted into the European Union (Withdrawal) Act 2018 as Part 1A of Schedule 7. The scrutiny requirements for the Citizens' Rights powers are in the European Union (Withdrawal Agreement) Act, Schedule 4.

[33] See n. 14, above, for examples.

each statute introduced to and enacted by Parliament. The experiment with sifting is coming to an end. The final section of this chapter evaluates the extent to which it still might continue to resonate.

## THE POSSIBLE LEGACY OF SIFTING

The analysis so far has been mainly pessimistic. Part 1 cast the scrutiny of delegated legislation as a constitutional problem in need of solution. Part 2 characterised the sifting process under EUWA as only a modest development which has, in any event, been abandoned in more recent legislation. Here, I try to excavate the parts of this analysis which might suggest that the developments discussed above may yet provide the foundation for an improvement in constitutional practice. For even modest and prematurely abandoned developments can leave a positive legacy.

An initial, and perhaps the significant way in which the experiment with the sifting process might have contributed to a sustained improvement in the scrutiny of delegated legislation has unfortunately already failed to materialise. I argued above that the main weakness of the approach was that it was superimposed on existing scrutiny procedures and not accompanied by any attempt to reform the underlying processes themselves. Still, the institutionalisation of the sifting process might nevertheless have indirectly prompted deeper change. In other contexts, the allocation of scrutiny processes can seem arbitrary or formulaic. Usually, the fact that a particular instrument is legally required to follow affirmative procedures does not single it out as meriting particular attention. It is there simply because a statute triggered its presence. On the other hand, a draft statutory instrument subject to affirmative procedures following sifting comes under that scrutiny because at least one parliamentary committee has published a reasoned opinion stating that it involves the kind of significant and political change which is only appropriate following parliamentary approval. The recommendation itself sets out the nature of that change and the ways in which it merits close attention. Sifted instruments, therefore, are not simply subject to affirmative procedures; rather they have been marked out as requiring heightened scrutiny. This special institutional status could well have been reflected in the way in which proposals were scrutinised. But it was not. Votes were not necessarily preceded by debate. When there were debates on sifted instruments, they had the same weaknesses as debates on ordinary affirmative instruments. There was no change to the effectiveness of the underlying procedures.

Consider this, haphazardly chosen, example of scrutiny of a sifted instrument: the European Research Infrastructure Consortium (Amendment) (EU

Exit) Regulations 2018. These amended the 'ERIC Regulation': retained EU law regulating international research collaborations.[34] In sifting, the (Commons) European Statutory Instruments Committee recommended affirmative procedures and stated two reasons for the recommendation: the need for further explanation of how the changes would facilitate post-Brexit participation by a (non-member state) United Kingdom in future ERIC research programmes, and a perceived need to further explore the continued, limited role of the ECJ suggested by the proposed legislation in these arrangements. In the explanatory note the government had insisted that these regulations made only technical changes to the law but the committee identified underlying policy considerations which – in their view – merited further examination.

In the resultant House of Commons committee examining the regulations, only four of those attending spoke at all. One of those four contributed nothing relevant and was chastised by the chair. The minister opened by closing down the parameters of the debate: 'I hope that we confine remarks in Committee to specific technical points on ERICs, rather than have a broader conversation about European science and innovation, which I am not going to answer today.'[35] The discussion did not address the ECJ point raised by the European Statutory Instruments Committee. There was no discussion of the policy underlying the regulations and the session ultimately deviated into the (real but separate) issue of the impact of changes to immigration on research in the United Kingdom. The meeting lasted thirty minutes. The regulations were subsequently approved by the Commons – without division, in proceedings which lasted less than ten seconds in total – at 1:05 am on Wednesday 5 December. This is neither negligence on the part of the participants, nor atypical. Delegated legislation committees simply are not an effective forum for the kind of scrutiny prompted by the sifting referral. And genuine engagement with the substance of delegated legislation is not part of Commons practice. This is how the scrutiny of delegated legislation typically happens in Parliament in general, and regulations made under EUWA simply fit into these established practices.

Secondly, and more positively, the origins of sifting are constitutionally significant and encouraging. They were amended into the bill during its passage through Parliament. As is well known, the circumstances under

---

[34] Regulation on the Community Legal Framework for a European Research Infrastructure Consortium (ERIC), Council Regulation (EC) No. 723/2009.
[35] House of Commons Delegated Legislation Committee on the Draft European Research Infrastructure Consortium (Amendment) (EU Exit) Regulations 2018, 3 December 2018, col. 4.

which this happened were particular as a minority government struggled to pass its flagship legislation, against strong resistance that included its own backbenches. So it is unusual that the government was essentially forced to tighten the scrutiny arrangements applicable to powers it delegated (to itself) in EUWA. This is one aspect of the wider story – which may well turn out to be sui generis – of the May government's travails in securing parliamentary cooperation with its Brexit agenda. But, even allowing for that caveat, the creation of the sifting process still matters. Parliament adverted to the possible exacerbation of a constitutional problem. And it innovated in response to that risk, creating novel institutional structures aimed at addressing it. One important lesson of the experience of sifting under EUWA is the confirmation that primary legislation can be the engine for reform in this area. And whilst the innovation was restricted both in application (only covering legislation under s. 8) and time (the delegated power and the processes connected with it will soon expire) it is in principle a generalisable development. This instance of sifting has only a relatively short shelf life, but the idea itself, and the possibility of its generalisation, will persist and the process under EUWA serves as a standing precedent of parliamentary innovation. In time, the sifting process under EUWA has the potential to come to be treated as a pilot project rather than a discrete historical experiment.

Next, the creation and the operation of the sifting process has put various issues connected to scrutiny of delegated legislation on the constitutional agenda, which itself leaves a valuable legacy. In particular, it focused attention directly on the question of what levels of parliamentary scrutiny are most appropriate for what kinds of delegated legislation, and how to identify the boundaries between what ought to be actively approved by Parliament and what can safely be left to the lesser safeguard of the risk of annulment. The sifting processes were organised around this specific issue, which resulted in significant attention. The question enjoyed a period of unprecedented prominence, and its institutionalisation into a system of written justifications, published committee recommendations, and government responses to those recommendations means that a substantial body of literature – institutional parliamentary literature – has now emerged.[36] This can be the foundation for future development of a principled approach to matching delegated powers with appropriate scrutiny procedures, either in Parent Acts themselves, or through future expansion, recreation or generalisation of the sifting

---

[36] For a systematisation of the principles emerging from this literature, see Jack Simson Caird and Ellis Patterson, *Brexit, Delegated Powers and Delegated Legislation: A Rule of Law Analysis of Parliamentary Scrutiny* (London: The Bingham Centre for the Rule of Law, 2020).

mechanisms. There is also a natural creep beyond this question, because asking whether something does or does not need parliamentary approval can sometimes lead to the answer that some things really need the kind of approval which can only be provided by the primary legislative process.[37] So the question underlying the sifting process is also a window on the wider issue of where to draw the line between the appropriate uses of primary and secondary legislation. Sifting has also, indirectly, focused attention on other dimensions of the problem with delegated legislation. It has highlighted the weaknesses in the underlying processes which it serves, and one way to improve the effectiveness of sifting would be to make deeper reforms aimed at improving those processes. The institutional experiences of designing, implementing, and participating in these processes is itself a valuable resource. It proves that these innovations can be made to function successfully and provides a source of learning on how to do them well; what worked, what did not and so on. A parliament that has reformed its processes once is well placed to undertake the task of reforming them again.

Next, the availability of resources for scrutinising delegated legislation has now been – quite emphatically – confirmed. In any context, a significant objection (which must always be taken seriously) to claims that Parliament could better discharge any of its multiple responsibilities is the fact that parliamentary resources are limited and already the subject of intense competition. But the experiment with sifting has shifted what we know Parliament can do. The availability of resources has been demonstrated; the challenge for the coming years is to maintain those resources and to find ways to direct them as effectively as possible. The demonstration that the resource problem can be overcome is a significant step towards tackling the problem with delegated legislation.

And finally – and perhaps most significantly – the operation of the sifting process demonstrated that institutional procedures of this kind can successfully change government behaviour. Initially, it was seen as a weakness of the sifting amendment that the process it created was not binding on the government. The committees involved had no power to force the government to accept their recommendations; there was no coercive element, and the statute even explicitly created a mechanism for government to explain any decisions to override the outcome of sifting. Lord Lisvane proposed (unsuccessfully) to

---

[37] In fact, the passage of EUWA through Parliament illustrates this possibility. In the original version of the bill (Schedule 7, para. 1(2)(a)) the creation of a new public authority was one of the triggers for affirmative procedures. But in the Act as eventually enacted (s. 8(7)(d)) the creation of public authorities had been moved to the list of exclusions from the scope of the delegated power; that is, such creation can now only be done through primary legislation.

further amend the bill to make it mandatory for government to respect sifting recommendations, on the grounds that a non-mandatory procedure would be 'better than nothing, but not much'.[38] But such fears ultimately proved to be unfounded. Government routinely accepted the recommendations of sifting committees, and a standard practice rapidly developed of withdrawing such instruments from the negative scrutiny track and republishing them as affirmative instruments. And the mechanics of the sifting process itself prompted a subtler change to the government's legislative behaviour. The statute requires the government to provide sifting committees with a memorandum setting out ministers' reasons for considering it appropriate to use negative procedures.[39] When the process first came into operation, the government initially adopted an extremely formalistic approach to the content of these statements. Essentially, they would cite the factors in the statute which would have triggered affirmative procedures, assert that they did not apply in this instance, and conclude that it was therefore appropriate to choose the negative track. So, the argument – routinely – was something like 'we are not obliged to seek parliamentary approval for this instrument, so we will not'. For example, the material part of the memorandum for the Trade Barriers (Revocation) (EU Exit) Regulations 2018 stated:

> In my view the Trade Barriers (Revocation) (EU Exit) Regulations 2018 should be subject to ... the negative procedure ... because the statutory instrument does not meet any of the criteria for affirmative resolution ...

This was followed by the list of triggers extracted from the statute, and then the conclusion:

> For all other matters the negative procedure can be used. This instrument does not involve any of the matters ... so the negative procedure will be used.

This amounted to a government refusal to engage properly with the process and the sifting committee acted quickly to nip it in the bud. Their report on that instrument –published in their very first round of recommendations – responded:

> The Committee ... note that the Minister's Opinion is based on an extremely narrow interpretation of the criteria for deciding on the appropriate procedure. We expect the Government to provide more information than simply confirming that the regulations do not implement changes specifically disallowed under the 'negative procedure' in the ... Act .... The Committee expects all Government departments to have regard to the criteria for

---

[38] *Hansard*, HL, vol. 791, col. 87, 8 May 2018.
[39] European Union (Withdrawal) Act Schedule 7, para. 3(3).

deciding on the appropriate procedure set out by both Houses and to provide adequate information and reasons in the form of Minister's Opinions, in line with its statutory duties, to allow the 'sifting' Committees to conduct their work effectively.[40]

And the government responded to this pressure. Subsequent ministerial statements defended more substantive reasons for favouring negative procedures. Compare, for example this later memorandum concerning the Consumer Protection (Enforcement) (Amendment etc.) (EU Exit) Regulations 2018:

> In my view the ... Regulations 2018 should be subject to annulment in pursuance of a resolution of either House of Parliament (i.e. the negative procedure) ... because: this instrument does not bring into effect a policy change in relation to the enforcement of consumer law, other than such changes as are necessary to:
>
> a) deal with the cessation of the reciprocal arrangements under the CPC Regulation and Injunctions Directive consequent of the UK ceasing to be an EU Member State – including removal of the right of EU bodies being Community enforcers under Part 8 of the 2002 Act to apply for enforcement orders under that Part;
> b) allow the 2002 Act and 2015 Act to function effectively in enabling enforcement of consumer legislation, including retained EU-derived domestic legislation and direct EU legislation, after EU exit – these changes include the removal of EU references which are not considered appropriate after the UK has left the EU.

This represented a significant change in the government's approach. The new style of justificatory statement sets out to explain, albeit in a perfunctory fashion, how the proposed measures fall short of the kind of policy change which necessitate deeper scrutiny. And the committee's early intervention resulted in this becoming normal practice.

At the outset there were fears that the government would not respect the outcome of the sifting process, and the government's early engagement with the scheme was attenuated. But both problems were overcome as committee recommendations acquired a kind of informal binding force over time and the government engaged more authentically and less formalistically in the process; thereby playing its part in the accumulation of institutional literature on the issue, as highlighted above.

---

[40] European Statutory Instruments Committee (1st Report of Session 2017–19), 2018 HC 1532, para. 4.3.

To summarise, there are at least four ways in which the experience of the sifting process has the potential to ground positive constitutional development in the future. It proved that parliamentary innovation on the issue can succeed; it put the issue of scrutiny of delegated legislation squarely on the parliamentary agenda; it demonstrated the availability of resources to improve scrutiny; and it showed that processes like this have the capacity to prompt improvement in government behaviour.

So, as argued in the second part of this chapter, whilst the direct impact of the scheme itself may well have been modest in the face of the scale of the problem with delegated legislation, this is counterbalanced by some significant reasons to treat the sifting experiment as the starting point for longer term improvement in the scrutiny of such legislation. The underlying problem remains; sifting was only a limited solution. And the direction of travel is not at present promising. But the sifting experience shows that the problem with delegated problem can be tackled, and it may have laid the foundations for future incremental progress. This will only be the case, however, if those foundations are built upon.

## 12

## Litigating Brexit

Christopher McCorkindale and Aileen McHarg

INTRODUCTION

The long process of deciding whether, and if so on what terms, to leave the European Union was one marked by hyper-litigation. In remarkable volume and with increasing frequency over time, a wide range of litigants either sought or threatened recourse to the courts – both in the United Kingdom and elsewhere in Europe – in an attempt to influence the process, substance and/or the politics of Brexit.

Such 'strategic litigation'[1] – 'the continuation of politics by other means'[2] – is not unknown in the United Kingdom: in their pioneering study of *Pressure Through Law*, Harlow and Rawlings document examples dating back to the eighteenth century, albeit they note an increased volume of pressure group litigation from the 1970s onwards.[3] Nevertheless, the use of strategic litigation during the Brexit process is, we argue, unusual in two main respects. First, the sheer intensity of litigation on a single issue over a relatively short period of time was, we believe, unprecedented in the UK context, as were the range and diversity of legal arguments and litigants involved. This was not a single, coordinated litigation strategy in pursuit of a clearly defined objective, but rather a reactive and opportunistic resort to litigation by parties with differing political motivations. This is all the more remarkable given that, in the UK context, decisions to change aspects of the constitution have traditionally been regarded as purely political. Secondly – in contrast with earlier attempts at

---

[1] We prefer the term 'strategic litigation' as a more encompassing label than similar terms like 'public interest litigation', 'test-case litigation', or 'cause lawyering'. See Michael Ramsden and Kris Gledhill, 'Defining Strategic Litigation' (2019) 38 *Civil Justice Quarterly* 407–26.
[2] Aidan O'Neill, 'Strategic Litigation before the CJEU: Pursuing Public Interest Litigation within the EU Judicial Architecture', paper delivered at NYU Paris, 7 March 2019, on file with the authors, p. 3.
[3] Carol Harlow and Richard Rawlings, *Pressure Through Law* (Abingdon: Routledge, 1992).

strategic litigation over EU membership, which were invariably rejected as non-justiciable and/or unarguable[4] – Brexit-related litigation had a surprising degree of success. Although the vast majority of the cases were rejected or abandoned, the process was punctuated by very high-profile victories which pushed at the boundaries of constitutional justiciability. Insofar as the factors encouraging hyper-litigation are applicable beyond the Brexit context, we believe that this may represent a further step-change in the use of strategic litigation in the UK constitutional context.

In this chapter, we do four things. First, we document the cases; identifying who, where, about what, and with what aims parties were litigating Brexit. Secondly, we discuss the impacts of the litigation, both in legal terms – seeking to identify why some cases succeeded where others did not – and in terms of their broader political effects. Thirdly, we try to account for hyper-litigation, identifying the various factors encouraging resort to the courts. Finally, we consider the likely long-term impacts of Brexit-related strategic litigation.

While many lawyers have welcomed – indeed, encouraged[5] – Brexit-related strategic litigation, often casting the courts as guardians of the constitution, we take a more sceptical view. First, we are doubtful about both the doctrinal and practical benefits of many of the cases, both as regards the handling of the Brexit process and on wider constitutional questions. Secondly, given the well-recognised tension that strategic litigation creates for the courts in terms of balancing the openness required to enable them to uphold the rule of law whilst avoiding being drawn too overtly into political controversies which might undermine their reputation for political impartiality,[6] we fear a backlash against strategic litigation from both the courts themselves and political actors.

---

[4] See, on the decision to join the (then) EEC: *Blackburn* v. *Attorney-General* [1971] 1 WLR 1037; *Jenkins* v. *Attorney-General, The Times*, 14 August 1971; *McWhirter* v. *Attorney General* [1972] CMLR 882; *Gibson* v. *Lord Advocate* 1975 SC 136. On the Maastricht Treaty: *McWhirter & Atherton* v. *Hurd and Maude*, Hexham Magistrates Court, 9 September 1993, unreported; *R* v. *Secretary of State for Foreign and Commonwealth Affairs, ex p Rees-Mogg* [1994] QB 552. On the draft Constitutional Treaty: *R* v. *Secretary of State for Foreign and Commonwealth Affairs ex p Southall* [2003] 3 CMLR 18. On the Nice Treaty: *McWhirter* v. *Secretary of State for Foreign and Commonwealth Affairs* [2003] EWCA (Civ) 384. On the Lisbon Treaty: *R (Wheeler)* v. *Office of the Prime Minister* [2008] 2 CMLR 57. On the European Arrest Warrant: *Wheeler* v. *Office of the Prime Minister* [2015] 1 CMLR 46.

[5] See, e.g., Richard Ekins and Graham Gee, 'Miller, Constitutional Realism, and the Politics of Brexit', in Mark Elliott, Jack Williams, and Alison L Young (eds.), *The UK Constitution after Miller: Brexit and Beyond* (Oxford: Hart Publishing, 2018); and see further below.

[6] See generally Harlow and Rawlings *Pressure Through Law*, chap. 7.

BREXIT-RELATED STRATEGIC LITIGATION

*The Case Sample*

Table 1 includes fifty-seven instances of Brexit-related strategic litigation conducted (though not necessarily concluded) between May 2015, when the EU referendum became a concrete prospect, and 31 January 2020, when the United Kingdom formally left the EU. Litigation was a prominent feature throughout the Brexit process, with two cases arising even before the referendum itself (*Tomescu* and *Shindler UK*), and applications being made within days of the referendum result in *Miller 1*. However, the bulk of the cases arose in 2019, peaking as the intended Brexit dates of 29 March and then 31 October approached. Unsurprisingly, most of the cases occurred in the United Kingdom's domestic courts, but we also found significant attempts to involve other European courts, either by raising actions before the EU General Court,[7] or in other EU member states, usually with the aim of securing preliminary references to the CJEU.[8]

The sample includes only cases in which at least a formal step towards litigation (such as issuing a pre-action letter) was taken, although not all cases were subsequently pursued to a hearing. And it includes only those cases which, in our judgement, were intended to have an impact, directly or indirectly on Brexit – whether by changing decision-making processes, affecting the substance of Brexit-related decisions, or simply influencing public opinion. We have therefore excluded cases arising contextually or defensively out of the Brexit process (such as commercial litigation, or appeals against Electoral Commission fines), and cases in which arguments about Brexit were tactically deployed in service of some non-Brexit-related objective (for example, to resist extradition).[9] We also excluded cases which were relevant to the politics of Brexit, but where we judged the connection to be too indirect to justify inclusion.

Cases were discovered primarily by paying close attention to news and social media reports about Brexit-related litigation. Some cases received

---

[7] *Fair Deal for Expats*; *Shindler EU1*; *Walker*; *Shindler EU2*; *Shindler EU3*.
[8] Two cases were raised in Ireland (*GLP Ireland*; *McCord Dublin*); one in the Netherlands (*Williams*) and three in France (*Watson*; *B*; *AB*). One preliminary reference was heard by the CJEU, referred by the Court of Session (*Wightman*).
[9] For differently constituted case samples, see Vaughne Miller and Sylvia de Mars, 'Brexit Questions in National and EU Courts', HC Library Briefing Paper, No. 8415 (1 November 2019); Steve Peers, 'Litigating Brexit – a Guide to the Case Law', EU Analysis Blog, 27 July 2020, http://eulawanalysis.blogspot.com/p/litigating-brexit-guide-to-case-law.html.

TABLE 1 Brexit-Related Strategic Litigation (by year of commencement)

| 2015 | 2016 | 2017 | 2018 | 2019 | 2020 |
|---|---|---|---|---|---|
| R (Tomescu) v. Lord President of the Council and Others [2015] EWHC 3293 (Admin) | R (Shindler) v. Chancellor of the Duchy of Lancaster [2016] 3 WLR 1196 (Shindler UK) | The Good Law Project and ors v. Ireland (GLP Ireland) | State of Netherlands v. Williams et al. Gerechtshof Amsterdam, 19 June 2018, ECLI:NL:GHAM-S:2018:2009, NJ 2018/460 | Trimble and ors v. Secretary of State for Exiting the European Union | AB v. Minister of the Interior ECLI:FR:CEOR-D:2020:438696.20200221 |
|  | R (Miller & dos Santos) v. Secretary of State for Exiting the European Union [2017] UKSC 5 (Miller 1) | Application for Judicial Review by Martyn Truss CO/3008/2017 | The UK Withdrawal from the European Union (Legal Continuity) (Scotland) Bill – A Reference by the Attorney General and the Advocate General for Scotland [2018] UKSC 64 | Watson et al. No 42834 442942, Conseil d'Etat, 1/7/20 | Watt v. Prime Minister and Advocate General for Scotland (Watt 2) |
|  | Reference re the matter of applications for judicial review by Agnew & Others and Raymond McCord [2017] UKSC 5 | Shindler and Others v. Council Case T-458/17, C-755/18 [2019] 2 CMLR 12 (Shindler EU1) | R (Webster) v. Secretary of State for Exiting the European Union [2019] 1 CMLR 8 | R (Good Law Project) v. Secretary of State for Health and Social Care [2019] EWCA Civ 1211 (GLP Serious Shortage Protocols) |  |
|  | Fair Deal for Expats v. Commission Case T-713/16 | R (Good Law Project) v. Electoral Commission [2018] EWHC 2414 (Admin) [2019] EWCA Civ 1567 (GLP Electoral Commission) |  | Ball v. Johnson [2019] EWHC 1709 |  |
|  |  |  |  | Leave Means Leave v. Minister for the Cabinet Office |  |
|  |  |  |  | Wolchover & Silver v. the Prime Minister |  |
|  |  |  |  | Cherry et al. v. Advocate General for Scotland [2019] UKSC 41 |  |
|  |  |  |  | McCord et al. v. Prime Minister and Secretary of State for Exiting the European Union [2019] NICA 49 (McCord et al.) |  |
|  |  |  |  | Shindler and ors v. Council Case T-541/19 (Shindler EU2) |  |
|  |  |  |  | R (Liberty) v. Prime Minister [2019] EWCA Civ 1761 |  |
|  |  |  |  | Vince et al. v. Prime Minister and Advocate General for Scotland [2019] CSIH 51 |  |

TABLE 1 (continued)

| 2015 | 2016 | 2017 | 2018 | 2019 | 2020 |
|---|---|---|---|---|---|
| | R (Yalland) v. Secretary of State for Exiting the European Union [2017] EWHC 630 (Admin) | Miller and International Workers Union of Great Britain v. HM Treasury R (Good Law Project Ltd) v. Secretary of State for Exiting the European Union [2018] EWHC 719 (Admin) (GLP Impact Studies) R (Hardy) v. Prime Minister CO/5012/2017 Wightman & Others v. Secretary of State for Exiting the European Union [2018] CSIH 62; Case C-621/18, [2019] QB 199 | R (Wilson) v. the Prime Minister and the Electoral Commission [2019] EWCA Civ 304 R (Good Law Project Ltd) v. Electoral Commission and Democratic Unionist Party (GLP DUP) Fair Vote UK v. Prime Minister Rush v. Information Commissioner and Cabinet Office | R (English Democrats) v. Prime Minister and Secretary of State for Exiting the European Union CO/1392/2019 Legg v. Prime Minister and Secretary of State for Exiting the European Union Allmann v. Prime Minister B v. Minister of the Interior ECLI: FR: CECH-R:2019:430008.2-019515 R (MCS & ClientEarth) v. Secretary of State for the | R (Fratila & Tanese) v. Secretary of State for Work and Pensions [2020] EWHC 998 (Admin) Shindler and Others v. Commission Case T-627/19 (Shindler EU3) JR90 R (Independent Workers Union of Great Britain and others v. Prime Minister (IWUGB 2) Public Law Project v. HM Treasury Maugham v. Advocate General for Scotland [2019] CSOH 80 |

McCord v. An Taoiseach & others (McCord Dublin)

Re McCord's Application for Judicial Review [2020] NICA 23 (McCord Border poll)

R (Watt) v. Prime Minister and President of the European Council CO/5050/2017 (Watt 1)

Environment Food and Rural Affairs [2019] EWHC 2682 (Admin)

Brake et al. v. Commissioner of the Metropolitan Police

Walker and Others v. Parliament and Council Case T-383/19; C-789/19

R (Keighley) v. British Broadcasting Corporation [2019] EWHC 3331 (Admin)

R (Miller) v. Prime Minister [2019] UKSC 41 (Miller 2)

R (thethreemillion) v. Prime Minister and Secretary of State for Exiting the European Union

Bryson v. Prime Minister

R (Liberal Democrats and Scottish National Party) v. ITV Broadcasting Ltd [2019] EWHC 3292 (Admin)

Liberal Democrats v. BBC (Lib Dems BBC)

The Bureau of Investigative Journalism v. Prime Minister (BIJ)

considerable publicity, but many did not and were essentially stumbled upon, or brought to our attention by the litigants themselves, by Brexit campaigners, and by other academics. We therefore make no claims as to the exhaustiveness of our sample. Citations or other official identifying numbers have been included in Table 1 where available, but these do not exist, or we have been unable to find them, for all cases.

## What Was Being Litigated?

Table 2 groups the cases into seven broad categories (although some cases appear more than once because they raised multiple issues).

Unsurprisingly, the largest group concerned various aspects of the withdrawal process under Art. 50 TFEU. Immediately following the referendum, in *Miller 1* and *Agnew & McCord*, the courts were asked to decide whether the United Kingdom's 'constitutional requirements' for a decision to leave the EU had been complied with. The Supreme Court's ruling that the UK government could not use the foreign affairs prerogative to trigger Art. 50, but required specific legislative authorisation, spawned a series of satellite cases. Some questioned the adequacy of the ensuing legislative response – the European Union (Notification of Withdrawal) Act 2017. *Yalland* (and later *Watt 2)* argued that the Act was not sufficient to authorise withdrawal from the EEA. Various cases claimed that, although the prime minister had been empowered to *notify* the European Council of the United Kingdom's decision to withdraw from the EU, no valid *decision* to withdraw had in fact been made (*Truss; Hardy; Watt 1; Webster; Watt 2*). Similarly, *Wilson* and *Wolchover* argued that the prime minister had improperly exercised the discretion to notify the United Kingdom's intention to withdraw conferred by the 2017 Act. Other 'child of *Miller*' cases argued that further legislation was required at later stages of the Brexit process – to authorise an extension to the Art. 50 negotiating period (*English Democrats; Legg*), to revoke the Art. 50 notification (*Allman*), or to authorise a 'no deal' Brexit (*Cherry et al.*). Other Art. 50 litigation sought to establish whether, and if so by whom, the United Kingdom's notification could be revoked (*GLP (Ireland); Wightman*) or whether an implementation period was permitted under Art. 50 (*Watt 1*). Litigation also challenged the EU's refusal to begin negotiations before the Art. 50 notification had been made (*Fair Deal for Expats*) and, conversely, the validity of the decision to open negotiations (*Shindler (EU1)*). In addition, clarification was sought regarding the effect of the first Art. 50 extension on the United Kingdom's participation in the May 2019 European Parliament elections (*Leave Means Leave*).

TABLE 2 *What Was Being Litigated?*

| Article 50 process | Conduct of the referendum | Government-parliament relations | Territorial constitution | Access to information and impartiality | Citizens' rights post-Brexit | Other substantive effects of Brexit |
|---|---|---|---|---|---|---|
| Miller 1 | Tomescu | Miller 1 | Miller 1 | GLP (Impact Studies) | Fair Deal for Expats | GLP (Serious Shortage Protocols) |
| Agnew & McCord | Shindler (UK) | Miller/IWUGB 1 | Agnew & McCord | Rush | Shindler (EU1) | MCS & ClientEarth |
| Fair Deal for Expats | Shindler (EU1) | Watt 1 | McCord (Dublin) | Keighley | Williams | |
| Yalland | GLP (Electoral Commission) | Miller 2 | McCord (Border poll) | Lib Dems & SNP | Watson et al. | |
| GLP (Ireland) | Wilson | Cherry et al. | Continuity Bill Reference | Lib Dems (BBC) | Leave Means Leave | |
| Truss | GLP (DUP) | McCord et al. | Trimble | BIJ | B | |
| Shindler (EU1) | Fair Vote UK | Liberty | McCord et al. | | Walker | |
| Hardy | Ball | Vince et al. | Bryson | | thethreemillion | |
| Wightman | Wolchover | JR 90 | Lib Dems & SNP | | Shindler (EU2) | |
| Watt 1 | Brake et al. | IWUGB 2 | Watt 2 | | Fratila | |
| Webster | BIJ | Public Law Project | | | Shindler (EU3) | |
| Wilson | | Maugham | | | AB | |
| Leave Means Leave | | | | | Watt 2 | |
| Wolchover | | | | | | |
| English Democrats | | | | | | |
| Legg | | | | | | |
| Allman | | | | | | |
| Cherry et al. | | | | | | |
| Watt 2 | | | | | | |

Process themes dominated the litigation more generally. Overlapping with the Art. 50 cases were those questioning the conduct of the referendum. One set of cases questioned the validity of the franchise, which excluded British expat voters (*Shindler (UK)*; *Shindler (EU1)*) and other EU nationals resident in the United Kingdom (*Tomescu*). The other set alleged various irregularities in the conduct of the referendum campaign, either trying to force action to be taken against those responsible (*GLP (Electoral Commission)*; *GLP (DUP)*; *Fair Vote UK*; *Ball*; *Brake et al.*; *BIJ*), or claiming that the irregularities made it unlawful to implement the referendum result (*Wilson*; *Wolchover*).

Another overlapping theme was the separation of powers between the UK Parliament and executive. In addition to the cases on the use of prerogative powers in the Art. 50 process, the government's loss of control of the House of Commons after the 2017 general election produced challenges on various other issues. These included: the Conservative/DUP confidence and supply agreement (*Miller/IWUGB 1*); the attempted prorogation of Parliament in September/October 2019 (*Miller 2*; *Cherry et al.*; *McCord et al.*); potential or alleged failures by the government to comply with statutory duties (*Vince*; *Liberty*; *JR90*; *IWUGB 2*; *Maugham*); the impact of Brexit on Queen's Consent (*Watt 1*); and the extent of ministerial powers to amend primary legislation (*Public Law Project*).

A fourth set of cases concerned the internal territorial impacts of Brexit. Again, most focused on process issues: the need for territorial consent to constitutional change (*Miller 1*; *Agnew & McCord*; *McCord et al.*; *Bryson*; *Watt 2*); the territorial distribution of powers to implement Brexit *(Continuity Bill Reference)*; issues of territorial representation (*Lib Dems & SNP* – which concerned the SNP's exclusion from leaders' debates at the 2019 general election); and the circumstances in which Irish reunification referendums might be held, as a possible consequence of Brexit (*McCord (Dublin)*; *McCord (Border Poll)*).

A final process-related theme concerned access to information. Three cases (*GLP (Impact Case Studies)*; *Rush*; *BIJ*) attempted to force the publication of Brexit-related information, and another three (*Keighley*; *Lib Dems & SNP*; *Lib Dems (BBC)*) raised questions of impartiality in Brexit-related broadcasting.

On matters of substance, the most frequently litigated issue was the impact of Brexit on citizens' rights. Some cases focused on the loss of EU citizenship rights generally (*Leave Means Leave*; *Watt 2*), or the rights of other EU nationals living in the United Kingdom *(thethreemillion; Fratila)*, but most concerned British citizens living elsewhere in the EU. In general, these cases aimed to preserve EU citizenship rights, but even here there was a particular emphasis on voting and other political process rights (*Shindler EU1*; *Leave Means Leave*; *B*; *thethreemillion*; *Shindler EU2*; *Shindler EU3*; *AB*). Also focusing on substantive issues, two of the territorial constitution cases challenged the constitutionality of the Northern Irish Protocol on grounds of its differential impact on Northern Ireland compared with Great Britain (*Trimble*; *Bryson*). Finally, two cases sought to challenge particular substantive policy decisions taken in consequence of Brexit (*GLP (Serious Shortages Protocol)*; *MCS & ClientEarth*).

Two general points stand out about the subject matter of the cases. First, there were multiple cases on some issues, either in sequence or in parallel (sometimes in different jurisdictions), or even combined in the same proceedings. For instance, the initial Art. 50 litigation involved two parallel sets of litigation in England and Northern Ireland, both combining cases initiated by different sets of litigants. The second point is the way some cases fed off or built upon one another. We have already noted how the successful outcome of *Miller 1* opened up a range of related challenges. Less directly, the lowering of the bar for formal justiciability in *Wightman* and for substantive justiciability in *Cherry* and *Miller 2* also encouraged and facilitated later cases. Thus, whereas the litigants in *Wightman* had struggled at first instance to establish that there was a live issue to be determined,[10] the more liberal approach taken on appeal meant that the petitioners in *Cherry* had no difficulty in securing permission for judicial review although their case was equally hypothetical when it was first raised. Similarly, the Supreme Court's decision in *Cherry/Miller 2* that the prorogation was justiciable despite raising issues of extreme political sensitivity, and that the challenge did not breach parliamentary privilege, undoubtedly encouraged subsequent litigation to force the prime minister to comply with the duty under the Benn-Burt Act[11] to seek a further extension to Brexit (*Vince*; *Liberty*; *JR90*; *IWUGB*), as well as the daring attempt in *Maugham* to claim that Parliament was barred from voting to approve the Withdrawal Agreement by s. 55 of the Taxation (Cross-Border Trade) Act 2018.

## Who Was Litigating?

Table 3 groups those initiating legislation, along with interested parties and intervenors,[12] into six categories.

---

[10] See [2018] CSOH 8; [2018] CSOH 61.
[11] The European Union (Withdrawal) (No. 2) Act 2019.
[12] Interventions were typically in support of the claimants. Exceptions include *Miller 1*, where the Attorney General for Northern Ireland intervened in support of the UK government; *Wightman*, where the European Council and Commission argued against a right of unilateral revocation of the Art. 50 notification; and the *Continuity Bill Reference*, where the Welsh and Northern Ireland Law Officers intervened in support of the Scottish government.

TABLE 3 Who Was Litigating? Claimants/Petitioners, Interested Parties and Interveners

| Institutional actors | Expats/EU nationals | Politicians/political parties | Lawyers | Campaigners/campaign groups | Others |
|---|---|---|---|---|---|
| Miller* | Tomescu | Agnew | Shindler (UK) | Tomescu | Miller |
| Agnew* | Shindler (UK) | Good Law Project (Ireland) | Good Law Project (Ireland)** | Trimble | Truss |
| Wightman* | Miller | Good Law Project (Impact Studies) | Good Law Project (Electoral Commission)** | Good Law Project (Serious Shortage Protocols)** | Hardy |
| Continuity Bill Reference | Fair Deal for Expats | Wightman | Agnew & McCord | Ball | Watt 1 |
| Miller 2* | Yalland | Trimble | Fair Deal for Expats | Leave Means Leave | McCord et al. |
| Walker**** | Shindler (EU1)*** | Brake et al. | Yalland | English Democrats | Vince |
| Cherry et al.* | Williams | Cherry et al. | Good Law Project (Ireland)** | Legg | JR 90 |
| | Wilson | Vince et al. | Shindler (EU1) | Allmann | Watt 2 |
| | Watson et al.*** | Lib Dems & SNP (ITV) | Good Law Project (Impact Studies)** | MCS & ClientEarth | |
| | B*** | Lib Dems (BBC) | Wightman* | Keighley | |
| | thethreemillion | | Webster | Miller 2 | |
| | Walker*** | | Good Law Project (DUP)** | thethreemillion | |
| | Shindler (EU2)*** | | Rush | Cherry et al.** | |
| | Fratila | | Good Law Project (Serious Shortage Protocols)** | McCord et al. | |
| | Shindler (EU3)*** | | Wolchover | Liberty | |
| | AB*** | | MCS & ClientEarth | Vince et al. | |
| | | | Cherry et al.** | Fratila | |
| | | | Vince et al.** | IWUGB 2 | |
| | | | Maugham** | Public Law Project | |
| | | | BIJ | Maugham | |
| | | | | Bryson | |
| | | | | BIJ | |

| | | | | Miller/IWUGB 1 | |
| | | | | McCord (Dublin) | |
| | | | | McCord (Border poll) | |
| | | | | Williams | |
| | | | | Webster | |
| | | | | Wilson | |
| | | | | Good Law Project (DUP)** | |
| | | | | Fair Vote UK | |

*Interveners **Jo Maugham QC ***Represented by Julien Fouchet ****Governments of Spain and Gibraltar as interveners

The largest set of cases – predictably – were brought by individual campaigners or campaign groups. The sizeable group involving other EU nationals or British expats is also unremarkable, given the amount of litigation on citizens' rights. By contrast, institutional actors featured mainly as respondents to litigation. There was only one instance of inter-institutional litigation – the *Continuity Bill Reference*, raised by the UK government against the Scottish government – although both domestic and foreign governments, as well as EU institutions, intervened in several cases. There were, however, a surprising number of cases involving individual sitting politicians, which is very rare in British politics (though more common in Northern Ireland). Also notable is the amount of litigation brought by lawyers themselves, either via cause lawyering groups (such as the Good Law Project (GLP), ClientEarth, the Public Law Project, and Liberty), or in their own name (*Shindler UK*; *Wightman*; *Rush*; *Wolchover*; *Cherry*; *Vince*; *Maugham*).

Echoing the pattern of repeat litigation noted above, there was also a pattern of repeat *litigators*. Gina Miller, Joanna Cherry QC MP, Jolyon Maugham QC, the Good Law Project, Harry Schindler, and Raymond McCord were all high-profile repeat players, along with other less prominent repeat litigators and/or intervenors. Indeed, the repeat player phenomenon was more pronounced than it appears, since behind many of the cases, as instigators and/or funders, were two entrepreneurial lawyers – Jolyon Maugham QC in the United Kingdom and Julien Fouchet in France.[13] We also find behind-the-scenes networks of mutual support, particularly through crowdfunding efforts. Further, as in previous examples of successful strategic litigation, there were clear instances of 'plaintiff stacking' – a tactic used to suggest to the court a broad constituency of support for the case.[14] This was most pronounced in *Cherry*, which ultimately had seventy-nine petitioners, including seventy-three MPs from a range of political parties.

## Why Were They Litigating?

Table 4 categorises the cases according to the litigants' political motivations. Again, this classification reflects our judgement about what the parties were aiming to achieve, based upon what they said about their reasons for litigating, as well as background information about their political views and objectives.

---

[13] This is by no means a new phenomenon – see Harlow and Rawlings, *Pressure Through Law*, p. 291.
[14] See Harlow and Rawlings, *Pressure Through Law*, pp. 195–6.

TABLE 4 Political Motivation

| Pro-Remain | Pro-Leave | Protection of NI peace process | Upholding parliamentary authority/executive subjection to law | Brexit outcomes | Quality of democratic process |
|---|---|---|---|---|---|
| Tomescu | Trimble | Agnew & McCord | Miller 1 | Fair Deal for Expats | Tomescu |
| Shindler (UK) | Leave Means Leave | McCord (Dublin) | Miller/IWUGB 1 | Yalland | Shindler (UK) |
| Miller 1* | English Democrats | McCord (Border poll) | Continuity Bill Reference | Williams | Shindler (EU1) |
| Agnew & McCord | Legg | Trimble | Miller 2 | Watson et al. | GLP (Electoral Commission) |
| Good Law Project (Serious Shortage Protocols) | Allman | McCord et al. | Cherry et al. | GLP (Serious Shortages Protocol) | GLP (Impact Studies) |
| Good Law Project (Ireland) | Keighley | Bryson | Liberty | B | Webster |
| Ball | Bryson | | Vince et al. | Walker | Wilson |
| Truss | | | JR90 | MCS & ClientEarth | GLP (DUP) |
| Wolchover | | | IWUGB 2 | Fratila | Fair Vote UK |
| Shindler (EU1) | | | Public Law Project | Shindler (EU3) | Rush |
| Cherry et al. | | | Maugham | AB | Ball |
| Good Law Project (Electoral Commission) | | | | Watt 2 | Wolchover |
| Vince | | | | | Brake et al. |
| IWUGB 2 | | | | | Keighley |
| Maugham | | | | | thethreemillion |
| Miller/IWUGB 1 | | | | | Shindler (EU2) |
| Lib Dems & SNP (ITV) Lib Dems (BBC) | | | | | Shindler (EU3) |
| Good Law Project (Impact Studies) | | | | | Lib Dems & SNP (ITV) |
| Hardy | | | | | Lib Dems (BBC) |
| Wightman | | | | | BIJ |
| Watt 1 | | | | | |
| Webster | | | | | |
| Wilson | | | | | |
| Watt 2 | | | | | |

* Dos Santos was a Leave voter, but the preponderance of *Miller* litigants were pro-Remain

Most cases can be crudely classified as either pro-Remain or pro-Leave, with the former clearly dominant. However, there was an uptick of pro-Leave cases in 2019 as the risk that Brexit would be postponed, or even abandoned altogether, increased. Nevertheless, both overlapping with and separate from these broad political motivations, litigants cited various more specific concerns. For instance, much of the focus on process was undoubtedly instrumental, as parties sought to shift decision-making into more politically favourable forums, to change the terms of debate by increasing the range of options available or undermining the political authority of the referendum, or simply to buy more time, for example by ensuring that a further extension to the withdrawal period was sought. However, there was also evidence of sincere concern with upholding what litigants saw as the rightful role of Parliament vis-à-vis the executive in the withdrawal process (for example, one of the parties in *Miller 1* – Dier Dos Santos – was in fact a Leave voter). Similarly, we find genuine concerns about the quality of democratic debate during the referendum and subsequent withdrawal process, and about the impact of Brexit on the Northern Ireland peace process. In some instances, these other motivations were probably *more* important than Brexit-related objectives. For example, Harry Shindler's various cases form part of long-standing campaign for the extension of expat voting rights, while Raymond McCord also has a history of Northern Ireland peace process-related litigation pre-dating Brexit. Finally, some litigation was (ostensibly at least) neutral on the question *whether* the United Kingdom should leave the EU, but nonetheless concerned with the *form* that Brexit should take – particularly, though not exclusively, regarding the protection of citizens' rights.

## OUTCOMES AND IMPACT

In relation to strategic litigation, legal outcomes and political impact must be assessed separately.[15] While a successful legal outcome may amplify the political impact of a case, as Harlow and Rawlings have said, the assumption 'that the sole motive for litigation is the desire to win' is often misplaced.[16] Even where litigation is doomed to fail, it might nevertheless be used, inter alia, to delay the implementation of policy or legislation, to attract publicity to a political cause, to exert political pressure, to 'harass' those in power, or to change or improve policy through settlement.[17] At the same time, strategic

---

[15] See generally Genevra Richardson and Maurice Sunkin, 'Judicial Review: Questions of Impact' (1996) *Public Law* 79–103; Harlow and Rawlings, *Pressure Through Law*, pp. 299–310.
[16] *Pressure Through Law*, p. 300.
[17] Ibid.

litigation might produce negative or unintended political impacts, such as an adverse ruling that narrows or closes off political channels for change or that strengthens the resolve of political opponents, or a positive ruling that generates significant political pushback or problematic side effects, or the effect of which is easily side-stepped.

### Legal Outcomes

As Table 5 indicates, only five cases in our sample resulted in a final judgment wholly or partially in the claimants' favour. One further case – *GLP (Electoral Commission)* – was initially successful, but reversed on appeal, while in *Public Law Project*, a pre-action letter was sufficient to secure the legal outcome sought.[18] In addition, *Vince* was instrumental in securing compliance with the Benn-Burt Act. Undertakings to that effect given by the government's lawyers were sufficient to persuade the first instance judge that there was no reasonable apprehension of breach of statutory duty.[19] However, on appeal, the court chose to continue rather than dismiss the case until it became clear whether the prime minister would, in fact, comply.

Nevertheless, the vast majority of cases were unsuccessful, with most either rejected at the permission, or equivalent admissibility, stage without a full hearing on the merits, or alternatively abandoned or suspended. Why, then, did some cases succeed where most failed? A number of factors can be identified which might affect the outcome of strategic litigation.

According to Harlow and Rawlings, 'Success [may] depend on skilful "forum shopping" for favourable judges.'[20] There is some evidence in our sample of deliberate forum shopping, for example in the two cases promoted by Jolyon Maugham QC on the revocability of the Art. 50 notification – *GLP (Dublin)* and *Wightman*. The matter appears to have been raised in Ireland initially in the belief that the request for a CJEU reference would be welcomed, but was discontinued when it became clear that the Irish government opposed the reference, and hence that proceedings were likely to be prolonged, expensive, and uncertain of success.[21] The issue was then reopened in *Wightman* in Edinburgh, again as a matter of conscious litigation strategy in

---

[18] HM Treasury agreed to revoke the Cross Border Trade (Public Notices) (EU Exit) Regulations 2019, SI 2019/1307 because they created a sub-delegated Henry VIII power which was ultra vires the parent statute.

[19] *Vince et al. v. Johnson and Lord Keen of Elie* [2019] CSOH 77.

[20] *Pressure Through Law*, p. 309.

[21] 'Dublin Case Update: Our Decision to Discontinue', Good Law Project, 30 May 2017, http://goodlawproject.org/update/dublin-case-update-3/.

TABLE 5 *Legal Outcomes*

| Successful | Rejected on merits | Rejected at permission/admissibility stage | Abandoned/suspended | Ongoing |
|---|---|---|---|---|
| Miller 1 | Shindler (UK) | Tomescu+ | Fair Deal for Expats | thethreemillion |
| Wightman | Agnew & McCord | Yalland* | Good Law Project (Ireland) | |
| Continuity Bill Reference | Good Law Project (Electoral Commission) | Truss+ | Miller/IWUGB 1 | |
| | | Shindler (EU1)** | Rush | |
| Cherry et al. | McCord (Border poll) | Good Law Project (Impact Studies)*** | Trimble | |
| Miller 2 | McCord et al. | Hardy*/**** | Leave Means Leave | |
| | Vince | McCord (Dublin)** | Wolchover | |
| | Fratila | Watt 1****/+ | Legg | |
| | AB | Williams* | Brake et al. | |
| | | Webster****/+ | JR90 | |
| | | Wilson ****/+ | Vince et al. | |
| | | Good Law Project (DUP)*/+ | Public Law Project | |
| | | Fair Vote UK*****/+ | Maughan | |
| | | Watson et al.+++ | Bryson | |
| | | Good Law Project (Serious Shortage Protocols)+ | Lib Dems (BBC) | |
| | | Ball++ | BIJ | |
| | | English Democrats+ | | |
| | | Allman+ | | |
| | | B+ | | |
| | | MCS & ClientEarth* | | |
| | | Walker** | | |
| | | Keighley****/+ | | |
| | | McCord et al.*/+++ | | |
| | | Shindler (EU2)** | | |
| | | Liberty*/++++ | | |
| | | IWUGB 2 ++++ | | |
| | | Shindler (EU3)+ | | |
| | | Lib Dems and SNP+* | | |
| | | Watt 2+ | | |

*Premature **Lack of Standing ***Failure to exhaust alternative remedy ****Out of time +Unarguable on the merits ++Quashed +++Non-justiciable ++++Repetitive of existing litigation +*Outwith scope of JR

the belief that Scotland's Remain vote meant that the case would receive a more sympathetic hearing than it would in London.[22] The success of *Wightman* then appears to have encouraged Maugham and others to bring further cases in Scotland in the latter stages of the Brexit process (*Cherry; Vince; Maugham; Watt 2*).[23] Whether the Scottish courts were, in fact, more sympathetic than the English courts is difficult to say. The cases were invariably *un*successful in the Outer House of the Court of Session, but more successful on appeal to the Inner House. Anecdotal evidence suggests that the Inner House may be more receptive to novel claims appealing to issues of principle. However, the case sample is too small to allow firm conclusions to be drawn.

Choice of litigants is a second important strategic consideration. Standing in the formal sense does not appear to have been a barrier in any domestic case, though several cases failed on this ground before the EU courts,[24] where the requirement of 'direct and individual concern' is a significant obstacle to strategic litigation.[25] So, too, did Raymond McCord's attempt to force the Irish government to publish its policy on a reunification referendum (*McCord (Dublin)*). Nevertheless, in *Wightman*, the litigants – members of the Scottish, UK, and European Parliaments from a range of political parties – were carefully chosen to send a message to the courts that they were representative 'of the wider body politic and civil society in Scotland', with a legitimate interest in seeking authoritative resolution of the legal issue at stake.[26] This was indeed a factor in persuading the Inner House to grant permission.[27] The identity of the litigant was also relevant in a negative sense in *Ball* – the attempted private prosecution of Boris Johnson for misconduct in public office due to misleading statements made during the referendum campaign. Given clear evidence of Marcus Ball's political motivations for bringing the prosecution, the High Court quashed the summons granted by the District Judge inter alia because it could detect no reasoning to support her conclusion that the prosecution was not vexatious.[28]

---

[22] O'Neill, 'Strategic Litigation', pp. 16–17.
[23] An additional consideration in *Cherry* was that the courts continued to sit in Scotland over the summer, allowing the case to be heard more quickly than the parallel proceedings in London in *Miller 2*. See Jo Maugham, 'Suspending Parliament is the act of a dictator. We can't allow it', Crowd Justice, www.crowdjustice.com/case/dont-suspend-parliament/.
[24] *Shindler (EU1), Walker* and *Shindler (EU2)*.
[25] See O'Neill, 'Strategic Litigation', pp. 4–8.
[26] O'Neill, 'Strategic Litigation', pp. 17–18.
[27] See [2018] CSIH 18 at para. 12. Although, in its substantive judgment, the Inner House was doubtful whether MSPs, and MEPs, as distinct from MPs, had standing – see [2018] CSIH 62 at para. 27.
[28] [2019] EWHC 1709 at paras. 41–46.

A more significant issue in our sample was the timing of litigation. Six cases were refused permission because they were out of time, while another seven were deemed premature (see Table 5). In addition, several cases were discontinued because they were effectively overtaken by events (*GLP (Impact Studies)*; *Rush*; *Trimble*; *Watson et al.*; *Leave Means Leave*; *Allman*; *Vince*; *Maugham*). However, evolving facts could also work in litigants' favour. For example, in *Wightman*, the enactment of the requirement in s. 13 of the European Union (Withdrawal) Act 2018 for the House of Commons to hold a 'meaningful vote' on the Withdrawal Agreement was material in persuading the Inner House to reverse the Lord Ordinary's decision that the issue of revoking the Art. 50 notification was purely hypothetical.[29] Similarly, in *Miller 2*, *Cherry*, and *Vince*, press reports during the course of proceedings casting doubt on whether the UK government would comply with the courts' rulings may have encouraged the higher courts to take a more robust line in those cases than the lower ones.

Nevertheless, the treatment of timing issues was not consistent. In *Yalland*, the Administrative Court refused to rule on evolving facts because,

> [where the] relevant legal and factual situations against which the various claims made will need to be assessed have not yet occurred ... the court cannot ... identify with precision, first, what, if any, justiciable issues will arise for adjudication by the courts and, secondly, the full factual and legal context in which any such issues will fall to be assessed.[30]

This dictum was subsequently relied upon by McCloskey LJ to refuse permission in *McCord et al.*, which sought to argue that a no-deal Brexit would breach the Northern Ireland Act 1998.[31] By contrast, as noted, the Inner House in *Vince* chose to continue the appeal to see if the issues would become live ones. Similarly, while the hypothetical nature of the claim was initially a barrier to the *Wightman* litigation, it was not even raised as an issue in *Miller 1* or *Cherry* (which gained permission before it became clear that Parliament would in fact be prorogued).

A final factor affecting success or failure is the nature of the legal claims being made. Table 5 shows that fourteen cases were refused permission or ruled inadmissible because they were unarguable on their merits. Similarly, the summons initially granted in *Ball* was quashed by the High Court because the essential ingredients of the offence of misconduct in public office were not

---

[29] [2018] CSIH 62 at para. 27.
[30] [2017] EWHC 630 (Admin) at paras. 48–51.
[31] [2019] NIQB 78 at para. 52. The court's reasoning was confirmed on appeal.

prima facie present. Three further cases were refused permission on the basis that essential elements of the claim were not made out (*GLP (Impact Studies)* – failure to exhaust alternative remedies; *McCord et al.* – issues not justiciable; *Lib Dems and SNP* – issue outwith the scope of judicial review). And influencing the decision to abandon some of the other cases must surely have been an appreciation that the legal arguments were weak.

However, it is too simplistic to see success or failure as directly linked to the strength or credibility of the claim. After all, many of the cases raised during the Brexit process, including those which ultimately succeeded, were highly speculative. In four out of the five successful cases, judges reached differing conclusions on their arguability and/or merits at different stages of the litigation; and although the fifth – the *Continuity Bill Reference* – produced a unanimous decision, the Supreme Court rejected most of the grounds on which the vires of the bill had been challenged. Conversely, some of the unsuccessful cases had heavyweight academic support.[32]

More important seems to be what Harlow and Rawlings term achieving a 'good fit' with the ideology of the law,[33] or as Feldman puts it, appealing to the judge's 'constitutional ethic'.[34] Thus, in keeping with the United Kingdom's prevailing constitutional ethic of representative democracy and responsible government,[35] those cases which succeeded either involved relatively straightforward exercises in statutory interpretation (i.e., giving effect to the intention of Parliament – *Continuity Bill Reference*)[36] or which sought to empower Parliament and parliamentarians against the executive – in *Miller 1*, by requiring statutory authorisation of the withdrawal process; in *Wightman*, by clarifying and extending the range of outcomes open to Parliament; and in *Miller 2/Cherry*, by insisting that Parliament must be allowed to exercise its constitutional function of overseeing the government's Brexit policy.

These latter three cases undoubtedly involved a degree of constitutional creativity – in *Miller 1*, by insisting in the face of legislative silence that a constitutional change of the magnitude of EU withdrawal must be authorised by Parliament; in *Wightman*, by pushing at the boundaries of reviewability of hypothetical decisions; and in *Miller 2/Cherry*, by significantly extending the scope of review of the prerogative, and by using

---

[32] See Table 6, below.
[33] *Pressure Through Law*, pp. 10, 307.
[34] David Feldman, 'Public Interest Litigation and Constitutional Theory in Comparative Perspective' (1992) 55 *Modern Law Review* 44–72.
[35] Ibid., p. 44.
[36] As did *GLP (Electoral Commission)*.

constitutional principle to discover limits to the prorogation power. Importantly, though, it was creativity of a 'constitutionally conservative' kind. Claims which would have required the courts to act outside their constitutional comfort zone – for example, to recognise principles of devolved consent, or the ability to regulate voting rights and electoral outcomes at common law – were invariably unsuccessful. Where the UK government sought to depart from accepted principles of devolution jurisprudence in the *Continuity Bill Reference*, its arguments were also rejected,[37] while in the proceedings before the CJEU in *Wightman*, it was a deliberate tactic to persuade the court that a power of unilateral revocation was the more *communautaire* interpretation of Art. 50.[38]

Conversely (with the initial exception of *Ball*), cases which involved a direct challenge to the legitimacy of political decisions or political conduct were unsuccessful. This again is consistent with the UK courts' prevailing constitutional ethic.[39] In both respects, therefore, the courts were careful – in highly politically charged territory – to limit their vulnerability to accusations of political decision-making.

## Political Impacts

What, then, of the political impacts of Brexit hyper-litigation?

As we might expect, even unsuccessful or abandoned cases sometimes had significant effects. In some instances, the mere prospect of litigation prompted the government to alter its position. In *Yalland*, for example, where permission was refused for prematurity, the prospect of subsequent litigation on whether the United Kingdom's withdrawal from the EEA was valid, seems to have caused the government to abandon its position that withdrawal from the EU meant automatic withdrawal from the EEA. The government argued instead that Brexit would deprive the United Kingdom's EEA membership of any practical effect, hence formal withdrawal was unnecessary. Following *GLP (Impact Studies)* and *Rush*, the litigants have argued that the legal proceedings influenced subsequent decisions by the government to put into the public domain information that it had previously been reluctant to publish. In the former case, GLP claimed that the government's partial release of Brexit impact case studies was influenced by – and pre-empted – its (consequently abandoned) legal action to force publication of that

---

[37] See Aileen McHarg and Christopher McCorkindale, 'The Supreme Court and Devolution: the Scottish Continuity Bill Reference' (2019) *Juridical Review* 190–97.
[38] O'Neill, 'Strategic Litigation', pp. 26–32.
[39] Feldman, 'Public Interest Litigation', p. 50.

information.⁴⁰ Similarly, in *Rush*, the claimant abandoned an appeal to the First Tier Tribunal to force disclosure, under the Freedom of Information Act 2000, of government mapping exercises on the impact of Brexit on north-south cooperation under the Belfast/Good Friday Agreement (the 1998 Agreement), when some of those documents were (in Rush's view, pre-emptively) published.⁴¹

Other unsuccessful cases nevertheless had the effect of mobilising political support for the litigants' cause. Most notably, a string of unsuccessful cases attacking the legitimacy of the referendum process – various GLP cases, *Webster, Wilson, Ball, Walchover* – seemed only to intensify the belief amongst 'ultra-Remainers' that Brexit itself was illegitimate. This arguably had the effect of focusing attention on the legitimacy of Brexit and away from the process by which Brexit would be delivered and the form it would take. In *GLP (Serious Shortages Protocol)*, we saw an attempt to leverage that political support back on the legal process in order to pre-empt an unsuccessful outcome or to influence a positive outcome. In a series of tweets, Jolyon Maugham drew his followers' attention not only to what he believed to be the 'pro-government' reputation of the judge, Swift J, who had refused permission on the papers but also – and more controversially – that of the judge, Supperstone J, who was *still to hear* the appeal against that refusal, urging the latter to 'defy his reputation' and do the right thing.⁴²

Finally, we saw in the course of Brexit litigation, and most clearly in cases around Brexit and the territorial constitution, that unsuccessful or abandoned cases could change the dynamics of the decision-making process. McCrudden and Halberstam, for example, have argued that the Supreme Court's treatment of Northern Ireland-specific issues in *McCord and Agnew* – downplaying the legal significance of constitutional protections afforded by the 1998 Agreement, and the need for legislative consent by the Northern Ireland Assembly to 'unpick' the existing devolution settlement – hardened the resolve of the EU-27 to prioritise 'sufficient progress' on the Ireland/Northern Ireland dimensions of Brexit in their Brexit negotiations with the United Kingdom.⁴³

⁴⁰ See this thread of tweets by Jolyon Maugham in which, owing to the government's release of the studies, he includes *GLP (Impact Studies)* (tweet 3 in the thread) as part of what he considers GLP's 'extraordinary record of success' (tweet 7) in the conduct of strategic litigation – Jo Maugham, @JolyonMaugham (23 March 2018), https://twitter.com/JolyonMaugham/status/977128368733859841.
⁴¹ Communication with the authors.
⁴² CJ McKinney, 'Jolyon Maugham QC suffers backlash on Twitter after calling High Court judge "pro-Government"', Legal Cheek, 26 March 2019, www.legalcheek.com/2019/03/jolyon-maugham-qc-suffers-backlash-on-twitter-after-calling-high-court-judge-pro-government/.
⁴³ Christopher McCrudden and Daniel Halberstam, '*Miller* and Northern Ireland: A Critical Constitutional Response' (2016–17) 8 *Supreme Court Yearbook* 299–343.

Similarly, it may be argued that the Supreme Court's approach to the Sewel Convention in *Miller 1* – depriving s. 2 of the Scotland Act 2016 of legal effect, thereby leaving the necessity of legislative consent to be determined in the political arena and, in so doing, signposting the weakness of the constitutional protections for devolution – encouraged the UK government to adopt a hard line on devolution issues during the passage of the subsequent Withdrawal Act.

Conversely, the political impacts of *successful* cases have been complex and – sometimes – less favourable to the parties than they might initially have appeared. In *Miller 1*, for example, the claimants won an important formal victory by requiring Parliament explicitly to authorise the government to trigger Art. 50. However, the political impact of the win was somewhat limited. First, Parliament's *use* of that power was simply to hand the government an unconditional discretion to trigger Art. 50, a decision which undermined Parliament's ability to control the conduct and terms of Brexit negotiations at an early stage. Secondly, the approach taken by the Supreme Court – downplaying the constitutional significance of the referendum and placing greater weight on Parliament's (politically, but not legally, consequent) decision to leave – closed off the possibility of later challenges to the legitimacy of the referendum process or result. Thirdly, the court's refusal to engage with the Sewel Convention undermined the capacity of the devolved governments to exert meaningful influence on the UK government.

In *Wightman*, the CJEU's ruling that a member state may unilaterally withdraw its Art. 50 notification in line with its own constitutional requirements had the desired effect of changing the political dynamics – with the (then) minority UK government shifting its rhetoric from 'no deal' to 'no Brexit' as the inevitable alternative to its Withdrawal Agreement. However, by adding to and further complicating the range of options on the table, it is arguable that the case contributed to the parliamentary stalemate that required the government to seek extensions in order to ward off the prospect of a 'no deal' Brexit by default.

In the *Continuity Bill Reference*, whilst the government was – ultimately – successful in defeating the Scottish government's bill,[44] this too came at a political cost. The UK government's use of the reference procedure to change the rules of the game – delaying the bill's submission for Royal Assent, and using that delay in order to amend the Scotland Act 1998 and *retrospectively* place the bill outwith competence – arguably handed the Scottish government a political and moral victory, whilst sparing it the practical headache of how to implement a parallel scheme.

[44] UK Withdrawal from the European Union (Legal Continuity) (Scotland) Bill 2018.

Finally, where the litigants in *Cherry/Miller 2* achieved a significant legal victory, the political impacts of that case were more complex. First, by restoring the status quo ante – an embattled minority government that had struggled to find support in Parliament for its flagship Brexit policies[45] – *Cherry/Miller 2* was arguably an important catalyst for the December 2019 general election at which the Conservative Party was returned to power with an eighty-seat majority. Secondly, whilst the Supreme Court Justices – aware of the political fallout that was sure to follow – were extremely careful to disguise the novelty of their judgment in orthodox reasoning and in defence of parliamentary democracy, the political responses to that judgment were unsurprisingly partisan. Amongst Remain supporters, there was an unhelpful outburst of 'court- (and Lady Hale-) worship', which was doubly problematic. On the one hand, the praise for judges as 'Heroes of the People'[46] by implication validated the infamous criticism of judges as 'Enemies of the People' by pro-Brexit supporters and media.[47] On the other hand, with the emotional, political, and constitutional stakes so high – and where hyper-litigation had been felt by the government to have disrupted its ability to deliver Brexit *on its terms* – the conditions were ripe for political pushback. This has manifested in the government's commissioning of an Independent Review of Administrative Law. The review panel has been set broad terms of reference to consider, inter alia, codification of the grounds of judicial review, the proper scope of judicial review, the impact and remedial effects of judicial review on government decision-making, as well as the 'stream-lining' of judicial review, including a return to the question of standing in public law cases.[48] Although set in ostensibly neutral terms, the desired outcome of the review is hinted at in the terms of reference. The panel, this said, 'should bear in mind how the legitimate interest in the citizen being able to challenge the lawfulness of executive action through the courts can be properly balanced with the role of the executive to govern effectively under the law'.[49] The agenda behind the

---

[45] See chapters by Howarth and Petrie in this volume.

[46] As one headline reacted to the Court of Session's decision in *Cherry*, see Jim Cormack, 'Heroes of the People', *Scotsman*, 12 September 2019, www.pressreader.com/uk/the-scotsman/20190912/281487868045940.

[47] James Slack, 'Enemies of the People: Fury over "out of touch" judges who have "declared war on democracy" by defying 17.4m Brexit voters and who could trigger constitutional crisis', *Daily Mail*, 3 November 2016, www.dailymail.co.uk/news/article-3903436/Enemies-people-Fury-touch-judges-defied-17-4m-Brexit-voters-trigger-constitutional-crisis.html.

[48] See further the government's press release announcing the review, gov.uk, 31 July 2020, www.gov.uk/government/news/government-launches-independent-panel-to-look-at-judicial-review.

[49] Ibid.

review has been made explicit too, in leaks that the government had instigated the review in order to 'curb' the powers of judicial review and in so doing 'prevent a repeat' of its 'humiliating defeat' in *Cherry/Miller* 2.[50]

### THE DRIVERS OF LITIGATION

Another question that requires attention is *why* Brexit has been the subject of hyper-litigation. The *potential* for litigation arises largely from the uncertainty that has defined the project. There has been uncertainty about the legitimacy and conduct of the referendum process, about the constitutional authority of the referendum result, about the constitutional boundaries between government and parliament, between central and devolved governments, and between the shape and various effects of a harder or softer Brexit. However, uncertainty can also play against the potential for success given the high constitutional stakes and the conduct of prolonged negotiations that leave issues locked in the political arena (for example, *Yalland*; *Williams*; *Trimble*; *Vince*). In addition, while uncertainty generates the potential for litigation, something more is needed to convert interesting legal questions into litigation. Within our case sample, we have identified several factors which *discourage* actors away from the political process and *encourage* potential litigants towards the legal process.

#### *Factors Discouraging Pursuit of Political Solutions*

A significant factor that has discouraged actors from pursuing their aims through the political process has been their feeling of political *exclusion*. We see this most clearly in the various challenges brought by those excluded from the UK Parliament, referendum, and European Parliament election franchises (*Tomescu*; *Shindler UK*; *Shindler EU 1*; *B*). Exclusion was a factor, too, in *Agnew & McCord* and *Miller 1* where it was felt that the UK government had marginalised the devolved institutions during withdrawal negotiations. The *Continuity Bill Reference*, initiated by the UK government's Law Officers,

---

[50] Gordon Rayner, 'Boris Johnson ready to curb the scope and power of judicial reviews', *Telegraph*, 24 July 2020, www.gov.uk/government/news/government-launches-independent-panel-to-look-at-judicial-review. As justice is devolved to Scotland and Northern Ireland, the review terms are mostly confined to judicial review in England and Wales. However, the prospect of push back does influence judicial thinking in other UK jurisdictions – see Lord Hope's warning to litigants in the Scottish courts to use strategic litigation responsibly or risk political backlash in 'A Judicial Perspective on Strategic Litigation' (paper delivered at the Development of Strategic Litigation Seminar hosted by the Faculty of Advocates and the Equality and Human Rights Commission, March 2014, on file with the authors).

was born of a double exclusion. On the one hand, the devolved institutions in Scotland and Wales were frustrated that their concerns about the proper return of competences from the EU had been ignored. This caused both governments to retaliate with indigenous Continuity Bills to apply in devolved areas, which were then referred to the Supreme Court.[51] On the other hand, the exclusion – by the Scottish government in the formulation of their Continuity Bill – of the UK Law Officers from the three-week pre-introduction period, when concerns about competence are usually addressed and resolved through political dialogue, left those concerns instead to be raised and addressed in the process of litigation.[52] Finally, in *Cherry/Miller 2* the use of prorogation by the executive to 'stymie' further parliamentary input into the Brexit process[53] was an important factor in pushing political actors away from the political process and towards litigation.

In *Cherry/Miller 2*, there were important additional factors in play that explain why so many MPs turned to law rather politics in their opposition to prorogation. Unlike *Wightman*, which was born of political stalemate, the politicians party to this litigation had political options on the table to face down prorogation. They might have pursued a vote of no confidence in the government, the passage of legislation to block or condition prorogation, a vote of contempt against the PM, or a Humble Address motion inviting the Queen to disregard the PM's advice.[54] However, a range of considerations – the pressures of time (reports that the PM had sought legal advice about prorogation were published just two weeks before its intended implementation),[55] and concerns about the efficacy of political remedies (for example, a no confidence vote leading to dissolution would have had a similar effect to prorogation; the PM might have ignored the contempt order, or advised the monarch to refuse Royal Consent to any legislation affecting the

---

[51] Albeit that the Welsh reference was abandoned due to the Welsh Assembly repealing its Continuity Act and consenting to concessions made to the UK bill.

[52] See Christopher McCorkindale and Janet Hiebert, 'Vetting Bills in the Scottish Parliament for Legislative Competence' (2017) 22 *Edinburgh Law Review* 319–51, esp. pp. 341–8. In Wales there is no equivalent practice of sharing bills with UK Law Officers prior to their introduction.

[53] *Cherry and others v. The Advocate General* [2019] CSIH 49, para. 55.

[54] See David Howarth, 'Threat of Prorogation: What Can the Commons Do?', LSE Blog, 29 August 2019, www.democraticaudit.com/2019/08/28/threat-of-prorogation-what-can-the-commons-do/ (noting the author's view that the chances of obtaining a legal remedy were slim).

[55] Toby Helm and Heather Stewart, 'Boris Johnson seeks legal advice on five week parliament closure ahead of Brexit', *Guardian*, 24 August 2019, www.theguardian.com/politics/2019/aug/24/johnson-seeks-legal-advice-parliament-closure.

prerogative power to prorogue)[56] seem to have motivated politicians to run political and legal strategies in tandem.

Another factor that has discouraged recourse to the political process has been the perception or the effects of elite control. This has resulted in litigation aimed at improving access to information held by government (*GLP (Impact Studies); Rush*) and the adequacy of consultation exercises conducted by government (*GLP (Serious Shortages Protocol)*), both of which are essential to wider public understanding and participation.

A final set of considerations has been disillusionment with the available political choices. In some instances, this has manifested in efforts to constrain or close off undesirable political choices through law (for example, recourse to the 1998 Agreement to contest the legality of the NI backstop (*Trimble*) and the revised border solution (*Bryson*)). Conversely, law has been used to open up new choices in the face of political stalemate (as with the prospect of unilateral Art. 50 revocation in *Wightman*). In other cases, litigants have sought to shift the locus of decision-making power to alternative forums where more desirable choices might present themselves (from the executive to Parliament in *Miller* 1 and *Yalland*, and in various challenges to the extension of Art. 50; from the devolved institutions to the centre in the *Continuity Bill Reference* and vice-versa in *Miller* 1; from the executive to the Court of Session in *Vince*).

## Factors Encouraging Pursuit of Legal Solutions

The very high profile, high stakes, and controversial nature of Brexit created a strong motivation for people to take action to advance their preferred outcome by whatever means were open to them. What, then, are the factors that push or pull those who are disillusioned with the political process towards the courts?

First, academic visibility and engagement – enabled by more immediate and accessible (to litigants and to practitioners) means of publication, such as widely read constitutional and EU law blogs, and incentivised by government and academic institutions by the measure and reward of research 'impact' – has made a measurable impact on litigation patterns. Table 6 shows the very high number of cases that have been triggered – or at least significantly informed – by academic engagement and discussion or that have involved direct input by academic experts.

---

[56] Howarth, 'Threat of Prorogation'.

TABLE 6 *Expert Involvement*

| Cases triggered by expert discussion | Direct expert involvement in litigation |
|---|---|
| *Miller 1* | *Miller 1* (Prof Dan Sarooshi) |
| *Agnew & McCord* | *Agnew & McCord* (Prof Chris McCrudden, Prof Gordon Anthony) |
| *Yalland* | |
| *Good Law Project (Ireland)* | *Wightman* (Prof Piet Eeckhout) |
| *Wightman* | *Wilson* (Prof Pavlos Eleftheriadis) |
| *Williams* | *GLP (Serious Shortage Protocol)* (Prof Tammy Harvey) |
| *Continuity Bill Reference* | |
| *Webster* | *Cherry* (Prof Kenneth Armstrong) |
| *Wilson* | *Cherry/Miller 2* (Public Law Project interveners) |
| *Trimble* | |
| *GLP (Serious Shortage Protocols)* | *Public Law Project* |
| *Leave Means Leave* | *Maugham* (Prof Alan Winters) |
| *Wolchover* | |
| *English Democrats* | |
| *Allman* | |
| *Miller 2* | |
| *Cherry et al.* | |
| *McCord et al.* | |
| *Liberty* | |
| *Vince et al.* | |
| *JR90* | |
| *IWUGB 2* | |

Secondly, as noted above, litigants were pulled to court by entrepreneurial lawyers generating arguments and seeking – indeed, in *Fair Deal for Expats*, advertising for – clients.

Thirdly, time pressures were an important factor in converting potential to actual cases. Because the Art. 50 negotiating periods were time limited – with a 'no deal' Brexit the default if those periods were to expire without a negotiated agreement or agreed extension – there were only limited windows of opportunity to influence the political process. This, in part, explains the number of unsuccessful and abandoned cases in the sample. Since there was a very fine window of opportunity to bring cases in which the issues had sufficiently crystallised to be reviewable, yet avoid bringing the courts into a head-on collision with high stakes political decisions that had already been made, this may have incentivised risky litigation in the hope that *some* of it might stick.[57] The political significance of time pressures also explains

---

[57] We are grateful to Adam Tucker for this point.

a number of cases that were taken with the aim of extending the time available for a successfully negotiated outcome, taken to mean a 'softer' Brexit (*Liberty*; *Vince*; *JR90*; *IWUGB* 2) or opposing any extension in order to make a 'harder' or 'no deal' Brexit the more likely outcome (for example, *English Democrats*; *Legg*).

Finally, the courts have become much more receptive in recent years to strategic litigation. Judges in the United Kingdom, and in particular those who sit in the Supreme Court, are much more comfortable with constitutional adjudication than they were in the past; standing at least for domestic cases has been significantly liberalised; and litigation costs are much less of a barrier than they once were. One factor here is the willingness of courts to make protective costs orders in public interest cases, which has been a feature of some Brexit cases. A much more significant factor, however, has been the emergence of crowdfunding.

In *Pressure Through Law*, Harlow and Rawlings exposed the tension in a system where clients' ability to raise public interest litigation greatly depended on their ability to secure funding from the state through legal aid.[58] Writing at a time when the provision of legal aid was, they thought, 'relatively generous',[59] they nevertheless considered that the legal aid system was individualist in its application and so tended to discourage group litigation.[60] In more recent years, there has been a steep decline in the percentage of judicial reviews funded by legal aid in England and Wales[61] and within our sample only the various McCord cases and *Bryson* – all arising in Northern Ireland – were funded in this way. Crowdfunding has emerged as a way to overcome cost barriers to strategic litigation for those who do not qualify for legal aid and who do not have the independent means or backing to pursue their rights or interests in court. Moreover, it does so in a way that allows potential litigants quickly to raise money more or less directly from the public and to establish channels of communication between themselves and their donors about the legal arguments to be advanced, the progress of the case, and how their money has been used. In other words, not only does crowdfunding fill the gap that legal aid reform has left behind, it does so in

---

[58] *Pressure Through Law*, p. 115.
[59] Ibid. pp. 115–20.
[60] Ibid.,
[61] See Joe Tomlinson, 'Crowdfunding Public Interest Judicial Reviews: A Risky New Resource and the Case for a Practical Ethics' (2019) *Public Law* 166–85. On the inadequacies of the Scottish Legal Aid regime for strategic litigants, see Mhairi Snowden and Janet Cormack, 'Discussion Paper: Overcoming Barriers to Public Interest Litigation in Scotland' (2018), esp. p. 13, https://scotland.shelter.org.uk/__data/assets/pdf_file/0005/1621526/Discussion_Paper_Overcoming_Barriers_Public_Interest_Litigation_Scotaland.pdf/_nocache.

a potentially democratising way that is more encouraging and enabling of group actions.

Although there were attempts to use crowdfunding in public interest cases before and outside of the Brexit context,[62] Table 7 demonstrates that crowdfunding has had a profound impact on the number of Brexit cases that have been brought. It has been a feature in at least twenty-seven of our fifty-seven cases (with public donations sought in at least a further four cases). In some instances, the sums involved have been very large indeed, reaching well into six figures. However, the sheer volume of cases has shone a light on ethical considerations around crowdfunding that remain to be addressed. In some cases, litigants have been able to raise significant sums of money to advance arguments that were always unlikely to succeed (for example, in *Ball*, £700,000 to support the failed private prosecution of Boris Johnson; in *Webster*, £190,000 to support a dubious challenge to the validity of the prime minister's Art. 50 notification). In highly emotive contexts such as Brexit, it seems that non-expert donors may part with their money on the basis of their emotional or political preferences rather than on the merits of the legal argument. At the same time, whilst there are examples of good practice with regard to the sharing of arguments and other key documents with donors, the democratising impact of crowdfunding is undermined in other instances[63] where very little is offered by way of arguments, documents or case updates. In addition, crowdfunding has drawn lawyers (and clients) inexperienced in judicial review into that space and this has caused some judicial pushback against lawyers who are therefore ill-prepared for such proceedings (*GLP (Electoral Commission)*) and against 'hopeless' arguments being pushed too far up the appeal chain (for example, the exceptional award of costs at the permission stage against the claimants in *Webster* and *Wilson*). Attention to the need for better regulation and scrutiny of crowdfunding in legal cases in order to realise its democratising potential might therefore be one more positive outcome of its intense use so soon in its development.[64]

## CONCLUSION: STRATEGIC LITIGATION AFTER BREXIT

In *Pressure Through Law*, Harlow and Rawlings challenge the view that the use of pressure through law is a 'modern phenomenon' that began in 1954 with

---

[62] An early, and high profile, use of crowdfunding of this kind was *Justice for Health v. Secretary of State for Health* [2016] EWHC 2338.

[63] Tomlinson, 'Crowdfunding Public Interest Judicial Reviews', esp. pp. 175–6, citing *Webster* as an example of a 'less well managed' example of a crowdfunded judicial review.

[64] Ibid.

TABLE 7 *Litigation Funding*

| Crowdfunded | Party-funded | Legal aid | Pro-bono | Other | Unknown |
|---|---|---|---|---|---|
| Miller 1 | Tomescu | McCord | Miller 1 | Williams | Shindler (UK) |
| Agnew | Miller 1 | McCord (Border poll) | Good Law Project (Impact Studies) | | Truss |
| Yalland | Agnew | McCord et al. | | | Hardy |
| Good Law Project (Ireland) | Fair Deal for Expats* | Bryson | Williams | | McCord (Dublin) |
| Ball | Continuity Bill Reference | | Watson | | Watt 1 |
| English Democrats | Rush | | thethreemillion | | Legg |
| Brake et al. | Leave Means Leave* | | Miller 2 | | B |
| Keighley | Wolchover* | | | | Walker |
| thethreemillion | Allman | | | | Miller 2 |
| Good Law Project (Electoral Commission) | MCS & ClientEarth* | | | | Shindler (EU2) |
| Cherry et al. | Miller 2 | | | | Fratila |
| Liberty | Vince | | | | Shindler (EU3) |
| Good Law Project (Impact Studies) | IWUGB 2 | | | | JR90 |
| Maugham | | | | | Lib Dems & SNP (ITV) |
| BIJ | | | | | |
| Williams | | | | | Lib Dems (BBC) |
| Webster | | | | | |
| Wilson | | | | | |
| Watt 2 (intention to seek) | | | | | |
| Good Law Project (DUP) | | | | | |
| Fair Vote UK | | | | | |
| Trimble | | | | | |
| Watson et al. | | | | | |

* Donations sought

Brown v. Board of Education of Topeka.[65] Instead, they say, pressure through law might be as old as the existence of pressure groups themselves.[66] Collectively, then, the cases that we have highlighted here take their place within a long tradition of strategic litigation used to influence a wider political context.

What is new, however, and what marks this body of strategic litigation out as being worthy of study on its own terms, is three-fold. First, it is clear that the unusual interplay of factors which gave rise to Brexit hyper-litigation will continue to feed efforts to influence Brexit even now that the United Kingdom has left the EU.[67] More interestingly, there is evidence already that these factors – and patterns of hyper-litigation – have spilled over from the Brexit context and into other areas of political controversy. In June 2020, a study by Tomlinson et al. found that there had been at least sixty-three cases (and counting) relating to aspects of the United Kingdom's response to the Covid-19 pandemic.[68] In Scotland, meanwhile, a legal challenge concerning the power to hold an independence referendum has drawn explicit inspiration from Brexit litigation, in particular the decision in *Cherry/Miller 2*.[69]

Secondly, Brexit hyper-litigation has had enormous constitutional impacts. It has expanded the scope of justiciability both in terms of substance (*Miller 1*; *Cherry/Miller 2*) and in terms of remedies (*Wightman*). It has extended judicial control over prerogative powers (to determine whether prerogative powers are engaged at all (*Miller 1*) as well as their lawful exercise (*Cherry/Miller 2*). And it has accelerated the advance of common law constitutionalism by recasting parliamentary sovereignty (*Continuity Bill Reference*; *Cherry/Miller 2*) and responsible government (*Cherry/Miller 2*) as substantive legal principles capable of judicial enforcement.

Thirdly, whilst hyper-litigation and judicial activism might be defended as necessary responses to the executive's unconstitutional behaviour, our case sample does not necessarily bear this out. Behind the majority of cases we find partisan political motivations disguised as constitutional concerns. This finding might not be surprising – but it is problematic. Overt politicisation of the courts by those bringing claims risks *undermining* respect for the rule of law, as

---

[65] 347 US 483 (1954).
[66] *Pressure Through Law*, p. 12.
[67] Peers, 'Litigating Brexit'.
[68] Joe Tomlinson, Jo Hynes, Jack Maxwell and Emma Marshall, 'Judicial Review during the COVID-19 Pandemic (Part III)', Administrative Law in the Common Law World Blog, 28 May 2020, https://adminlawblog.org/2020/05/28/joe-tomlinson-jo-hynes-jack-maxwell-and-emma-marshall-judicial-review-during-the-covid-19-pandemic-part-ii/.
[69] See Forward as One's crowdfund page in support of their 'People's Action on Section 30', www.crowdjustice.com/case/pas30/.

highly partisan reactions to *Miller 1* and *Cherry/Miller 2* demonstrate. Indeed, the final irony of Brexit hyper-litigation is that its legacy might not be the use of legal techniques by lawyers and their clients to advance political positions, nor the development by the judiciary of a richer common law constitutionalism – but the hollowing out, by a 'humiliated' government, of judicial review itself.

# 13

## The Law Officers: The Relationship between Executive Lawyers and Executive Power in Ireland and the United Kingdom

Conor Casey

### INTRODUCTION

The United Kingdom's decision to invoke Art. 50 of the Treaty on European Union triggered serious ripples across its constitutional order, including repeat clashes between Parliament and the government. This friction reached a crescendo in 2018, following the former's unprecedented decision to hold the latter in contempt for refusing to obey its request to publish the Attorney General's full legal advice on the government's draft Withdrawal Agreement with the EU.[1] One of the many interesting constitutional issues thrown into sharp focus by this event, was the important relationship between executive power and the legal advice-giving role of executive lawyers. This is not a relationship unique to the UK legal order. Across many divergent constitutional orders, the executive branch binds itself to the constitutional or legal advice tendered by its legal advisors, despite there being no formal rule of law requiring it to do so.[2] In many ways, the work of executive legal advisors can have as great an impact on what government decides to do – or not do – than the decisions of the courts.[3] This serves to tie legal advisors closely to executive action, and makes their work an important variable to consider when assessing the power of the executive.

Using the United Kingdom[4] and Ireland as illustrative examples, this chapter considers how the work of executive lawyers interacts with executive

---

[1] 'British government found in contempt of parliament', RTE News, 5 December 2018, www.rte.ie/news/brexit/2018/1204/1014950-brexit/.
[2] David Luban, *Legal Ethics and Human Dignity* (Cambridge: Cambridge University Press, 2007), p. 196.
[3] Ben Yong, *Government Lawyers and the Provision of Legal Advice within Whitehall* (London: The Constitution Unit, 2013), p. 16.
[4] For the purposes of this essay, I refer to the executive lawyers who provide advice to the UK government. However, it is worth noting the devolved executives in Northern Ireland, Wales, and Scotland have their own dedicated legal advisors.

authority. I argue that their legal advice can be important in supporting the executive's political narratives about the basis for controversial policy action or inaction. I give an account of how legal advice is deployed by the executive to enhance the legal credibility and political legitimacy of contested and controversial political positions. My observations are necessarily tentative, given the high level of confidentiality surrounding executive legal advice. But I argue that the work of senior executive lawyers clearly deserves further exploration. Its relationship to exercises of public power deserves greater positive and normative scrutiny, both within each system I discuss and from a comparative public law perspective more broadly.

## STRUCTURE OF WORK OF EXECUTIVE LAWYERS

### United Kingdom

Legal advice to the executive in the United Kingdom is characterised by a fusion of pluralism and centralisation. In some respects, provision of legal advice is highly porous; with several government departments relying primarily on internal legal advisors for a majority of their advice. In these departments, routine legal problems are mostly dealt with by its own internal legal staff.[5] In other respects, provision of legal advice is centralised, given that a majority of government departments rely on the same provider for legal advice: the Government Legal Department (GLD), which has a staff complement of over 2000[6] and is headed by the Treasury Solicitor.[7]

At the apex of government legal advisors stand several lawyers: the Attorney General for England and Wales (AG), Solicitor General for England and Wales (who advises both the UK and Welsh governments),[8] and the Advocate General for Scotland (who advises the UK government on Scots law). These lawyers are collectively known as the Law Officers.[9] Today, the main function of the Law Officers is to serve as legal advisors to the Crown via her prime

---

[5] Elwyn Jones, 'The Office of Attorney-General' (1969) 27 *Cambridge Law Journal* 43–53, p. 46.
[6] *Workforce Management Information for GLD, AGO and HMCPSI 2018/19* 24 May 2018, https://www.gov.uk/government/publications/workforce-management-information-for-gld-ago-and-hmcpsi-201819.
[7] Barry K. Winetrobe, 'Legal Advice and Representation for Parliament' in Dawn Oliver and Gavin Drewry (eds.), *The Law and Parliament* (London: Butterworths, 1998) p. 95.
[8] The AG of England and Wales also holds the Office of Advocate General for Northern Ireland and advises the UK government on Northern Irish law.
[9] J. L. J. Edwards, *The Attorney General, Politics and the Public Interest* (London: Sweet & Maxwell, 1984), pp. 1–11; Peter Archer, 'The role of the law officers', 339 *Fabian Research Series* (November 1978) 1–32, p. 3.

minister and the cabinet. The Law Officers are, by convention, members of government but not members of cabinet.[10] Traditionally, AGs attended cabinet meetings on request as a need for advice arose,[11] however, recent AGs have reported that there is now an 'expectation' that they will attend every cabinet meeting.[12] The Law Officers act as a quasi-centralised source for legal advice for all government departments, helping to coordinate executive legal policy concerning the most difficult, pressing, and sensitive legal and political issues.[13] The cabinet office's Ministerial Code specifies that the Law Officers must be consulted in the following cases: if the legal consequences of action by the government have important policy repercussions; if a department legal advisor is unsure of the legality or constitutionality of legislation; if the vires of subordinate legislation is in dispute; or where two or more departmental advisors are in disagreement.[14] There is thus no legally grounded central control over the provision of legal advice,[15] but instead a convention that the AG's advice be sought in certain serious circumstances and accepted as authoritative when provided.[16]

## *Ireland*

The Irish Attorney General is given constitutional status in Ireland by Art. 30 of the Irish Constitution, which provides that the AG is 'the adviser of the Government in matters of law and legal opinion'.[17] Unlike the AG in the United Kingdom, the Irish AG typically attends all cabinet meetings.[18] The AG has almost always been a lawyer of eminence and long standing and has frequently been a member of, or had some political affiliation with, one of the

---

[10] The AG has not been a member of cabinet since 1928.
[11] Jones, 'The Office of Attorney-General', p. 47; S. C. Silkin, 'The Function and Position of the Attorney-General in the United Kingdom' (1978) 12 *Bracton Law Journal* 29–39, p. 34.
[12] Conor McCormick and Graeme Cowie, 'The Law Officers: A Constitutional and Functional Overview' HC Library Briefing Paper, No. 08919 (28 May 2020), p. 49.
[13] Silkin, 'The Function and Position of the Attorney-General', p. 34.
[14] *Ministerial Code: A Code of Conduct and Guidance on Procedures for Ministers* (London: Cabinet Office, 2001), para. 22.
[15] Edwards, *The Attorney General*, p. 192.
[16] Terence Daintith and Alan Page, *The Executive in the Constitution: Structure, Autonomy and Internal Control* (Oxford: Oxford University Press, 1999), p. 323; *Ministerial Code* (London: Cabinet Office, 2019), para. 2.10.
[17] See Art. 30.1 and 30.4 (1937). See James Casey, *The Irish Law Officers: Roles and Responsibilities of the Attorney General and the Director of Public Prosecutors* (Dublin: Round Hall Ltd., 1996).
[18] He or she is formally appointed by the president, but the nomination is made by the Taoiseach, and the president has no discretion to refuse to make the appointment.

parties in government.[19] The Attorney General's office acts as a centralised provider of legal advice for the cabinet and all government departments; it is staffed by career civil servants, who are generally former practising lawyers of some years' experience.

## PROCEDURES GOVERNING PROVISION OF ADVICE

### United Kingdom

The work of executive legal advisors is deeply integrated into departmental policy making and advice tendered by them is generally accepted by government departments.[20] In instances where advice is questioned; where there is inter-departmental disagreement; or where the advice raises issues of importance, legal advice can be referred to the Law Officers for resolution. A request may also be made directly to the AG at cabinet level, particularly if it involves an issue on which the prime minister has taken a policy lead.[21] The Law Officers' decision is, by convention, accepted as binding;[22] making it the last word on internal legal questions for the executive.[23]

### Ireland

According to the Irish Government's Cabinet Handbook, before policy proposals are brought to cabinet for discussion, they must undergo consultation with three bodies: the Taoiseach's office, the Department of Finance, and the Attorney General's office.[24] If this advice is not obtained, any policy proposal to government may be withdrawn by the Taoiseach in consultation with the AG. In this way, the AG is intimately involved in the formulation of policy from its inception, and no policy with significant legal dimensions can take shape without his or her guidance.[25] Indeed, the most recent former

---

[19] Casey, *The Irish Law Officers*, p. 305.
[20] Daintith and Page, *The Executive in the Constitution*, p. 323.
[21] Ibid., p. 302.
[22] A. H. Dennis, 'Place of the Official Lawyer in the Constitution'; (1925) 41 *Law Quarterly Review* 378–88, p. 387.
[23] Daintith and Page, *The Executive in the Constitution*, p. 308.
[24] *Cabinet Handbook*, Government of Ireland, March 2019, p. 32.
[25] David Kenny and Conor Casey, 'A One Person Supreme Court? The Attorney General, Constitutional Advice to Government, and the Case for Transparency' (2020) 42 *Dublin University Law* Journal 89–118.

incumbent has described the Attorney General's office as a 'hub' through which almost everything of major governmental importance passes.[26]

## SUBSTANTIVE NORMS GOVERNING ADVICE PROVISION

### United Kingdom

Given the confidentiality surrounding legal advice, it is hard to be definitive about the substantive norms governing its provision.[27] However, the self-professed ideal pursued by the Law Officers is to offer impartial detached advice in the manner of counsel's advice to any client: to give an objective analysis of the law as they see it.[28] One previous holder of the office suggested that while it cannot be denied that the Law Officers are highly political animals, given that they are ministers and parliamentarians, they have always striven for impartiality and detachment when giving legal advice.[29]

But many have speculated about how the political nature of the Law Officers influences their work.[30] Some maintain that the advice of the Attorney General is more likely to be accepted and respected by ministers precisely because it comes from one of their own – a political actor who understands the wider political and policy context in which they operate – as opposed to advice from an externally sourced technocrat without a political background.[31] Others take a less sanguine view of the AG's fusion of political and advisory roles, and strongly argue that it inevitably hinders provision of independent and impartial advice. Jowell, for example, argues the dual party political and legal functions of the AG invariably invites conflicts[32] and 'inevitably lends itself to charges of political bias in legal decisions' of high salience to the executive. [33]

---

[26] Anne Marie-Hardiman, 'The Lawyer at the Centre' (2017) 22 *The Bar Review* 124–7.
[27] Neil Walker, 'The Antinomies of the Law Officers' in Maurice Sunkin and Sebastian Payne (eds.), *The Nature of the Crown: A Legal and Political Analysis* (Oxford: Oxford University Press, 1999), p. 159.
[28] Daintith and Page, *The Executive in the Constitution*, p. 297.
[29] Jones, 'The Office of Attorney-General', p. 50.
[30] Gabrielle Appleby, 'Reform of the Attorney General: comparing Britain and Australia' (2016) *Public Law* 573–94, p. 585.
[31] Appleby, 'Reform of the Attorney General, p. 585.
[32] Walker, 'The Antinomies of the Law Officers'; House of Commons Justice Committee, *Constitutional Role of the Attorney General* (5th Report of Session 2006–7), HC 306, pp. 22–4.
[33] Jeffrey Jowell QC, 'Politics and the Law: Constitutional Balance or Institutional Confusion', JUSTICE Tom Sargant Memorial Annual Lecture, 17 October 2006, p. 11.

## Ireland

The substantive norms underpinning legal review in Ireland are also shrouded in confidentiality. It is unclear what standard the AG applies when assessing the constitutionality of legislation or executive action; whether, for example, it takes a departmentalist approach to legal interpretation like its US counterpart which takes a stance on the law that is more favourable to the executive than a court.[34] It seems from what evidence is available, however, that advice generally focuses on risk assessment that mimics the courts – having regard to the probability of the act being invalidated.[35]

### PUBLICATION OF ADVICE

### United Kingdom

Confidentiality pervades executive legal advice in the United Kingdom[36] as there is a strong convention against disclosing the Law Officers' advice.[37] Indeed, it has been suggested that the very fact that advice has been sought and given cannot be disclosed;[38] a convention which is included in the current Ministerial Code.[39] There is also a debate about whether the consent of the AG is required before advice can be disclosed, or whether the minister in receipt of legal advice can disclose it without such consent.[40] Despite the convention contained in the Ministerial Guide, legal advice has been disclosed in a handful of exceptional circumstances.[41]

### Ireland

As in the United Kingdom, the advice of the Irish AG is rarely released for parliamentarians to assess and scrutinise. In contrast, the *fact* of the advice – that the AG has advised that some policy is constitutional or not – is often

---

[34] See Robert Post and Reve Siegel, 'Popular Constitutionalism, Departmentalism and Judicial Supremacy' (2004) 94 *California Law Review* 1027–44.
[35] Kenny and Casey, 'A One Person Supreme Court?', p. 96.
[36] Legal advice to government is covered by the exemption for legal professional privilege in s. 42 of the Freedom of Information Act 2000.
[37] K. A. Kyriakides, 'The Advisory Functions of the Attorney-General' (2003) 1 *Hertfordshire Law Journal* 73–94, p. 76.
[38] Jones, 'The Office of Attorney-General', p. 48.
[39] *Ministerial Code* (London: Cabinet Office, 2019), para. 2.13.
[40] Matthew Windsor, 'Government Legal Advisers through the Ethics Looking Glass' in David Feldman (ed.), *Law in Politics, Politics in Law* (London: Bloomsbury, 2015), p. 133.
[41] Yong, *Government Lawyers and the Provision of Legal Advice within Whitehall*, p. 62.

disclosed if an issue is politically controversial and questioned in Parliament. The opinion of governments on the publication of the AG's advice has clearly hardened in recent years, and the convention which was that the advice is not generally published has become that it can never be published. In 2011, then Taoiseach Enda Kenny stated to the Dáil he was not considering any change to the current practice of not publishing AG's advice, and noted he could not personally recall an instance where advice had been published.[42] In 2018, when publishing a short précis of the AG's advice on the wording of the abortion referendum, then Taoiseach Leo Varadkar described the move as 'unprecedented'.[43] The comments of these former Taoisigh implicitly reflect the high levels of confidentiality the government maintains over advice.

But it would be incorrect to state that AG's advice has *never* been published, given that advice of the AG *was* published on several occasions when it suited the government to do so, even on issues of high political controversy such as the wording of the 1983 abortion referendum proposal.[44] It is thus more accurate to say that advice is published by the executive when it is most politically expedient to do so.[45] Irish officials' general attitude of confidentiality towards legal advice has several effects, the main one being that parliamentarians and the public cannot assess the cogency and quality of the AG's advice, nor the sincerity of the government's stated reliance on it.[46]

## IMPACT ON EXECUTIVE POWER

### Legal Advice Important to Political Credibility and Legitimacy

Legal advice is deeply embedded in the policy-making process of the two systems considered here. One consequence of this is that the work of executive lawyers can have a real impact on the scope of executive discretion, potentially directing executive actors away from courses of action they might otherwise consider more politically expedient, wise, or lawful.[47] This raises important questions about the incentives driving the executive to structure policymaking in a manner which binds its political discretion and ability to achieve its

---

[42] Dáil Éireann Debate, 31st Dáil, vol. 732, no. 4, 18 May 2011.
[43] Kenny and Casey, 'A One Person Supreme Court?', pp. 89–118.
[44] See David Kenny and Conor Casey, 'Shadow Constitutional Review: The Dark-Side of Political Pre-Enactment Review in Ireland and Japan' (2020) 18 *International Journal of Constitutional Law* 51–77, p. 65.
[45] For examples see Casey, *The Irish Law Officers*, pp. 120–40.
[46] Ruadhan MacCormaic, *The Supreme Court* (Dublin: Penguin Books, 2016), p. 7.
[47] Daintith and Page, *The Executive in the Constitution*, pp. 306–7.

substantive goals. In other words, why would the executive bind itself to the work of executive legal advisors at all?

The importance of executive lawyers to policymaking in these systems is undoubtedly partly linked to the fact governments wish to avoid the costs of political embarrassment and disruption that might come with judicial invalidation or rebuke.[48] Its importance is also linked to the connection between legality and political legitimacy in constitutional democracies. The fact of commitment to legality by political actors like 'voters, officials, political parties, interest groups, and social movements'[49] has strong political and social force, which limits the bounds of executive discretion.[50] Consider, for example, recent political anger that followed rumours the UK government would not request an extension to the Brexit withdrawal from the European Council as stipulated in the European Union (Withdrawal) (No. 2) Act 2019, an Act the passage of which was fiercely opposed by the government.[51] Backbenchers and opposition MPs warned of immediate impeachment proceedings if the statutory directive was not followed, a warning that emerged immediately after the mere suggestion the government might take a course of illegality.[52]

Whether one thinks it a positive or negative development, in the United Kingdom and Ireland it is clear that 'law and legality are now ever-present considerations in the policy and decision-making process. Government cannot escape from the reach of the law – if it ever could.'[53] The public revelation that an executive official adopted a contentious policy decision contrary to legal advice, or without seeking advice in the first instance, would very likely invite political backlash for showing insufficient respect for legal constraints and the rule of law.[54] The explosive political fall out from the Chilcott Inquiry and the allegation the executive tried to circumvent Attorney General Goldsmith's initial legal advice on the illegality of invading Iraq is a good

[48] Kenny and Casey, 'Shadow Constitutional Review', p. 54.
[49] See Eric A. Posner and Adrian Vermeule, 'Demystifying Schmitt' in Jens Meierhenrich and Oliver Simons (eds.), *The Oxford Handbook of Carl Schmitt* (Oxford University Press, 2016), p. 165.
[50] Aziz Huq, 'Binding the Executive (by Law or by Politics)' (2012) 79 *University of Chicago Law Review* 777–836, p. 807.
[51] Oliver Garner 'The Benn-Burt Extension Act: A roadblock to a No-deal Brexit?' UK Constitutional Law Blog, 13 September 2019, https://ukconstitutionallaw.org/2019/09/13/oliver-garner-the-benn-burt-extension-act-a-roadblock-to-a-no-deal-brexit/.
[52] 'Brexit extension: 'Impeach Boris Johnson if law ignored' BBC News website, 9 September 2019, www.bbc.co.uk/news/uk-wales-politics-49628435.
[53] Yong, *Government Lawyers and the Provision of Legal Advice within Whitehall*, p. 94.
[54] Daintith and Page, *The Executive in the Constitution*, p. 302; Barry K. Winetrobe, 'Legal Advice and Representation for Parliament', p. 99.

example of the fact that, even if legal constraints *can* be ignored or circumvented, such action will come at immense cost to political credibility and reputation when revealed.[55] There are thus clear incentives for executive actors to seek advice from their advisors, particularly on contentious issues, to guard against the negative political consequences of perceived illegality.[56] Moreover, and perhaps more significantly, the normative force accorded to legality and commitment to the rule of law more generally means that executive officials are also likely to have internalised the view that the law must be taken very seriously as an aspect of political morality.[57] The rarity of reported cases of governments deliberately acting contrary to legal advice might suggest the existence of an overwhelming expectation that clear legal advice will be followed, and that to do otherwise would be offensive to core values of political morality in each system.[58]

Theresa May's failed attempt to secure parliamentary approval for her draft Withdrawal Agreement with the EU provides a vivid case study of the potent effect legal advice can have, and of how dedication to legality is not limited to issues of low political salience. The draft Withdrawal Agreement encountered parliamentary resistance partly due to a fear that elements of the agreement would be immensely difficult to disengage from, if the EU and United Kingdom were unable to negotiate a permanent agreement for their prospective relationship. In particular, the Northern Ireland protocol (or 'backstop') caused considerable consternation amongst influential backbenchers in her own party, her Democratic Unionist Party confidence and supply partners, and members of the opposition.[59]

Legal advice given by Attorney General Geoffrey Cox in respect of the backstop arrangement gave little reassurance in respect of such concerns. The AG's interpretation was that if the United Kingdom and EU simply could not conclude a future trade deal, which would prevent the backstop from coming into effect, then the United Kingdom would have no lawful means of exiting the backstop unilaterally under international law.[60] In March 2019, the government agreed several additional instruments and declarations with the EU

---

[55] James Blitz, 'Why the attorney-general will matter on Brexit', *Financial Times*, 26 October, 2018, www.ft.com/content/813612fe-d914-11e8-ab8e-6beodcf18713.
[56] Daintith and Page, *The Executive in the Constitution*, p. 302.
[57] Daphna Renan, 'Presidential Norms and Article II' (2018) 131 *Harvard Law Review* 2187–282, p. 2199.
[58] Daintith and Page, *The Executive in the Constitution*, p. 328.
[59] See 'The UK's EU Withdrawal Agreement' HC Research Briefing Paper No. 08453 (11 April 2019).
[60] Geoffrey Cox AG, 'Legal Effect of the Protocol on Ireland/Northern Ireland', Attorney General's Office, 13 November 2018.

to assuage concern that the backstop would endure indefinitely, with a clear hope the AG might alter his legal advice accordingly. However, despite these additions, the AG stated that the Protocol on Ireland/Northern Ireland still could not be legally unilaterally terminated by the United Kingdom save in very limited circumstances.[61] AG Cox's advice on the protocol and its international law implications clearly proved a major obstacle to May's ability to gain support for the agreement. Parliamentarians from the opposition benches, her confidence and supply partners, and her own party all explicitly cited the legal risk identified in the advice as a reason to reject the agreement.[62] The prime minister could no doubt have replaced the AG and forum shopped for legal advice until a more helpfully permissive legal opinion was found, harmonising the law with the executive's preferred policy outcome. But this course of action would clearly have left her open to severe political criticism on the basis that such a manoeuvre represented a cynical circumvention of legal constraints.

But legal advice does not just limit the scope of executive policy discretion. It can be used by governments to build political narratives which help legitimise their policy positions. For a start, even if legal advice does not always favour the executive's preferred course of action, the *fact* that the executive's policies are consistently subject to legal review can provide a source of critical political credibility.[63] Such credibility is central to effective use of executive power as, without it, the executive's ability to employ its authority is impaired and might receive public, legislative, or judicial pushback.[64] The work of executive lawyers builds this credibility, and the executive commitment to binding itself to its legal advisors' articulation of legality constitutes a form of 'reputation-building'.[65] Binding itself to legal advice signals to other political actors that the executive is committed to acting in accordance with law, and is willing to sacrifice some freedom of action to do this. While elite actors, political opponents, or the electorate might viscerally dispute a government policy on ethical or moral grounds, they cannot as easily attack it on legal or constitutional grounds if a perception exists that it has undergone robust and detached scrutiny for compliance with legality. This is particularly the case

---

[61] Geoffrey Cox AG, 'Legal Opinion on Joint Instrument and Unilateral Declaration concerning the Withdrawal Agreement', Attorney General's Office, 12 March 2019, para. 19.
[62] Rowena Mason and Rajeev Syal, 'ERG signals it could back May's Brexit deal if legal advice is clearer', *Guardian*, 13 March 2019, www.theguardian.com/politics/2019/mar/13/erg-signals-it-could-back-may-brexit-deal-legal-advice-is-clearer.
[63] Richard Pildes, 'Law and the President' (2012) 125 *Harvard Law Review* 1389–1424, p. 1390.
[64] Adrian Vermuele and Eric A. Posner, 'The Credible Executive' (2007) 74 *University of Chicago Law Review* 865–913, p. 913.
[65] Daphna Renan, 'The Law Presidents Make' (2017) 103 *Virginia Law Review* 805–904, p. 818.

when advice is not published, and its cogency cannot be assessed in depth. In this section, I offer several examples in the United Kingdom and Ireland which I argue highlight how the government can lean on executive legal advice to build political narratives which help bolster the legitimacy of controversial policy positions.

### Use of Legal Advice to Legitimise Executive Action in United Kingdom

As noted above, the importance of legal advice to executive policymaking can impact upon the resolution of policy issues of high salience to the political executive. A notable recent example of governments explicitly leaning on legal advice to help legitimate intensely controversial political decisions can be seen over the course of several debates over the use of armed force. For example, the importance of legality to the executive's political credibility can be discerned in the now well-trodden controversy surrounding the advice outlined by Attorney General Lord Goldsmith on the legality of the 2003 British invasion of Iraq. As is well documented, intense debate raged over whether the AG was placed under political pressure by senior executive figures to give legal advice helpful to the government's intention to invade Iraq.[66] Prior to invasion, it was widely accepted within UK political circles that the AG's legal clearance would be required before military force could be deployed.[67] Indeed, Prime Minister Blair himself stated during his testimony to the Iraq Inquiry that it was 'absolutely clear' that if the AG 'in the end had said, "This cannot be justified lawfully", we would have been unable to take action'.[68] The AG's advice that there was a reasonable case for invading Iraq was thus crucial to the government's attempt to legitimise its immensely controversial decision.[69]

Since the conflict in Iraq, the executive has on several subsequent occasions heavily relied on advice given to it by the AG to anchor the political legitimacy

---

[66] Robert Verkaik, 'Goldsmith under pressure from legal profession over impartiality' Independent, 29 April 2005, www.independent.co.uk/news/uk/crime/goldsmith-under-pressure-from-legal-profession-over-impartiality-3903.html.
[67] Matthew Windsor, 'The Special Responsibility of Government Lawyers and the Iraq Inquiry' (2016) 87 The British Yearbook of International Law 159–76, p. 161.
[68] Transcript of evidence given by the Rt Hon Tony Blair, National Archives, 29 January 2010, p. 150, https://webarchive.nationalarchives.gov.uk/20171123123234/http://www.iraqinquiry.org.uk/the-evidence/witnesses/b/rt-hon-tony-blair/.
[69] Rebecca Moosavian and Conall Mallory, 'How Tony Blair, Jack Straw and Lord Goldsmith come out of the Chilcot Report', The Conversation, 19 July 2016, https://theconversation.com/how-tony-blair-jack-straw-and-lord-goldsmith-come-out-of-the-chilcot-report-62252.

of armed action, advice which involved invocation of 'almost every conceivable legal justification for the use of force'.[70] For instance, in November 2015, then Prime Minister David Cameron sought parliamentary support for extending airstrikes into ISIS held territory in Syria. Prominent amongst his justifications for military action was that intervention had a strong legal, as well as moral, basis.[71] The prime minister explicitly told MPs he had been advised there was no barrier in international law to extending the United Kingdom's support for the Iraqi government against ISIS into Syria,[72] being at pains to argue the government had a clear legal basis for military action founded on the right of self-defence recognised in Art. 51 of the United Nations Charter.[73] However, in response to calls for the government to publish the advice in full, the prime minister pointed to long-standing convention that legal advice given by Law Officers to the government was not disclosed publicly.[74]

Around the same time, it emerged that the executive authorised a lethal drone-strike on a UK citizen fighting with ISIS. In a statement to the Commons, then Prime Minister Cameron said he 'had been killed in an act of self-defence, to protect the British people from a direct threat of terrorist attacks being plotted and directed'.[75] The prime minister argued that under Art. 51 of the UN Charter, the drone strike was legal as an imminent necessity to prevent an attack against the United Kingdom. The prime minister leaned on the AG's advice that there was a clear legal basis in international law, namely the United Kingdom's inherent right to take necessary and proportionate action to defend itself against terrorist attack.[76] The AG declined, however, to disclose to a parliamentary committee the legal test that had been applied when advising that there was a clear legal basis for the drone strike.[77] Despite the fact the 'limits of self-defence against a terrorist group under international law are contested and difficult to fulfil' and that

---

[70] Colin Murray and Aoife O'Donoghue, 'Toward Unilateralism? House of Commons Oversight of the Use of Force' (2016) 65 *International and Comparative Law Quarterly* 305–41, p. 306; Windsor, 'The Special Responsibility of Government Lawyers', p. 3.

[71] Prime Minister's Office, 'Memorandum to the Foreign Affairs Select Committee Prime Minister's Response to the Foreign Affairs Select Committee's Second Report of Session 2015–16: The Extension of Offensive British Military Operations to Syria', November 2015, pp. 5–17.

[72] Murray and O'Donoghue, 'Toward Unilateralism?', p. 334.

[73] *Hansard*, HC, cols. 1489–94, 26 November 2015.

[74] Murray and O'Donoghue, 'Toward Unilateralism?', p. 339.

[75] UK Parliament Joint Committee on Human Rights, 'The Government's policy on the use of drones for targeted killing' (2nd Report of Session 2015–16) HL Paper 141 HC 574, para. 1.3.

[76] Murray and O'Donoghue, 'Toward Unilateralism?', p. 335.

[77] Joint Committee on Human Rights, 'The Government's policy on the use of drones for targeted killing', para. 3.12.

parliamentary oversight of such 'claims is all but impossible' without access to legal advice, the AG's advice remained withheld.[78]

Following the use of chemical weapons by Syrian Armed Forces against civilians in 2018, the United Kingdom participated in deterrent retaliatory strikes alongside France and the United States. Prime Minister Theresa May responded to critique of her failure to seek parliamentary approval by insisting the action was 'moral and legal'[79] and swiftly released a brief summary of the legal position justifying the strikes.[80] But again, a full legal opinion was not forthcoming for scrutiny by parliament or the public despite the AG's advice on legality being central to political argument over the rights and wrongs of military action.[81]

Some commentators argue that the legal justifications proffered in these instances, insofar as they could be criticised in the absence of disclosure of full legal advice, were based on 'legally dubious ... doctrines',[82] which merely clothed contentious executive action in a cloak of 'superficially impressive legalese'.[83] Whatever the merits of the advice, what is important for the purposes of this chapter is that legal advice can be used by government to try and legitimise controversial decisions in the eyes of political actors and the public, alongside more openly moral arguments about executive action.

## Use of Legal Advice to Legitimise Executive Action in Ireland

Similar examples of the government using executive legal advice to help legitimise controversial political positions can also be found in Ireland. Between 2011–2016, the then Fine Gael/Labour Coalition government faced several calls by factions in the Oireachtas and pro-choice advocacy groups to allow a fatal foetal abnormality exception to Ireland's then strict abortion regime. On each occasion, the government reported that the AG had advised any such move would be unconstitutional by virtue of Art. 40.3.3.[84] In 2015, then Minister for Health Leo Varadkar, went so far as to state that the fact of

---

[78] Murray and O'Donoghue, 'Toward Unilateralism?', p. 335.
[79] 'Syria air strikes: Theresa May says action 'moral and legal', BBC News website, 16 April 2018, www.bbc.co.uk/news/uk-politics-43775728.
[80] Prime Minister's Office, 'Syria action – UK government legal position', 14 April 2018.
[81] 'Syria air strikes: UK publishes legal case for military action', BBC News website, 14 April 2018, www.bbc.co.uk/news/uk-43770102.
[82] Murray and O'Donoghue, 'Toward Unilateralism?', p. 340.
[83] Murray and O'Donoghue, 'Toward Unilateralism?', p. 306.
[84] Michael O'Regan, 'Government defeats Daly's abortion Bill with big majority', *Irish Times*, 10 February 2015, www.irishtimes.com/news/politics/oireachtas/government-defeats-daly-s-abortion-bill-with-big-majority-1.2099035.

the matter was that the government *could not* introduce any legislation to the Oireachtas if the AG had advised it was unconstitutional, effectively turning her advice into an ex ante binding rule of law.[85] Members of the socially liberal Labour Party, who had long campaigned for liberalising Ireland's abortion regime, were whipped to vote *against the bill* based on this advice.[86] The AG's unpublished opinion on the measure's illegality was liberally deployed by the government to help justify the legitimacy of effectively ending debate on the possibility of legislative reform of abortion law, one of Ireland's most volatile political issues at the time.[87]

Between 2011 and 2020, the then Fine Gael/Labour Coalition and Fine Gael minority administrations also faced a deepening homelessness crisis. Both received criticism for their alleged lack of robust action. On several occasions, the government claimed to face very severe limitations on legislative action due to the AG's advice on constitutional property rights. The government asserted that several backbencher proposals to tackle the growing housing and homelessness crisis, from rent freezes to greater protections against eviction, were all stymied by the AG's advice.[88] The AG's stated position on many of these proposals has been hotly contested on the basis that under Supreme Court precedent, property rights can be highly qualified in the interests of the common good and social justice.[89]

As the advice was not published, the cogency of the AG's reasoning, or how the government portrayed the AG's reasoning, could not be assessed. Some commentators suggested that the AG may have given highly cautious advice based on a conservative reading of judicial precedent.[90] Others speculated that the executive could have *presented* the AG's advice in an overly cautious manner to provide favourable legal cover for what was, in reality, ideological preference for market-based solutions to the housing crisis and an unwillingness to undertake aggressive state action.[91] The most persuasive reading of

---

[85] Dáil Éireann Debate, 31st Dáil, vol. 886, no.4, 6 February 2015.
[86] Lucinda Creighton, 'Why an attorney general's advice should be public: Governments should not use secret legal advice as an excuse for policy U-turns' *Irish Times*, 6 April 2015, www.irishtimes.com/opinion/lucinda-creighton-why-most-attorney-general-advice-needs-to-be-made-public-1.2165942.
[87] Fiona DeLondras, 'Fatal Foetal Abnormality, Irish Constitutional Law, and Mellet v Ireland' (2016) 24 *Medical Law Review* 591–607, p. 598.
[88] See Kenny and Casey, 'Shadow Constitutional Review', p. 67.
[89] Gerard Hogan, Gerard Whyte, David Kenny and Rachael Walsh, *Kelly: The Irish Constitution* (Dublin: Bloomsbury Professional, 5th edn., 2018), p. xvii.
[90] Rachael Walsh, 'Opinion on the Implications of Constitutional Property Rights for Responses to the Housing Crisis', Academia, www.academia.edu/41273377/Opinion_on_the_Implications_of_Constitutional_Property_Rights_for_Responses_to_the_Housing_Crisis.
[91] Kenny and Casey, 'Shadow Constitutional Review', p. 51.

case-law and leading academic commentary undoubtedly suggested that there was ample scope to pursue many of the measures rejected by government.[92] Despite this, the AG's unpublished advice was repeatedly used by the executive to bolster the political legitimacy of its policy inaction, while simultaneously undercutting the legitimacy of rejected opposition policies on the basis that they were unconstitutional.[93]

Irish governments have also recently relied on the advice of the AG to justify controversial positions which embraced a wide conception of executive power.[94] One example came to light after a revealing exchange in late 2019, when then Taoiseach Leo Varadkar told the Dáil it would not be appropriate to issue a 'money message' for a private members bill pursuant to Art. 17.2 of the constitution,[95] if he was advised by the AG that the bill was unconstitutional, or contrary to European law or to any international treaties.[96] Article 17 provides that only the executive may introduce a bill of financial significance, but certainly does not envisage the entire sweep of the Oireachtas' law-making function being conditional on the executive's views on a bill's legality.[97] This interpretation effectively provides the executive with a veto authority over which private members bills receive a money message, and thus continue to proceed through the legislative process. This interpretation, and the authority it vests in the executive and AG, is striking because it is clearly beyond the textual scope or purpose of Art. 17.2, which was never intended to vest a generic veto over the legislative activity of the Oireachtas in the executive and the AG.[98]

---

[92] Hogan, Whyte, Kenny and Walsh, *Kelly: The Irish Constitution* p. xvii.
[93] David Kenny and Conor Casey, 'The Resilience of Executive Dominance in Westminster Systems: Ireland 2016–2019' (2021) *Public Law* (forthcoming).
[94] Eoin Daly, 'Reappraising judicial supremacy in the Irish constitutional tradition', in Hickey, Cahillane and Gallen (eds.), *Judges, Politics and the Irish Constitution* (Manchester: Manchester University Press, 2017), p. 40.
[95] Article 17.2 provides that 'no law shall be enacted, for the appropriation of revenue or other public moneys unless the purpose of the appropriation shall have been recommended to Dáil Éireann by a message from the Government signed by the Taoiseach'. This means that laws of significant financial consequence can be enacted unless the purpose of the law is consented to by the Taoiseach.
[96] Dáil Éireann Debate, 32nd Dáil, vol. 990, no. 5, 4 December 2019.
[97] See David Kenny and Eoin Daly, 'Opinion on the Constitutional Limits of the "Money Message" Procedure under Article 17.2 of the Constitution of Ireland', May 2019, Academia, www.academia.edu/40448056/Opinion_on_the_Constitutional_Limits_of_the_Money_Message_Procedure_under_Article_17.2_of_the_Constitution_of_Ireland.
[98] Kenny and Casey, 'A One Person Supreme Court?', p. 104; Walsh, 'Opinion on the Implications of Constitutional Property Rights'; Gerard Hogan, Gerry Whyte, David Kenny and Rachel Walsh, *Kelly: The Irish Constitution* (Dublin: Bloomsbury Professional, 5th edn., 2018) p. xvii.

Perhaps a starker example came during the 2020 general election. While the polling date was set for 8 February 2020, uncertainty emerged following the sudden death of a candidate in the Tipperary constituency. Section 62 of the Electoral Act 1992 provides that in such circumstances, 'all acts done in connection with the election (other than the nomination of the surviving candidates) are void and that a fresh election will be held'. On foot of this provision, the returning officer for the constituency postponed the polling date. However, Art. 16.3.2 of the constitution states that a general election must be held not later than thirty days after the dissolution of the Dáil. Applying the 1992 Act and restarting the electoral process in Tipperary, would take the poll outside that time period. Evidently concerned that postponement of the poll could leave the whole election open to challenge as a breach of Art. 16.3.2, the government issued a 'special difficulty order' purporting to suspend operation of s. 62 and allow the poll to continue in early February. The government justified the legitimacy of this decision by citing the advice of the AG, who seemingly advised that, contrary to clear legislative provision in s. 62, the poll should go ahead on the basis that suspending it was unconstitutional having regard to 16.3.2.

Even if s. 62 is of dubious constitutionality, the government's actions represented an unprecedented exercise of executive authority.[99] The government and AG are, of course, entitled to hold the view that a given statutory provision is unconstitutional. But the constitution explicitly vests the power to invalidate unconstitutional laws in the Superior Courts, and it is a bedrock tenet of the Irish constitutional order that the executive cannot suspend a duly enacted statute, whether through its Art. 28 executive power,[100] or by relying on a statutory administrative power.[101] In order to justify its actions, which involved an unusually broad assertion of executive authority, the legitimating quality of AG's advice was again critical, and heavily leaned on by the government.[102] An alternative, and less contentious approach, would have been for the AG to apply to the High Court in his capacity as guardian of the public interest to secure an injunction in relation to the objection, and possibly allow the Superior Courts to assess the constitutionality of s. 62.

---

[99] Gerard Hogan and Hilary Hogan, 'Legal and Constitutional Issues Emerging from the 2020 General Election' (2020) 63 *Irish Jurist* 113–42, p. 116.
[100] Conor Casey, 'Underexplored Corners: Inherent Executive Power in the Irish Constitutional Order' (2017) 40 *Dublin University Law Journal* 1–36, p. 28.
[101] Hogan, Whyte, Kenny and Walsh, *Kelly: The Irish Constitution*, para. 4.2.27.
[102] Kenny and Casey, 'The Resilience of Executive Dominance'.

## CONCLUSION

I suggest the above examples show how legal advice is used by UK and Irish executives to increase the perceived political legitimacy of controversial policy positions – sometimes just as much as openly ethical or moral arguments. This has been the case even where the AG's arguments in favour of the executive appeared, from what information was available, stretched or strained in light of the 'best view' of the demands of constitutional or international law as assessed by an independent judicial tribunal.[103] The executive's use of legal advice as a tool of legitimisation, I suggest, is linked to what the professional work of executive lawyers represents in each system – dedication and respect for the rule of law and its boundaries – which remain critically important for maintaining legitimacy in constitutional democracies.[104] Any political actor can *assert* that a policy they wish to undertake is perfectly lawful, or one that they do not wish to take is unlawful, but the legitimising force legal advice has in the eyes of political actors and the public comes from the fact lawyers are understood to be articulating the bounds of what the law allows, 'using tools of professional legal craft and expertise' which insulate them from partisan political pressures.[105]

But as the advice is frequently highly confidential it can be hard to know if the executive in each system is ever using it as dubious legalistic cover. Hard to know, for example, whether an executive lawyer has allowed ideological loyalty or political pressure to cloud independence, or whether advice has been exaggerated to present a legal position as firm, when it is in fact equivocal. In either case, the result could be a substantial bolstering of the executive's position through the use of contestable legal advice; allowing the executive to deploy the 'technicalities of legal discourse' to place a 'seal of legitimacy' on political decisions.[106]

### *Executive Lawyers and Political Choices*

Executive lawyers clearly play an important, yet relatively overlooked, role in relation to exercises of public power by the executive. In this final section

---

[103] Jack Goldsmith contrasts two different approaches that executive lawyers in the USA have taken to legal interpretation. One, which carries an 'obligation neutrally to interpret the law as seriously as a court' would, he calls the 'best view'. This approach can be contrasted with the 'reasonable legal position' approach which requires less – that a legal argument merely be plausible and taken in good faith. Jack Goldsmith, 'Executive Branch Crisis Lawyering and the "Best View" of the Law' (2018) 31 *The Georgetown Journal of Legal Ethics* 261–76, p. 263.
[104] See Aziz Huq, 'Binding the Executive'.
[105] Kenny and Casey, 'Shadow Constitutional Review', p. 63.
[106] Tanja Aalberts and Lianne Boer, 'Entering the Invisible College: Defeating Lawyers on their Own Turf (2018) 87 *The British Yearbook of International Law* 177–95, p. 193.

I would like to set down some potential avenues for further exploration. I suggest that, in any assessment of the overall impact of the work of executive lawyers on executive power and policymaking, we must take into account the fact that they are not an exogenous constraint imposed on the executive, but a mechanism which can be structured in a manner most suitable to it. To conclude, I offer two brief examples of structural choices which deserve greater exploration from public law scholarship: control over the disclosure of legal advice and the norms influencing the appointment of personnel.

### Non-Disclosure Useful to Executive

The UK and Irish governments exercise high levels of informational control over the legal advice they receive. The advantage for the executive of opting for high levels of control over disclosure appears to be that it can hamstring legality-based critiques of its agenda and policy positions. This is because the near-blanket insistence on non-disclosure of legal advice, or the provision of only a minimalist summary of advice, clearly narrows scope for parliamentary or popular scrutiny. If the substantive legal basis for asserting legal compliance or non-compliance were published, it could open avenues for greater scrutiny of controversial government policies, particularly those explicitly tied to contestable assessments of the Law Officers.[107] As Renan observes, if the assessment is contestable (as many legal issues invariably will be), disclosure can create 'controversy, distract from other priorities, or put ... policies at risk'.[108]

Consider, for example, the political backdrop to the recent UK Supreme Court judgment in *The UK Withdrawal From the European Union (Legal Continuity) (Scotland) Bill – A Reference by the Attorney General and the Advocate General for Scotland* case.[109] In February 2018, the Scottish Government introduced the UK Withdrawal from the European Union (Legal Continuity) (Scotland) Bill to the Scottish Parliament. The bill largely mirrored the analogous Withdrawal Bill before the UK Parliament, but differed on several points which Holyrood took issue with. One disagreement was over the precise way in which EU law would continue to have effect in Scotland and the procedures governing the manner in which ministers could make regulations to modify EU law following Brexit. Under the Scotland Act 1998, all bills must be accompanied by a statement from the relevant sponsoring minister that

---

[107] Ben Yong, Greg Davies and Cristina Leston-Bandeira 'Tacticians, Stewards, and Professionals: The Politics of Publishing Select Committee Legal Advice' (2019) *Journal of Law & Society* 367–95, p. 371.
[108] Daphna Reena, 'The Law Presidents Make', p. 805.
[109] [2018] UKSC 64. I thank Aileen McHarg for bringing this case to my attention.

they are within the legislative competence of the Scottish Parliament. The Presiding Officer of the Scottish Parliament must also to issue a certificate stating whether the bill is within the Parliament's competence. In this instance, debate broke out between these actors about whether the bill was within devolved competence. The Scottish government's chief legal advisor – the Lord Advocate – published a statement to the Scottish Parliament outlining his legal position that the bill was not incompatible; whereas the Presiding Officer published a contrary statement suggesting it was ultra vires.

The fact that both conflicting legal opinions and their rationales were publicly available, and hence subject to scrutiny, made it easier for the UK government not to accept the assessment of the Lord Advocate and simply give their 'devolution counterparts the benefit of the doubt' on the bill's legality.[110] Instead, the UK government and its Law Officers were able to scrutinise the legal advice, and the latter were then able present their own conflicting legal position, which served as justification for exercising discretion pursuant to s. 33(1) Scotland Act 1998 to refer the question of legislative competence to the UK Supreme Court.[111] This 'nuclear'[112] option had not been employed by the UK Law Officers hitherto, and was undoubtedly facilitated by their ability to scrutinise the basis for their Scottish counterparts' position on legislative competence. From the Law Officers' perspective, this position was ultra vires for touching upon international relations and upsetting the 'constitutional framework underpinning the devolution settlement'.[113] In the end, the arguments of the UK Law Officers were almost entirely rejected by the Supreme Court. But merits of the conflicting opinions aside, the disclosure of legal advice in this context expanded scope for debate about its legal cogency and accordingly, the policy it underpinned. This same debate would not have been possible if the legal advice remained behind a veil of confidentiality.[114]

---

[110] Christopher McCorkindale and Aileen McHarg 'Continuity and Confusion: Legislating for Brexit in Scotland and Wales (Part II)', UK Constitutional Law Blog, 7 March 2018, https://ukconstitutionallaw.org/2018/03/07/christopher-mccorkindale-and-aileen-mcharg-continuity-and-confusion-legislating-for-brexit-in-scotland-and-wales-part-ii/.

[111] McCorkindale and McHarg, 'Continuity and Confusion'.

[112] Ibid

[113] [2018] UKSC 64 at para. 25; Christopher McCorkindale and Aileen McHarg, 'Continuity and Confusion: Towards Clarity? – The Supreme Court and the Scottish Continuity Bill', UK Constitutional Law Blog, 20 December 2018, https://ukconstitutionallaw.org/2018/12/20/chris-mccorkindale-and-aileen-mcharg-continuity-and-confusion-towards-clarity-the-supreme-court-and-the-scottish-continuity-bill/.

[114] Chris McCorkindale and Janet Hiebert, 'Vetting Bills in the Scottish Parliament for Legislative Competence' (2017) 21 *Edinburgh Law Review* 319–51, p. 329.

The general ability of the executive to control and structure the extent, form, manner, and timing of disclosure of advice thus seems to be a potentially powerful political tool. It opens up space for legal advice to be leaned on by the executive to pursue and legitimise political aims, secure in the knowledge that in the vast majority of circumstances, it will remain immune from contestation. Conversely, as Goldsmith has argued in the context of the United States, the semi-regular publication of executive legal advice has been essential in helping the press, the academy, and legislature scrutinise legal advice for 'accuracy, persuasion, and consistency' and to criticise and 'possibly correct self-serving or mistaken or excessive interpretations'.[115] Further research from a comparative perspective is necessary to probe whether increased transparency and disclosure of legal advice help, as Goldsmith suggests, to deter possible misrepresentation of legal advice by the executive, or the provision of political motivated and legally dubious advice by its lawyers.

## Norms Governing Appointment

The norms underpinning the executive's appointment of its leading lawyers, and an appointee's self-understanding of their constitutional role, are also likely to be of relevance to questions of the overall impact of executive legal advice. The overview of the work of the Law Officers presented in this essay justifies the observation that the role of the executive legal advisor in the UK and Ireland is characterised by an institutional tension between being both an ideologically sympathetic political appointee and an impartial legal advisor. This institutional tension raises several questions worthy of further research from a comparative perspective. For example, does it make a sizeable difference to the impact of legal advice on executive authority whether advisors are appointed more for their ideological compatibility than technocratic competence? In both Ireland and the United Kingdom, only the Law Officers themselves are appointed on an explicitly political basis and they lead a team of career civil servants who serve across different political administrations. In the United States, however, the Office of Legal Counsel (OLC) is mostly staffed by political appointees who vacate office upon the appointment of a new president. A frequent complaint levelled at OLC lawyers by many commentators is that their work is excessively clouded by political ideology. Indeed, some go as far as accusing the OLC of enabling 'plebiscitary

---

[115] Jack Goldsmith, 'The Irrelevance of Prerogative Power and the Evils of Secret Legal Interpretation' in Clement Fatovic and Benjamin Kleinman (eds.), *Extralegal Power and Legitimacy: Perspectives on Prerogative* (Oxford: Oxford University Press, 2013) p. 228.

Caesarism' by providing undeserved legal cover for aggressive claims of executive power behind the legitimacy of the constitution.[116] Do explicitly political appointees have more of an empowering impact than those appointed more for the perceived mastery of legal craft? Are highly politicised executive lawyers an important component in facilitating 'executive aggrandisement' in established constitutional democracies?[117]

Conversely, do systems where the appointment of apex executive lawyers is expected to be technocratic and independent of political considerations – as with the Japanese Cabinet Legislation Bureau for example[118] – help rein in more exuberant assertions of executive authority? It is also worth asking whether a highly technocratic model, where lawyers only sanction as lawful policies consistent with the 'best' view of the law a court might reach, risks developing its own pathologies. To paraphrase a question recently posed by Appleby and Olijnyk: does this kind of system lead to an inappropriately 'constitutionally conservative' approach to policy development which risks 'constitutional – and potentially social – stagnation'?[119]

Further comparative study might show that, depending on what norms underpin their appointment, executive lawyers are more likely to operate either as a legalistic brake, or a constitutional accelerator for executive power. Indeed, depending on the conventions, norms, and structure within which they operate, executive lawyers may take on wildly different roles, from Machiavellian counsellors and hired guns moving mountains to provide executive policy proposals with a shield of legal legitimacy, on the one hand, to the conscience of the administrator tasked with 'speaking law to power' and denying the executive flimsy legal justification to shore up the legitimacy of its policies, on the other.[120] Whatever the ultimate answer, given their impact on the allocation and use of public power, these questions seem worthy of further engagement from a domestic and comparative perspective.

---

[116] Gerhard Casper, 'Caesarism in Democratic Politics: Reflections on Max Weber', Robert G. Wesson Lecture in International Relations Theory and Practice, The Freeman Spogli Institute for International Studies at Stanford University, 13 March 2007, p. 23.

[117] See Tarunabh Khaitan, 'Executive aggrandizement in established democracies: A crisis of liberal democratic constitutionalism' (2019) 17 *International Journal of Constitutional Law* 342–56.

[118] See Hajime Yamamoto, 'Interpretation of the Pacifist Article of the Constitution by the Bureau of Cabinet Legislation: A New Source of Constitutional Law' (2017) 22 *Washington International Law Journal* 99–125, p. 111.

[119] Gabrielle Appleby and Anna Olijnyk, 'Executive Policy Development and Constitutional Norms: Practice and Perceptions' (2020) *International Journal of Constitutional Law* (forthcoming) 1–34, p. 8.

[120] Windsor, 'Government Legal Advisers', p. 117.

# 14

# In Search of the Constitution

## Martin Loughlin

### INTRODUCTION

Who nowadays would dare to write about 'the great juggle' of the constitution? No longer is it possible to follow the traditional method of steering a steady course between expounding and eulogising.[1] Today, the virtues of the constitution's continuity cannot be extolled without admitting the value of continuous change.[2] Nor can one celebrate its pageantry without acknowledging power politics.[3] A century ago, Sir Maurice Amos could proclaim that of all the achievements of more than a thousand years of English civilisation, 'none is a more proper subject for national pride than our living tradition of constitutional government'. True to his name, Amos confidently prophesied 'that when the historian of the remote future comes to estimate the contribution of England to the common stock of civilisation, his principal emphasis will be laid upon our political constitution'.[4] It would take some courage for a constitutional historian to defend the constitution in such terms today.

---

[1] A. V. Dicey, *Introduction to the Study of the Law of the Constitution* (London: Macmillan, 8th edn., 1915), pp. 3–4: 'The constitutional lawyer is called upon to perform the part neither of a critic nor an apologist, nor of a eulogist, but simply of an expounder.'

[2] David L. Keir, *The Constitutional History of Modern Britain, 1485–1937* (London: A & C Black, 1938), p. 1: 'Continuity has been the dominant characteristic in the development of English government. Its institutions, though unprotected by the fundamental or organic laws which safeguard the "rigid" constitutions of most other states, have preserved the same general appearance throughout their history, and have been regulated in their working by principles which can be regarded as constant.'

[3] Richard Cobden, 'The great juggle of the English constitution. A thing of monopolies, churchcraft and sinecures, armorial hocus-pocus, primogeniture and pageantry' (1838), cited in John A. Hawgood, *Modern Constitutions Since 1787* (London: Macmillan, 1939), p. 284.

[4] Sir Maurice Amos, *The English Constitution* (London: Longmans, Green & Co. 1930), p. 14. See also A. F. Pollard, *The Evolution of Parliament* (London: Longmans, Green & Co. 1920), p. 3: 'Parliamentary institutions have, in fact, been incomparably the greatest gift of the English people to the civilization of the world.'

It seems almost impossible to convey the importance that this 'living tradition of constitutional government' once held in the consciousness of the political class. One reason for this is uncertainty about its supposedly fixed characteristics. With procedures and practices varying in importance according to changing social, economic, and political conditions, all attempts at establishing a 'constitutional status' for any of them are now contentious. In 1936, Ivor Jennings claimed that the constitution 'is changing so rapidly that it is difficult to keep pace with it', but John Griffith's later quip that the constitution is simply 'what happens' now seems much nearer the mark.[5]

The challenge is compounded by a worldwide tendency to subject ever greater swathes of political decision-making to the processes of constitutional review. This has emboldened scholars facing the declining authority of traditional practices to promote imaginative – and ideologically motivated – reconstructions of the constitution as hierarchically ordered fundamental law. In these fluid circumstances, all attempts at presenting an account of the constitution are hazardous. My primary objective will therefore be not to try and explain the thing in itself but only to reveal its various discordant meanings.

For this purpose, I present a simplified history of constitutional development to demonstrate that the conventional meaning of the word 'constitution' varies over time and is informed by prevailing political concerns. My aim is to show that the key concern in accentuating a specific conception of the constitution in each of the six main phases of modern development has been to bolster governmental authority in the face of changes that might erode it. I conclude that we now face a period of constitutional anxiety, one that is largely attributable to the fact that certain persistent and deep-seated ambiguities about the nature of the state supposedly constituted by this constitution can no longer be suppressed.

## PHASE I: THE ARISTOCRATIC SETTLEMENT, 1689–1867

The English constitution was settled in the period between the Revolution of 1689 and the accession of George I in 1714. The 1689 Revolution marked the final resolution of the civil war that had gripped the country in the mid-seventeenth century. Although this revolution was essentially conservative – its ostensible objective being to restore the balances of the ancient constitution – its impact was radical. It was the world's first modern revolution.[6]

---

[5] W. Ivor Jennings, *Cabinet Government* (Cambridge: Cambridge University Press, 1936), p. xii; J. A. G. Griffith, 'The Political Constitution' (1979) 42 *Modern Law Review* 1–21, p. 19.

[6] Steve Pincus, *1688: The First Modern Revolution* (New Haven: Yale University Press, 2009).

Wresting power from the monarch in a revolutionary manoeuvre, the aristocracy finessed the seventeenth-century struggles over sovereignty between Crown and Parliament by claiming that sovereignty vests in a composite entity, 'the Crown-in-Parliament'.[7] No longer was Parliament merely an institution which, by petitioning for the redress of grievances, sought to hold government to account. In this new configuration, Parliament, in partnership with government, became the key institution in a modern state-building project.[8]

This unique arrangement meant that Britain followed a different path from those European countries that modernised their states through the medium of absolutism.[9] Other states had to undertake a fundamental reconstitution of their regimes following revolutionary upheaval, but the British were able to modernise their state through incremental reforms.

Constitutional eulogists attribute this exceptional path of development to some distinctive genius in the art of governing, but the reality is more complicated. The century following the 1689 Revolution, during which the essential practices of parliamentary government were established, was a period in which the English state, through incorporating unions, expanded into a British state,[10] and evolved from an agricultural into an industrial and commercial nation. The state that in the seventeenth century had been relatively weak and insular was transformed into a major European power. On these social and economic foundations, Britain rapidly established itself as the world's dominant trading economy and leading imperial power.[11]

It was on these same foundations that the landed class was able to establish a consensus on governing practices. At its core, was the arrangement by which two major parties, operating as government and opposition, were formed

---

[7] Sir William Blackstone, *Commentaries on the Laws of England* (Oxford: Clarendon Press, 1776), vol. 1.
[8] John Brewer, *The Sinews of Power: War, Money and the English State, 1688–1783* (New York: Knopf, 1989); Dale Hoak and Mordechai Finegold (eds.), *The World of William and Mary: Anglo-Dutch Perspectives on the Revolution of 1688–1689* (Stanford: Stanford University Press, 1996); Jonathan Scott, *England's Troubles: Seventeenth-Century English Political Instability in a European Context* (Cambridge: Cambridge University Press, 2000).
[9] Thomas Ertman, *Birth of the Leviathan: Building States and Regimes in Medieval and Early Modern Europe* (Cambridge: Cambridge University Press, 1997).
[10] The kingdom of Great Britain was established in 1707 by the Treaty of Union between England and Scotland and then the United Kingdom of Great Britain and Ireland was formed in 1800, by the Act of Union with Ireland.
[11] See Douglas North and Barry R Weingast, 'Constitutions and Commitment: The Evolution of Institutions Governing Public Choice in Seventeenth-Century England'; (1989) 49 *J. of Economic History* 803–32; Geoffrey Holmes, *The Making of a Great Power: Late Stuart and Early Georgian Britain, 1660–1722* (London: Longman, 1993).

within a Parliament holding full authority. But what enabled ministries to be made and overthrown within a framework of common loyalty to the Crown was the fact that, despite differences in party allegiance, members of the governing class shared a common background with common values and religious beliefs, received the same schooling, intermarried, moved in the same circles, and drew on the same common stock of ideas. Whether Whig or Tory – whether English, Scottish, or Welsh – they believed in the essentials of commercial and imperial action and in the need to protect life, liberty, and property from undue governmental interference. This flexible and evolving constitution rested on a bedrock of specific material interests which it was the fixed policy of the state to protect. And because the wealth and power of the country was growing so rapidly, a policy of making concessions and adjustments was easily adopted.

These are the material factors that helped to shape the basic characteristics of the modern constitution. Its distinctive practices evolved due to the community of interests of a landed class monopolising governing power. When Walter Bagehot wrote *The English Constitution* in the mid-nineteenth century, his aim was to show that this special arrangement of parliamentary practices was the product of unique historical circumstances. He therefore sought 'to disabuse his readers of the quaint notion that English-style parliamentary institutions could be exported to other countries, irrespective of national differences, differences of character, and differences of historical development'.[12]

It was this development that prompted Arthur Balfour, an Eton-educated Scot with more than fifty years of experience in politics, to claim in his Introduction to the 1928 edition of Bagehot that 'our whole political machinery presupposes a people so fundamentally at one that they can safely afford to bicker; and so sure of their own moderation that they are not dangerously disturbed by the never-ending din of political conflict'.[13] But, as Harold Laski quipped, Balfour's 'only recorded contact with the working-class ... was with his valet and his chauffeur', which tells us pretty much all we need to know about the 'people' on whom that claim was based.[14]

The much-feted flexible constitution was erected on the foundation of institutionalised aristocratic rule. Deliberation over its practices was confined

---

[12] Miles Taylor, 'Introduction' to Walter Bagehot, *The English Constitution* (Oxford: Oxford University Press, 2001), p. xv.

[13] Arthur J. Balfour, 'Introduction' to Walter Bagehot, *The English Constitution* (Oxford: Oxford University Press, 1928), p. xxiv.

[14] Harold J. Laski, *Reflections on the Revolution of Our Times* (London: Allen & Unwin, 1943), p. 34.

to those entrusted with the powers of rule. That the Victorians invariably called it the 'English' constitution was not indiscriminate. The constitution was the product of the manner of 'making the English nation and the English state'.[15] 'Constitution' meant the constitution of the state, with the idea of 'the state' incorporating the patterns of the collective political life of its society, its established religious outlook, and the spirit of its laws. In this sense it is an English constitution, though one that incorporated England and Wales, but in a broader cultural and religious sense it can also be understood as a British constitution. 'It was', explains Linda Colley, 'their common investment in Protestantism that first allowed the English, the Welsh and the Scots to become fused together, and to remain so, despite their many cultural divergences.'[16]

## PHASE II: THE THREAT OF DEMOCRATISATION, 1829–1928

The deep-seated aristocratic and religious basis of the constitution explains why the movement to reform the franchise in Britain became the most contentious constitutional question of the nineteenth century.

Reform was first raised by Ireland's incorporation into the United Kingdom in 1800. Arrogantly promoted to maintain the security of the country and the empire,[17] incorporation raised the question of the status of Catholics within the newly expanded state. Having been excluded since the 1689 Revolution from voting, holding office or being members of Parliament, Catholic emancipation had always been resisted on the ground that it posed a threat to Britain's constitutional identity. But a political crisis generated by an Irish Catholic political reform movement, led in 1829 to a Tory Parliament – in the face of stiff opposition that included the king – passing a Catholic Emancipation Act.

Given the Protestant foundations of the post-1689 settlement, Colley asks: 'What would emerge as a national cement in its stead?'[18] The short answer is that the cement was to be supplied by the gradual democratisation of Parliament and local government. But incorporation of Ireland into the British state turned out to be problematic. The first cracks in the Protestant foundations appeared in 1865 when the Church of Ireland was disestablished,[19] but the most vexatious

---

[15] Pollard, *The Evolution of Parliament*, n. 4 above, p. 4.
[16] Linda Colley, *Britons: Forging the Nation 1707–1837* (London: Pimlico, 1992), p. 368.
[17] Patrick Geoghegan, *The Irish Act of Union: A Study in High Politics, 1789–1801* (Dublin: Gill & Macmillan, 2001), esp. chap. 1.
[18] Colley, *Britons: Forging the Nation 1707–1837*, p. 334.
[19] Irish Church Act 1869. Before 1869, though commanding the allegiance of a very small minority of the Irish population, the Church had not only sent bishops to the House of Lords but also collected tithes from the Irish population.

issue of the latter half of the century was the question of Irish Home Rule. This was finally conceded in the Government of Ireland Act 1914 but then suspended because of the war. This delay triggered the Easter Rising in 1916 and then led, in quick succession, to the electoral success of Sinn Féin, the formation of the Dáil, the Irish War of Independence in 1919–21, and the Anglo-Irish Treaty by which Ireland – with the exception of six counties of Northern Ireland, four of which had Protestant and Unionist majorities – broke away from the United Kingdom.[20]

Returning to the wider British struggle for electoral reform, we can see that the breakthrough was made with the Reform Act 1832. This was the outcome of a movement that emphasised the positive impact of reform: in place of an irresponsible Parliament governing in favour of its own class, the nation might be united and renewed. Yet, since the Act gave the vote to less than 20 per cent of the adult male population, the phase of aristocratic settlement might reasonably be said to extend to 1867. But the constitutional significance of the Reform Act lay just as much in the realisation that a haphazardly evolved and bewilderingly complex system of parliamentary representation could be reformed through the ordinary process of legislation. The 1832 Act was no great democratising measure, but it nevertheless radically reformed the basis of the electoral system.

The Reform Act of 1867, which extended the franchise to the urban male working class, proved to be just as contentious. It was promoted by a Tory government led by Benjamin Disraeli, who was prepared to make this great 'leap in the dark' once he realised that Britain remained a highly deferential society and the Tories need not fear for their continued dominance. Yet it was Disraeli himself who, in his novel *Sybil*, had written about a Britain consisting of 'two nations' not sharing a common language, ignorant of each other's habits and feelings, and with no unity of outlook.[21] That this was orthodoxy among Britain's governing class goes some way towards explaining why most 'enlightened' opinion of the time remained vehemently opposed to electoral reform.

Sir Henry Maine had warned that 'the gradual establishment of the masses in power is the blackest omen for all legislation founded on scientific opinion'.[22] Bagehot, too, believed that the masses were not fit to govern. Arguing in his celebrated study of the constitution in 1865–7 that further

---

[20] See Alvin Jackson, *Home Rule: An Irish history, 1800–2000* (New York: Oxford University Press, 2003).
[21] Benjamin Disraeli, *Sybil, or the Two Nations* (London: Henry Colburn, 1845).
[22] Henry Sumner Maine, *Popular Government* (London: John Murray, 1885), p. 98.

electoral reform would result in bringing into Parliament men 'entrapped into something they do not comprehend' leaving the institution 'more heterogeneous' but 'more vacillating and timid', he found his world turned upside down the moment his study was published in book form.[23] He felt obliged to publish an extended Introduction to the second edition in 1872, in which he wrote ponderously that 'the future of this country depends on the happy working of a delicate experiment' and spoke of his fear of the corruption that would follow once 'our political parties ... bid for the support of the working man'.[24] Dicey had initially been more sanguine. Expressing horror at the coming of an 'era of collectivism' in the last decades of the nineteenth century, he retained a residual faith in reform only because England was still 'a deferential country'.[25] But when the Liberal government 1906–14 not only promoted social reform but also challenged aristocratic power through the Parliament Act 1911, he realised his error; the 1911 Act, Dicey declaimed, had 'destroyed our last effective constitutional safeguard'.[26]

After the war, the Labour Party, formed at the turn of the twentieth century to provide parliamentary representation of the working classes, quickly replaced the Liberals in the two-party parliamentary arrangement. Significantly, the prestige and authority of the established system of parliamentary government was such that Labour never challenged it. They sought to bring about social reform by winning parliamentary power rather than by reforming the constitution. By 1928, when universal suffrage was achieved, Labour had already had a brief taste of power, in 1924, as a minority government, and was firmly set on the parliamentary road to socialism.

Labour's emergence as a parliamentary force helped to sustain the idea that, with the coming of democracy, the institutions of government would be responsive to the will of electoral majorities. Yet this obscured the extent to

---

[23] Bagehot, *The English Constitution* (Oxford: Oxford University Press, 2001), pp. 196–7. The work was originally published as a series of articles in the *Fortnightly Review* between May 1865 and January 1867.

[24] Walter Bagehot, *The English Constitution* (Glasgow: Collins, RHS Crossman edn., 1963), pp. 275, 277.

[25] A. V. Dicey, *Lectures on the Relation between Law and Public Opinion in England during the Nineteenth Century* (London: Macmillan, 1905), p. 57.

[26] See, e.g., A. V. Dicey, 'The Parliament Act, 1911, and the Destruction of all Constitutional Safeguards' in Sir William R. Anson et al., *Rights of Citizenship: A Survey of Safeguards for the People* (London: Frederick Warne & Co., 1912), 81–107, pp. 81–2: 'The first truth is that the Parliament Act has destroyed our last effective constitutional safeguard. The second truth is that the whole experience of every country, which enjoys popular government, proves that the absence of constitutional safeguards imperils the prosperity of the State. The last truth is that the absence of constitutional safeguards is full of danger to England; for it enables a party, or a coalition of parties, to usurp the sovereignty of the nation.'

which the power institutionalised through the old aristocratic settlement remained a dominating force. Parliamentary democracy may have been formally established, but most institutions of state – the monarchy, the Lords, the judiciary, the civil service, and the defence forces – remained firmly under the control of a narrow elite immersed in the aristocratic traditions of rule.

But the century marking incremental democratisation at least saw the emergence of a more discrete conception of the constitution. Whereas in the aristocratic settlement the constitution represented an entire hierarchical form of collective public life, the struggles over the franchise and related reforms led to the appearance of a more formal understanding of 'the constitution'. The constitution, Dicey explained, referred essentially to that set of rules 'which directly or indirectly affect the distribution or the exercise of the sovereign power in the state'.[27] This conception was not universally accepted: indeed, it was ridiculed by scholars who complained that 'our constitutional history has been perverted at the hands of lawyers'.[28] But there can be no doubting that a more formal conception of the term had entered public consciousness.

## PHASE III: MODERNISING THE MACHINERY OF GOVERNMENT, 1914–79

The establishment of parliamentary democracy coincided with the emergence of the activist state. Many of the developments consequential on this process, not least the growth of administration, ran contrary to the classical liberal values that underpinned traditional parliamentary practices. The most dramatic shift in governmental activity occurred during the First World War, when the government had been obliged to commandeer the nation's entire resources for the war effort. The government became 'the chief consumer of the nation and set itself up as the final arbiter of production and distribution'.[29] This level of government expenditure may have been scaled back at the end of the war but it never reverted to that of the status quo *ante bellum*. The era of collective planning had begun.

---

[27] A. V. Dicey, *Introduction to the Study of the Law of the Constitution* (London: Macmillan, 8th edn., 1915), p. 22.
[28] Edward A. Freeman, *The Growth of the English Constitution from the Earliest Times* (London: Macmillan, 1876), p. x.
[29] W. H. Greenleaf, *The British Political Tradition*, Vol. 1, *The Rise of Collectivism* (London: Routledge, 1983), p. 54.

The era opened with intense ideological disputes among lawyers concerning the allocation of legislative and judicial powers to government bodies. In an intemperate outburst, Lord Hewart CJ railed against a bureaucratic encroachment on ordinary life that was instituting a 'new despotism' of 'administrative lawlessness'.[30] But the critical constitutional issues were of a more basic structural character. The most important question was whether the traditional practices of parliamentary government possessed the capacities needed to respond to the technological challenges of big government, and the issue dominated mid-century debate. Consider, for example, Leo Amery's *Thoughts on the Constitution*. Drawing on a long career in politics, Amery concluded that 'the arteries of our constitutional system are already suffering from acute high blood-pressure at a time when the brain and body which they serve are being summoned to ever greater exertions'. Acknowledging their adaptability in the past, he nevertheless doubted they could withstand 'the more intense strains of the near future without a complete breakdown ending in violent revolutionary change or in progressive paralysis'.[31]

The growth of big government arising from the emergence of a welfare state and the nationalisation of the energy and transport sectors had produced a highly centralised system of government. This seemed to be a necessary consequence of modernisation in a parliamentary state. 'Without an efficient instrument for planning at the centre', noted Amery, 'nothing but confusion, congestion, and eventual disaster can result'.[32] But this outcome had resulted in the creation of big bureaucracies – central departments and public corporations – that often seemed insufficiently responsive to changing needs.

Although Amery called his reflections 'constitutional', his concerns focused entirely on the adequacy of the machinery of government to the tasks at hand. His thoughts were not constitutional in the traditional sense of reflecting on the collective life of the nation, nor in the more formal sense of inquiring into the rules by which the sovereign powers of the state are exercised. The specific conception of 'constitution' with which he was working questioned whether the 'machinery of government' was up to the task of 'social and economic reconstruction'.[33]

This became the dominant motif of constitutional reflection in this phase of modern development. From the Haldane Committee on the machinery of government in 1918, through Donoughmore on executive powers to legislate

---

[30] Rt Hon Lord Hewart of Bury, *The New Despotism* (London: Benn, 1928).
[31] Leo Amery, *Thoughts on the Constitution* (London: Oxford University Press, 1947), p. ix.
[32] Ibid., p. x.
[33] Ibid., p. 104.

in 1932, the Franks Committee on administrative tribunals in 1957, the Fulton Report on the civil service in 1968, and the Kilbrandon Report on centralised government in 1973, the constitution was treated as synonymous with the machinery of government.[34] Consider, for example, Kilbrandon's Report of the *Royal Commission on the Constitution*. Notwithstanding its wide-ranging title, its official task was much narrower: it was to 'examine the present functions of the central legislature and government in the several countries, nations and regions of the United Kingdom' and consider whether 'any changes are desirable in those functions or otherwise in present constitutional and economic relationships'.[35] And the commission duly stuck to that specific task and avoided engagement with more general considerations.[36]

Kilbrandon's orientation chimed with the concerns of the day. During the 1970s, political analyses – variously expressed as a fiscal crisis of the state, an imbalance between production and consumption, a growing institutional sclerosis, or of governmental overload imposing too great a regulatory burden[37] – all indicated that the critical constitutional question was that of governmental effectiveness. Gone were the days of eulogising 'the matchless constitution' or worrying whether its traditional values were being eroded as a result of modern developments. Eulogy was replaced by a growing consensus that the traditional arrangements through which Britain had made the transition to modernity were now coming to the end of their useful life. And without the catalyst of 'revolutionary change', the prospect, as Amery had foretold, was one of 'progressive paralysis'.

---

[34] Ministry of Reconstruction, *Report of the Machinery of Government Committee* (chair: Viscount Haldane) (London: HMSO, 1918); *Report of the Committee on Ministers' Powers* (chair: Earl of Donoughmore) Cmd 4060 (London: HMSO, 1932); *Report of the Committee on Administrative Tribunals and Inquiries* (chair: Sir Oliver Franks) Cmnd 218 (London: HMSO, 1957); *Report of the Committee on the Civil Service* (chair: Lord Fulton) Cmnd 3638 (London: HMSO, 1968); *Royal Commission on the Constitution 1969–1973, Vol.1 Report* (chair: Lord Kilbrandon) Cmnd 5460 (London: HMSO, 1973).

[35] *Royal Commission on the Constitution*, para. 11.

[36] *Royal Commission on the Constitution*, para. 14: 'On the most sweeping interpretation, it might be argued that these terms of reference open the way to a root and branch examination of the whole of the British constitution ... Our own conclusion was that such a wide review was not intended, and would not be practicable.'

[37] James O'Connor, *The Fiscal Crisis of the State* (New York: St Martin's Press, 1973); Roger Bacon and Walter Eltis, *Britain's Economic Problem: Too Few Producers* (London: Macmillan, 1976); Mancur Olson, *The Rise and Decline of Nations. Economic Growth, Stagflation and Social Rigidities* (New Haven: Yale University Press, 1982); Anthony King, 'Overload: problems of governing in the 1970s' (1975) 23 *Political Studies* 284–96; James Douglas, 'The Overloaded Crown' (1976) 6 *Brit. J. of Political Science* 483–505; S. H. Beer, *Britain Against Itself: The Political Contradictions of Collectivism* (New York: Norton, 1982).

Towards the end of this phase, analyses began to appear proposing fundamental reform by the adoption of a modern type of constitution.[38] Of this genre, the most interesting was Nevil Johnson's *In Search of the Constitution*. Johnson's thesis was that the authority of 'one of the world's reputedly most stable political orders has weakened so much that it is apparently no longer capable of resolving many of the problems of the society'.[39] And it was not just policies but the foundations of these institutions that were deficient: the issue was constitutional. A serious gap between theory and reality had emerged because 'much of the traditional language of the British Constitution ... has lost its vitality'.[40] Those who invoke the traditional idea of the constitution, he argued, simply sustain outworn myths, while those who present the constitution as a body of rules can no longer justify political authority. The contemporary problem is that of 'the atrophy of any language in which we can talk of constitutional issues'. He concluded that we are left 'floundering in a world of pure pragmatism'.[41]

## PHASE IV: FREE ECONOMY AND STRONG STATE, 1979-97

In 1979, a response to the threat of 'progressive paralysis' came in the form of the 'revolutionary change' ushered in by the election of the Thatcher government. Through four successive terms, Conservative governments addressed the constitutional problem, not in Nevil Johnson's conception but simply as a 'machinery of government' matter.[42] The revolution — strictly, a counter-revolution — sought to resolve the problem of governmental effectiveness by rolling back the state. Their aim was to perforate the boundary between the state and the market by privatising nationalised industries and other public bodies, imposing market

---

[38] See Leslie Scarman, *English Law: The New Dimension* (London: Stevens, 1974); Michael Zander, *A Bill of Rights?* (London: Sweet & Maxwell, 1975); Lord Hailsham, *The Dilemma of Democracy: Diagnosis and Prescription* (Glasgow: Collins, 1978), esp. chap. 20, 'Elective Dictatorship'; Nevil Johnson, *In Search of the Constitution: Reflections of State and Society in Britain* (Oxford: Pergamon Press, 1977).

[39] Johnson *In Search of the Constitution*, p. 1.

[40] Ibid., p. 26.

[41] Ibid., p. 29.

[42] In his Dimbleby Lecture on 'Elective dictatorship' (*The Listener*, 21 October 1976, 496-500), Lord Hailsham had advocated the need for fundamental constitutional reform. Appointed Lord Chancellor in the first Thatcher government, he did nothing to pursue this agenda and by 1991 was rejecting the proposal for a bill of rights, arguing that 'we are probably the most successful political society that has ever existed'. *Who's Who Magazine*, Summer 1991; cited in Ferdinand Mount, *The British Constitution Now* (London: Heinemann, 1992), p. 3.

disciplines on public bodies that remained, and instituting a clear distinction between policy and delivery.[43]

This radical programme eroded the idea that public service provision differed in any way from the provision of widgets in the market. But it threw up a dilemma. The 'free economy' could not be promoted without riding roughshod over traditional practices of parliamentary government and instrumentalising the power of law and policymaking.[44] A programme intended to remedy deficiencies in the constitution as governmental machinery (the phase III concept as described above) could be implemented only by further destroying constitutional traditions (the phase I concept) and converting constitutive rules (the phase II concept) into regulative rules, rules conceived as tools of government.

The programme may not have been fully realised but it did project a novel conception of the constitution. The policy of establishing 'the free economy' through 'the strong state' was actually a British variant of the German ordoliberal 'economic constitutionalism'. The ordoliberals had recognised that, far from evolving spontaneously, free markets had to be created by positive action and that to survive they needed legal protection maintained by the central state. A strong state was needed to establish the regulatory framework that enables markets to function efficiently. The key task became one of establishing an economic constitution in which the state is vested with strong but constitutionally limited powers to maintain free markets.[45]

Although running counter to the traditional conception of the constitution, steps towards promoting this programme had already been taken with Britain's accession to what is now the European Union (EU). When the Conservatives took the United Kingdom into the European Economic Community in 1973, the constitutional implications of membership were little discussed. It was commonly believed that we were joining a common market, and the venture was part of the modernising government programme. The European project may have had two strands – achievement of a single market and the establishment of a federation – but it was then assumed that existing veto powers were sufficient to protect Britain's national interests.

---

[43] From the many studies, see only: Christopher D. Foster and Francis J. Plowden, *The State Under Stress: Can the Hollow State be Good Government?* (Buckingham: Open University Press, 1996).

[44] On the impact in the context of central-local government relations see Martin Loughlin, *Legality and Locality: The Role of Law in Central-Local Government Relations* (Oxford: Clarendon Press, 1996), esp. chap. 7.

[45] See Alan Peacock and Hans Willgerodt (eds.), *Germany's Social Market Economy* (London: Macmillan, 1989).

The structure and policies of the EU – based on the protection of economic freedoms (the four freedoms of movement of capital, labour, goods, and services), the promotion of undistorted competition, and latterly on the maintenance of stable currencies then a single currency (EMS and subsequently EMU) – were closely attuned to the Conservative government's reform agenda. From the late 1980s the European project gained pace, mainly because of the Single European Act 1986 which had secured the internal market by removing non-tariff barriers to trade. The Thatcher government supported many of these developments because they imposed the ordoliberal discipline of 'free economy and strong state'. It was not then realised that completion of the internal market also strengthened the EU federal project. The constitutional aspects of this development therefore did not come to the fore until the next developmental phase.

### PHASE V: CONSTITUTIONAL MODERNISATION, 1997–2015

When Labour came to power in 1997, they did not reverse the Conservatives' project of establishing economic constitutionalism. Instead, having witnessed the degree to which the implementation of the 'free economy/strong state' programme had eroded traditional constitutional practices, they embraced many of the claims made by movements such as Charter 88 and the Scottish Constitutional Convention of 1989–95 on the need for Britain to establish a modern type of constitutional framework.[46] Labour thus placed the theme of constitutional modernisation at the centre of their programme for government. But rather than focusing on modernising the machinery of government (phase III), they sought a new constitutional compact between government and citizen.

The various reforms – the devolution of legislative and executive powers to Scotland, Wales, and Northern Ireland; the enactment of a Human Rights Act and a Freedom of Information Act; reform of the House of Lords and the establishment of a Supreme Court for the United Kingdom in the Constitutional Reform Act 2005 – have been widely studied and will not be examined here.[47] My point is that only in this phase of development were

---

[46] See, e.g., on Charter 88: David Erdos, 'Charter 88 and the Constitutional Reform Movement: A Retrospective' (2009) 62 *Parliamentary Affairs* 537–51; on the Scottish Constitutional Convention: Owen Dudley Edwards (ed.), *A Claim of Right for Scotland* (Edinburgh: Polygon, 1989); Report to the Scottish People by the Scottish Constitutional Convention, *Towards Scotland's Parliament* (Edinburgh, 1990); on general analysis: David Marquand, *The Unprincipled Society: New Demands and Old Politics* (London: Fontana, 1988); Will Hutton, *The State We're In* (London: Jonathan Cape, 1995).

[47] See, e.g., the essays in Sir Jeffrey Jowell and Colm O'Cinneide (eds.), *The Changing Constitution* (Oxford: Oxford University Press, 9th edn. 2019).

governmental reforms introduced that were orientated towards establishing a modern constitutional framework of fundamental law.

Taking their cue from these parliamentary initiatives, the judges also began to innovate. Those in the vanguard asserted that the constitution is 'in its essentials the creation of the common law'.[48] Reformulating the constitution as a 'common law constitution', they maintained that the constitution rather than Parliament is sovereign, and assumed as their key task the explication of the constitution as an ordered system of principles. Consequently, they held that there are such things as 'fundamental constitutional rights' which the judiciary must be vigilant to protect, and 'constitutional statutes' which Parliament cannot repeal implicitly.[49] The trajectory was clear. As Laws LJ stated in 2002: 'In its present state of evolution, the British system may be said to stand at an intermediate stage between parliamentary supremacy and constitutional supremacy.'[50]

Labour's modernising agenda, it might be noted, was underpinned by Britain's participation in the venture of continuing European integration. The Thatcher regime had responded to the threat of 'progressive paralysis' by looking to Europe to bolster their reform agenda of aligning government agencies more closely to the market. Labour, by contrast, saw European integration as a means of bringing the British constitution more closely into alignment with modern constitutional democracies. In both programmes, the judiciary has been empowered to review legislation to ensure compatibility with European Union law, to adopt teleological modes of reasoning antithetical to traditional common law methods, to make a categorial distinction between constitutional statutes and ordinary legislation, and to devise a continental-type distinction between public and private law.

But the project of European integration extends much further. The United Kingdom has been able to adopt what it is in effect a bill of rights without the need for public deliberation. Integration into the Council of Europe regime strengthened the case for replacing the Judicial Committee of the House of Lords with an independently constituted Supreme Court. And the existence of a common European governing framework has helped the United Kingdom to set in place a dynamic scheme for devolving governmental powers to its Celtic regions and provided a supporting structure for the unique cross-border arrangements that formed part of the peace settlement in Northern Ireland.

---

[48] Sir John Laws, 'Law and Democracy' (1995) *Public Law* 72–93, p. 92.
[49] *Thoburn v. Sunderland City Council* [2003] QB 151; *HS2 Action Alliance v. The Secretary of State for Transport* [2014] UKSC 3.
[50] *Secretary of State for the Home Department v. Roth* [2002] 1 CMLR 52 at para. 71.

Britain's constitutional arrangements were incrementally modernised by participation in the European federal framework. And just as the strategy of deepening integration was pursued by European elites without consulting their publics, so too was the British political elite able to effect these constitutional changes without elaborate constituent deliberation. Participation in the common project of European integration became the means by which progressive institutional paralysis was avoided.

This phase of development also embraces the work of the coalition government of 2010–15.[51] The Liberal Democrats had demanded an ambitious programme of constitutional reform as the precondition for entering into a coalition with the Conservatives. Their joint 'Programme for Government' opened with the dramatic statement: 'The Government believes that our political system is broken.'[52] But the implementation of this reform programme was little short of disastrous. Fixed term parliaments were adopted (with awkward consequences for the following phase), together with further incremental devolution of powers to Wales and Scotland. But there was no voting reform, no constituency equalisation, no further reform of the House of Lords, and no reform or repeal of the Human Rights Act. What replaced these was the use of referendums, not just for voting reform but also – though not at the initiative of Westminster – on Scottish independence in 2014. In 2010, the Liberal Democrats had committed themselves to 'an in/out referendum' on the EU the next time a fundamental change in UK-EU relations was needed. The Conservatives had pledged that no further transfer of powers to the EU would occur without a referendum, which became law with the EU Act 2011. This was the harbinger of things to come.

### PHASE VI: PARALYSIS, 2015–19

In the 2015 election, the Conservatives, contrary to expectations, gained an overall majority of twelve and were able to form a majority government. This gave them the freedom to implement their manifesto pledges, including holding 'an in/out referendum' on EU membership. David Cameron, the prime minister, gave this high priority and after seeking concessions from the EU, in June 2016 held a referendum which, again contrary to expectations, resulted in a majority (52–48%) voting to leave. The government had been

---

[51] For an overall assessment see Martin Loughlin and Cal Viney, 'The Coalition and the Constitution' in Anthony Selden and Mike Finn (eds.), *The Coalition Effect* (Cambridge: Cambridge University Press, 2015), pp. 59–86.

[52] 'The Coalition: Our Programme for Government', Cabinet Office, May 2010, s. 24, www.gov.uk/government/publications/the-coalition-documentation.

completely unprepared for this outcome, having undertaken no detailed work to deal with the consequences. Thus began a series of developments which reveal the truth of Amery's mid-twentieth century forecast that continuous incremental development would lead to progressive paralysis. In the crises of authority that unfolded, each of the conceptions of constitution that had been influential in earlier phases found advocates, yet none commanded broad support. Constitutional analysis was reduced to political argument.

Following the referendum, Cameron resigned and was replaced by Theresa May. May at first indicated that she had no intention of going back to the polls, but within the year surprised everyone by doing just that, claiming the need to acquire a strong mandate to negotiate Brexit. Held on 8 June 2017, this election – once more contrary to forecasts – led to the Conservatives losing their majority and being obliged to enter into a 'confidence and supply agreement' with Northern Ireland's Democratic Unionist Party (DUP). The constitutional aspects of what followed must be sketched in the barest of outlines.

First, however ineptly, Parliament had consciously transferred decision-making authority on membership of the EU to the electorate in the 2016 referendum. Anyone examining the parliamentary debates on the bill authorising the referendum can be left in no doubt about that. But around three-quarters of MPs had voted to remain in the EU, including most of Cameron's cabinet and a majority of Conservative MPs. The government was therefore in the position of having to deliver an outcome it had neither supported nor expected and to negotiate a parliament in which the great majority had voted to remain. This unique situation generated not just a crisis of parliamentary representation, with Leave and Remain voters being inadequately represented by their constituency MPs, but, given serious splits in the ranks of the governing party, it also created a crisis of governmental authority. Both major parties attempted to minimise these problems by pledging at the 2017 general election to respect the referendum outcome but the impact of that was weakened when the government lost its overall majority and was forced to enter into an agreement with the DUP.

Because of the parliamentary arithmetic, traditional practices of parliamentary government in negotiating Brexit were placed under severe strain and at times entirely broke down. The efficacy of a system of parliamentary government depends on the maintenance of party discipline and of the two-party arrangement of government and opposition. But because Brexit divided MPs across party lines, that discipline proved almost impossible to maintain. Neither the conduct of parliamentary business nor collective cabinet responsibility operated according to the normal conventions.[53]

After failing to get her Withdrawal Agreement through the Commons, May was replaced by Boris Johnson. Johnson's tumultuous premiership has stretched the conventions of constitutional practice almost to breaking point. Parliament adjourned for its 2019 summer recess on the day following his appointment, reconvening on Tuesday 3 September. In the interim, at a Privy Council meeting on 28 August, the Queen, on the advice of her PM, ordered that Parliament be prorogued from 9 September until 14 October. When Parliament reconvened on 3 September, the PM's insistence on leaving the EU on 31 October led to revolt among his party members and, having lost his majority, he lost a series of major votes in the first week following the summer adjournment. This led to the unprecedented action of Parliament, with the Speaker's support,[54] taking control of the House of Commons Order Paper. The Opposition then introduced a bill mandating the PM to request a further extension until 31 January 2020 if a renegotiated Withdrawal Agreement was not adopted by 19 October. This bill passed all its Commons stages that same day and received the Royal Assent on Monday 9 September.[55] In effect, Parliament had taken over the functions of the government.

In this chaos, no authoritative expression of constitutional understanding could be determined. Did it depend on traditional practices and precedents, or on the formal rules, or on certain fundamental principles? Into this void, notably in the two *Miller* cases, stepped the judiciary. The first *Miller* case generated a great deal of political heat but in constitutional terms the issue was relatively uncontroversial: could the Art. 50 TEU notification to the EU signalling its decision to withdraw be exercised by the government through its treaty-making prerogative powers or did it require parliamentary sanction? Parliament had not complained about the government's intended use of its prerogative powers but a group of citizens challenged the decision by judicial review. In a high-profile case the Supreme Court held that, since rights were

---

[53] See, e.g., Speaker rulings on Standing Order 24, which is used to seek an emergency debate but not generally used to debate a substantive motion. The Speaker twice ruled to permit a motion on seeking extensions rather than risk a no-deal exit from the EU: EU (Withdrawal) (No 5) Bill (Cooper-Letwin, April 2019) and EU (Withdrawal) (No 6) Bill (Benn, September 2019). These became the EU (Withdrawal) Act 2019 and EU (Withdrawal) (No 2) Act 2019 respectively. On collective cabinet responsibility, see: R. B. Taylor, 'Brexit and collective cabinet responsibility: why the Convention is still working', LSE Brexit Blog, 20 May 2019, https://blogs.lse.ac.uk/brexit/2019/05/20/brexit-and-collective-responsibility-why-the-convention-is-still-working/.

[54] See n. 53, above, regarding the Benn Bill.

[55] EU (Withdrawal) (No 2) Act 2019.

affected by the notification, authorisation by Act of Parliament was required.[56] If the litigants were anticipating that Parliament would vote down the proposed Art. 50 notification, their hopes were soon frustrated; given that the government held an overall majority, the Act authorising the PM to issue the notification was speedily enacted.[57]

The second *Miller* case concerned the legality of the prorogation, an issue that proved much more controversial. There is no statute or convention regulating the length of any prorogation; it normally lasts seven to ten days, although in 1930, for example, Parliament had been prorogued from 1 August until 28 October.[58] Prorogation has also been used on occasion for the purpose of gaining political advantage.[59] By September 2019 the Parliamentary session, which normally lasts a year, had been running since 21 June 2017; longer than any in the previous forty years, and this was attributable to the political dynamics of negotiating Brexit. But the government justified this prorogation on the grounds that there was not much new legislative business to conduct, that the new ministry needed time to devise a new legislative programme, and that the thirty-four calendar days proposed included the conference period when Parliament is typically adjourned for three weeks. It therefore claimed that only seven to ten sitting days would be lost and that Parliament would be in session before the critical EU Council meeting of 17–18 October, leaving time for debate and new legislation if necessary before 31 October.[60] Some parliamentarians, including the Speaker,[61] called the prorogation a 'constitutional outrage', but no parliamentary action was taken to overturn this in the week before it was prorogued.

---

[56] *R (Miller) v. Secretary of State for Exiting the European Union* [2017] UKSC 5.

[57] Introduced on 26 January, two days after the Supreme Court ruling, the bill was fast tracked, and received the Royal Assent on 16 March 2017: European Union (Notification of Withdrawal) Act 2017.

[58] *R (Miller) v. Prime Minister* [2019] EWHC 2381 (QB) at para. 54.

[59] *Miller*, ibid., at para. 55: 'One of the most notable examples of that was its use to facilitate the speedy passage of what became the Parliament Act 1949. Under s. 2 of the Parliament Act 1911 a non-money bill could only be enacted without the consent of the House of Lords if it was passed in three successive sessions by the House of Commons. In order to procure the speedy enactment of the 1949 Act the Government arranged for a session of minimal length in 1948. Parliament was prorogued on 13 September 1948 to the following day. Following the passage of the Parliament Bill by the House of Commons, it was then prorogued again on 25 October 1948.'

[60] *Miller*, ibid., at para. 13.

[61] Kate Proctor, 'Boris Johnson's move to prorogue parliament a "constitutional outrage" says Speaker' *Guardian*, 28 August 2019, www.theguardian.com/politics/2019/aug/28/boris-johnsons-move-to-prorogue-parliament-a-constitutional-outrage-says-speaker.

The legality of the prorogation was then challenged in both the English and Scottish courts. Initially, a specially constituted Divisional Court held that the issue was not justiciable but the Inner House of Court of Session determined otherwise. These two discrepant rulings were appealed to the Supreme Court. In a single judgment, the eleven-member court unanimously held that a decision to prorogue Parliament would be unlawful 'if the prorogation has the effect of frustrating or preventing, without reasonable justification, the ability of Parliament to carry out its constitutional functions as a legislature and as the body responsible for the supervision of the executive'.[62] Finding this to be the case, the court declared that the PM acted outside his powers in advising prorogation, that this vitiated the Order-in-Council, and that the actual prorogation, 'which was as if the Commissioners had walked into Parliament with a blank piece of paper', was similarly 'unlawful, null and of no effect'.[63]

There are many contentious aspects of this ruling.[64] But its main constitutional significance lies in the way the court interpreted its ruling that 'the boundaries of a prerogative power relating to the operation of Parliament are ... determined by the fundamental principles of our constitutional law'.[65] It held that the two most relevant constitutional principles are those of parliamentary sovereignty and parliamentary accountability and, invoking these principles to determine the limit of the power of prorogation, it concluded that the PM's advice in this case was unlawful. In effect, the court had converted such political practices as parliamentary accountability into normative principles and then claimed authority to act as the authoritative interpreter of their meaning. In so doing, the Supreme Court was asserting that the British constitution comprises a structure of legal principles which it is their responsibility to protect.

This last turbulent phase of constitutional development came to an abrupt end in December 2019. Although the PM claimed he would never seek an extension beyond 31 October, a letter mandated by the EU (Withdrawal) (No 2) Act was indeed sent, albeit unsigned, alongside a note stating that the government did not feel a further extension would serve any purpose. Nonetheless, a flexible extension was granted until 31 January 2020. At this point, the Liberal Democrats and SNP indicated they were prepared to

---

[62] *R (Miller) v. Prime Minister/Cherry v. Advocate General* [2019] UKSC 41 at para. 50.
[63] Ibid., at para. 69.
[64] See Martin Loughlin, 'The Case of Prorogation: The UK Constitutional Council's ruling on appeal from the judgment of the Supreme Court', *Policy Exchange*, 15 October 2019, https://policyexchange.org.uk/publication/the-case-of-prorogation/.
[65] *R (Miller) v. Prime Minister/Cherry v. Advocate General* [2019] UKSC 41 at para. 38.

support a general election and the bill providing for this was duly enacted on 31 October. The Early Parliamentary General Election Act 2019, authorising a general election on 12 December, thus circumvented the need for a two-thirds majority under the Fixed-term Parliaments Act 2011. In that general election, the Conservatives were returned with a large overall majority of eighty, the United Kingdom formally left the EU at the end of January, and the phase of paralysis appeared to have come to an end.

CONCLUSION: A CONSTITUTION IN SEARCH OF A SUBJECT

This inquiry 'in search of the constitution' has shown that the term 'constitution' acquires different meanings across the various phases of modern governmental development. Traditionally, it meant the manner of collective life of society, its religious convictions and the spirit of its laws as much as the structure of its governing arrangements (1689–1867). Then, following intense debate over reform of the franchise, the constitution came to be defined more formally as the set of rules that directly or indirectly affected the exercise of the sovereign power of the state (1829–1928). Later, concerns about its adaptability to twentieth-century requirements led to this more limited conception being equated to the institutional machinery of government (1914–79), and in the late-twentieth century the term was harnessed to a project of establishing an order that could maintain free markets and fair competition (1979–97). Finally, in the twenty-first century the claim that the constitution should be conceived as establishing an overarching normative framework of legal principles gained greater support (1997–2015).

Each of these conceptions has played a role in shaping modern understanding, each has become the dominant conception at certain moments, but none has acquired hegemonic authority. The 'constitution', it can be concluded, is evidently not a 'thing' to be discovered; it is a term around which competing interests struggle to establish the authority of their own favoured view.

There is, however, one basic aspect of the inquiry that, to this point, has been sidestepped. This has been an inquiry in search of a constitution that lacks a subject. In modern understanding, the subject of the constitution is readily identifiable: constitutions are constitutions of 'the state'. In our own case, however, the entity around which these competing ideas of the constitution revolve remains thoroughly ambivalent.

The grand tradition of constitutional scholarship that embraces Magna Carta, the Glorious Revolution, and the genius of the common law does relate to a specific subject, but that subject is the English state. That tradition extols the aristocratic constitution of an English state that, through conquest, extended across the territory of England and Wales. The problem arises because the entity formed by the Anglo-Scottish Union of 1707 is a much more ambiguous construction. Established as a parliamentary union, it left not only the arrangements of parliamentary politics but also the underlying structure of English social and political practices unaffected, just as the distinctive character of Scots institutions relating to law, religion, and education were retained intact. Viewed from the outside, a new state was formed, and this state went on to build a British Empire that stretched across the globe. But conceived internally, the state, understood as the union of territory, people and ruling authority, was a much more ramshackle edifice from which it has proved difficult to discern a distinctively 'British' constitutional identity.[66]

This inability to forge such an identity seems to be one reason why, during the nineteenth century, a more restricted conception of the constitution as a set of formal rules emerged. After all, we can more readily accept the existence of a British state once our conception of that entity narrows and its character is revealed simply by studying the rules through which governing authority is exercised. And it is telling that the classic work of the period, Dicey's *Law of the Constitution*, avoids precise specification of his subject. The constitutional law he examines is that of English law and this leads him, not quite correctly, to refer to Her Majesty's Government as the 'executive of England', to elaborate basic principles that he believes to 'pervade the whole of the English constitution', and to assert that the Act of Union 1707 has no greater claim to be considered 'a supreme law' than the Dentists Act 1878.[67] The idea of a 'British' constitution might carry more traction as an account of its underlying practices, not least because England, Scotland, and Wales share

---

[66] See J. G. A. Pocock, 'The Limits and Divisions of British History: In Search of the Unknown Subject' (1982) 87 *American Historical Review* 311–46, p. 313: 'Because the effective determinants of power lay in England, the history of the Anglo-Scottish Union is English history – not because the relations of power to society in Scotland were assimilated to those in England but because they were excluded and could be largely ignored. English historians of the period have, therefore, no need to study Scottish history, and Scottish historians interested in *verità effettuale* might do better to study English history than Scottish. This indeed seems to have been the decision of the great Scottish historians from Hume to Macaulay, who with one accord aimed at an understanding of English (and European) history more sophisticated than any the English could construct for themselves ... To write the history of Britain, viewed as the interaction of several peoples and several histories, does not seem to have struck them as *effettuale*; nor did they continue to write Scottish history as a series of social and political processes, still taking place within "Britain" and forming part of its history.'

[67] Dicey, *Law of the Constitution*, pp. 8, 402, 141. On the Scottish debates generated by this conception of the constitution, and especially the fundamental legal principle of parliamentary sovereignty, see Colin Kidd, *Union and Unionism: Political Thought in Scotland, 1500–2000* (Cambridge: Cambridge University Press, 2008), chap. 3.

in common a Protestant religious, cultural, and (perhaps) political identity. But this British conception mainly comes to the fore externally as an expression of the common imperial project.[68]

The Union with Ireland was an altogether different affair. Formally, a state called the United Kingdom of Great Britain and Ireland was established, comprising a defined territory and a centralised ruling authority. But the attempt to integrate Ireland into the idea of the British state by establishing a unity of a people was stillborn. The subsequent partition of Ireland following the Irish revolution of the early twentieth century left the state reconfigured as the United Kingdom of Great Britain and Northern Ireland. But whether in a juridical sense the six counties of Northern Ireland actually forms part of the British state is debateable: the troubled history of the province, its special governmental and security arrangements, the acknowledgement by the British of its right to reunite with the rest of Ireland when signalled by a majority of its population, and the unique governing arrangements established in accordance with the peace settlement in 1998 all suggest that the province has not been integrated into the formation of the British state.

The ambivalence of these processes of state formation might explain why throughout the twentieth century the term 'constitution' was equated with 'machinery of government'. Focusing on surface matters concerning the efficacy of governing arrangements saved us from having to delve deeper into these matters. And later, when European integration was pursued as a response to the loss of empire, the difficulties were only exacerbated: notwithstanding the pursuit of 'constitutional modernisation', harmonisation of British arrangements with member states that have adopted modern constitutions simply threw into relief the lack of any settled constitution. Finally, those who have responded to this problem by promoting the notion that ours is a 'common law constitution' seem blind to the fact that this is either a project to resurrect an English constitution or it is an invention of that most certain of the moral sciences, scholastic rationalism.

This developmental trajectory suggests that we are facing nothing short of a crisis of constitutional identity. Responding to some of the problems thrown up in the final phase of paralysis, the Conservative administration elected in December 2019 pledged to establish a Constitution, Democracy and Rights Commission.[69] But once the government had been confronted by the

---

[68] It might be noted that Dicey's only references to Britain are to the British Empire (ibid., pp. xxxiv–xxxv) and to the British North America Act 1867 (ibid., pp. 161–3).

[69] *Get Brexit Done. Unleash Britain's Potential*, The Conservative and Unionist Manifesto 2019 (London: Conservative Party, 2019), pp. 47–8.

Coronavirus crisis this was placed on hold and might never be launched. In any case, the issues on which it was likely to focus – fixed-term parliaments, electoral matters, prerogative powers, the House of Lords, the Human Rights Act, access to justice and judicial review – are hardly fundamental to the key issue of constitutional identity. Unless the basic issue of the nature of the state is addressed, other reforms seem almost futile.

# Index

abortion, 102, 194, 298, 304
Act(s) of Union 1707, 333
Act(s) of Union 1800, 315
Alliance Party, 87, 90, 93, 94, 106
Anglo-Irish Agreement, 114, 125, 134
Anglo-Irish Treaty, 11, 318
Asquith, Herbert, 11

Bagehot, Walter, 121, 222, 316, 318
Barnier, Michel, 72
Belfast/Good Friday Agreement, 2, 10, 12, 13, 64, 72–3, 75–7, 80–2, 84–5, 86, 90–1, 93–102, 105, 106, 108–10, 114–28, 129, 131–3, 137, 139, 141, 144, 145, 147, 169, 193, 280
Bercow, John, 229, 230, 231
Blair, Tony, 21, 91, 204, 211, 220, 302
border poll, 93, 94, 99, 100, 101, 103, 104, 106, 111, 117, 153
Brexit Party, 5, 203
Brexit Trilemma, 13
British Commonwealth of Nations, 11, 69, 146, 235
British monarch, 146, 176, 220, 227–8, 230–4, 284, 315, 329
British-Irish Council, 134
British-Irish Intergovernmental Conference, 134
Britishness, 9, 91
Brown, Gordon, 204, 220

Cabinet Handbook, 295
Cabinet Office Ministerial Guide, 297
Cameron, David, 187, 192, 195, 196, 197, 211, 216, 303, 327–8
Canada, 11, 47, 155, 163, 164, 165, 167
Catholics, 100, 103, 158, 317

Charter 88, 325
China, 7
citizenship, 2, 8, 76, 101, 111, 120, 121, 123, 124, 147, 191, 268
Common Agricultural Policy, 33
Common Travel Area, 75, 93
confidence votes, 202, 220, 224, 231–4, 237, 268, 284, 300, 301, 328
Conservative Party, 65, 75, 78, 79, 195, 198, 204, 214, 216, 223, 232, 282
constituent power, 108–11, 115, 188
Constitution of the Irish Free State, 11
constitutional convention, 176, 177, 189
Corbyn, Jeremy, 200–1, 204, 214
Council of Europe, 326
Covid-19, 335
Cox, Geoffrey, 300, 301
Cummings, Dominic, 203
Customs Union, 13, 73, 76, 78

d'Hondt system, 136
Dáil Éireann, 11, 131, 136, 139, 147, 187, 298, 306, 307, 318
Davidson, Ruth, 207
de Gaulle, Charles, 4
de Valera, Éamon, 11, 159
Delors, Jacques, 5
Democratic Unionist Party, 66, 74, 77–9, 84, 87–9, 91–7, 101–4, 115, 118, 125, 135, 199, 224, 268, 300, 328
Denmark, 4
Department for Exiting the EU, 197, 202
Dicey, Albert Venn, 121, 186, 319, 320, 333, 334

English identity, 205
English Votes for English Laws, 143

equality, 99, 100, 101, 124, 132, 140, 158, 162, 197
Erskine May, 230
European Commission, 32, 33
European Constitution, 6
European Convention on Human Rights, 22, 29, 35, 133
European Court of Justice, 6, 32, 35, 36, 37, 73, 120, 198
European Parliament, 75, 88, 266, 283
European single market, 1, 206
European Union (Withdrawal Agreement) Act 2020, 9, 240, 251–2
European Union (Withdrawal) (No. 2) Act 2019, 226, 299
European Union (Withdrawal) Act 2018, 9, 55, 224, 230, 231, 240, 245, 277

Farage, Nigel, 195, 203
Fianna Fáil, 106, 114, 126, 153
Fine Gael, 106, 114, 126, 153, 304, 305
Fiscal Compact Treaty, 139, 140
Fixed-term Parliaments Act 2011, 199, 233, 234, 332
Foster, Arlene, 101, 105, 156
France, 90, 262, 271, 304

Germany, 24, 26, 90
Green Party, 106, 135

Haughey, Charles, 114
Heath, Edward, 7, 112
Henry VIII powers, 241, 249, 274
Hobbes, Thomas, 222, 237
House of Commons, 143, 218, 225, 233, 242–3, 254, 268, 277, 329, 330
House of Lords, 35, 178, 242–4, 317, 325, 326, 327, 330, 335
Human Rights Act, 16, 62, 121, 122, 247, 325, 327, 335
Hume, John, 88–90, 98, 108–15, 118, 119, 121, 125, 128

*In re McCord*, 126, 127
India, 163
Irish Home Rule, 129, 318
Irish language, 146
Irish Sea, 65, 66, 74, 77–9, 92, 106

Johnson, Boris, 7, 13, 64, 65, 66, 78, 79, 86, 92, 93, 98, 106, 196, 197, 202–3, 276, 288, 329
Johnson, Nevil, 323

Joint Committee of the Irish Human Rights and Equality Commission, 75
Juncker, Jean-Claude, 5, 32

Kenny, Enda, 298

Labour Party (Ireland), 114, 305
Labour Party (UK), 5, 30, 199, 200, 204, 210, 319
Liberal Democrats, 201, 203, 207, 221, 327, 331
Lisbon Treaty, 12, 32, 35, 198, 261
Long, Naomi, 90

Maastricht Treaty, 5, 31, 32, 261
Macmillan, Harold, 7, 223
Mallon, Séamus, 104
May, Theresa, 9, 17, 78, 92, 120, 122, 196, 202, 300, 301, 304, 328
McGuinness, Martin, 101, 102
media, 103–4, 180, 198, 200, 211, 212, 213, 220, 262, 282
Miliband, Ed, 200, 204
*Miller (No 1)*, 36, 43, 44, 50, 53, 54, 55, 57, 59, 269, 290, 291
*Miller (No 2) Cherry*, 225, 226, 228, 234, 269, 271, 276, 277, 278, 282–4, 290, 291

NATO, 208
Nesbitt, Mike, 92, 105
Netherlands, 236, 237, 262
New Decade, New Approach Agreement, 122, 131, 154
Nice Treaty, 12, 89, 261
Northern Ireland Act 1998, 108, 116, 132, 277
Northern Ireland Assembly, 101, 102, 110, 115, 137, 142, 169, 280
Northern Ireland backstop, 77–9, 84, 92, 93, 94, 98, 232, 285, 300, 301
Northern Ireland Human Rights Commission, 76, 82, 122

Oireachtas, 11, 131, 137, 138, 139, 140, 141, 143, 147, 184, 185, 188, 191, 304, 306
Ordoliberalism, 324, 325

Paisley Jnr, Ian, 101
Paisley, Ian, 88, 115, 117, 125
Parliament of Northern Ireland, 110, 111
parliamentary accountability, 226, 331
parliamentary sovereignty, 27, 41, 47, 51, 62, 108, 123, 178, 226, 241, 331, 333
People's Vote campaign, 203

Plaid Cymru, 52
political authority, 175, 176, 182, 214, 215, 273, 323
political constitutionalism, 148
popular sovereignty, 18, 175–80, 182–90, 194, 208, 235
populism, 175, 179–87, 190–1, 194, 196, 213–14, 238
Presiding Officer of the Northern Ireland Assembly, 136
Presiding Officer of the Scottish Parliament, 48, 310
prorogation of Parliament, 39, 203, 225, 226, 268, 269, 277, 279, 284, 285, 329–31
Protestants, 10, 131, 157
Protocol on Ireland/Northern Ireland, 32, 40, 66, 79, 83, 85, 124, 133, 251, 269, 300, 301

Robinson, Peter, 97, 104, 118, 125
royal prerogative, 16, 198, 224, 225, 228, 231, 266, 268, 278, 285, 290, 329, 331, 335
Russell, Michael, 56

Salmond, Alex, 207
same-sex marriage, 102, 161
Scotland Act 1998, 47–9, 54, 57, 281, 309, 310
Scotland Act 2016, 49, 54, 209, 281
*Scottish Continuity Bill Reference*, 28, 41, 43, 44, 56–9, 269, 271, 278–9, 281, 283, 285, 290, 309
Scottish National Party, 51, 52, 205–10, 215, 219, 268, 331
Scottish Parliament, 31, 47–52, 54–9, 62, 97, 142, 205, 208–10, 309, 310
SDLP, 93, 111, 113, 119, 135
Seanad Éireann, 131, 147, 187
separation of powers, 14, 161, 217, 241, 268
Sewel Convention, 29, 30, 37, 41, 49–62, 141, 142, 209, 210, 281
Sinn Féin, 74, 79, 89, 93–5, 97, 99–104, 106, 113, 118, 119, 135, 153, 318

Social Democratic and Labour Party, 79, 88–90, 93, 104, 111, 112, 135
South Africa, 163
Spain, 46
Speaker of the House of Commons, 227, 229–31, 329, 330
St Andrews Agreement, 142
sterling, 208
Sturgeon, Nicola, 56, 206, 207
subsidiarity, 6, 21, 22, 23, 25, 26, 30–41
supraconstitutional, 184

Taoiseach, 104, 131, 147, 159, 193, 265, 294, 295, 298, 306
territorial claim to Northern Ireland, 11, 13, 14, 96, 112
territorial constitution, 10, 27, 30, 35, 44, 54, 57, 58, 178, 269, 280
Thatcher, Margaret, 7, 114, 214, 323, 325, 326
Traditional Unionist Voice, 97
Trimble, David, 116

Ulster Unionist Party, 74, 79, 87, 88, 89, 92, 93, 98, 105, 115, 135, 166
United Kingdom Independence Party, 181, 195, 198, 200, 203–5, 216
United States of America, 5, 6, 7, 155, 159, 163, 165, 190, 212, 304, 311

Varadkar, Leo, 65, 104, 298, 304, 306
Villiers, Theresa, 91

Wales Act 2017, 28, 49
Welsh Assembly, 38, 55, 284
West Lothian Question, 143, 150
*Wightman*, 269, 274–9, 281, 284, 285, 290
Withdrawal Agreement, 4, 12, 59, 64, 66, 71, 78–80, 92, 124, 133, 177, 202, 203, 224, 227, 245, 247, 251, 269, 277, 281, 292, 300, 329
World Trade Organisation, 64, 70, 72, 73, 76, 78, 79, 82–5
Wright Committee, 218, 220, 222